AWS
Cloud Practitioner
Exam Guide

Mastering AWS identity, compute, storage, networking, and database fundamentals for cloud practitioner success

Gabriele Mastrapasqua

bpb

www.bpbonline.com

First Edition 2025

Copyright © BPB Publications, India

ISBN: 978-93-65897-876

To View Complete
BPB Publications Catalogue
Scan the QR Code:

www.bpbonline.com

Dedicated to

*My Girlfriend **Karina**, my beloved parents
and my two dogs **Ector** and **Iro***

About the Author

Gabriele Mastrapasqua is a cloud engineer and a solution architect, specialised in AWS Cloud services and development in different kinds of realities, from startups to consultancies to bigger enterprises, creating scalable solutions. He has worked as a developer and architect for 15+ years on some high traffic web services in the ad-tech media, fintech, insurance and e-learning space and has been using AWS for 6 years. He is dedicated to work with small cross-functional teams using TypeScript, Python and Java. He is a self-learner and started working at 18 years of age. He started to work on Java applications and firmwares in C ARM microcontrollers. After all these years, he has the same passion to discover new things and learn new programming languages.

About the Reviewers

❖ **Vinoth Kumar Arumugam** is a seasoned network architect with a wealth of experience in data center networking, cloud, and hyper-converged infrastructure. Holding the prestigious CCIE R&S certification (#28720), he brings extensive hands-on expertise in network testing, design, deployment, debugging, development, and automation. Vinoth has successfully led numerous high-performance global teams in testing, automation, technical sales, and data center deployment.

Currently, he is part of Dell Technologies' CTIO Organization, where he leads AI-driven solutions.

❖ **Udhaya Chandran Shanmugam** is a seasoned technology leader with over 17 years of experience in the networking industry and cloud technologies. Holding a CCIE Emeritus (#28467) certification, he possesses deep technical expertise in network design, development, implementation, and testing.

His career progression at prominent companies like Cognizant Technology Solutions and Dell Technologies demonstrates a strong track record of successfully delivering complex networking solutions and cloud architectures, driving quantifiable improvements in team performance and product quality. His expertise extends to AI-driven solutions and cloud connectivity, showcasing his adaptability and forward-thinking approach.

Currently serving as a technical staff member (engineering technologist) at Dell Technologies, Udhay combines technical proficiency with leadership skills, consistently delivering exceptional results in a highly competitive landscape.

With extensive experience in designing, developing, and deploying complex cloud architectures, Udhay is well-equipped to assess the accuracy, clarity, and practical relevance of technical content. As a reviewer, he offers a discerning eye for detail and a critical assessment of the technical accuracy, clarity, and overall impact of books within his area of expertise.

❖ **Harshavardhan Nerella** is a distinguished cloud engineer at a Fortune 500 company, with over seven years of expertise in cloud computing, cloud-native solutions, and Kubernetes. He holds multiple prestigious certifications, including AWS Certified Solutions Architect - Professional, Certified Kubernetes Administrator, and Certified Kubernetes Application Developer.

Beyond his professional work, Harshavardhan is deeply engaged in research and technical community contributions. He has published research papers in esteemed journals and conferences and has authored articles featured in DZone Spotlight. As a technical book reviewer, he has contributed to publications such as Logs and Telemetry, Terraform Made Easy, and CyberSecure™: An Essential Guide to Protecting Your Digital World.

Harshavardhan is a senior member of IEEE and a fellow at IICSPA and IAEME, recognizing his contributions to the field of cloud computing, Kubernetes and enterprise technology. His commitment to advancing the industry extends to serving as a peer reviewer for IEEE, Springer, and ACM conferences, as well as judging prestigious competitions such as Princeton Research Day, Technovation and many more. He is also a highly sought-after mentor and interview coach on ADPList, where he ranks in the top 1% of mentors.

Acknowledgement

There are a few people I want to thank for the support they have given me during the writing of this book. First and foremost, I would like to thank my girlfriend and my parents for continuously encouraging me to write the book. I could have never completed this book without their support.

My gratitude also goes to the team at BPB Publications for being very professional and supportive, and improving the overall experience of this book.

Also, I want to thank all the technical editors who gave me suggestions to better this book.

Preface

This book will provide you with all the information that is required to understand AWS services to pass AWS Cloud Practitioner Certification exam, which is now updated to new version CLF-C02. It also will give you a solid foundation to choose when and why to use some specific AWS services based on the requirements of your job. This book explain the qualities of the cloud and will give you, as an individual or a company, a competitive advantage for the strong security guarantees, the elastic provisioning of servers, the speed of development and safeguards given by AWS. We will discover the main computing model, the billing and costs associated and all the other possible AWS services that the exam can ask you.

After reading this book, you will be able to follow the best practices suggested by AWS and will improve your work and the quality of your architectures for years to come. This book will help you pass AWS Cloud Practitioner Certification and to start your new career as a cloud engineer, a solution architect, a DevOps, support/help desk for the best cloud available.

Chapter 1: Cloud Introduction - This chapter introduces cloud computing, defines its core concepts, and outlines the benefits of adopting a cloud-based approach. It presents an overview of Amazon Web Services, its key offerings, and the potential advantages of transitioning to a cloud provider. The chapter provides a broad overview of the main functionalities available on AWS, grouped into its major service areas. It also explains the different deployment topologies supported by cloud providers, highlighting their advantages and disadvantages. At the end, the chapter outlines the foundational pillars of the AWS Well-Architected Framework with a focus on designing scalable, reliable, and secure solutions within the AWS environment.

Chapter 2: AWS Global Infrastructures and Main Services - This chapter provides a high level overview of AWS's global capabilities, focusing on how it operates across multiple regions and **Availability Zones (AZs)** to support deployments around the world. It highlights how AWS ensures high availability through its use of AZs and Global Infrastructure. We will also explore the main macro areas where AWS excels, along with the most commonly used services. Detailed descriptions of individual services will follow in the next chapters. Additionally, you will be introduced to AWS Global CloudFront **content delivery network (CDN)**, along with options and features related to edge locations that AWS users can leverage to optimize performance and reduce latency.

Chapter 3: AWS Identity Access Management - This chapter provides a more detailed overview of how AWS manages users, roles, and groups. It focuses on the various features and options available for AWS users, emphasizing best security practices such as MFA and different types of access, including access tokens. It also highlights the tools available to monitor IAM security, check users' last access times, and review the types of policies applied.

Chapter 4: AWS Compute Services - This chapter covers EC2 as AWS's primary compute service, detailing instance types, billing options (on-demand, reserved, spot), and instance classes for different workloads like GPU, compute, memory-optimized. It discusses supported operating systems such as Windows, Linux and architectures like x86, ARM. ECS is introduced as the service for running Docker containers, integrated with ECR for image management. The chapter explains AWS Lambda, the serverless compute service, and its impact on system architecture, with use cases, pros, cons, and event-driven triggers. Finally, it discusses other AWS compute services, comparing their use cases, pros, cons, and pricing models.

Chapter 5: AWS Storage Services - This chapter highlights S3 as one of AWS's best services, explaining its role as an object storage solution. It covers the different storage options available, such as Glacier and Standard, and outlines the pricing model. The chapter also explores how S3 can be used for web hosting static assets. Additionally, it introduces other useful storage services like EBS and EFS, explaining their roles in storing data for various use cases.

Chapter 6: AWS Database Services - This chapter covers AWS's relational database solution explaining its meaning and history. It details database options like PostgreSQL, SQL Server, MySQL, and introduces Aurora. DynamoDB, AWS's NoSQL key-value database is discussed with options like on-demand, provisioned, auto scaling, and features such as main and sort keys, along with global distributions. Redshift, AWS's primary data warehouse is introduced for analytical purposes, along with big data and analytics services. The chapter also highlights other AWS big data services and databases, sparking interest in various solutions, from graph databases to document databases, and their use cases.

Chapter 7: AWS Networking - This chapter explains what a VPC is and how it provides users with security and networking guardrails in AWS. It covers the common use cases for AWS networking and the various options available, including networking features and configurations. Additionally, the chapter explores other networking services, such as VPNs and Direct Connect, and how they help in establishing secure, reliable connections between on-premises environments and AWS.

Chapter 8: AWS Security - This chapter provides a detailed explanation of AWS shared responsibility model, outlining what it means for users and the responsibilities of AWS. It covers SLAs and safeguards AWS guarantees. The chapter also discusses security measures at the networking level and how AWS services can enhance security at the data level, particularly through key management. It explains how to comply with regulations such as EU GDPR, HIPAA and demonstrates how to monitor AWS user activity and operations using CloudTrail.

Chapter 9: AWS Content Delivery and Global Applications - This chapter explains the concepts, usage, and pricing of Route 53. It also covers what a content delivery network CDN is, along with the usage and pricing of CloudFront. Additionally, the chapter explores other AWS services designed for global distribution.

Chapter 10: AWS Events and Messages - This chapter explains the SQS service, pricing model, and use cases. It also covers the different types of queues and discusses why they are essential in applications for managing asynchronous communication. It also describes the SNS service, its pricing model, and its role in pub/sub messaging with event buses, highlighting why this service is valuable in applications. Additionally, the chapter explores other messaging and event-driven services, including Kinesis, MQ, and EventBridge, detailing their use cases and pricing models, and explaining when to choose these alternatives for specific application needs.

Chapter 11: AWS Cloud Monitoring - This chapter explains the main functionalities of CloudWatch, including custom alarms, metrics, and dashboards for monitoring AWS resources. It also covers the features, highlighting its usefulness for auditing and tracking user activity across AWS services. Additionally, the chapter introduces other monitoring and diagnostic services, such as X-Ray for tracing application performance, CodeGuru for code quality analysis, and AWS Health for personalized alerts and information about AWS service events impacting your environment.

Chapter 12: AWS Cloud Deployment and IaC - This chapter explains the main features of CloudFormation, its use cases. It also covers AWS CDK, highlighting its key features and use cases as an alternative to CloudFormation for defining infrastructure. Additionally, the chapter explores AWS's CI/CD services, including CodeCommit, CodePipeline, and CodeBuild, detailing how they streamline the software development lifecycle. It also discusses the advantages of using these services and the associated costs.

Chapter 13: AWS Billing and Organizations - This chapter outlines the pricing models for various AWS services along with AWS Billing and Cost Explorer for managing and analyzing costs. It also covers AWS Organizations, explaining its use cases and how it allows you to segment companies or create sub-level organizational units for better management and control of resources across different teams or departments.

Chapter 14: AWS Advanced Identity Services - This chapter explains the main features of AWS Cognito, including its use cases for user authentication, authorization, and management. It covers federation and single sign-on capabilities, allowing seamless access across multiple applications. Additionally, the chapter explores other AWS services for authentication and authorization, highlighting their roles in securing applications and managing user access across different environments.

Chapter 15: Machine Learning and Other AWS Services - This chapter explores other AWS services used for machine learning, highlighting their capabilities and use cases in building intelligent applications. It also covers a range of AWS compute services, focusing on more specialized use cases. The chapter provides a comprehensive overview of AWS's diverse compute options, showcasing the full spectrum of possibilities for leveraging AWS infrastructure to meet various application needs.

Chapter 16: Preparing for the Exam - This chapter provides additional resources for readers to test and study for the exam. It includes tips on how to effectively prepare for exam day, covering common installations and best practices to follow. The chapter also prepares the reader for proctored exam inspections, outlining what to expect. It also offers advice on how to access discounts or take the exam, ensuring a cost-effective path to certification.

Code Bundle and Coloured Images

Please follow the link to download the
Code Bundle and the *Coloured Images* of the book:

https://rebrand.ly/4npikj0

The code bundle for the book is also hosted on GitHub at
https://github.com/bpbpublications/AWS-Cloud-Practitioner-Exam-Guide.
In case there's an update to the code, it will be updated on the existing GitHub repository.

We have code bundles from our rich catalogue of books and videos available at
https://github.com/bpbpublications. Check them out!

Errata

We take immense pride in our work at BPB Publications and follow best practices to ensure the accuracy of our content to provide with an indulging reading experience to our subscribers. Our readers are our mirrors, and we use their inputs to reflect and improve upon human errors, if any, that may have occurred during the publishing processes involved. To let us maintain the quality and help us reach out to any readers who might be having difficulties due to any unforeseen errors, please write to us at :

errata@bpbonline.com

Your support, suggestions and feedbacks are highly appreciated by the BPB Publications' Family.

Did you know that BPB offers eBook versions of every book published, with PDF and ePub files available? You can upgrade to the eBook version at www.bpbonline. com and as a print book customer, you are entitled to a discount on the eBook copy. Get in touch with us at :

business@bpbonline.com for more details.

At **www.bpbonline.com**, you can also read a collection of free technical articles, sign up for a range of free newsletters, and receive exclusive discounts and offers on BPB books and eBooks.

Piracy

If you come across any illegal copies of our works in any form on the internet, we would be grateful if you would provide us with the location address or website name. Please contact us at **business@bpbonline.com** with a link to the material.

If you are interested in becoming an author

If there is a topic that you have expertise in, and you are interested in either writing or contributing to a book, please visit **www.bpbonline.com**. We have worked with thousands of developers and tech professionals, just like you, to help them share their insights with the global tech community. You can make a general application, apply for a specific hot topic that we are recruiting an author for, or submit your own idea.

Reviews

Please leave a review. Once you have read and used this book, why not leave a review on the site that you purchased it from? Potential readers can then see and use your unbiased opinion to make purchase decisions. We at BPB can understand what you think about our products, and our authors can see your feedback on their book. Thank you!

For more information about BPB, please visit **www.bpbonline.com**.

Join our book's Discord space

Join the book's Discord Workspace for Latest updates, Offers, Tech happenings around the world, New Release and Sessions with the Authors:

https://discord.bpbonline.com

Table of Contents

CHAPTER 1

Cloud Introduction

Introduction

Amazon Web Services (**AWS**) is a cloud computing platform that provides a wide range of cloud-based services and solutions to individuals and businesses. It gives security, scalability, and a vast range of services for all possible use cases. AWS is a company created by *Amazon* (**http://amazon.com**) and was launched in 2006. Since then, it has grown to become one of the most popular cloud computing platforms in the world and the first public cloud used in business.

AWS revolutionized the concept of deployment and infrastructure as what was used before, bringing new concepts like pay on demand, elastic compute, and auto scaling, giving a better and solid **service level agreement** (**SLA**) of services and offering better security all around. All those features can be used in small startups and difficult use cases like in the enterprise.

AWS was the first cloud provider, the first product bringing us concepts such as Cloud, Serverless, Elastic compute, and so on. AWS is the biggest and most important cloud as it is the most comprehensive in terms of services offered and also because it is the fastest in innovating its offering year by year.

As of today, 2023, based on different professional surveys, AWS is the most used cloud provider for startups and enterprises worldwide. For example, the Stack Overflow survey of 2023 gives AWS (as in the previous years) the primate of the most used cloud by IT professionals:

https://survey.stackoverflow.co/2023/#most-popular-technologies-platform-prof

Structure

In this chapter, we will cover the following topics:

- History of AWS
- Cloud computing
- Elastic computing
- Advantages of AWS
- Deployment types
- AWS Cloud Practitioner exam
- Benefits of AWS Cloud services

Objectives

This chapter will give the reader a high level view of the main AWS services, and we will gain an insight into basic cloud concepts. Starting from the history of AWS, we will then explore different use cases and why choosing a cloud provider like AWS could benefit you and your team. Then, we will see how the AWS Cloud Practitioner exam is structured, how it could be useful for the reader and their career, and the main domains that you need to know to pass the exam. Finishing this chapter will help you to start to understand the main terms and services of AWS, create your first AWS account, and understand all the main topics of the exam. This is an introductory step for all the topics discussed in the next chapters.

History of AWS

The story of AWS began in the early 2000s, when Amazon.com, under the leadership of *Jeff Bezos*, recognized the need for a more efficient and scalable way to manage its vast IT infrastructure and to improve the speed of development of new services from his team of engineers. AWS could be described as a spin-off from Amazon.com, built as another company dedicated to reproducing the same scalable services used for Amazon.com.

Genesis and inception (2002-2006)

The company's existing IT infrastructure struggled to keep up with this growth, leading to challenges in maintaining a high level of engineering velocity. As Amazon expanded its product range, the need for faster development cycles, efficient deployment, and seamless scalability became significant. Amazon recognized that its existing approach to IT infrastructure was hindering its engineers' ability to innovate and iterate quickly. Traditional data centers were labor-intensive to manage and required substantial upfront investments. The result was slow development cycles, stifled innovation, and a growing gap between engineering potential and reality.

To address these challenges, Amazon began developing internal tools and services that leveraged cloud computing principles. These tools allowed Amazon's engineers to provision resources on demand, experiment more freely, and accelerate development cycles. Over time, it became evident that these solutions had the potential to revolutionize not only Amazon's own operations but the entire industry.

In 2002, the concept of AWS emerged. By transforming their internal tools into external services, Amazon aimed to provide other businesses with the same technological advantages that had helped streamline their own operations. This marked the inception of AWS and the birth of cloud computing as a transformative force.

Launching the cloud (2006-2010)

The pivotal moment arrived in March 2006 with the launch of Amazon's **Simple Storage Service (S3)**, which offered developers a scalable and reliable storage solution in the cloud. This marked the official entry of AWS into the market. A year later, Amazon **Elastic Compute Cloud (EC2)** was unveiled, allowing users to rent virtualized computing resources on demand. These services ignited a revolution, providing businesses with unprecedented flexibility and scalability.

Diversification and expansion (2010-2014)

AWS quickly broadened its service portfolio. Amazon introduced services like Amazon SimpleDB, a highly available NoSQL data store, and AWS Elastic Beanstalk, a **Platform-as-a-Service (PaaS)** offering. The introduction of these services demonstrated AWS's commitment to catering to a diverse range of application needs, from databases to application deployment.

Enterprise adoption and dominance (2014-2017)

As AWS matured, it became evident that cloud computing was not just for startups and small businesses. Major enterprises started migrating their critical workloads to AWS, driven by its reliability, scalability, and cost-effectiveness. In 2015, AWS achieved an annual revenue run rate of $7.3 billion, solidifying its position as the dominant player in the cloud market.

Innovation and specialization (2017-2020)

AWS continued to innovate and release new services at a rapid pace. It ventured into specialized areas such as **artificial intelligence (AI)** and **machine learning (ML)** with services like Amazon Polly, Rekognition, and SageMaker. AWS Marketplace also emerged, offering third-party software and services to complement the AWS ecosystem.

Beyond cloud infrastructure (2020-2023)

In recent years, AWS expanded its focus beyond traditional cloud infrastructure. It delved into space with AWS Ground Station, providing satellite communication capabilities, and made significant strides in edge computing with services like AWS Greengrass. Acquiring companies like Annapurna Labs and CloudEndure further strengthened its technological prowess.

From its humble beginnings as an internal initiative to its status as a technology powerhouse, AWS's journey has been one of innovation, expansion, and transformation. It has not only revolutionized the way businesses approach IT infrastructure but has also played a pivotal role in shaping the very nature of technology deployment and scalability.

As we move forward, the legacy of AWS will undoubtedly continue to evolve, driving new standards and possibilities in the tech industry. With its ongoing commitment to customer-centricity and innovation, AWS remains at the forefront of the digital revolution, inspiring businesses and individuals to dream big and harness the power of the cloud.

Cloud computing

Cloud computing is a technology that enables businesses and individuals to access powerful computing resources on demand without having to invest in expensive hardware and infrastructure. Instead, they can rent resources from cloud providers like AWS, which has a vast global network of data centers that offer scalable and flexible services.

Cloud computing offers several advantages over traditional on-premises computing. Firstly, it allows businesses to scale their resources up or down depending on their needs, pay only for what they use, and avoid the costs and complexities of managing their infrastructure. With cloud computing, businesses can scale and create applications that can be accessed near the location of their users from anywhere in the world, thanks to AWS geographically distributed networks (AWS Region) and AWS CloudFront **content delivery network (CDNs)**. This provides significant flexibility for businesses and their customers, even if the business is working with customers coming from various geographical locations around the world.

Also, cloud computing offers businesses a significant advantage over traditional on-premises computing systems in terms of security. With cloud computing, businesses can benefit from the latest security technology and infrastructure maintained and updated by the cloud provider, freeing them from the costs and complexities of managing their own security systems.

Elastic computing

Elastic computing encompasses the capacity to seamlessly modify the allocation of computing resources, such as CPU and memory, to adapt to fluctuating workloads experienced by your applications and services. This flexibility ensures that your system can efficiently scale up or down as demand varies. This elasticity allows you to scale up or down as needed, ensuring your applications can handle varying traffic levels efficiently. AWS offers services like Amazon EC2 that exemplify this concept by providing resizable virtual servers that you can launch or terminate based on your use cases.

The Elastic term in AWS enables companies to have the flexibility and adaptability of various cloud resources beyond just computing, including storage, databases, and networking. An elastic infrastructure allows you to provision and de-provision resources quickly, automate scaling based on conditions or policies, and optimize cost and performance by dynamically adjusting resources. This elasticity is a fundamental characteristic of cloud computing, allowing you to align your IT infrastructure with your specific business needs and effectively manage costs.

Benefits of cloud computing

Cloud computing has several advantages, including scalability, cost savings, flexibility, and security. One of the primary advantages of cloud computing is its scalability. Businesses can quickly and easily increase or decrease their computing resources as demand fluctuates. This can be particularly beneficial for businesses with seasonal or unpredictable workloads, like black Fridays for e-commerce, a flow of new signups for a mobile app from socials, startups with new customers giving them new data to handle, big data workloads on Apache Spark and other big data frameworks, ML tasks, big enterprises in need to handle a big new customer dataset and new traffic, and so on.

So, the cloud enables enterprises big and small to handle the unpredictable: the spikes in traffic that an application can see if it gains traction and users, but also to make engineers faster in handling new projects and workloads; also it enables working on a solid base for the infrastructure, so a cloud as AWS could improve the velocity of the development team but also improve the handling of new user demands.

Cloud computing also saves businesses money on hardware and infrastructure costs by only paying for the resources they use. They do not have to invest in expensive servers, storage, and networking equipment that they may not fully utilize. Instead, they can rent resources from cloud providers like AWS, which offers a wide range of services that cater to businesses of all sizes.

Another advantage of cloud computing is its flexibility. It allows businesses to spin up instances on demand around the world near the location of their users, based upon the needs of the business, and create servers in seconds instead of waiting hours or days as we can see with on-premises setups. This is possible thanks to all the features of a cloud like AWS, like integrating with on-premises setups, accessing and creating secure credentials for storage and credentials for users in a team, creating secure connections using VPN, and secure direct connection to the resources on the cloud and on-premises servers.

Cloud computing is also highly secure, with cloud providers like AWS offering the latest security technology and infrastructure to protect businesses' sensitive data and applications. AWS strongly focuses on security and compliance, with various tools and features to help businesses protect their data and applications. These span different areas, from encryption on data at rest to data in transit, and also for credentials management and password rotation policies. All the best practices are here to be used in AWS.

Advantages of the cloud over on-premises hosting

Cloud computing offers several advantages over traditional on-premises computing. Firstly, it allows businesses to scale their resources up or down depending on their needs, pay only for what they use, and avoid the costs and complexities of managing their infrastructure.

Furthermore, cloud computing offers businesses a significant advantage over traditional on-premises computing systems in terms of security. With cloud computing, businesses can benefit from the latest security technology and infrastructure maintained and updated by the cloud provider, freeing them from the costs and complexities of managing their own security systems. This is a big issue for companies, as updating and maintaining infrastructure is costly and time-consuming. With AWS, you could have the latest security update for distribution on Linux or Windows free of charge, with automatic updates of all the instances you run.

Another point to take into consideration is the cost of managing the infrastructure, whether it is on-premises or in the cloud. As a company or a small team of developers in a startup, you must handle all the infrastructure in an on-premises setup. This will be more additional work to handle all the servers that are needed to serve your application; you will need a way to handle the provisioning of the servers with the correct updates and packages needed for security updates; you will need to handle all the security of all the networking infrastructure like subnets, firewalls, API Gateways, auth credentials services, you will also need to handle the scaling and backups for the databases you will use, and so on.

In an on-premises setup, you lose all the properties of elastic computing, so you will not be able to easily create new servers on demand based on your workload and your configuration.

This means that for a company, all this extra work will come as a new and additional cost associated only with running the application in production. You will need a dedicated team of expert **system administrators** (**SysAdmins**) or DevOps engineers to handle all the possible use cases and failure scenarios.

This all means that you will need to over-provision the servers to handle possible spikes and handle the normal workload, and having more costs associated with only running your application, committing to a setup that is difficult to scale and improve in time.

So, your business will be relegated to the speed of your team to improve the setup when a cloud like AWS could give you all those features and save money on hardware and infrastructure costs by only paying for the resources you use.

No need to invest in expensive servers, storage, and networking equipment that you may not fully utilize. Instead, you can rent resources from cloud providers like AWS, which offers a wide range of services that cater to businesses of all sizes.

Advantages of Amazon Web Services

AWS is one of the leading cloud computing providers, offering a wide range of services that cater to businesses of all sizes. One of the key advantages of AWS is its global network of data centers, which allows businesses to access resources from anywhere in the world and their users; with a global network, AWS could serve your application all around the world with low latencies.

AWS offers various managed services, including computing, storage, databases, analytics, machine learning, and more. These services are highly scalable and flexible, allowing businesses to adapt to changing needs easily.

AWS is also known for its reliability and high availability, with a SLA that guarantees a certain level of uptime. AWS also offers significant cost savings for businesses, particularly those looking to move away from on-premises computing.

AWS strongly focuses on security and compliance, with various tools and features to help businesses protect their data and applications. AWS also offers a range of certifications and compliance programs to help businesses meet regulatory requirements. This means that working in AWS will enable a company to be ready and compliant with GDPR, HIPAA, etc., following their best practices and guidelines.

Managed service

Managed services are web services that are fully managed (at the level of infrastructure, scalability, provisioning, and operations) by a cloud provider like AWS for its customers.

AWS offers a wide range of managed services that help businesses offload the operational overhead associated with managing infrastructure, applications, databases, and various other components. These managed services are designed to simplify the deployment, operation, and scaling of IT resources in the AWS Cloud.

Some key characteristics of managed services in AWS include:

- **Fully managed**: AWS takes care of the operational aspects, such as server provisioning, configuration, patching, and monitoring, allowing customers to focus on using the service rather than managing it.

- **High availability**: AWS-managed services are typically designed for high availability and Fault-tolerance, leveraging AWS's Global Infrastructure and redundancy features.

- **Scalability**: Customers can easily scale AWS-managed services up or down to accommodate changes in demand without needing significant manual intervention.

- **Security**: AWS places a strong emphasis on security, and many managed services come with built-in security features, encryption, and access controls. AWS also provides tools and best practices for further enhancing security.

- **Pay-as-you-go pricing**: Managed services often follow a pay-as-you-go pricing model, where customers pay only for the resources they consume, helping to control costs.

Examples of AWS-managed services include:

- **Amazon Relational Database Service**: A managed database service supporting engines like MySQL, PostgreSQL, and Oracle.

- **Amazon Elastic Beanstalk**: A PaaS offering that simplifies the deployment and management of web applications.

- **Amazon Redshift**: A fully managed data warehousing service for analyzing large datasets.

- **Amazon SageMaker**: A managed machine learning service that makes it easier to build, train, and deploy machine learning models.

- **AWS Lambda**: A serverless computing service that automatically scales to handle event-driven workloads.

- **Amazon S3**: A scalable and highly available object storage service.

- **Amazon Polly**: A text-to-speech service that converts text into lifelike speech.

These managed services in AWS allow organizations to leverage AWS's infrastructure and expertise while reducing the operational burden and cost associated with managing these services independently. It enables businesses to focus on their core applications and services, driving innovation and agility in the cloud.

AWS versus other cloud providers

One of the reasons why AWS stands out compared to other cloud providers is its wide range of services and tools and its global presence. AWS boasts an extensive Global Infrastructure with data centers in numerous Regions worldwide, offering unmatched scalability, redundancy, and low-latency access.

AWS offers a suite of services that cater to businesses of all sizes, from startups to large enterprises. This includes computing, storage, databases, analytics, ML, and more.

Another reason why AWS is a top choice for businesses is its reliability and high availability. AWS has a SLA that guarantees a certain level of uptime and has a strong reputation for providing reliable and stable services.

Then, AWS provides a vast array of services and features that cover almost every aspect of cloud computing, from computing and storage to ML and IoT. This comprehensive portfolio allows businesses to build, deploy, and manage various applications and workloads, making AWS a one-stop shop for cloud solutions. Additionally, AWS's commitment to innovation means continually introducing new services and enhancements to stay at the forefront of the industry.

Furthermore, AWS's strong security measures, compliance certifications, and robust network infrastructure make it a trusted choice for organizations with stringent security and compliance requirements. The AWS Well-Architected Framework also guides customers in building secure, high-performing, and efficient infrastructure for their applications.

AWS stands out due to its extensive global presence, comprehensive service offerings, commitment to innovation, and robust security measures. These factors have contributed to its widespread adoption and continued leadership in the cloud computing industry.

Deployment types

Here, we compare a cloud as AWS, hybrid cloud, and on-premises setup, which needs to be considered what an organization needs.

Here is a comparison across several key dimensions:

Infrastructure ownership and location

Let us explore the different Infrastructure ownership possibilities, meaning whether you use your own equipment or rent from a provider like AWS:**AWS (Cloud)**: AWS is a public cloud service provider, which means you do not own the physical infrastructure. Your applications and data run on AWS's global network of data centers, renting the infrastructure:

- **Hybrid cloud**: Hybrid cloud combines public cloud (like AWS) and private cloud / on-premises infrastructure. You have control over on-premises resources and leverage the public cloud as needed.

- **On-premises**: On-premises infrastructure means you own and maintain your servers, storage, and networking equipment within your data centers.

Scalability

Scalability means the ability to handle more users, traffic, or data by adding more resources (like servers, storage, or processing power) without compromising performance. It is ensured that your web application can handle ten users smoothly or a million:

- **AWS (Cloud)**: Cloud environments, including AWS, offer virtually unlimited scalability. You can easily scale resources up or down to accommodate changing workloads.

- **Hybrid cloud**: Scalability in hybrid environments depends on how seamlessly you can integrate and burst into the public cloud from your private infrastructure.

- **On-premises**: Scaling on-premises infrastructure often involves purchasing and provisioning new hardware, which can be time-consuming and costly.

Costs

Costs refer to the money spent on using cloud services like servers, storage, databases, and networking. These costs depend on factors like how much computing power you use, how much data you store, and how much traffic your app gets:

- **AWS (Cloud)**: Cloud costs are typically based on usage, making it easier to align costs with the actual resource consumption of your business.

- **Hybrid cloud**: Costs can vary depending on your hybrid setup. You may incur costs for both on-premises infrastructure and cloud services.

- **On-premises**: On-premises infrastructure has upfront capital expenses and ongoing operational costs for maintenance, power, cooling, and space.

Flexibility and agility

Flexibility and agility mean the ability to easily scale, adapt, and modify resources or features based on user needs, traffic changes, or business requirements and how much time is required to make those changes. This includes scaling servers up or down, switching between different services, and integrating new tools without major disruptions:

- **AWS (Cloud)**: Cloud environments provide great flexibility and agility, enabling rapid deployment of resources and services.

- **Hybrid cloud**: Hybrid setups allow you to leverage the agility of the cloud while retaining control over sensitive or legacy systems.

- **On-premises**: On-premises environments can be less agile, as hardware provisioning and configuration changes can take time.

Security and compliance

Keeping data safe from cyber threats (like hackers) and following legal rules or industry standards (like GDPR or HIPAA). Security includes things like encryption, firewalls, and access controls, while compliance ensures that the app meets specific regulations to avoid fines or legal issues:

- **AWS (Cloud)**: AWS offers robust security features and compliance certifications. Security responsibilities are shared between AWS and the customer.

- **Hybrid cloud**: Security and compliance depend on the specific hybrid configuration. Properly configured, hybrid clouds can meet security and compliance requirements.

- **On-premises**: You have full control over security on-premises, but it requires significant investment in security measures and compliance efforts.

Management and maintenance

Management and maintenance mean keeping the system running smoothly by fixing bugs, updating software, improving security, and ensuring performance stays optimal. It includes regular updates, security patches, server monitoring, and sometimes temporary downtime for upgrades.

- **AWS (Cloud)**: AWS handles infrastructure management and maintenance tasks, such as patching, updates, and hardware replacement.

- **Hybrid cloud**: Management is a mix of AWS's management and your responsibility for on-premises resources.

- **On-premises**: You are responsible for all aspects of management and maintenance, including hardware upkeep and software updates.

Disaster recovery and redundancy

Disaster recovery and redundancy mean having backup systems and plans to keep your app running smoothly, even if something goes wrong (like server crashes, cyberattacks, or natural disasters). Redundancy ensures there are duplicate systems ready to take over instantly, while disaster recovery is the process of restoring data and services quickly after a failure:

- **AWS (Cloud)**: AWS offers built-in disaster recovery and redundancy options for some of the services offered. AWS uses a Shared Responsibility model, so the SysAdmins or DevOps in your company are up to configure some AWS configurations effectively in order to reach the desired solution and the level of security you need, the redundancy of the databases but also the recovery from data losses for databases or S3 files, the scaling level for compute instances, the security parts for all the AWS services you use etc. When creating a setup of the AWS public cloud infrastructure, including data replication and automated backup solutions for different services, the administrators need to configure AWS properly to have the perfect SLA and disaster recovery solution you want. AWS use this shared responsibility model to give the professionals the power and flexibility to choose how the systems and infrastructure should work, but it is fundamental for any AWS administrator to know what it is needed to create the perfect setup to mitigate all the possible data losses, to create a redundancy system, and have a disaster recovery plan.

- **Hybrid cloud**: Hybrid environments can be designed to include disaster recovery strategies across both on-premises and cloud components.

- **On-premises**: Disaster recovery on-premises requires substantial planning and investment in redundancy and backup solutions.

So, the choice between AWS, a hybrid cloud, and on-premises infrastructure depends on your organization's specific requirements, budget, and long-term strategy.

Many organizations are adopting an all-cloud approach to balance the benefits of scalability and agility with the control, security, and velocity of their teams.

Some organizations use the hybrid approach to reuse old legacy services and use cloud services on demand for some more intensive workloads.

Some organizations implement custom on-premises solutions to cut down on their cloud expenses. However, they may inadvertently end up overspending on DevOps teams responsible for server provisioning and security. Additionally, it is common for them to allocate more servers and storage capacity than necessary to handle potential spikes in their application's traffic.

AWS Cloud Practitioner exam

This exam is the most entry-level AWS offers to certify your skills. The main purpose of this exam is to validate basic knowledge of cloud concepts and to check a basic understanding of all the main AWS services described in this book. The exam covers a wide range of topics, including AWS Cloud architecture, basic security and compliance, AWS pricing and billing, and core AWS services such as computing, storage, and databases. The exam aims to assess candidates' ability to define what the AWS Cloud is and the basic Global Infrastructure, identify key AWS services, and understand basic security and compliance aspects of the AWS platform. It is a foundation for individuals who want to pursue more specialized and advanced AWS Certifications, helping them gain confidence and credibility in cloud computing practices. Passing the AWS Certified Cloud Practitioner exam demonstrates that an individual has a solid understanding of AWS fundamentals and is well-prepared to work with AWS services and solutions.

Importance of the AWS Cloud Practitioner exam

Taking the AWS Certified Cloud Practitioner exam can significantly benefit and enhance your professionalism in several ways:

- **Demonstrates fundamental knowledge**: Passing the AWS Certified Cloud Practitioner exam validates your understanding of fundamental cloud computing concepts and AWS services. It shows you have a strong foundation in cloud technology, which is becoming increasingly important in today's IT landscape.

- **Increased credibility**: Earning a recognized certification from a reputable organization like AWS adds credibility to your professional profile. It provides third-party verification of your skills and knowledge, which can be particularly valuable when seeking new job opportunities or promotions.

- **Career advancement**: AWS Certifications are highly regarded by employers. Having the AWS Certified Cloud Practitioner credential on your resume can open doors to new job roles and career advancement opportunities. It can also help you stand out in a competitive job market.

- **Better earning potential**: Professionals with AWS Certifications often command higher salaries than those without. Employers are willing to pay more for individuals who can demonstrate their expertise and commitment to cloud technology through certifications.

- **Skills validation**: The certification process involves rigorous training and studying, which ensures you acquire the necessary skills and knowledge to work effectively with AWS Cloud services. This validation can boost your confidence and make you a more proficient Cloud Practitioner.

- **Stay current with technology**: AWS regularly updates its services and features. To maintain your certification, you must stay current with these changes, which encourages continuous learning and keeps your skills up-to-date. This commitment to staying informed benefits both you and your employer.

- **Improved problem-solving**: Preparing for the exam requires you to delve into real-world scenarios and solve complex problems using AWS services. This experience can improve your problem-solving skills, making you more effective at addressing challenges in your professional role.

- **Networking opportunities**: AWS Certifications often come with membership in the AWS Certified Global Community, providing opportunities to network with other certified professionals, share experiences, and gain insights into best practices.

- **Employer benefits**: Your employer can also benefit from your AWS Certification. They can leverage your expertise to optimize their AWS infrastructure, reduce costs, and enhance security, ultimately improving the organization's efficiency and competitiveness.

- **Global recognition**: AWS Certifications are recognized worldwide, making it easier for you to pursue international job opportunities or collaborate on global projects. Your certification serves as a universal indicator of your cloud proficiency.

Exam description and main domains asked

The examination will have a maximum duration of two hours and will be scored out of 1000 points. To successfully pass the exam, a minimum of 700 points is required. Each question may present either single or multiple choices for candidates to select from.

The main sections of the exam, as per the update of September 2023 (CLF-C02), **https://d1.awsstatic.com/training-and-certification/docs-cloud-practitioner/AWS-Certified-Cloud-Practitioner_Exam-Guide_C02.pdf** will be:

- **Domain 1**: Cloud Concepts (24% of scored content)
- **Domain 2**: Security and Compliance (30% of scored content)
- **Domain 3**: Cloud Technology and Services (34% of scored content)
- **Domain 4**: Billing, Pricing, and Support (12% of scored content)

The percentages represent that the exam will focus more on some domains than others.

The AWS Certified Cloud Practitioner (CLF-C02) exam will ask you all about the main AWS services described in this book and commonly used. It will also test the exam taker on optimizing costs and efficiency on AWS, following the AWS Well-Architected Framework guidelines and best practices.

Domain 1: Cloud concepts

In Domain 1 of the AWS Certified Cloud Practitioner exam, candidates are introduced to fundamental cloud computing concepts that serve as the foundation for understanding AWS and its services. This domain covers essential topics such as the advantages of cloud computing, the different cloud service models (PaaS, and software as a service), and deployment models (public, private, and hybrid clouds).

Additionally, candidates will learn about the AWS Global Infrastructure, which includes Regions, Availability Zones, and edge locations. Understanding these concepts is crucial as they provide the context needed to grasp how AWS services are designed and deployed to meet the diverse needs of organizations.

Furthermore, Domain 1 delves into key cloud-related terminology and principles, including elasticity, scalability, and the shared responsibility model for security.

It emphasizes the importance of cost optimization through cloud services and highlights the role of AWS Well-Architected Framework as a resource for best practices in cloud architecture.

Overall, Domain 1 sets the stage for candidates to develop a strong conceptual understanding of cloud computing. It serves as the basis for their journey into AWS Certification and deeper exploration of the cloud ecosystem.

The questions are covered from the following topics:

- The advantages of using AWS are cost efficiency, global reach, and scalability.

- Understanding the pillars of the well-architected framework (for example, operational excellence, security, reliability, performance efficiency, cost optimization, and sustainability).

- Main strategies for cloud adoptions and migrations following the AWS Cloud Adoption Framework **https://aws.amazon.com/cloud-adoption-framework/**. Those are guidelines that help organizations to start in AWS or to migrate existing infrastructure to the cloud.

- Understand cloud economics: the cost savings associated when using a Cloud, the difference between a fixed cost and variable cost, the different methods of pricing for each AWS main service, and how a service will bill your organization (for example, issuing EC2 instances for a fixed reserved yearly plan is different in price instead of using on-demand EC2 instances billed by hours), understand the concept of rightsizing (means choose the correct size for the services you use based on your workload so that the excess can be reduced and so reduce the cost associated).

- Identifying managed AWS services (for example, Amazon DynamoDB, Amazon RDS, **Amazon Elastic Container Service** (**Amazon ECS**), **Amazon Elastic Kubernetes Service** (**Amazon EKS**), and so on).

- Identifying benefits of automation (for example, provisioning and configuration management with AWS CloudFormation).

Domain 2: Security and compliance

Domain 2 of the AWS Certified Cloud Practitioner exam focuses on assessing your knowledge and understanding of fundamental security and compliance concepts within the AWS Cloud environment. In this domain, candidates are expected to grasp the importance of security best practices and compliance in cloud computing.

You will be evaluated on your ability to identify and describe, at a high level, AWS security services and features, such as **Identity and Access Management (IAM)**, **Virtual Private Cloud (VPC)**, and encryption mechanisms. Furthermore, the domain covers the shared responsibility model, where you should comprehend the division of security responsibilities between AWS and the customer, emphasizing the need for customers to secure their applications and data in the cloud.

Additionally, this domain delves into compliance frameworks and regulations that AWS adheres to, including the **General Data Protection Regulation (GDPR)** and the **Health Insurance Portability and Accountability Act (HIPAA)**.

Candidates must recognize the significance of compliance in various industries and understand how AWS services can help customers meet compliance requirements. Overall, Domain 2 aims to ensure that AWS Certified Cloud Practitioners have a strong foundation in security and compliance principles, enabling them to make informed decisions and implement secure cloud solutions in alignment with industry standards and best practices.

For this domain, the significant topics for the exam are:

- **AWS shared responsibility model**: What is the AWS shared responsibility model, and how does it integrate into different AWS services (for example, AWS Lambda, AWS EC2, AWS RDS.

- **AWS Compliance offered**: GDPR, HIPAA, and the security best practices offered by a cloud (for example, encryption), and the AWS services used for compliance (for example, monitoring with Amazon CloudWatch; auditing with AWS CloudTrail, AWS Audit Manager, and AWS Config; reporting with access reports).

- **Main features of AWS IAM**: Protecting the root account, the principle of least privilege, user management in AWS IAM, usage of user groups and policies, Single sign, **multi-factor authentication (MFA)**.

- **AWS security**: Offering like VPC, Network ACLs, firewalls (AWS WAF), AWS Trusted Advisor.

Domain 3: Cloud technology and services

In Domain 3 of the AWS Certified Cloud Practitioner exam, titled *Cloud Technology and Services*, candidates are evaluated on their knowledge and understanding of the core cloud computing technologies and services provided by AWS.

This domain delves into the fundamental concepts and components of AWS's cloud infrastructure. It covers a wide range of topics, including computing, storage, databases, and networking services offered by AWS.

Candidates are expected to demonstrate their comprehension of key concepts such as virtualization, elasticity, and scalability, as well as the ability to differentiate between various AWS services and identify use cases for each.

Furthermore, in this domain, candidates are assessed on their grasp of the AWS Global Infrastructure, which includes Regions, Availability Zones, and edge locations, and how these components contribute to creating highly available and fault-tolerant cloud solutions.

For this domain, the important points of the exam will be:

- Deciding between options such as programmatic access (for example, APIs, SDKs, CLI), the AWS Management Console, and **infrastructure as code (IaC)**.

- Identifying different deployment models (for example, cloud, hybrid, on-premises).

- Identifying connectivity options (for example, AWS VPN, AWS Direct Connect, public internet).

- AWS Regions knowledge, Availability Zones, edge locations.

- High availability concept, recognizing the appropriate use of different EC2 instance types (for example, compute optimized, storage optimized), understanding and knowing when to choose different container options (for example, Amazon ECS, Amazon EKS), recognizing the appropriate use of different serverless compute options (for example, AWS Fargate, Lambda).

- Recognizing that auto scaling provides elasticity and identifying the purposes of load balancers.

- AWS database services and the options offered for database migrations, know when to choose to host a database using EC2 vs. a managed service like RDS, know the difference between a relational database like RDS, a NoSQL like DynamoDB, an in-memory database like Redis or Memcached.

- Identify AWS network services like VPC components (subnets, gateways), and VPC security like ACLs and security groups.

- Identify the use case for Route 53 for DNS, CloudFront, Global Accelerator for edge services, network connectivity like VPN, Direct Connect.

- Identify AWS storage services like S3, EBS, EFS, and different class of storage.

- Identify AWS AI/ML services like AWS Kendra, Lex, SageMaker.

- Identifying the services for data analytics (for example, Amazon Athena, Amazon Kinesis, AWS Glue, and Amazon QuickSight).

- Know why to use other services like: SQS, SNS, EventBridge for messaging, SES for emails, other tools for development and deployment like CodeBuild, CodeDeploy, and so on.

Domain 4: Billing, pricing, and support

The fourth domain of the exam focuses on essential aspects of managing the cost of AWS services and understanding the various pricing models and support plans available to AWS customers. In this domain, candidates are expected to demonstrate their knowledge of AWS Billing and Cost Management tools, such as AWS Cost Explorer and AWS Budgets, which enable organizations to monitor, analyze, and optimize their AWS spending.

Additionally, the exam takers need to understand the key principles of AWS pricing, including the pay-as-you-go model, Reserved Instances, and Spot Instances, to make informed decisions about cost-effective resource allocation.

Candidates must be well-versed in the concepts of AWS Billing and pricing to manage their AWS resources while staying within budget effectively. This knowledge ensures they can make informed decisions about which AWS services to use, how to leverage pricing models to reduce costs, and how to access AWS support resources when needed.

For this domain, the exam covers the following topics:

- Compute purchasing options (for example, On-Demand Instances, Reserved Instances, Spot Instances, Savings Plans, Dedicated Hosts, Dedicated Instances, Capacity Reservations), prices of data transfers, storage options, and tiers

- Understand how to check bills and price usage in AWS using AWS Budgets, AWS Cost Explorer, and basic usage of AWS Pricing Calculator.

- Understanding AWS Organizations' consolidated billing and allocation of costs.

- Know how to find information and help in AWS, like AWS Support Center, AWS official documentation from the main website, and AWS whitepapers and blog posts.

Sitting for the exam

The AWS Certified Cloud Practitioner exam is typically available in two different modes, online using your PC or through:

- **Testing center (in-person) exam**:
  - This mode involves taking the AWS Cloud Practitioner exam at a physical testing center, a Pearson VUE, or a PSI exam center.
  - Candidates schedule their exam at a nearby testing center through the Pearson VUE or PSI website.
  - You must visit the testing center on your scheduled date and time to take the exam in a proctored environment.
  - The in-person exam is monitored by a proctor to ensure exam security and compliance with exam rules and policies.

- **Online proctored exam**:
  - AWS also offers an online proctored exam option for the AWS Certified Cloud Practitioner exam.
  - With the online proctored exam, you can take the test from the comfort of your own home or office, provided you meet the technical requirements and have a quiet, secure, and well-lit environment.
  - You will need a computer with a webcam and microphone, a stable internet connection, and a compatible web browser.

o The online proctored exam is monitored remotely by a proctor who ensures exam integrity and adherence to exam guidelines.

Candidates can choose the exam mode that best suits their preferences and circumstances. The in-person and online proctored exams are designed to maintain exam security and integrity while providing candidates with flexibility in how and where they take the exam.

Note that AWS exam delivery methods and policies may evolve, so we recommend visiting the official AWS Certification website or contacting AWS Certification support for the most up-to-date information on exam modes, requirements, and procedures.

For more information and to sign up for a new AWS exam, please visit: **https://www.aws. training/Certification**

AWS Well-Architected Framework

The AWS Well-Architected Framework is a set of best practices and guidelines to help customers build secure, high-performing, resilient, and efficient infrastructure for their applications and workloads. It serves as a blueprint for designing and operating reliable systems in the AWS Cloud environment.

The framework consists of architectural principles, design patterns, and recommendations that enable organizations to make informed decisions about their cloud architecture.

The well-architected framework is organized into six key pillars:

- **Operational excellence**: This pillar focuses on optimizing operations to deliver business value continuously. It emphasizes automating tasks, monitoring systems, and maintaining operational health. By implementing best practices in this pillar, organizations can improve their ability to manage and troubleshoot their AWS resources effectively.

- **Security**: Security is paramount in the cloud, and this pillar provides guidance on protecting data, systems, and assets. It covers IAM, encryption, network security, and compliance. By following these security principles, organizations can create a robust security posture in their AWS environments.

- **Reliability**: The reliability pillar ensures systems operate smoothly and consistently. It emphasizes Fault-tolerance, disaster recovery, and the ability to recover from failures quickly. By designing for reliability, organizations can minimize downtime and provide a better user experience.

- **Performance efficiency**: This pillar focuses on optimizing resource utilization and achieving desired performance outcomes. It includes guidance on selecting the right instance types, scaling applications efficiently, and optimizing storage and databases for performance. Following these recommendations helps organizations get the most value from their AWS resources.

- **Cost optimization**: Cost optimization is essential for controlling expenses in the cloud. This pillar provides strategies for optimizing AWS costs, including usage analysis, resource optimization, and cost-effective pricing models. It helps organizations align their cloud spending with their business goals.

- **Sustainability**: improve and calculate the impact on the environment your business has using cloud services. In the context of constructing cloud workloads with sustainability at the forefront, this pillar involves understanding the environmental implications of service utilization, quantifying these impacts across the entire lifecycle of the workload, and implementing design principles and optimal practices to mitigate these effects.

The AWS Well-Architected Framework is a valuable tool for organizations looking to build and operate cloud workloads that are secure, efficient, and resilient. By applying the principles and best practices from each pillar, businesses can make informed decisions, reduce risks, and create scalable and reliable cloud architectures that meet their specific needs and objectives. AWS also offers a **Well-Architected Review (WAR)** program, allowing customers to engage with AWS experts to assess and improve their architecture based on the framework's guidelines.

Benefits of AWS Cloud services

The startup ecosystem is a dynamic and challenging environment where innovation thrives, and ambitious entrepreneurs seek to disrupt traditional industries with new ideas. In this fast-paced landscape, technology infrastructure plays a crucial role in determining the success of startups. AWS, the leading cloud computing provider, offers a wealth of benefits tailored to meet the unique needs of startups.

AWS has all the services one could ask to build a modern and new IT startup, for example, services for machine learning, big data processing, IoT, real-time analytics and ingestion, etc. And offering unique properties such as elastic computing, security, compliance, and high availability, AWS offers only for startups the program AWS Activate **https://aws. amazon.com/startups** where a startup joining the program could have granted from 1,000 to 100,000 $ in AWS credits, usable for cloud spending in a new created AWS account for the company and to build the infrastructure around the new startup.

Startups grow in terms of users and usage, and so a cloud like AWS could grow with them in the quest to conquer a new market, so the unique properties of a cloud could only benefit a startup in the early stage.

Having the infrastructure on AWS with the options to choose the instance sizes, the scalability, etc., is fundamental for a fast-paced business like a startup.

To recap, AWS provides several advantages that cater to the needs of startups:

- **Cost-efficiency**: AWS's pay-as-you-go pricing model means startups can avoid substantial upfront infrastructure costs. This enables them to allocate resources where they are most needed, like product development and marketing.

- **Scalability**: Startups often experience rapid growth, and AWS allows them to scale their infrastructure seamlessly. Whether they need to handle a sudden surge in users or expand into new regions, AWS offers the flexibility to adjust resources accordingly.

- **Vast service portfolio**: AWS provides a wide range of services, from computing and storage to AI, machine learning, and data analytics. This enables startups to access advanced technologies without significant in-house expertise.

- **AWS Activate**: AWS offers the AWS Activate program, which provides credits, technical support, and resources to eligible startups. This program can help reduce initial infrastructure costs and provide valuable technical guidance.

- **Global reach**: AWS has data centers in multiple Regions worldwide. This global presence ensures startups can provide low-latency access to users wherever they are located, enhancing the user experience.

- **Security and compliance**: AWS offers a robust security framework and compliance certifications, easing the burden of security compliance for startups. This helps build trust with customers and investors. Why is this important? For some startups working in big data and AdTech media, using a compliant service is fundamental to success, as they must comply with GDPR, HIPAA, etc.

Advantages of using AWS for enterprises

Enterprises, with their large-scale operations and complex IT requirements, also find AWS highly advantageous:

- **Cost optimization**: AWS provides tools and services for optimizing costs through resource monitoring, automatic scaling, and cost allocation. Enterprises can achieve significant cost savings by fine-tuning their infrastructure.

- **Scalability and elasticity**: AWS's ability to scale resources on demand is essential for enterprises dealing with fluctuating workloads. This elasticity ensures that IT resources can match the demands of the business.

- **High availability and disaster recovery**: AWS offers high availability solutions and disaster recovery options, reducing downtime and ensuring business continuity, which is critical for enterprises.

- **Migration services**: Enterprises often work on-premises or using different cloud providers, AWS offers multiple services to help migrate some or all workloads to the AWS Cloud, enabling enterprises to use different clouds if needed for a business perspective or changing from one to another effortlessly.

- **Hybrid and multi-cloud deployments**: Enterprises can build hybrid and multi-cloud architectures with AWS, allowing them to integrate their existing on-premises infrastructure with cloud resources, providing flexibility and continuity.

- **Security and compliance**: AWS provides a robust security model and adheres to numerous compliance certifications. This is crucial for enterprises, especially those in regulated industries like finance and healthcare. Compliance is a big theme for enterprises; complying to GDPR, HIPAA, etc., is a requirement for most of their businesses.

- **Analytics and big data**: AWS offers a suite of analytics and big data tools, enabling enterprises to derive actionable insights from their data, improve decision-making, and drive innovation.

- **Managed services**: AWS provides managed services for various databases, AI/ML, and other specialized functions. This reduces the operational burden on enterprises, allowing them to focus on core business activities.

- **Enterprise support**: AWS offers a range of support plans, including dedicated technical account managers, for enterprises. This ensures timely assistance and expertise.

Advantages of using AWS for developers

Using AWS offers a multitude of advantages for developers from a career perspective.

First, AWS provides a vast and ever-expanding ecosystem of cloud services, making it an ideal platform for developers to build, deploy, and scale applications. This exposure to cutting-edge technology not only enhances a developer's skill set but also keeps them in high demand in the job market.

Thanks to the cloud, like AWS, there are new exciting roles in the developer sphere, like cloud engineer, cloud architect, cloud DevOps, and so on.

Also, AWS Certifications validate a developer's expertise in cloud computing, boosting their credibility and earning potential.

Additionally, AWS continuously invests in training and resources, enabling developers to stay current with industry trends and emerging technologies.

So, to recap, AWS empowers developers to thrive in their careers by providing them with the tools, knowledge, and opportunities needed to excel in the ever-evolving world of cloud computing.

Free Tier in AWS

You can check the Free Tier for AWS services here: **https://aws.amazon.com/free/**

Some services are free for the first twelve months of your newly created AWS account, and others are always free. Using the official webpage is always suggested to know the latest updates in the Free Tier, and you can filter and check out all the services and limits offered.

Here is a list of some of the Free Tier's services in the first twelve months for a new account (and some are always free, like AWS Lambda with 1 million free requests per month— check the AWS website for updated information):

- **Amazon EC2 (Elastic Compute Cloud)**: Limited to 750 hours of Linux or Windows t2.micro instances per month.

- **Amazon S3 (Simple Storage Service)**: 5 GB of Standard storage, 20,000 GET and 2,000 PUT requests with Standard storage per month.

- **Amazon RDS (Relational Database Service)**: 750 hours of db.t2.micro instances running MySQL, PostgreSQL, MariaDB, or Oracle (subject to Region availability) per month.

- **AWS Lambda**: 1 million free requests and up to 3.2 million seconds of monthly compute time.

- **Amazon CloudWatch**: Basic monitoring and 10 custom metrics and 10 alarms per month.

- **Amazon CloudFront**: 1 TB data transfer out, 10 million requests, 2 million edge function invocation per month.

- **Amazon SES (Simple Email Service)**: 62,000 outgoing or 10,000 incoming email messages monthly.

- **Amazon SQS (Simple Queue Service)**: 1 million requests per month.

- **Amazon SNS (Simple Notification Service)**: 1 million events published, 100,000 HTTP/S endpoints, and 1,000 email deliveries per month.

- **Amazon DynamoDB**: 25 GB of indexed storage, 25 provisioned write capacity units, and 25 provisioned read capacity units per month.

- **AWS CodeBuild**: 100 build minutes per month.

- **AWS CodePipeline**: 1 active pipeline per month.

- **AWS Step Functions**: 4,000 free state transitions per month.

- **Amazon Comprehend**: 50,000 units of text per month.

- **AWS Glue**: 2 million free job runs per month and 1 million free development endpoint minutes per month.

- **AWS Elastic Beanstalk**: 750 hours of t2.micro instances per month.

- **AWS Data Transfer**: A limited amount of free data transfer between AWS services within the same region.

- **AWS Key Management Service (KMS)**: Some free usage for managing cryptographic keys.

- **Recap**: Benefits of AWS Cloud services.

There are several key benefits of using AWS:

- **Scalability**: One of the primary benefits of AWS is its scalability. Users can quickly and easily scale their computing resources up or down as needed. This means that businesses can easily handle spikes in traffic without having to invest in additional hardware. AWS offers auto scaling capabilities that can automatically adjust computing resources based on demand.

- **Flexibility**: AWS is also highly flexible, allowing users to choose from various services to meet their needs. This flexibility also makes it easy to integrate with existing software and infrastructure. AWS provides various tools and services that can be used to create customized solutions for specific business needs.

- **Cost-effective**: AWS is highly cost-effective, as users only pay for the resources they use. This means that businesses can easily adjust their computing costs to match their budget without having to worry about investing in hardware that they may not need. AWS offers a pay-as-you-go pricing model, where users are only charged for the resources they use, without any upfront costs.

- **Security**: AWS also offers a high level of security, with advanced security features and protocols to keep user data and applications safe. AWS complies with industry standards, such as HIPAA, PCI DSS, and ISO 27001, ensuring that data is secure and meets regulatory requirements.

- **Reliability**: AWS is known for its high reliability and uptime. AWS has multiple data centers located in different Regions, which allows for automatic failover in case of a hardware or software failure. Businesses can rely on AWS to keep their applications and services running.

- **Innovation and growth**: AWS is constantly innovating and expanding its services, providing new tools and capabilities to help businesses meet their evolving needs. AWS has a strong focus on customer needs and feedback, and as a result, is always working to improve and enhance its services to meet those needs.

Main AWS services

AWS offers a wide range of services, including:

- **Compute**: AWS offers two classes of computing services types, used for different categories of problems and scaling levels a business can need. We can use AWS services that are provisioned as a virtual server instances (VPS) named in AWS as **Elastic Compute Cloud** (**EC2**), but they need some configurations to be used correctly; or we can use services that are provisioned automatically (named serverless in AWS) that are more easy to be used and to cofigure, but with specific restrictions and limits when used instead of the more hard to configure but more free to use services in the first category. In AWS, we got for the first class of services some services like the powerful **virtual private servers** (**VPS**) named EC2 instances, or ECS (Elastic Cloud Service for Docker containers), or EMR (Elastic Map Reduce Apache Spark clusters for big data processing and ETL), etc. All those AWS compute services use the EC2 virtual servers under the hood. Those services need to be configured and managed correctly from a specialist like a SysAdmins or a DevOps and you will need to configure all the details for a cluster of servers to create a working environment, for example you will need to configure options needed for scaling the instances and how scale the instances, and other specific configuration needed to make them work fine. AWS also offers other services (usually called **serverless**, so without a server to handle and configure for you as a customer of AWS) where the management of the scaling and setup of the servers is automatic and handled by AWS, for example we have AWS Lambda (Serverless functions) or AWS Glue (Serverless big data processing and ETL using Apache Spark as in EMR), which allows AWS users to run the business logic code without provisioning or managing servers, so they can think only about the application at hand, instead on thinking on how to provision and configure the servers needed to process the work. AWS also offers container services, such as ECS and EKS, that allow users to run and manage Docker containers.

- **Storage**: AWS offers a variety of storage options, including S3, which provides object storage for various data types, and EBS, which provides block-level storage volumes for use with EC2 instances. AWS also offers file storage services, such as Amazon **Elastic File System** (**EFS**), that allow users to store and access files in the cloud.

- **Databases**: AWS offers various database services, including Amazon **Relational Database Service** (**RDS**), which provides managed relational databases, and Amazon DynamoDB, which provides a fast and flexible NoSQL database. AWS also offers various database services, such as Amazon Aurora, Amazon DocumentDB, and Amazon Neptune, that can be used for various use cases.

- **Networking**: AWS also offers a range of networking services, including Amazon **Virtual Private Cloud** (**VPC**), which allows users to launch AWS resources into a virtual network, and Amazon Route 53, which provides a scalable DNS web service. AWS also offers a range of security and compliance services, such as AWS IAM and AWS KMS, that can be used to manage user access and encrypt data.

- **Analytics**: AWS offers various analytics services, including Amazon Kinesis, which allows users to collect, process, and analyze real-time streaming data, and Amazon Redshift, which provides a fast and scalable data warehouse. AWS also offers various other analytics services, such as Amazon QuickSight and Amazon EMR, that can be used to analyze and visualize data.

- **Machine learning**: AWS offers various machine learning services, including Amazon SageMaker, which allows users to build, train, and deploy machine learning models at scale, and Amazon Rekognition, which provides image and video analysis. AWS also offers various machine learning services, such as Amazon Comprehend, Amazon Transcribe, and Amazon Translate, that can be used for various use cases.

- **Internet of Things**: AWS offers various services for the IoT, including AWS IoT Core, which allows users to connect and manage IoT devices, and AWS IoT Greengrass, which extends AWS to devices in the field. AWS also offers various IoT services, such as Amazon FreeRTOS, Amazon IoT Analytics, and Amazon IoT Device Defender, that can be used for various use cases.

AWS is a powerful and flexible cloud computing platform that offers a wide range of services and solutions to individuals and businesses. With its scalability, flexibility, cost-effectiveness, reliability, and security features, it is a popular choice for those looking to build and deploy applications and services in the cloud. AWS continues to innovate and expand its services, providing new tools and capabilities to help businesses meet their evolving needs. As a result, AWS has become an essential part of the technology stack for many businesses worldwide.

Learning and starting to use AWS

To better understand and improve your knowledge on AWS topics you could research the free resources listed here. It is also suggested to try the AWS Console creating a new account, to get a feel of the UI and the main services offered.

AWS Documentation

To find more information about AWS in their official documentation, you can follow these steps:

- **AWS Documentation homepage**: Visit the AWS Documentation homepage at **https://docs.aws.amazon.com/**. This is the starting point for accessing all AWS Documentation resources.

- **Getting Started guides**: If you are new to AWS, look for Getting Started guides for various services. These guides provide step-by-step instructions to help you get up and running quickly.

- **Tutorials and sample code**: AWS provides tutorials and sample code to help you understand how to use their services effectively. Look for the *Tutorials* section in the navigation menu.

- **API reference**: If you are a developer, you can find detailed API reference documentation for AWS services here: **https://docs.aws.amazon.com/general/latest/gr/Welcome.html.** This is useful for integrating AWS services into your applications.

- **AWS Blogs and forums**: For community and expert insights, visit the AWS Blogs (**https://aws.amazon.com/blogs/**) and Forums (**https://repost.aws/**). These can be valuable sources of information and discussion on AWS-related topics.

- **AWS YouTube channel**: AWS also has an official *YouTube* channel here, where you can find video tutorials, webinars, and other educational content.

- **AWS Certification resources**: If you are preparing for AWS Certifications, AWS provides exam guides and sample questions to help you study. You can find more information and getting started guides here: **https://aws.amazon.com/certification/**.

AWS Educate

You could use the service AWS Educate for free to access courses and labs with a virtual AWS account where you could test your learning here:

https://aws.amazon.com/education/awseducate/

All the labs and courses are free of charge, even if you have another AWS account; using AWS Educate will enable a temporary AWS account when using labs to test and try the AWS Console (main UI) and some AWS services.

There are Getting Started courses and Labs like:

- Introduction to AWS Management Console

- Introduction to Cloud 101

- Other basic courses for Compute, Storage, Serverless, Security, etc.

- Courses for machine learning, Databases, etc.

AWS Cloud Quest

Another free resource to learn AWS is AWS Cloud Quest:

https://aws.amazon.com/training/digital/aws-cloud-quest/, an interactive 3D RPG game where you use AWS services to play the game in a virtual city.

Players embark on a virtual journey through a fictional world, encountering various cloud-related challenges and puzzles. To progress in the game, participants must solve AWS-specific tasks, explore AWS services, and acquire hands-on experience with cloud computing concepts. Cloud Quest not only tests players' knowledge but also enhances their understanding of AWS services, architectures, and best practices. This gamified learning approach fosters a deeper comprehension of cloud technologies while making the process enjoyable and rewarding.

AWS Console

You can create a new AWS account by following these steps:

1. **Creating an AWS account**:

    a. Start by visiting the AWS website (**https://aws.amazon.com/**) and click the **Create an AWS Account** button.

    b. Follow the prompts to provide your email address, as shown in *Figure 1.1*:

Figure 1.1: *Insert your email for a new AWS account*

    c. Follow the prompts to provide a password in *Figure 1.2* and account information:

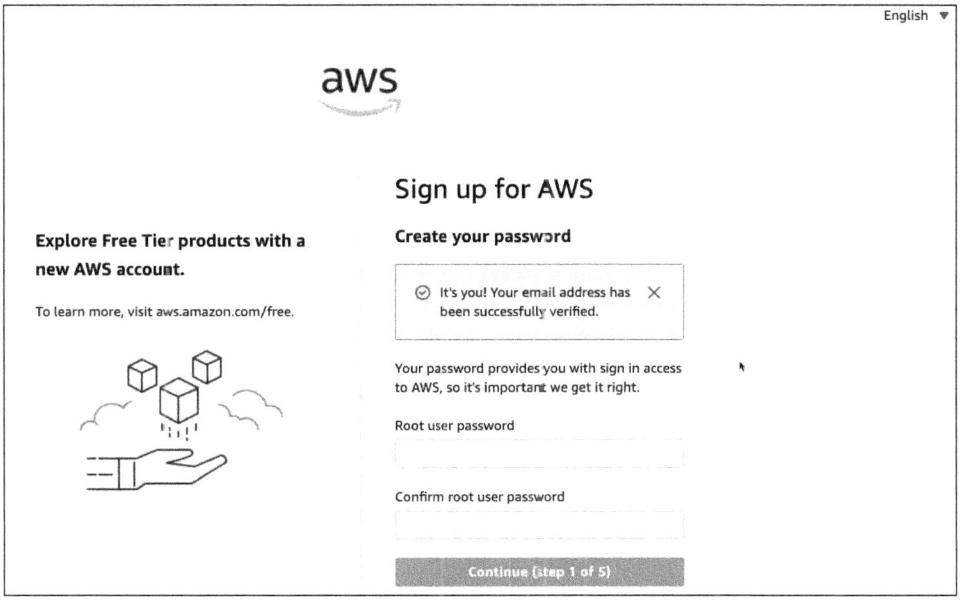

Figure 1.2: *Insert your root password*

d. You will need to provide payment information for billing purposes, as shown in *Figure 1.3*. AWS offers a Free Tier with limited resources, allowing you to explore many services for free within certain usage limits. Take a look at the following figure:

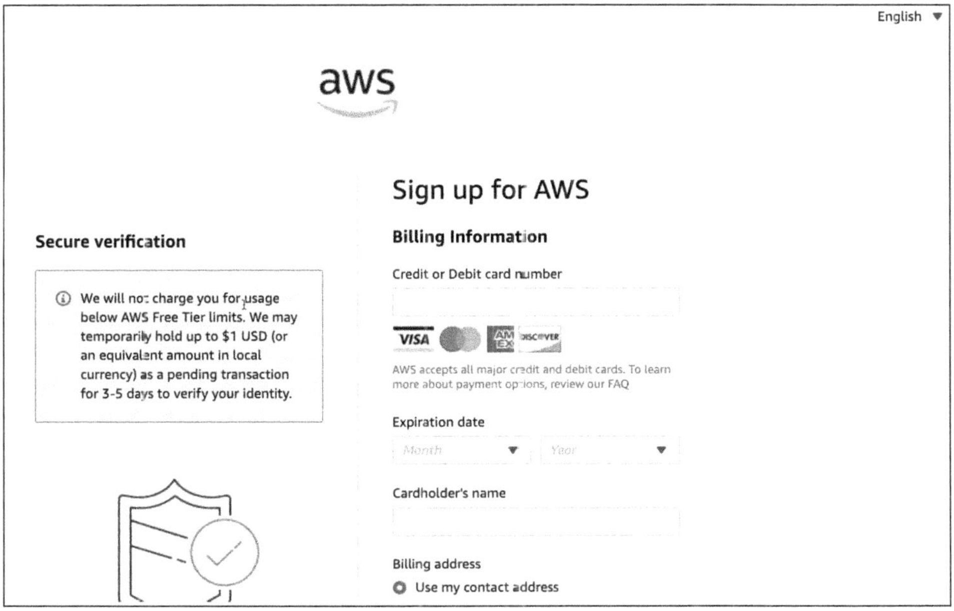

Figure 1.3: *Insert your credit card data*

e.   Verify your identity as shown in *Figure 1.4:*

Figure 1.4: Verify your identity using SMS or a voice call

f.   After successful registration, you will receive a verification email. Follow the instructions to verify your email address.

g.   Once your email is verified, you can sign in to your newly created AWS account, as shown in *Figure 1.5:*

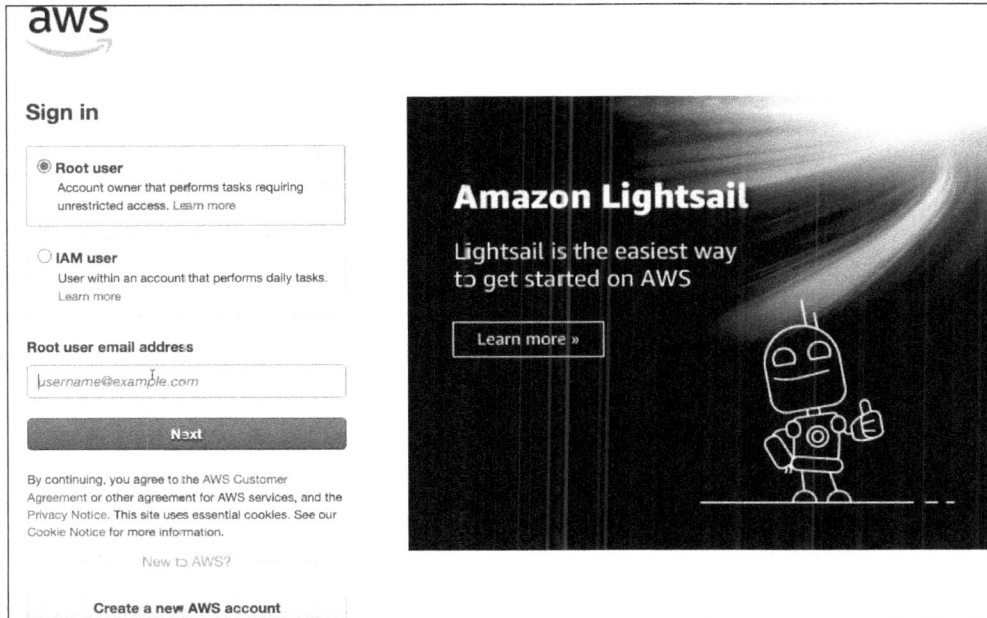

Figure 1.5: Login as a root email account

2. **Navigating the AWS Management Console**:

   a. After signing in, you will be taken to the AWS Management Console, which is the central hub for managing AWS services, see *Figure 1.6*:

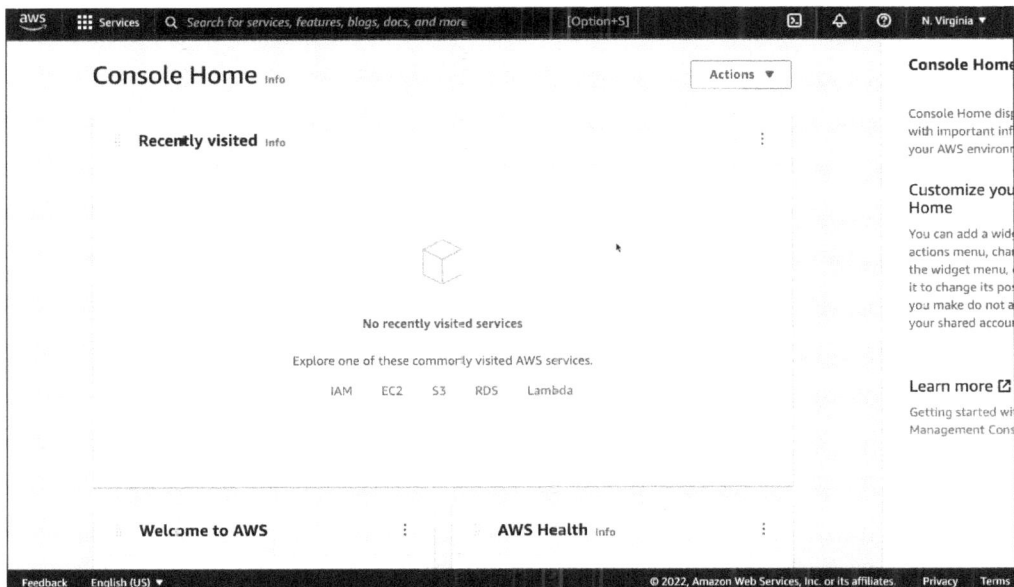

Figure 1.6: AWS Console first access

b. The console has a sidebar on the left and the main content area on the right.

c. The services are categorized by type (for example, Compute, Storage, Databases) in the sidebar.

d. To access a specific service, click on its category, and a list of related services will appear. Click on the service you want to use.

e. Each service has its dashboard, and you can create, configure, and manage resources within that service from its dashboard.

f. You can use the search bar at the top to quickly find specific services or resources.

g. The top-right corner displays your account name and provides access to important settings like billing and security.

3. **Using the AWS dashboard:**

a. Once you have selected a service, you will typically find a dashboard with options to create and manage resources. For example, in Amazon EC2, you can launch virtual servers EC2 instances, manage security groups, and Setup networking.

b. Each service's dashboard may have a different layout and options, so it is essential to consult the documentation or tutorials specific to the service you want to use.

c. You can also access key resources and information, such as billing, IAM, and the AWS Marketplace, from the main AWS Management Console page.

4. **Identity and Access Management:**

a. AWS IAM allows you to manage user accounts, roles, and permissions. It is crucial for security and access control.

b. To configure IAM, go to the Services menu, find Security, Identity and Compliance, and click on IAM.

5. **Billing and Cost Management:**

a. Monitoring your AWS usage and costs is essential. You can access billing information and Setup billing alerts by going to the Services menu, selecting Billing and Cost Management, and then Cost Explorer.

6. **Support and documentation:**

a. AWS provides extensive documentation and support resources. You can access documentation, support plans, and the AWS Knowledge Center from the AWS Management Console's top navigation.

Remember that AWS services can vary significantly in complexity, so consult the documentation and tutorials relevant to the specific services you plan to use. As cited before, AWS also offers a Free Tier with limited usage for many services, allowing you to experiment and learn without incurring charges.

Conclusion

This chapter has given you a basic understanding of AWS and cloud concepts. In the next chapter, we will explore every key service needed to take and pass the exam. The AWS Certified Cloud Practitioner exam, as discussed, serves as a vital entry point for individuals aiming to validate their knowledge of AWS basics. To successfully tackle the exam, one must grasp key concepts such as AWS infrastructure, core services, security measures, and pricing models. Moreover, practical experience and hands-on familiarity with AWS services through labs and projects greatly enhance your chances of success. By obtaining the AWS Certified Cloud Practitioner certification, individuals not only validate their cloud knowledge but also open doors to more advanced AWS Certifications, setting a solid foundation for a successful career in cloud computing.

In the next chapter, we will learn more about the AWS Global Infrastructure. We will learn the key components and services that enable companies to deploy their applications around the globe at specific locations. We will explore AWS Regions, Availability Zones, CloudFront (the main CDN service), Route 53 (the main DNS service), we will talk about the most used and common AWS services used for compute, networking and storage, and finally we will see what AWS accounts are and for what they are used.

Join our book's Discord space

Join the book's Discord Workspace for Latest updates, Offers, Tech happenings around the world, New Release and Sessions with the Authors:

https://discord.bpbonline.com

CHAPTER 2
AWS Global Infrastructures and Main Services

Introduction

Amazon Web Services (**AWS**) offers globally distributed services that enable companies to deploy their web applications in specific areas (or so-called Region in AWS terms) around the globe, so you can have your web sites and applications near your users, or replicate the same services using multiple AWS Regions and **Availability Zones** (**AZs**). More specifically a Region is a local geographical area like *Ireland, North Virginia, Frankfurt*, and so on. An AZ is the segregation of a single Region into multiple sections, and you could choose to deploy in a single AZ or multiple. To obtain more safeguards in terms of high availability is always suggested you use multiple AZs.

AWS offers multiple services to scale your application globally and distribute it around the world. For example, AWS offers CloudFront which is a **content delivery network** (**CDN**) so you can serve your static assets like CSS, images, HTML, files, etc., within the least distance from a user request, accelerating the response times. You could also serve some dynamic content from this CDN, using lambda and edge functions.

Also, AWS offer Route 53, the main product used for **Domain Name System** (**DNS**) where you can register new **top level domains** (**TLDs**) names like .com, .net, and so on; you could host and manage them using custom DNS records including **canonical name** (**CNAME**), A records, MX records, etc. Route traffic using specific criteria to direct your user requests to the appropriate resource. You could health check your endpoints using Route 53 (for example to load balancers and web servers) so you can know periodically if some service is working or not.

Structure

The chapter discusses the following topics:

- AWS Regions
- AWS Availability Zones
- AWS Regions list
- AWS Local Zones and Availability Zones
- Example of RDS high availability
- Recap of AWS Regions and AZs
- Overview of AWS main services
- Managing access with AWS IAM
- Overview of AWS CDN and edge locations
- AWS edge location vs regional location

Objectives

In this chapter, our objectives are to delve into the fundamental concepts of AWS infrastructure, beginning with an exploration of AWS Regions and AZs. We aim to elucidate the significance of AWS Regions as geographically isolated locations comprising multiple AZs, each engineered to provide high availability and Fault-tolerance. By examining the AWS Regions list, readers will gain insight into the global reach and strategic placement of AWS data centers. Furthermore, we will delineate the distinction between AWS Local Zones and AZs, elucidating how Local Zones extend AWS infrastructure to specific geographic areas while maintaining low latency for select services.

Additionally, we endeavor to provide an overview of AWS core services, including compute, storage, and database solutions. By understanding these pillars of AWS infrastructure, readers will grasp the versatility and scalability offered by services such as Amazon **Elastic Compute Cloud (EC2)**, **Simple Storage Service (S3)**, and **Relational Database Service (RDS)**. Complementing this, we will outline the structure of AWS accounts, guiding readers through the process of creating and managing accounts to access AWS services securely. Lastly, we will shed light on AWS CDN and edge locations, elucidating how AWS optimizes content delivery through strategically positioned edge locations worldwide, enhancing the performance and reliability of web applications and content distribution. Through these objectives, readers will develop a comprehensive understanding of AWS infrastructure and its pivotal role in modern cloud computing architectures.

AWS Regions

One of the fundamental concepts in AWS infrastructure is the notion of AWS Regions. AWS divides the world into geographic areas called **Regions**, each of which is a separate and isolated infrastructure with multiple data centers.

Each AWS Region is essentially a separate and independent data center cluster equipped with its own networking, power, and cooling facilities. These Regions are strategically distributed across different continents and countries to serve AWS customers globally.

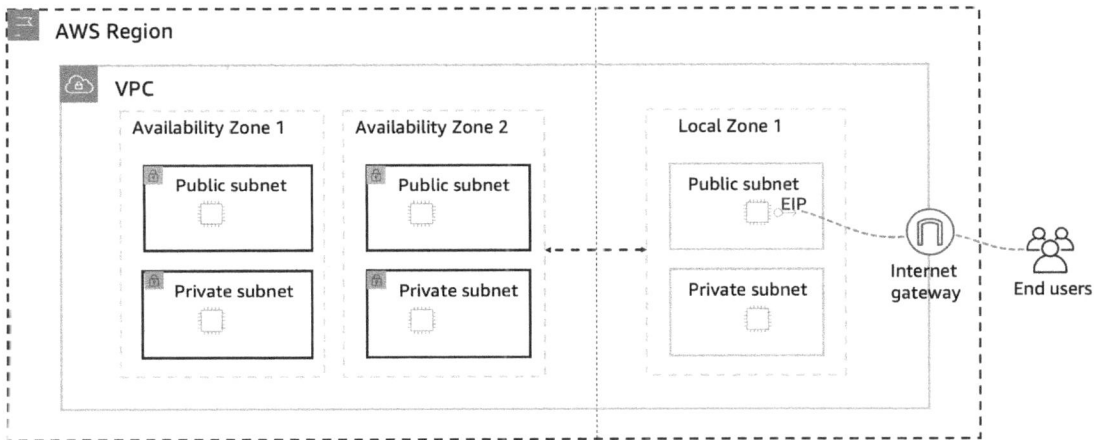

Figure 2.1: *AWS Regions, AZs, and Local Zones*

(*Source*: *AWS Documentation*)

One of the key purposes of AWS Regions is to provide geographic redundancy and data sovereignty options for customers. Organizations can choose to deploy their applications and data in specific AWS Regions to comply with data privacy regulations and ensure that their data is stored within a particular geographic area. Additionally, AWS Regions are designed for high availability and Fault-tolerance, with multiple AZs within each Region, allowing customers to build resilient and highly available architectures by distributing their resources across multiple AZs. AWS customers can leverage the services and infrastructure available within each Region to build, scale, and operate their cloud-based applications and services while benefiting from the AWS global network backbone for fast and reliable connectivity.

In particular, AWS Regions have the following features:

- **Geographic distribution**: AWS Regions are located in different parts of the world to serve customers globally. At the time of writing this book, AWS has 33 Regions worldwide, with more under development each year. You can see the updated map of all AWS Regions around the world here: **https://aws.amazon.com/about-aws/global-infrastructure**.

- **Isolation**: Each AWS Region is designed to be isolated from the others. This means that resources deployed in one Region are physically separated from those in another Region. This isolation is crucial for compliance, data sovereignty, and Fault-tolerance.

- **Availability**: AWS Regions are designed to provide high availability and Fault-tolerance. AWS aims to ensure that services within a Region are highly available and resilient to failures.

High availability introduction

High availability refers to a system or infrastructure's ability to remain operational and accessible for an extended period, often measured as a percentage of uptime, typically expressed in terms of nines (for example, 99.9% uptime). A highly available system experiences minimal downtime and is resilient to failures, ensuring that services or applications remain accessible to users even in the face of hardware failures, software glitches, or other unforeseen disruptions. The goal of achieving high availability is to minimize service interruptions, maintain user satisfaction, and prevent financial losses or reputational damage that can result from downtime.

To achieve high availability, organizations typically implement redundancy and Fault-tolerance measures. This involves duplicating critical components, such as servers, networking equipment, and data storage, and deploying them in a way that allows for seamless failover in case of a failure. Additionally, load balancing, monitoring, and automated recovery mechanisms are often used to distribute traffic, detect issues, and quickly restore services. High availability is essential in various industries and applications, including e-commerce websites, financial services, healthcare systems, and critical infrastructure, where downtime can have significant consequences like loss of information acquisition, loss of revenue for the company, user churn, etc.

So, to recap, high availability focuses on ensuring that a system is consistently operational and accessible to users over an extended period.

Fault-tolerance introduction

Fault-tolerance is a critical concept in computing and engineering that refers to a system's ability to continue functioning and providing its intended services or operations even in the presence of hardware failures, software errors, or unexpected disruptions. Essentially, it is a measure of a system's resilience to faults or failures. A fault-tolerant system is designed to detect, isolate, and mitigate failures to ensure that they do not lead to a complete system outage or loss of critical functionality. Achieving Fault-tolerance typically involves redundancy, error detection, and error recovery mechanisms to maintain continuous service availability.

In practical terms, Fault-tolerance is essential for systems that require high availability and reliability, such as data centers, telecommunications networks, aircraft control systems, and financial trading platforms. Redundancy plays a central role in Fault-tolerance by duplicating critical components, services, or data across multiple systems or resources. When a failure occurs in one part of the system, the redundant component takes over seamlessly, preventing downtime or data loss. The ultimate goal of Fault-tolerance is to minimize the impact of failures on the overall system, ensuring uninterrupted operation and data integrity even in the face of adversity.

So, to recap, Fault-tolerance focuses on the ability of a system to understand failures and to continue functioning without disruption in the presence of hardware or software failures.

In summary, Fault-tolerance emphasizes a system's ability to continue functioning despite failures, while high availability focuses on ensuring uninterrupted and reliable access to services over time. Both concepts are critical in modern computing to meet the demands of users and businesses for robust and resilient systems.

AWS Availability Zones

Within each AWS Region, there are multiple AZs. AZs are essentially data centers or clusters of data centers within a Region. They are connected with low latency, high-throughput networks. The primary purpose of AZs is to provide redundancy and Fault-tolerance within a Region and to provide high availability and Fault-tolerance for AWS services and resources.

The main features of AZs are as follows:

- **Isolation**: Each AZ is isolated from the others in terms of power, networking, and cooling. This isolation helps ensure that a failure in one AZ does not affect the others.

- **Resilience**: AWS designs AZs to be fault tolerant. This means that even if one AZ experiences an issue, the others continue to operate, providing high availability for your applications.

- **High availability**: AZs are a critical component for achieving high availability in AWS. By distributing your application resources across multiple AZs, you can minimize downtime and ensure your application remains accessible even in the face of infrastructure failures.

By distributing application components across multiple AZs, customers can ensure that their systems remain operational even in the face of infrastructure failures, such as power outages, network issues, or hardware failures.

AWS customers can deploy their applications and resources across multiple AZs to achieve greater resilience. When services are designed for Multi-AZ deployment, they automatically replicate data and resources between AZs, ensuring redundancy and minimizing downtime. In the event of a failure in one AZ, traffic can be routed to healthy resources in another AZ, allowing applications to continue running with minimal disruption.

This approach is crucial for all applications that require high availability, as it helps protect against single points of failure and ensures that customers can provide uninterrupted services to their users.

AWS Regions list

AWS provides a list of all available Regions in the AWS Management Console and through the AWS **Command Line Interface** (**CLI**). You can programmatically retrieve this list using AWS SDKs as well. The list includes details about each Region, such as the Region code, name, and the services available in that Region. AWS uses code names to describe a Region; for example, Frankfurt is eu-central-1, North Virginia is us-east-1, etc.

For example, using the AWS CLI, you can list AWS Regions with the following command:

```
aws EC2 describe-Regions
```

This command will provide you with a list of all AWS Regions and their respective details.

AWS Local Zones and Availability Zones

AWS Local Zones are an extension of AWS Regions, designed to provide low latency access to AWS services in specific geographic areas.

Unlike traditional AZs, which are located within a single Region, Local Zones are essentially data centers situated near densely populated areas where there is a high demand for low latency access to AWS services. These Local Zones are connected to the parent AWS Region but function as isolated entities, allowing customers to run applications requiring single-digit millisecond latency and access a subset of AWS services locally.

This design helps businesses and developers meet performance requirements by positioning resources closer to end-users, enhancing the user experience for applications that require real-time responses, such as gaming, media and entertainment, and financial services applications.

While traditional AZs are strategically placed within a Region for redundancy and Fault-tolerance, Local Zones target specific locations outside the primary Region. This setup enables customers to seamlessly extend their applications and workloads into these high-demand, latency-sensitive areas without compromising on performance.

With Local Zones, customers can leverage the same tools, APIs, and security controls available in the parent Region. They can easily deploy and manage applications in Local Zones while maintaining a consistent experience with the rest of their AWS infrastructure. This flexibility is particularly valuable for businesses operating in metropolitan areas with stringent latency requirements, ensuring that they can deliver responsive and reliable services to their users.

In summary, AWS Local Zones are localized extensions of AWS Regions, strategically positioned near urban centers to address the need for low latency access to AWS services. Unlike traditional AZs, Local Zones cater to specific geographic areas outside the primary Region, enabling businesses to deploy latency-sensitive applications closer to end-users. This architecture enhances the overall user experience by reducing latency, ensuring seamless performance for applications that demand real-time responsiveness.

Example of RDS high availability

Amazon RDS is a managed database service offered by AWS. It provides support for several popular database engines, such as MySQL, PostgreSQL, and SQL Server. You could deploy an RDS instance using a single AZ, but this is useful for price optimization, for example, in a development environment.

Achieving high availability with RDS involves using its Multi-AZ deployment option. This is more failure-safe, production-ready, and used usually as a standard for production environments.

Suppose you have a critical application that relies on a PostgreSQL database hosted on Amazon RDS, and high availability is a top priority.

Here is how you would configure a Multi-AZ deployment for RDS:

1. **Create an RDS DB instance**: Using the AWS Management Console or CLI, create an RDS DB instance with PostgreSQL as the database engine. During the setup, choose the Multi-AZ deployment option.

2. **Specify configuration**: Configure the database instance with the necessary settings, including instance type, storage, security groups, and database options.

3. **Choose AZ**: Let RDS automatically select the primary and secondary AZs within the chosen Region.

4. **Database replication**: RDS will automatically create a synchronous replica of your database in the secondary AZ.

5. **DNS endpoint**: Connect your application to the DNS endpoint provided by RDS. RDS will handle the failover process if the primary instance encounters issues.

With this setup, if there is a failure in the primary AZ, Amazon RDS will seamlessly promote the standby instance in the secondary AZ to become the new primary. Your application can continue operating with minimal disruption, ensuring high availability and data durability.

Recap of AWS Regions and AZs

In summary, AWS Regions and AZs are foundational to AWS's Global Infrastructure, providing geographic isolation and high availability. Using a Multi-AZ deployment is a simple way to achieve high availability for your relational databases or web services, ensuring your critical applications remain accessible and resilient to infrastructure failures.

You can also use Multi-AZ when you launch an EC2 instance. You can choose to deploy it in a specific AZ within a Region, or you can let AWS automatically distribute your instances across multiple AZs for high availability.

By deploying your instances in multiple AZs, you can ensure that your application remains available even if one of the AZs experiences an outage.

AWS provides services like **Elastic Load Balancing** (**ELB**) and Amazon RDS Multi-AZ deployments that work seamlessly with instances across different AZs to enhance the reliability and availability of your applications.

Overview of AWS main services

AWS is a comprehensive cloud computing platform provided by Amazon. It offers a wide array of services that cater to different computing needs. Among these services, compute, storage, networking, and database services are fundamental and extensively used by businesses and developers worldwide.

Compute services

AWS provides various compute services, such as Amazon EC2, which allows users to rent virtual servers on the cloud. EC2 instances come in various types optimized for different use cases, providing flexibility and scalability for computing resources.

Most other compute services use under-the-hood EC2 to run your application, like **Elastic Container Service** (**ECS**) or **Elastic Kubernetes Service** (**EKS**) managed Kubernetes for running Docker containers, AWS Elastic Beanstalk (that offers a simpler setup to run a fleet of EC2 with auto scaling, a balancer, and so on).

Other kinds of compute services are serverless like AWS Lambda (allows you to run code without provisioning or managing servers. You can upload your code, and Lambda automatically scales your application in response to incoming traffic), AWS Step Functions (is a serverless workflow service that lets you coordinate multiple AWS services into serverless workflows), AWS App Runner (a managed service to easily run Docker containers without thinking about infrastructure and servers). In all those cases, you do not need to think of instances or EC2 or sizing the correct instance size for your applications, as this is all handled by AWS.

Storage services

AWS offers versatile storage solutions, including Amazon S3 for object storage, used to store files and as a service to easily fetch those files even from different services and applications, Amazon **Elastic Block Store** (**EBS**) for block storage (they are dynamic disks that can be attached to an EC2 instance and used inside your server, and are resizable), and Amazon S3 Glacier for long-term archival of files. These services enable users to store and retrieve any amount of data at any time, ensuring durability and security.

Networking services

AWS networking services facilitate the creation and management of networks in the cloud. Amazon **Virtual Private Cloud** (**VPC**) allows users to create isolated networks within the AWS Cloud, providing complete control over the virtual networking environment. AWS Direct Connect establishes a dedicated network connection from the user's premises to AWS, ensuring secure and high-performance access to AWS services. AWS also offers all you could need to Setup a secure and scalable networking solution, like Route 53 for DNS, Elastic IP for static IP addresses, security based on ACLs and cloud Firewalls, and load balancers using AWS ELB.

Database services

AWS offers managed database services like Amazon RDS for relational databases, supporting a wide range of database engines like Postgres, MySQL, SQL server, and so on. AWS also offers different kinds of NoSQL databases like Amazon DynamoDB for a fast key-value database, AWS ElasticCache for having a managed Redis or Memcached (usually used for caching purposes), and Amazon Redshift for a fast and scalable data warehousing. These services handle administrative tasks, such as provisioning, patching, backup, recovery, and scaling, allowing users to focus on application development rather than database management.

Overview of AWS accounts

An AWS account is your passport to the cloud. It is a secure space within the AWS environment that grants you access to a vast array of cloud computing resources. These resources range from computing power with services like Amazon EC2 and storage solutions like Amazon S3 to advanced machine learning capabilities and everything in between. Your AWS account is not just a technical entity; it is a strategic asset, empowering businesses to innovate, scale, and transform in the digital age.

Significance of AWS accounts

Here is a list of key points about AWS accounts:

- **Gateway to the cloud**: An AWS account is your gateway to the virtually limitless cloud infrastructure provided by Amazon. It opens the door to a world where computational power, storage, and sophisticated applications are available at your fingertips.

- **Customization and control**: AWS accounts offer unparalleled customization options. They allow businesses to configure their cloud environment precisely to their needs, ensuring optimal performance, security, and cost efficiency.

- **Scalability and flexibility**: With an AWS account, businesses can scale their resources up or down based on demand. Whether you are a startup or an enterprise, you can tailor your infrastructure to match your current requirements, thus optimizing costs and performance.

- **Security and compliance**: AWS accounts come with robust security features and compliance certifications. Amazon data centers adhere to the highest industry standards, ensuring the safety and integrity of your data.

- **Innovation accelerator**: By removing the constraints of physical infrastructure, AWS accounts empower businesses to innovate rapidly. Whether you are developing cutting-edge applications, running data analytics, or implementing machine learning algorithms, AWS provides the tools and resources you need to innovate at speed.

Creating an AWS account

Creating an AWS account is a straightforward process. By visiting the AWS website, businesses and individuals can initiate the account creation process. During this process, users provide necessary information, such as email addresses and payment details, and Setup their account preferences. Once verified, the account is ready for use.

Managing your AWS account

Managing an AWS account is as crucial as creating one. AWS offers a user-friendly console and a powerful set of management tools. From the AWS Management Console, users can create, configure, and monitor their cloud resources. Additionally, AWS **Identity and Access Management (IAM)** allows for precise control over who can access specific resources, enhancing security and compliance.

Managing multiple AWS accounts

AWS accounts can be made multiple times under a root account of your main AWS account, like a tree hierarchy with the root as the main and other accounts as leaves.

Usually, companies use multiple AWS accounts to segregate different environments. For example, in a classical IT company, it is common to see the usage of an AWS account for a development environment, another AWS account for a production environment, and so on.

This is used and needed to administer correctly, separate all the AWS resources in an organized way, and create different sets of security rules and access levels for all the users of those AWS accounts and their AWS resources.

This is useful for security purposes and to better administer AWS user permissions and resources for every single environment.

For example, a common practice is to create a development/testing and production environment using different AWS accounts for the same web application.

Following the DevOps best practices and the twelve-factor rule **https://12factor.net/dev-prod-parity**, we could create the same infrastructure on the two accounts to keep development and production as similar as possible.

Thanks to this setup, a company could reduce the time spent to deploy new features for its web application, reducing the risk of breaking changes when updating the infrastructure and the code running the web application.

Managing access with AWS IAM

In the dynamic realm of cloud computing, security is paramount. AWS IAM service provides a robust framework for managing access and permissions within AWS accounts. IAM allows businesses to control who can access their AWS resources and what actions they can perform. By defining granular permissions, businesses can ensure that only authorized personnel can manipulate resources, enhancing both security and compliance.

IAM enables the creation of users, groups, and roles, each with specific permissions tailored to their responsibilities. For instance, administrators can create user accounts for developers, permitting them to manage resources within specific services like AWS Lambda or Amazon S3. Simultaneously, IAM roles can be defined, allowing temporary access to services and resources.

This fine-grained control not only strengthens security but also facilitates the principle of least privilege, ensuring users only have the permissions necessary for their tasks.

Moreover, IAM integrates seamlessly with other AWS services, enabling businesses to extend their security policies across various resources. Through **multi-factor authentication (MFA)**, password policies, and encryption features, IAM fortifies the AWS account, making it a robust fortress in the digital landscape.

AWS Organizations: Structuring your AWS resources

As businesses expand their cloud footprint, managing multiple AWS accounts efficiently becomes essential. AWS Organizations are a service designed to address this need, allowing businesses to manage multiple AWS accounts as a single entity. This service simplifies the complexity of managing diverse accounts, providing a unified approach for security, compliance, and billing.

AWS Organizations enables the creation of **organizational units (OUs)**, allowing businesses to group accounts based on their organizational hierarchy or application structure. Each OU can have its own policies, simplifying management for large enterprises with diverse teams working on various projects. Additionally, AWS Organizations facilitate consolidated billing, streamlining financial management by providing a single payment for all accounts within the organization.

Furthermore, AWS Organizations enhance security by enabling the application of **service control policies** (**SCPs**). SCPs act as guardrails, defining which services and actions are accessible within each account. This ensures a standardized security posture across all accounts, reducing the risk of misconfigurations and unauthorized access.

In summary, AWS accounts, IAM, and AWS Organizations are integral components of AWS accounts, providing the tools and frameworks necessary to maintain robust security, fine-grained access control, and streamlined management in the cloud. Together, these services empower businesses to harness the full potential of AWS while ensuring a secure and compliant cloud environment.

Overview of AWS CDN and edge locations

AWS CDN is a globally distributed network of servers designed to deliver content quickly and efficiently to users worldwide. It works by caching content at various edge locations strategically positioned around the globe. When a user requests content, the CDN routes the request to the nearest edge location, reducing latency and improving the overall user experience. AWS CDN offers high reliability and scalability, making it ideal for delivering static and dynamic content, such as web pages, images, videos, and applications, to a global audience.

AWS edge locations are key components of its CDN infrastructure. These are data centers located in major cities and strategic locations around the world, enabling AWS to bring content closer to end-users and reduce the distance data needs to travel. Each edge location is equipped with caching servers that store frequently accessed content, optimizing content delivery speed and performance. By leveraging AWS edge locations, businesses can enhance the availability and performance of their applications and websites, ensuring a seamless user experience regardless of geographic location.

Route 53 scalable Domain Name System service

AWS Route 53 is a scalable DNS web service designed to route end-user requests to endpoints globally. It translates friendly domain names like **https://www.example.com/** into IP addresses that computers use to identify each other on the network.

Route 53 is highly reliable and scalable, and provides domain registration and management services in addition to DNS routing:

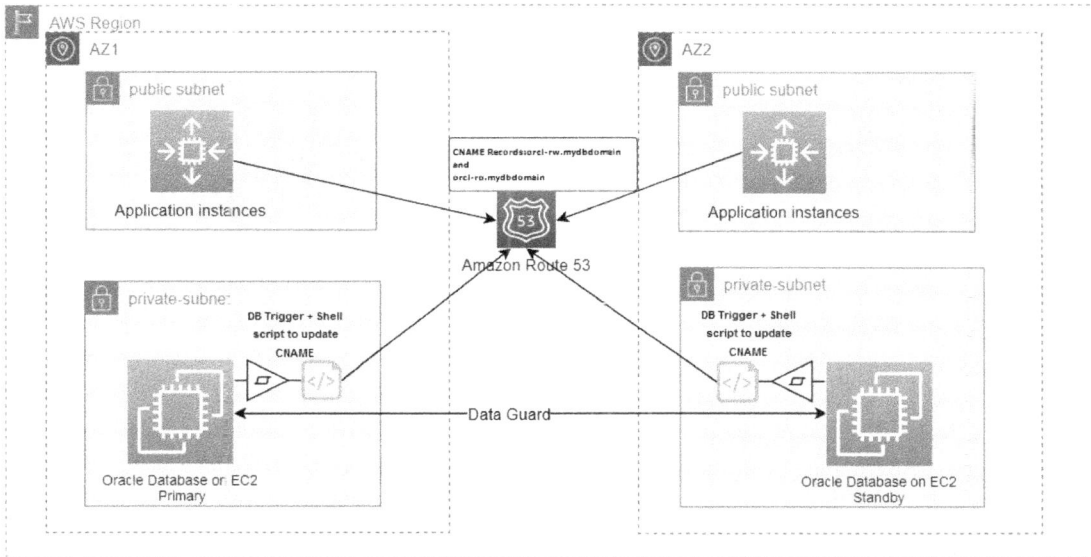

Figure 2.2: AWS Route 53

(**Source**: *AWS Documentation*)

The key features of AWS Route 53 are as follows:

- **DNS management**: Allows businesses to manage the DNS records of their domains, such as a record, CNAME records, and MX records.

- **Global traffic routing**: Routes traffic based on multiple routing policies, including geolocation, latency, weighted, and failover, ensuring high availability and Fault-tolerance.

- **Health checks**: Monitors the health and performance of endpoints and automatically adjusts traffic based on the health check results.

- **Domain registration**: Provides domain registration services, allowing businesses to search, register, and manage domain names directly from the AWS Management Console.

The use cases are as follows:

- **Highly available web applications**: Distributes traffic across multiple endpoints to ensure high availability and reliability of web applications.

- **Global content delivery**: Routes users to the nearest edge location, optimizing content delivery through integration with AWS CDN.

- **Disaster recovery**: Enables failover to backup endpoints or resources in the event of an outage, ensuring continuous operation of critical services.

CloudFront

AWS provides a robust CDN service that accelerates the delivery of web content to users across the globe. AWS CloudFront optimizes the delivery of static and dynamic content, including web pages, images, videos, scripts, and APIs, by caching this content at edge locations strategically placed around the world:

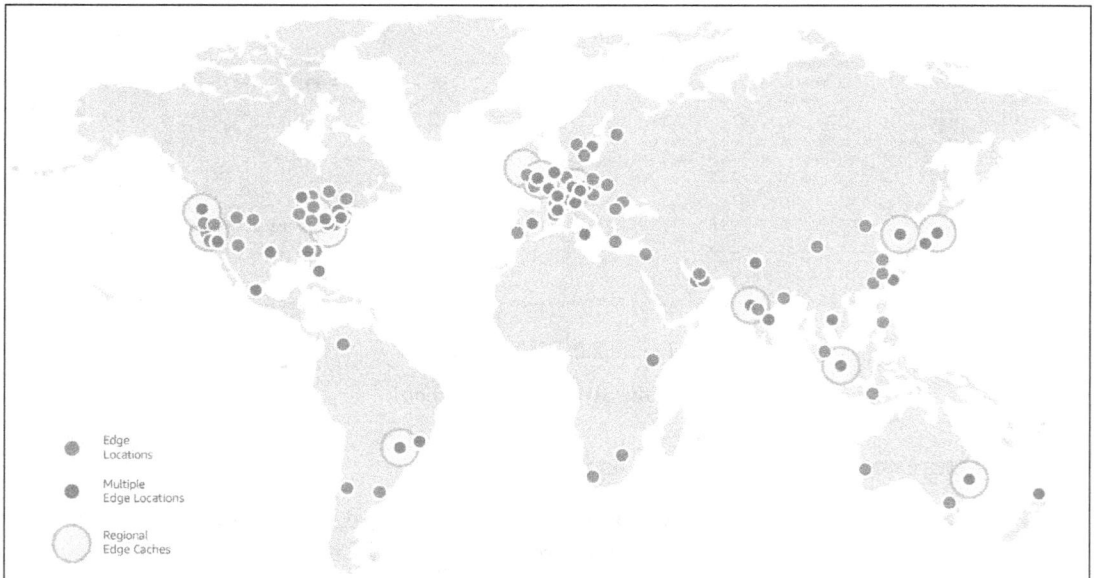

Figure 2.3: AWS global CDN network

(*Source*: AWS Documentation)

The key features of AWS CDN are as follows:

- **Global reach**: AWS CDN leverages a vast network of edge locations worldwide, ensuring low latency content delivery to users regardless of their geographic location.

- **High performance**: Content is served from edge locations, reducing latency and improving the load times of websites and applications.

- **Security**: AWS CDN offers **distributed denial of service (DDoS)** protection and **Secure Sockets Layer/Transport Layer Security (SSL/TLS)** encryption, enhancing the security of content during transit.

- **Scalability**: It automatically scales to handle varying levels of traffic, ensuring consistent performance under any load.

- **Cost-effectiveness**: The pay-as-you-go pricing model allows businesses to pay only for the data transfer and requests they use, making it a cost-effective solution for content delivery.

  The use cases are as follows:

- **Website acceleration**: Speeds up websites by serving content from the nearest edge location to users.

- **Video streaming**: This delivers high-quality video content with low latency and reduced buffering.

- **Software distribution**: Accelerates software distribution by caching installation files and updates.

- **Secure content delivery**: Ensures secure and encrypted delivery of sensitive content.

AWS edge locations and their significance

AWS edge locations are data centers situated in various parts of the world. They act as caching endpoints for the AWS CDN service. These locations are specifically designed to cache and deliver content with low latency to end-users.

The key features of edge locations areas can be listed as follows:

- **Reduced latency**: Edge locations reduce the time it takes to load content by caching it closer to the end-users, minimizing the round-trip time.

- **Improved user experience**: Faster loading times enhance user experience, leading to higher user engagement and customer satisfaction.

- **Resilience**: Distributing content across multiple edge locations ensures redundancy and Fault-tolerance. If one location experiences issues, traffic is automatically rerouted to other available locations.

- **Support for dynamic content**: Edge locations not only cache static content but also support dynamic content delivery, enabling real-time data processing and personalized content delivery.

AWS CloudFront seamlessly integrates with edge locations, enabling businesses to distribute content efficiently. Content is cached at these edge locations and delivered to users based on proximity, ensuring optimal performance.

AWS edge locations vs regional edge locations

Edge locations refer to the numerous data centers dispersed globally in major cities and Regions. These edge locations serve as caching points where content is temporarily stored to reduce latency for end-users. They play a crucial role in delivering content quickly by ensuring that users can access data from a server that is physically closer to them, significantly improving load times for websites and applications. Edge locations handle tasks like content caching, SSL/TLS termination, and some basic content delivery functionalities, directly enhancing user experience.

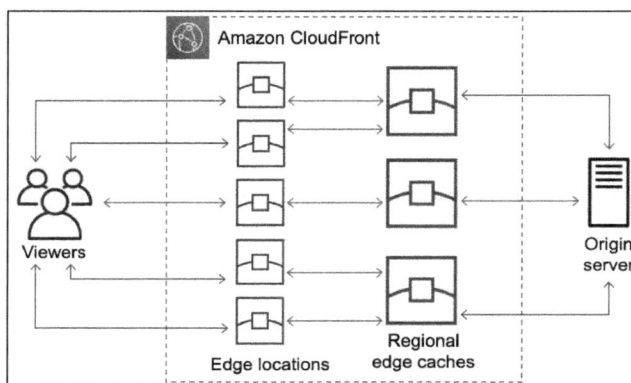

Figure 2.4: *AWS CloudFront locations*

(*Source*: *AWS Documentation*)

On the other hand, regional edge locations are a higher tier in Amazon CloudFront's infrastructure. Unlike standard edge locations, regional edge locations are fewer in number and strategically located in Regions rather than cities.

They are designed to provide more advanced services and capabilities, including functions like AWS **Web Application Firewall** (**WAF**) and AWS Lambda@Edge, which allow developers to execute custom code in response to CloudFront events.

These regional edge locations are responsible for more complex tasks related to content delivery, security, and customization, making them an integral part of CloudFront's ability to offer advanced features and tailored solutions to businesses and developers.

AWS CloudFront edge functions

AWS CloudFront edge functions allow developers to run lightweight serverless functions at the edge locations of the CloudFront CDN. These functions execute in response to CloudFront events, such as viewer requests or origin responses, allowing you to customize the content delivered to users without the need for a centralized server.

Edge functions enable dynamic content generation, security enhancements, and personalization at the edge, improving user experience and reducing the load on origin servers.

The benefits of CloudFront integration with edge functions are as follows:

- **Low latency**: Edge functions run closer to end-users, reducing latency and improving response times for dynamic content generation.

- **Scalability**: It automatically scales based on demand, handling varying levels of traffic efficiently.

- **Cost-effective**: Pay only for the compute time and resources used by the functions, ensuring cost-effectiveness for dynamic content processing.

- **Simplified architecture**: Offloads processing tasks from the origin server, simplifying the overall architecture and reducing the load on backend systems.

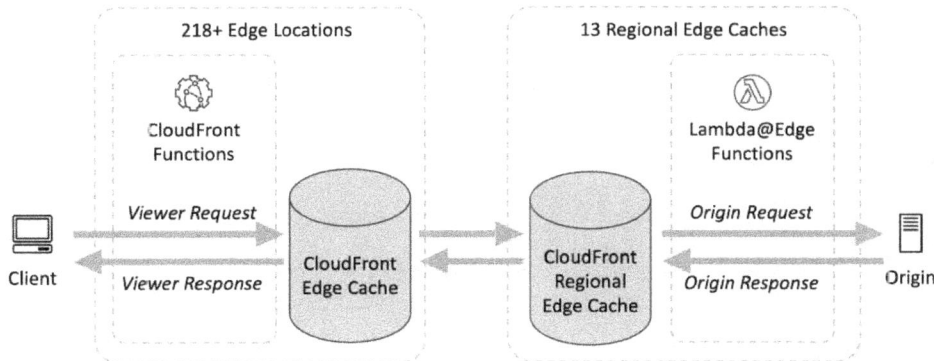

Figure 2.5: *AWS CloudFront edge locations and function types*

(**Source**: *AWS Documentation*)

CloudFront Functions versus Lambda@Edge functions

AWS CloudFront Functions and Lambda@Edge are both serverless compute services provided by AWS that operate at the edge locations of the CloudFront CDN. They enable developers to customize and enhance the content delivery process, but they differ in their integration and functionality.

CloudFront Functions are a lightweight, stateless, and scalable compute service specifically designed to run directly at the CloudFront edge locations. They allow developers to manipulate and customize the content delivery process by writing JavaScript functions that execute in response to CloudFront events. These events include viewer requests, origin requests, viewer responses, and origin responses. CloudFront Functions are ideal for tasks such as header manipulation, URL rewriting, and response generation. They are designed to be simple, cost-effective, and efficient for use cases where real-time content customization is required without the need for a backend server.

Lambda@Edge, on the other hand, is a more general-purpose compute service that allows you to run Lambda functions in response to CloudFront events. While similar to CloudFront Functions, Lambda@Edge provides more flexibility and allows you to execute more complex computations using the full capabilities of AWS Lambda. Lambda@Edge functions can be triggered by viewer request, origin request, origin response, and viewer response events.

They are suitable for a wide range of use cases, including authentication, dynamic content generation, and complex request and response manipulation.

Lambda@Edge functions have access to other AWS services and resources, making them powerful for sophisticated edge computing tasks. However, they are typically best suited for scenarios that require more advanced processing capabilities and integration with other AWS services.

So, to recap, both services are serverless functions, similar to AWS Lambda, but more limited for use cases and power of standard AWS Lambda. Also, the key difference between the two is that CloudFront Functions run on the CDN so can run in the global network of cities near a user, are less powerful but faster to respond because of this reduced distance from a user location request and AWS global network, and you are limited on only some use cases when using them.

Lambda@Edge instead runs using regional edge locations, so they are near your other AWS regional resources and could interact with them. It is more powerful thanks to this integration, but more limited in terms of being near the user location requests and, finally, potentially slower than CloudFront Functions to manipulate or answer a request.

Also using them, works per Region, so if you will need to architect a solution where you need to handle the same functionality for different user locations, for example, requests coming from *Asia* and from *Europe*, you will need to deploy the same function in at least two different AWS Regions to be more near the user request and to reduce latency. In this scenario, the same applies also to all the AWS regional resources that you will use, for example, EC2, RDS, etc.

Differences between types of edge functions

CloudFront Functions can be categorized as viewer functions or origin functions. Each of them can handle an HTTP request or response event coming on CloudFront:

- **Viewer functions**:
    - **Viewer request functions**: They execute when CloudFront receives a viewer request before it is sent to the origin. Useful for tasks like authentication, URL rewriting, or blocking malicious requests.

o **Viewer response functions**: They execute after CloudFront receives the response from the origin but before it is sent to the viewer. Common use cases include content manipulation, header modifications, or A/B testing.

- **Origin functions**:

  o **Origin request functions**: They execute when CloudFront sends a request to the origin. It can be used for tasks like request normalization, cache key customization, or origin switching.

  o **Origin response functions**: They execute after CloudFront receives the response from the origin but before it is cached or forwarded to the viewer. They are useful for content transformation, image optimization, or response header modifications.

Main differences between viewer functions and origin functions:

- **Timing**: Viewer functions operate at the edge after the request is received from the viewer or before the response is sent to the viewer. Origin functions operate at the edge during interactions with the origin server.

- **Use cases**: Viewer functions are typically used for tasks related to user requests and responses. Origin functions are focused on interactions with the origin server and the responses from the origin.

Use cases and best practices for edge functions

The use cases for edge functions are as follows:

- **Dynamic content generation**: Generate personalized content, such as recommendations or user-specific data, at the edge in real-time.

- **Security enhancements**: Implement security policies, such as access control or threat detection, to filter and block malicious traffic.

- **Content optimization**: Compress, resize, or format images and other assets to optimize content for various devices and network conditions.

- **Real-time analytics**: Capture and process analytics data at the edge to gain insights into user behavior and website performance.

The best practices for edge functions are as follows:

- **Optimize function code**: Keep functions lightweight and efficient to reduce execution time and costs.

- **Use caching wisely**: Leverage caching mechanisms for frequently used data to reduce the number of function executions.

- **Error handling**: Implement robust error handling to ensure graceful degradation in case of function failures.

- **Testing and monitoring**: Thoroughly test functions in a staging environment and monitor their performance and resource usage in production.

- **Security measures**: Implement security best practices, such as input validation and authentication, to prevent common vulnerabilities.

Incorporating AWS CloudFront with edge functions provides developers with a powerful toolset to enhance the performance, security, and customization capabilities of their applications, ensuring a seamless and optimized user experience for global audiences.

Conclusion

This chapter has explored the main AWS Global Infrastructure and the most common compute and storage services offered by AWS. AWS has established itself as a global leader in cloud computing, boasting an extensive network of Regions and AZs strategically located around the world. This expansive infrastructure enables AWS to deliver high availability, low latency, and scalability to businesses of all sizes. The wide array of compute and storage services offered by AWS caters to diverse needs, from basic virtual servers to advanced machine learning algorithms. With services like Amazon EC2, S3, and RDS, organizations can efficiently store, process, and analyze data at scale, empowering them to innovate and grow in today's digital landscape.

Moreover, AWS CDN and edge locations play a pivotal role in enhancing the performance and reliability of applications and websites. By caching content closer to end-users through edge locations, AWS minimizes latency and accelerates content delivery, resulting in an improved user experience. This global network of edge locations ensures that businesses can reach their customers with speed and consistency, regardless of their geographical location.

In essence, AWS Regions, Global Infrastructure, compute and storage services, along with its CDN and edge locations, collectively form a robust ecosystem that underpins the modern digital economy. As businesses increasingly rely on cloud services to drive innovation and efficiency, AWS remains at the forefront, providing the tools and infrastructure necessary to navigate the complexities of today's interconnected world.

In the next chapter, we will explore AWS IAM service and how to manage users and permissions in AWS.

Points to remember

- **AWS Regions**:
    - AWS operates in multiple geographical regions worldwide, each comprising multiple AZs.

- Regions are isolated from each other, offering redundancy and Fault-tolerance.
- Users can choose a region to host their resources based on latency, regulatory requirements, and data sovereignty.

- **Global Infrastructure**:
  - AWS has a global network infrastructure designed for reliability, scalability, and low latency.
  - It includes **points of presence** (**PoPs**), edge locations, and regional edge caches to optimize content delivery and improve user experience.
  - The backbone of AWS global network is built on high-speed private links, ensuring fast and secure data transfer.

- **AWS accounts**:
  - An AWS account is a fundamental entity for accessing AWS services and resources.
  - Users can create multiple AWS accounts to separate billing, resources, and permissions.
  - AWS Organizations allows for centralized management of multiple AWS accounts, enabling consolidated billing, security policies, and resource sharing.

- **CDN**:
  - AWS CloudFront is a globally distributed CDN service that accelerates the delivery of content (for example, web pages, videos, applications) to users.
  - It caches content at edge locations closest to end-users, reducing latency and improving performance.
  - CloudFront integrates seamlessly with other AWS services like S3, EC2, and Lambda, enabling efficient content delivery from various origins.

- **Edge locations**:
  - Edge locations are endpoints for AWS CloudFront and AWS Lambda@Edge.
  - They are located in major cities worldwide and serve requests directly to users, reducing the distance data travels and improving speed.
  - Edge locations also act as entry points for AWS services, enhancing the performance of dynamic content and APIs.

Exercises

1. **What are an AWS Region?**

    a. A collection of AZs in a geographic area.

    b. A single data center location.

    c. A specific AWS service.

    d. A virtual private network.

2. **How does AWS ensure high availability and Fault-tolerance?**

    a. By replicating data across multiple Regions.

    b. By relying on a single data center.

    c. By limiting the number of AZs within a Region.

    d. By using only one type of server hardware.

3. **What is AWS Global Infrastructure composed of?**

    a. Data centers located only in the United States.

    b. A network of interconnected Regions and edge locations.

    c. A single centralized server farm.

    d. Local servers accessible only within specific countries.

4. **How are AWS accounts managed?**

    a. Each account is isolated and managed independently.

    b. All accounts share the same resources.

    c. There is only one master account for all users.

    d. Accounts cannot be created or deleted.

5. **What is AWS CloudFront?**

    a. A virtual private network service.

    b. An on-premises server solution.

    c. A CDN service.

    d. A database management service.

6. **What is the purpose of AWS Edge Functions?**

    a. To manage virtual private networks.

    b. To process and respond to requests at the edge of the AWS network.

    c.   To regulate access to AWS resources

    d.   To provide cloud-based storage solutions.

7. **How does CloudFront enhance website performance?**

    a.   By slowing down content delivery.

    b.   By routing traffic through fewer servers.

    c.   By caching content closer to users.

    d.   By limiting access to certain Regions.

8. **Which AWS service is suitable for distributing dynamic content with low latency?**

    a.   AWS CloudTrail

    b.   AWS Lambda

    c.   AWS CloudFront

    d.   AWS S3

9. **How does AWS handle data replication across Regions?**

    a.   By storing data in a single Region for efficiency.

    b.   By transmitting data unencrypted between Regions.

    c.   By replicating data asynchronously across Regions.

    d.   By not allowing data replication across Regions.

10. **What is the primary benefit of using multiple AWS Regions?**

    a.   Reduced cost.

    b.   Increased Fault-tolerance and disaster recovery capabilities.

    c.   Faster data processing.

    d.   Limited scalability.

Answers

1. a

2. a

3. b

4. a

5. c

6. b

7. c

8. b

9. c

10. b

Key terms

- AWS Region
- AWS Availability Zone
- AWS EC2
- AWS RDS
- AWS S3
- AWS account
- Content delivery network
- AWS CloudFront
- AWS CloudFront edge functions
- AWS CloudFront Lambda@Edge

Join our book's Discord space

Join the book's Discord Workspace for Latest updates, Offers, Tech happenings around the world, New Release and Sessions with the Authors:

https://discord.bpbonline.com

CHAPTER 3

AWS Identity Access Management

Introduction

Amazon Web Services (AWS) Identity and Access Management (IAM) is a robust and secure cloud service that allows you to control access to various AWS resources without compromising security. IAM enables you to create and manage users, groups, roles, and policies to grant permissions to users and groups within your AWS account.

In this section, we will delve into IAM users and how they function within the AWS ecosystem.

Structure

In this chapter, we will cover the following topics:

- IAM users
- IAM groups
- Understanding IAM roles and policies
- Best practices of using AWS IAM
- Introduction to common predefined IAM roles
- Examples of predefined IAM roles and their usage

- Introduction to IAM custom policies
- AWS IAM security best practices
- Introduction to AWS CLI and AWS SDK
- AWS CLI in detail
- AWS SDK in detail
- AWS CloudShell
- Important security considerations on managing AWS IAM users
- Introduction to AWS IAM security tools
- IAM credential report
- IAM access advisor
- AWS IAM shared responsibility model
- AWS guarantees and administrator responsibilities
- Security level of AWS IAM

Objectives

This chapter aims to equip readers with essential skills to create and manage user identities, set permissions and policies, and establish secure access controls. Readers are guided through the process of configuring IAM users, groups, roles, and policies, ensuring the principle of least privilege is applied effectively. Additionally, the chapter delves into best practices for securing AWS resources by implementing **multi-factor authentication** (**MFA**), identity federation, and other advanced IAM features. Also, we will talk about IAM Access keys and their usage with AWS **Command Line Interface** (**CLI**) and AWS **software development kit** (**SDK**) libraries.

By the end of the chapter, readers are expected to have a comprehensive understanding of AWS IAM, enabling them to design secure, scalable, and efficient cloud infrastructures while adhering to industry standard security protocols.

Identity and Access Management users

IAM users are entities within your AWS account that represent the individuals, applications, or services that interact with your AWS resources. Each IAM user has a unique set of security credentials, including a username and password, access key, or **Secure Shell** (**SSH**) key pair. Users can be added, managed, and removed, and their permissions can be finely tuned to restrict access to specific AWS services and actions.

IAM users are fundamental to maintaining security within your AWS infrastructure. By assigning unique credentials to each user, you can track their activities and control their access permissions. For instance, you can create separate users for developers, system administrators, and third-party services, ensuring that they only have access to the resources they need for their tasks.

In the next section of this page, we will explore IAM groups and how they simplify the management of permissions for multiple users.

Identity and Access Management groups

IAM groups are collections of IAM users. Instead of managing permissions for each individual user, you can organize users into groups and assign permissions to the groups. This streamlines the process of granting access, especially in large organizations where numerous users require similar permissions.

Groups enable you to define common sets of permissions for different job functions. For example, you can create a group called **developers** and assign permissions related to development tools and resources. Any user added to the developers group inherits the specified permissions, reducing the administrative overhead of managing permissions for each developer individually.

IAM groups enhance security and simplify access management. When an employee's role changes, you can simply move them to a different group, adjusting their permissions accordingly. This flexibility ensures that users have the appropriate level of access throughout their tenure within the organization.

Understanding IAM roles and policies

IAM roles provide a secure way to delegate permissions to entities within and outside your AWS account, such as applications running on Amazon EC2 instances or users from a different AWS account.

IAM policies, on the other hand, are JSON documents that define permissions and can be attached to users, groups, or roles, controlling what actions they can perform on which resources.

IAM roles

IAM roles are similar to users, but instead of being associated with specific individuals or groups, roles are assumed by entities like AWS services or users from different AWS accounts.

Roles are particularly useful in scenarios where you need to grant permissions to entities that you do not directly control. For example, you can create a role that allows an EC2 instance to read data from an Amazon S3 bucket without embedding any credentials within the instance.

They are temporary and can be assumed by users or services when needed. This temporary nature enhances security by minimizing the exposure of sensitive credentials. Roles can also have specific policies attached, defining the exact actions that can be performed when the role is assumed.

IAM roles play a critical role in enabling secure interactions between various AWS services and resources, enhancing flexibility and reducing security risks associated with static credentials.

IAM policies

IAM policies are the building blocks of access control within AWS IAM. A policy is a JSON document that defines permissions, allowing or denying actions on specified resources. Policies can be attached to users, groups, and roles, dictating what actions these entities can perform.

They are versatile and can be as broad or granular as required, providing fine-grained access control.

This is an example of the format of an IAM policy:

```
{
    "Version": "2012-10-17",
    "Statement": [
        {
            "Effect": "Allow",
            "Action": [
                "s3:ListBucket",
                "s3:GetObject"
            ],
            "Resource": [
                "arn:aws:s3:::*",
                "arn:aws:s3:::*/*"
            ]
        }
    ]
}
```

IAM policies consist of elements such as actions, resources, effects, principals and conditions:

- Actions specify the actions that are allowed or denied (for example `s3:GetObject`).

- Resources define the AWS resources the policy affects (for example, ARN of an S3 bucket).

- Effects can be either allow or deny, indicating whether the specified actions are permitted or prohibited.

- Principals include IAM users, roles, federated users, and services that act on behalf of users or applications. Principals are essential in defining who is authenticated and authorized to use AWS resources.

- Conditions allow you to further refine policies based on factors such as IP addresses or request timestamps.

Policies are central to IAM's security model. By crafting well-defined policies, you can ensure that users, groups, and roles have precisely the right permissions they need, following the principle of least privilege. This principal limits user access rights for specific resources to the bare minimum necessary to complete their jobs, reducing the potential impact of security breaches.

Best practices of using AWS IAM

In this final section, let us examine some best practices related to AWS IAM:

- **Follow the principle of least privilege**: Grant only the permissions necessary for users, groups, and roles to perform their tasks. Regularly review and adjust permissions based on job roles and responsibilities.

- **Use IAM roles for EC2 instances**: When granting permissions to applications running on EC2 instances, use IAM roles instead of embedding access keys within the instances. Roles enhance security by reducing credential exposure.

- **Enable MFA**: Require MFA for all users to add a layer of security to their AWS accounts, making it significantly harder for unauthorized users to gain access.

- **Regularly rotate access keys**: It is better not to use access keys in AWS because they pose a security risk if exposed as they can have a long-term expiration. Instead, AWS recommends using IAM roles, which provide temporary security credentials and reduce the risk of long-term credentials being compromised. But If you are using access keys, regularly rotate them to mitigate the risk associated with compromised or leaked credentials

- **Monitor IAM activity**: Setup AWS CloudTrail to log IAM events, allowing you to track user activities and changes to permissions. Monitoring IAM activity helps in identifying and responding to potential security threats.

Introduction to common predefined IAM roles

In AWS, IAM roles can be created as custom new roles where you can define every permission per AWS service you need, or you could use pre-configured policies that help in defining a set of permissions for different job functions within an organization.

These predefined roles simplify the process of managing permissions for common use cases such as developers, administrators, DevOps engineers, and read-only users.

Also, using such predefined roles in IAM helps the AWS administrator to better handle different scenarios and user roles and responsibilities and use common setups already provided by AWS. This helps improve the security and reusability of roles, as we already have every edge case covered for every AWS service.

In this section, we will explore some of the commonly used predefined IAM roles and provide examples of how these roles can be utilized across different roles within an organization.

IAM roles for developers

Developers often require access to AWS services for tasks such as creating and managing EC2 instances, accessing S3 buckets, and configuring databases. A predefined IAM role for developers group might include permissions like **EC2:CreateInstance**, **s3:GetObject**, and **rds:DescribeDBInstances**. By attaching this role to developers, they can effectively work on developing applications and managing related AWS resources without having excessive privileges.

For example, a developer assumes an IAM role that grants permissions to deploy applications on EC2 instances, read data from specific S3 buckets, and write logs to CloudWatch Logs. With these permissions, the developer can deploy applications and access necessary resources without having access to sensitive data or critical infrastructure configurations.

IAM roles for administrators

Administrators require broader access across various AWS services to manage user accounts, configure security settings, and monitor activities. A predefined IAM role for administrators might include permissions like **iam:CreateUser**, **EC2:DescribeInstances**, **cloudwatch:GetMetricStatistics**, and **sns:Publish**. This role allows administrators to effectively manage the AWS environment, including creating and managing IAM users, monitoring resource usage, and handling notifications.

For example, an administrator assumes an IAM role that grants permissions to create and manage IAM users, view EC2 instance details for troubleshooting, access CloudWatch metrics for monitoring, and send notifications using **Simple Notification Service** (**SNS**). With these permissions, the administrator can maintain user accounts, monitor system performance, and respond to incidents promptly.

IAM roles for DevOps engineers

DevOps engineers focus on automating deployment processes, managing infrastructure as code, and ensuring seamless integration between development ard operations. A predefined IAM role for DevOps engineers might include permissions like **cloudformation:CreateStack**, **lambda:InvokeFunction**, and **EC2:ModifyInstanceAttribute**. These permissions allow DevOps engineers to automate infrastructure deployments, invoke serverless functions, and modify instance configurations as needed.

For example, a DevOps engineer assumes an IAM role that grants permissions to create and manage CloudFormation stacks for infrastructure deployment, invoke AWS Lambda functions for automated tasks, and modify EC2 instance attributes for dynamic scaling. With these permissions, DevOps engineers can automate the deployment process, manage serverless applications, and optimize resource utilization based on demand.

IAM roles for read-only users

Read-only users need access to monitor and view resources without the ability to make changes. A predefined IAM role for read-only users might include permissions like **cloudwatch:GetMetricStatistics**, **EC2:DescribeInstances**, **s3:GetObject**, and **iam:GetUser**. This role allows read-only users to view metrics, check EC2 instance details, access specific S3 objects, and retrieve user information without altering any resources.

Example: A read-only user assumes an IAM role that grants permissions to view CloudWatch metrics for monitoring, retrieve information about EC2 instances for status checks, access specific objects within S3 buckets for analysis, and view user details using IAM. With these permissions, read-only users can stay informed about the system's status and access necessary data without risking accidental modifications.

Examples of predefined IAM roles and their usage

Following the example above, for different user roles or job functionality like developer users, administrator users, DevOps users, read-only users, etc., you could use those predefined AWS IAM Roles to give each the correct permissions.

Here are some commonly used pre-configured AWS IAM roles for different job functions:

Useful IAM roles for developers

Developers usually needs full access to some resources and services to work and update the code running on AWS, for example some commons roles assigned to developers are:

- **AWSLambda_FullAccess**: Allows developers to create, update, and delete Lambda functions.

- **AmazonS3FullAccess**: Provides full access to Amazon S3 buckets and objects, allowing developers to read, write, and delete data.

- **AmazonDynamoDBFullAccess**: Grants full access to Amazon DynamoDB tables and data, enabling developers to perform CRUD operations.

- **AmazonEC2FullAccess**: Provides complete access to Amazon EC2 instances, allowing developers to create, modify, and terminate instances.

- **AWSCodeCommitFullAccess**: Grants full access to AWS CodeCommit, enabling developers to manage and version control their source code.

Useful IAM roles for administrators

Administrators are power users that usually needs to control some key aspect of the AWS environment like managing users on IAM, handling the creation or update for most resources on the AWS account like databases and VPC. Usually the administrators are the most powerful users with the most permissions on an AWS account, enabling other user types like devops or developers to access the account. Some example roles are:

- **AdministratorAccess**: Provides full access to all AWS services and resources, allowing administrators to manage the entire AWS environment.

- **IAMFullAccess**: Grants full access to IAM, enabling administrators to create, modify, and delete IAM users, groups, and roles.

- **AmazonVPCFullAccess**: Provides complete access to Amazon **Virtual Private Cloud (VPC)**, allowing administrators to create and manage VPC resources.

- **AmazonRDSFullAccess**: Grants full access to Amazon RDS resources, allowing administrators to manage RDS instances and databases.

- **AmazonRoute53FullAccess**: Provides full access to Amazon Route 53, allowing administrators to manage DNS records and domains.

Useful IAM roles for DevOps

Devops are power users that needs to control some key aspect of the AWS environment for handling deployments artifacts, code builds, code repositories, Docker container registries, logs and metrics, etc. They are enablers for other developer teams to handle parts of automation and infrastructure. Some example roles are:

- **AWSCodeDeploy_FullAccess**: Allows DevOps engineers to create and manage CodeDeploy applications, deployment groups, and deployments.

- **AWSCodePipeline_FullAccess**: Provides full access to AWS CodePipeline, allowing DevOps engineers to create and manage continuous delivery pipelines.

- **AmazonEC2ContainerRegistryFullAccess**: Grants full access to Amazon **Elastic Container Registry (ECR)**, enabling DevOps engineers to manage Docker container images.

- **AWSLambda_FullAccess**: Allows DevOps engineers to create, update, and manage Lambda functions.

- **AmazonECS_FullAccess**: Provides full access to Amazon **Elastic Container Service (ECS)**, allowing DevOps engineers to create and manage containerized applications.

Useful IAM roles for read-only users

Read-only users are users with limited permissions to only see some of the resources in an AWS account. Usually those kinds of users are useful in an organization to show some AWS services like reading logs of some applications on CloudWatch but disabling them to alter those resources. Some example roles are:

- **ReadOnlyAccess**: Provides read-only access to most AWS services and resources, allowing users to view configurations and monitor resources.

- **AmazonEC2ReadOnlyAccess**: Allows read-only access to Amazon EC2 instances, providing information on instances without modifying them.

- **AmazonS3ReadOnlyAccess**: Grants read-only access to Amazon S3 buckets and objects, allowing users to view and download data.

- **CloudWatchReadOnlyAccess**: Provides read-only access to Amazon CloudWatch, enabling users to view monitoring metrics and alarms.

- **AWSConfigReadOnlyAccess**: Allows read-only access to AWS Config, allowing users to view resource configuration history and configuration snapshots.

These predefined roles help streamline access management for developers, administrators, DevOps engineers, and read-only users, ensuring that they have the necessary permissions to perform their tasks efficiently and securely.

Introduction to IAM custom policies

AWS IAM allows you to create custom policies to define specific permissions for users, groups, or roles in your AWS environment. Custom policies provide a way to tailor access control precisely according to your organization's requirements.

Here, we will explore the process of creating IAM custom policies and discuss some key aspects involved.

Creating custom policies

Creating custom IAM policies in AWS involves a few straightforward steps. Here is a detailed description of the process:

Step 1: Sign in to the AWS Management Console

1. Sign in to the AWS Management Console using your AWS account credentials.

2. Make sure that you have the necessary IAM permissions to create custom policies, as IAM policies are critical for controlling access to AWS resources.

Step 2: Access the IAM dashboard

1. Once you are logged in, navigate to the AWS IAM dashboard by searching for **IAM** in the AWS Management Console search bar or by finding it under the **Security, Identity, & Compliance** section.

2. Click on **IAM** to access the IAM dashboard.

Step 3: Create a custom policy

1. In the IAM dashboard, click on **Policies** in the left-hand navigation pane.

2. On the **Policies** page, click the **Create policy** button.

Step 4: Build the policy document

1. In the **Create policy** wizard, you have two options: You can either use the visual policy editor or use the JSON editor. For more control and precision, it is recommended to use the JSON editor.

2. Click the **JSON** tab to open the JSON editor.

Step 5: Define the policy

1. In the JSON editor, you define the policy using JSON syntax. The policy must include the following elements:

    a. **Version**: The policy language version. Use **2012-10-17** for the latest version.

    b. **Statement**: An array of policy statements, where each statement defines the permissions for a specific action on specific resources.

    c. **Inside each statement, you specify**:

        i. **Effect**: Whether to allow or deny the action (**Allow** or **Deny**).

        ii. **Action**: The list of actions to be allowed or denied. These should be specified as an array of strings.

        iii. **Resource**: The AWS resources to which the policy statement applies. Specify these using **Amazon Resource Names** (**ARNs**). You can use wildcards (*****) to match multiple resources.

Here is an example of a custom policy JSON document:

```
{
  "Version": "2012-10-17",
  "Statement": [
    {
      "Effect": "Allow",
      "Action": [
        "s3:GetObject",
        "s3:ListBucket"
      ],
      "Resource": [
        "arn:aws:s3:::example-bucket",
        "arn:aws:s3:::example-bucket/*"
      ]
    }
  ]
}
```

In this example, the policy allows the **s3:GetObject** and **s3:ListBucket** actions on the specified Amazon S3 bucket (**example-bucket**) and its objects.

Step 6: Review and validate

1. After defining the policy in the JSON editor, you can validate the policy by clicking the **Validate policy** button. This helps ensure that the JSON is correctly formatted and follows AWS policy language syntax.

Step 7: Name and describe the policy

1. Once you have defined and validated the policy, you need to provide a name and description for the policy to make it easily identifiable.

2. Fill in the **Name** and **Description** fields.

Step 8: Review and create the policy

1. Review the policy details to ensure they match your intended permissions.

2. Click the **Create policy** button to create the custom policy.

Step 9: Attach the policy to users, groups, or roles

1. After creating the policy, you can attach it to users, groups, or roles in your AWS account.

2. To attach the policy, go to the **Users, Groups,** or **Roles** section in the IAM dashboard, select the desired identity, and then attach the policy.

You have successfully created a custom IAM policy in AWS. This policy can now be used to grant or restrict permissions for the associated users, groups, or roles within your AWS environment.

AWS IAM security best practices

Here we show some AWS IAM security best practices following AWS best security standards and suggestions:

Setting up multi-factor authentication for an AWS user

Setting up MFA for your AWS users and roles is a best practice and suggested by AWS. It will give you another level of security when a user needs to access your AWS account. MFA adds an extra layer of security to your AWS accounts and resources. Here is why activating MFA on users is crucial:

- **Enhanced security**: MFA significantly enhances security by requiring users to provide multiple forms of verification before accessing an account. In addition to the traditional username and password, users must also provide a second authentication factor, which can be a **time-based one-time password (TOTP)** from an authenticator app, a hardware token, or even a biometric factor like a fingerprint. This makes it exponentially harder for unauthorized individuals to gain access, even if they manage to obtain the user's password.

- **Mitigating credential theft**: With the rise of phishing attacks and data breaches, passwords are frequently compromised. MFA provides an additional barrier, making it much more challenging for attackers to misuse stolen credentials. Even if an attacker has the user's password, they would still need the secondary authentication factor to gain access.

- **Compliance requirements**: Many industries and regulatory standards (such as *Payment Card Industry Data Security Standard (PCI DSS)*, *Health Insurance Portability and Accountability Act (HIPAA)*, and *General Data Protection Regulation (GDPR)*) mandate the use of MFA to protect sensitive data. By enabling MFA, organizations can ensure compliance with these regulations and avoid potential penalties or legal issues related to data breaches.

- **Protecting business-critical applications**: MFA is especially crucial for accessing critical applications and services. In a cloud environment like AWS, where businesses store vast amounts of data and run mission-critical applications, having an additional layer of security is paramount to prevent unauthorized access or data manipulation.

- **Securing privileged accounts**: Users with elevated privileges, such as administrators and developers, have access to sensitive configurations and data. MFA ensures that these accounts are more secure, reducing the risk associated with misuse or accidental modifications of critical settings.

- **Account recovery and trust**: In case a user forgets their password or loses access due to some other reason, MFA can be used as part of the account recovery process, adding an extra layer of trust when verifying the user's identity.

- **Setting a security standard**: By mandating MFA for all users, organizations set a security standard that emphasizes the importance of robust authentication practices. It creates a culture of security awareness among employees and users.

In summary, enabling MFA on users accounts is essential for safeguarding sensitive data, meeting compliance requirements, preventing unauthorized access, and maintaining the security and integrity of AWS resources and services.

Follow the steps to activate MFA on an AWS user:

Step 1: **Sign in to AWS Management Console**:

1. Sign in to the AWS Management Console using your AWS account credentials.

Step 2: **Access IAM dashboard**:

1. Navigate to the IAM service by searching for **IAM** in the AWS Management Console search bar.

2. In the IAM dashboard, select **Users** from the left-hand navigation pane.

Step 3: **Select the user**:

1. Click on the username of the user for whom you want to enable MFA.

2. In the **Security credentials** tab, locate the **Assigned MFA device** section and click on **Manage MFA device**.

Step 4: **Choose MFA device**:

1. **Choose the type of MFA device**: **Virtual MFA device** (such as *Google Authenticator* or *Authy*) or **U2F security key** (a physical device).

2. Follow the on-screen instructions to configure the selected MFA device. For virtual MFA, you will need to scan the QR code with your authenticator app or enter the provided secret key.

Setting up single sign-on in AWS

AWS **Single Sign-On** (**SSO**) is a cloud service that simplifies managing SSO access to multiple AWS accounts and business applications. It enables users to sign in once and gain access to all assigned accounts and applications from a centralized portal.

SSO solutions have become increasingly popular in organizations of all sizes due to their ability to streamline access management, enhance security, and improve user productivity.

Here are why many organizations opt for SSO in their AWS environments:

- **Centralized access control**: SSO allows organizations to centralize access control. With a single set of credentials, users can access multiple applications and services, including AWS resources. This centralization simplifies the process of granting, updating, and revoking access permissions, making it easier for IT administrators to manage user accounts.

- **Improved user experience**: Users benefit from a more seamless and convenient experience. Once authenticated through SSO, they can access various AWS services and applications without needing separate login credentials for each one. This streamlines the login process and reduces the number of passwords users need to remember, enhancing user productivity.

- **Enhanced security**: SSO solutions often come with robust security features, such as MFA and adaptive authentication. MFA adds an extra layer of security by requiring users to provide additional verification, making it more challenging for unauthorized users to gain access. Adaptive authentication analyzes user behavior and context to determine the level of authentication required, adding flexibility and security.

- **Efficient onboarding and offboarding**: When new employees join an organization, or when existing employees leave, SSO simplifies the onboarding and offboarding processes. IT administrators can provision and deprovision user access to AWS services centrally, ensuring that employees have the right access levels from day one and that access is promptly revoked when they leave the organization.

- **Compliance and audit trail**: SSO solutions often provide robust auditing capabilities. They maintain detailed logs of user activities and access attempts, offering organizations valuable insights into user behavior. These logs are crucial for compliance purposes, helping organizations adhere to regulatory requirements by demonstrating who accessed what resources and when.

- **Integration capabilities**: SSO solutions can integrate with existing **identity providers** (**IdPs**) and directories, such as *Microsoft Active Directory* or *LDAP systems*. This integration streamlines user management processes, allowing organizations to leverage their existing identity infrastructure and extend it to cloud services like AWS.

- **Simplified password policies**: By using SSO, organizations can enforce strong password policies and authentication standards within the SSO solution itself. Users only need to remember one strong password for the SSO platform, reducing the likelihood of weak passwords or password reuse across multiple services.

- **Scalability and flexibility**: SSO solutions are designed to scale with the organization. As the number of users and applications grows, SSO can accommodate the increased load seamlessly. Additionally, SSO solutions often support a wide range of applications and services, making it flexible for organizations with diverse technology stacks.

By leveraging SSO, organizations can optimize their AWS environment, promoting security and productivity across the entire organization.

Follow the steps to enable SSO in your AWS account:

Step 1: Access AWS SSO dashboard:

1. Navigate to the AWS SSO service by searching for **SSO** in the AWS Management Console search bar.

2. In the SSO dashboard, click on **Applications** from the left-hand navigation pane.

Step 2: Add an application:

1. Click on **Add a new application**.

2. Select the application type (such as AWS SSO application or External SAML) and follow the prompts to configure the application. You might need to provide metadata URLs or other details depending on the application type.

Step 3: Assign users:

1. After configuring the application, assign users or groups to the application.

2. Click on the **Assign users** button and select the users or groups that should have access to the application.

Generating access keys for an IAM user

It is better not to use access keys in AWS because they pose a security risk if exposed as they can have a long-term expiration. Instead, AWS recommends using IAM roles, which provide temporary security credentials and reduce the risk of long-term credentials being compromised. As said before, if you need to use access keys, remember to always rotate them after some time.

Generating access keys for an IAM user in AWS is essential for several reasons:

- **Programmatic access**: Access keys are necessary if you want to interact with AWS programmatically through APIs, SDKs, or CLIs. These keys allow you to automate various tasks, such as deploying applications, managing resources, or integrating AWS services with third-party applications.

- **Secure authentication**: Access keys, coupled with the secret access key, provide a secure way to authenticate requests made to AWS services. When you generate access keys, you create a pair: An access key ID and a secret access key. While the access key ID is public and can be shared, the secret access key must be kept confidential. These keys act as a form of authentication, ensuring that only authorized users or applications can access AWS resources.

- **Granular permissions**: Access keys are associated with IAM policies that define specific permissions for users or applications. By generating access keys and attaching policies, you can enforce the principle of least privilege, granting only the necessary permissions to perform specific tasks. This granular control enhances security by restricting unnecessary access.

- **Temporary credentials**: Access keys can also be used to generate temporary security credentials. Temporary security credentials are often used in scenarios like cross-account access or temporary access to services. Temporary credentials are time-limited, reducing the risk of misuse if they are accidentally exposed.

- **Integrating third-party applications**: Many third-party applications and tools integrate with AWS services. Access keys are often required to establish secure connections between these applications and your AWS resources. By generating access keys, you enable seamless integration without compromising security.

- **Enhanced security practices**: Access keys allow organizations to implement security best practices, such as rotating credentials regularly. Regularly rotating access keys reduces the exposure window in case the keys are compromised. AWS provides tools and services to manage the rotation of access keys automatically.

- **Compliance requirements**: Certain regulatory standards and compliance frameworks require organizations to have strict access control policies, including the use of access keys. Generating access keys and following secure practices around their usage can help organizations meet these compliance requirements.

- **Non-interactive access**: Access keys enable non-interactive access to AWS resources. This means that applications and scripts can access AWS services without requiring human intervention. Automated processes can run without manual input, allowing for efficient and continuous operations.

Generating access keys for IAM users is a fundamental practice for securely managing and automating AWS resources in a wide range of use cases.

Follow the steps to activate an access key for a user in your AWS account:

Step 1: Access IAM dashboard:

1. Navigate to the IAM service by searching for **IAM** in the AWS Management Console search bar.

2. In the IAM dashboard, select **Users** from the left-hand navigation pane.

Step 2: Select the user:

1. Click on the username of the user for whom you want to create access keys.

2. In the **Security credentials** tab, locate the **Access keys** section and click on **Create access key**.

Step 3: **Download access keys**:

1. After clicking **Create access key**, AWS will generate an access key ID and a secret access key.

2. Download the CSV file containing these access keys. This file is crucial; it contains sensitive information and should be stored securely.

Introduction to AWS CLI and AWS SDK

AWS CLI is a powerful command line tool provided by AWS that allows users to interact with AWS services directly from the command line. It provides a unified interface for managing various AWS services and resources, making it efficient for developers, system administrators, and DevOps professionals to automate tasks, configure settings, and manage infrastructure on AWS.

Usually, AWS CLI and AWS SDK are used by access keys and IAM roles, to give the DevOps or developer a permanent access to AWS resources. Those keys are then required to use the CLI or the SDK to reach AWS services on the cloud and every user needs to Setup their PC to use them correctly.

Following are the key features of AWS CLI:

- **Unified command structure**: AWS CLI offers a consistent and intuitive command structure, allowing users to interact with different AWS services using simple commands and parameters.

- **Scripting and automation**: AWS CLI facilitates automation by enabling users to script and automate AWS tasks. This capability is invaluable for creating custom solutions and integrating AWS services into existing workflows.

- **Output customization**: Users can customize the output format of AWS CLI commands, making it easier to parse and integrate the output into scripts or other tools.

Overview of AWS software development kit

AWS SDKs are a collection of software tools and libraries provided by AWS to help developers build applications that interact with AWS services. These SDKs are available for various programming languages, including Python, Java, JavaScript, .NET, and more, making it easier for developers to work with AWS services in their preferred programming language.

AWS Command Line Interface in detail

The AWS CLI is a powerful tool designed to provide developers and system administrators with a streamlined way to interact with AWS from the command line. It offers a comprehensive set of commands that allow users to manage various AWS services, including compute, storage, networking, database, and more, directly from their terminal or command prompt. With the AWS CLI, users can perform a wide range of tasks, such as launching EC2 instances, managing S3 buckets, configuring IAM roles, and deploying serverless applications, all without the need for a graphical user interface.

One of the key benefits of the AWS CLI is its flexibility and automation capabilities. By leveraging the CLI's commands and scripting capabilities, users can automate routine tasks, create custom workflows, and integrate AWS services into their existing automation pipelines. This not only improves efficiency but also enables the seamless integration of AWS resources into complex workflows and applications. Additionally, the AWS CLI is continuously updated and maintained by AWS, ensuring compatibility with the latest AWS services and features, and providing users with access to cutting-edge tools and technologies for managing their cloud infrastructure. Overall, the AWS CLI is an essential tool for anyone working with AWS, offering a fast, efficient, and scriptable way to interact with AWS services from the command line.

Installation and configuration

Users can install AWS CLI on their local machines and configure it with their AWS credentials, allowing secure access to AWS services. Configuration includes specifying the AWS access key, secret key, default region, and output format.

Basic commands and usage

AWS CLI provides a wide range of commands for different services, such as EC2, S3, Lambda, and more. Users can create, configure, and manage resources using commands like `aws EC2 create-instance`, `aws s3 cp`, and `aws lambda create-function`.

AWS CLI advanced features

- **Profiles and multiple environments**: AWS CLI supports profiles, allowing users to switch between different AWS accounts and environments seamlessly. This feature is particularly useful for developers and administrators managing multiple AWS environments.

- **Query and filter options**: Users can query and filter AWS CLI output using `--query` and `--filter` options, enabling precise control over the data retrieved from AWS services.

- **Synchronization and transfer commands**: AWS CLI offers synchronization commands (`aws s3 sync`) that facilitate efficient transfer and synchronization of files and directories between local systems and Amazon S3 buckets.

AWS software development kit in detail

The AWS SDK is a comprehensive collection of tools, libraries, and APIs provided by AWS to streamline the process of integrating AWS services into applications and services. Designed to facilitate developers in building, deploying, and managing applications on the AWS platform, the SDK offers support for multiple programming languages, including Java, Python, JavaScript, .NET, Ruby, Go. and more. This versatility enables developers to leverage the AWS ecosystem regardless of their preferred programming language, enhancing flexibility and accessibility across diverse development environments.

With the AWS SDK, developers gain access to a vast array of AWS services ranging from compute, storage, and databases to machine learning, analytics, and IoT. Through intuitive APIs and client libraries, developers can interact with these services programmatically, enabling seamless integration of AWS functionalities into their applications. Whether provisioning cloud resources, managing data storage, orchestrating serverless workflows, or leveraging advanced AI capabilities, the SDK provides the necessary tools and abstractions to simplify development tasks and accelerate time-to-market. Moreover, the SDK is regularly updated to incorporate new features, enhancements, and optimizations, ensuring developers have access to the latest advancements and best practices for building robust, scalable, and secure applications on the AWS Cloud infrastructure.

SDK installation and configuration

Developers can install and configure AWS SDKs in their development environments, integrating them into their projects. Configuration involves setting up AWS credentials and selecting the desired region.

SDK usage in code

The AWS SDK is a comprehensive set of libraries and tools provided by AWS to facilitate interaction with AWS services programmatically. As we talked before, this SDK supports various programming languages such as Java, Python, JavaScript (Node.js). Ruby, and more, allowing developers to integrate AWS services seamlessly into their applications.

It offers a wide range of functionalities, including managing resources like EC2 instances, S3 buckets, DynamoDB tables, and more, as well as accessing AWS APIs for tasks like sending emails, processing data, and deploying applications. The AWS SDK simplifies and accelerates development by abstracting away the complexities of interacting with AWS services directly, handling authentication, request signing, and error handling, thus enabling developers to focus on building and innovating their applications without worrying about low-level implementation details. Additionally, it provides robust documentation, code samples, and community support, making it an indispensable tool for developers looking to leverage the power and scalability of AWS services in their projects.

Let us explore some example usage of what we can do with the AWS SDK! We will use python, one of the easiest to learn and successful language in the market. To interact with AWS, we will use the library **boto3**, that is a library to communicate to AWS from python so we can access AWS resources programmatically.

Creating AWS service clients

Developers can create service clients using the SDK, enabling them to interact with AWS services programmatically. For example, in Python, developers can create an S3 client using the Boto3 SDK.

```
import boto3

s3_client = boto3.client('s3')
```

Making API requests

Developers can make API requests to AWS services using SDK methods. For instance, to list objects in an S3 bucket, developers can use the following Boto3 code snippet:

```
response = s3_client.list_objects(Bucket='my-bucket-name')
print(response)
```

Error handling and asynchronous operations

AWS SDKs provide robust error handling mechanisms, allowing developers to handle various error scenarios gracefully. Additionally, SDKs support asynchronous operations, enhancing the efficiency of applications that interact with AWS services.

AWS SDK features and benefits

- **Built-in retry logic**: AWS SDKs include built-in retry logic, which automatically retries requests in case of transient failures, ensuring the reliability of applications.

- **Integration with AWS services**: SDKs provide seamless integration with various AWS services, enabling developers to work with services like AWS Lambda, DynamoDB, and Amazon S3 effortlessly.

- **Language-specific features**: Each SDK offers language-specific features and idiomatic interfaces, allowing developers to write code in a way that is natural for the programming language they are using, enhancing developer productivity.

- **Setting up AWS CLI**: Setting up AWS CLI or AWS SDK on a user's PC involves several steps to enable seamless interaction with AWS services.

Below are the methods of setting up AWS CLI and AWS SDK on a user's PC:

Installation

You can find AWS SDK documentation for multiple programming languages here, under the section developer resources: **https://aws.amazon.com/developer/tools/**

For Windows:

1. Download the AWS CLI installer for Windows from the official AWS CLI website.
2. Run the installer and follow the installation prompts.

For macOS:

1. Install AWS CLI using Homebrew by running `brew install awscli` in the Terminal.

For Linux:

1. Use the package manager (for example, **apt** for Ubuntu) to install AWS CLI. For example, on Ubuntu, run `sudo apt-get install awscli`.

Configuration

Run **aws configure** command:

1. Open the terminal or command prompt and type **aws configure**.
2. Enter your AWS Access Key ID, Secret Access Key, default region, and desired output format.

Verification

To verify the setup, run a simple AWS CLI command, such as **aws s3 ls**, to list your S3 buckets. If configured correctly, it should return a list of your S3 buckets.

Setting up AWS SDK

Here we show how to setup AWS SDK in your local environment to communicate with AWS services.

Choose the right SDK

Select the appropriate AWS SDK based on the programming language you are using (for example, Boto3 for Python, AWS SDK for JavaScript).

Installation

Using package managers:

- For Python (Boto3), install the SDK using **pip**:

  `pip install boto3`.

- For JavaScript (AWS SDK for JavaScript), install using **npm**:
- ` npm install aws-sdk`.

Using integrated development environments (IDEs):

Many IDEs, such as PyCharm and Visual Studio Code, have built-in support for AWS SDKs. You can install SDKs and manage dependencies directly within the IDE.

Configuration

- **AWS credentials**: Provide AWS credentials in your code using methods provided by the SDK. These credentials include AWS access key ID and secret access key.

- **AWS Region**: Set the desired AWS Region in your code to ensure your SDK interacts with the correct region.

Verification

Write a simple code snippet to interact with an AWS service (for example, create an S3 bucket, read from a DynamoDB table). If the code runs successfully and interacts with the service, your SDK setup is correct.

Remember, always follow the principle of least privilege. When configuring IAM users for CLI or SDK access, provide only the necessary permissions required for the specific tasks to enhance security.

Conclusion on AWS CLI and AWS SDK

AWS CLI and AWS SDKs are powerful tools that enable users and developers to interact with AWS services efficiently. Whether through the command line or in code, these tools provide flexibility, automation capabilities, and extensive features, empowering users and developers to manage AWS resources and build robust applications in the cloud.

AWS CloudShell

AWS CloudShell is a browser-based Shell provided by AWS, enabling users to manage AWS resources directly from the AWS Management Console. With CloudShell, users have access to a pre-configured shell environment, eliminating the need to install and configure command line tools. Here is an overview of its features and benefits:

- **Seamless access to AWS resources**: CloudShell provides direct access to AWS services and resources without the hassle of setting up credentials or managing configurations. It comes pre-authenticated with the user's existing AWS Console credentials, ensuring a seamless experience.

- **Pre-installed AWS CLI and SDKs**: CloudShell comes with pre-installed AWS CLI and various AWS SDKs. Users can instantly run AWS CLI commands and SDK code without any setup, making it ideal for quick tasks and scripting.

- **Persistent storage**: Each CloudShell session includes persistent storage of up to 1 GB, allowing users to store scripts, configuration files, and other resources securely. This persistent storage ensures that important files are retained across sessions.

- **Security and compliance**: CloudShell provides a secure and compliant environment for executing commands. It runs within an Amazon VPC with AWS IAM integration, ensuring robust security controls and compliance with AWS best practices.

- **Convenience and efficiency**: CloudShell's browser-based interface means users can access it from anywhere with internet connectivity, enhancing convenience and flexibility. It is particularly useful for scenarios where installing and configuring command line tools on local machines might be challenging, such as in shared or public computing environments.

- **Integration with AWS services**: CloudShell seamlessly integrates with other AWS services, enabling users to interact with resources directly from the shell. It can be used in conjunction with services like AWS Systems Manager, AWS Lambda, and AWS Step Functions, allowing for powerful automation and orchestration capabilities.

AWS CloudShell simplifies the management of AWS resources by providing a hassle-free, pre-configured shell environment directly within the AWS Management Console. Its seamless access, pre-installed tools, security features, and integration capabilities make it a valuable tool for developers, system administrators, and other AWS users, enhancing their productivity and simplifying their workflows.

Important security considerations on managing AWS IAM users

Managing AWS IAM users involve critical security considerations due to the substantial impact user access can have on the security posture of an organization's AWS environment. One of the primary concerns is least privilege access, ensuring that users have the minimum level of permissions necessary to perform their tasks.

Overly permissive access can lead to accidental or intentional misuse of resources, potentially resulting in data breaches, data loss, or infrastructure disruptions. Organizations must regularly review and refine permissions, adhering to the principle of least privilege, to mitigate these risks.

Another crucial security consideration revolves around credential management. This includes practices like enforcing strong password policies, enabling MFA to add an extra layer of security, and rotating access keys and secret keys regularly.

Compromised credentials are a significant security threat, as they can lead to unauthorized access and misuse of resources. Proper management of access keys, secret keys, and other authentication methods ensures that even if credentials are somehow leaked, they become useless after a short period due to rotation practices. Furthermore, organizations should closely monitor user activities and configure logging and auditing to detect and respond to any suspicious or unauthorized actions promptly. Security considerations in managing IAM users are essential to maintaining the integrity, confidentiality, and availability of AWS resources and data.

Checklist for the best IAM security to remember:

- Always secure MFA devices and access keys.
- Regularly rotate access keys for enhanced security.
- For SSO applications, follow best practices specific to the IdP and application configuration.
- Implement policies to enforce secure practices and restrict unnecessary permissions for your AWS services and AWS accounts.

Introduction to AWS IAM security tools

AWS IAM is a powerful tool that enables you to manage access to your AWS services securely. IAM allows you to create and manage AWS users and groups and use permissions to allow and deny their access to AWS resources. In addition to managing users and groups, IAM provides a range of security tools and features to enhance the security of your AWS environment.

Importance of IAM security

Securing your AWS environment is critical to protecting sensitive data, ensuring compliance, and preventing unauthorized access. IAM security tools play a vital role in achieving these objectives. This document explores two key IAM security tools: IAM credential report and IAM access advisor.

IAM credential report

The IAM credential report is a valuable tool provided by AWS IAM that gives you a detailed overview of the status of your IAM users and their respective security credentials. This report provides information about user access, their password policies, and the status of access keys.

Key features and benefits

- **Access key details**: The report includes information about access keys, such as their creation date, their status (active or inactive), and the last time they were used. This data is crucial for identifying and managing unused or outdated access keys, reducing the attack surface.

- **Password policy compliance**: IAM credential report also highlights the adherence of IAM users to your specified password policies. It provides insights into password complexity, ensuring that users follow the required security standards.

- **Security best practices**: By regularly reviewing the IAM credential report, you can enforce security best practices such as rotating access keys periodically, ensuring MFA is enabled, and monitoring password policy compliance.

Use cases

- **Security auditing and compliance**: IAM credential report is invaluable for security audits and compliance checks. Organizations can ensure that IAM users adhere to security policies and standards set by industry regulations and internal security guidelines.

- **Incident response**: In the event of a security incident, the report helps security teams identify compromised or suspicious accounts quickly. By promptly deactivating compromised access keys, organizations can mitigate potential risks.

IAM access advisor

IAM access advisor provides insights into how your IAM policies are being used across AWS services. It shows which services an IAM principal can access and which actions they can perform within those services.

Key features and benefits

- **Usage patterns**: Access advisor analyzes historical data to provide usage patterns. It helps organizations understand which permissions are necessary for users' day-to-day tasks and identify unnecessary or overly permissive policies.

- **Least privilege principle**: By leveraging IAM access advisor, organizations can implement the principle of least privilege effectively. This principle ensures that users have only the permissions necessary to perform their specific tasks, reducing the risk of unauthorized access.

- **Resource optimization**: Access advisor aids in optimizing resources by identifying unused or underutilized permissions. By removing unnecessary permissions, organizations can enhance security and reduce the attack surface.

Use cases

- **Policy refinement**: Access advisor data empowers organizations to refine policies based on actual usage. This refinement ensures that policies align with users' requirements while maintaining security, improving operational efficiency.

- **Security enhancements**: By identifying and removing unused or overly permissive policies, access advisor significantly enhances the security posture of an organization. It minimizes the risk of privilege escalation attacks and unauthorized access attempts.

  In conclusion, IAM credential report and IAM access advisor are integral components of AWS IAM's robust security arsenal. These tools not only provide critical insights into your IAM environment but also enable proactive security measures, policy refinement, and adherence to the principle of least privilege. By leveraging these tools effectively, organizations can enhance their security posture, ensuring secure and compliant usage of AWS resources.

AWS IAM shared responsibility model

AWS operates on a shared responsibility model, wherein AWS manages and controls the components from the host operating system and virtualization layer down to the physical security of the facilities in which the service operates. However, the customer is responsible for securing their data in the cloud, which includes configuring and managing access controls appropriately. In the context of AWS IAM, this shared responsibility model holds true.

AWS guarantees and administrator responsibilities

AWS provides a robust set of services and infrastructure to support the needs of businesses and developers globally. AWS guarantees high availability, scalability, and security through its data centers distributed across various regions worldwide. With its **service level agreements (SLAs)**, AWS commits to specific uptime percentages for its services, ensuring reliability and continuity of operations. However, administrators bear the responsibility of configuring and managing their AWS environments effectively. This includes tasks such as setting up security measures, implementing access controls, monitoring resource usage, optimizing performance, and ensuring compliance with industry standards and regulations. Additionally, administrators must stay updated with AWS best practices, promptly address any issues or vulnerabilities, and plan for disaster recovery to uphold the integrity and efficiency of their AWS deployments.

AWS guarantees in IAM Security

AWS guarantees the security and durability of the infrastructure that runs its services, including IAM. AWS ensures that IAM services are highly available, fault-tolerant, and resilient. Additionally, AWS provides various security features and best practices that customers can utilize, such as encryption, MFA, and detailed logging and monitoring tools.

In summary, AWS in the shared responsibility model guarantees for IAM:

- Infrastructure security (global network security) of all their networking tools and services

- Configuration and vulnerability analysis of all the services they offer, not only IAM

- Compliance validation: AWS continuously monitor IAM for security vulnerabilities and check compliance deviations to maintain a secure IAM environment.

Let us discover these points in more detail:

AWS guarantees for Infrastructure level

AWS ensures comprehensive infrastructure security to protect IAM services, including physical, network, and operational safeguards, to maintain high availability and rapid incident response:

- **Physical security**: AWS guarantees the physical security of its data centers, protecting IAM-related infrastructure against unauthorized access, theft, and natural disasters.

- **Network security**: AWS ensures network security, safeguarding the networks that host IAM services against common cyber threats such as DDoS attacks and network intrusion attempts.

- **Data center controls**: AWS implements strict access controls and monitoring within its data centers, ensuring that only authorized personnel have physical or virtual access to the systems hosting IAM services.

- **Availability and redundancy**: AWS provides high availability and redundancy for IAM services, guaranteeing a certain level of uptime and availability to customers.

- **Incident response**: AWS has incident response procedures in place to handle security events that may impact IAM services, ensuring timely detection, mitigation, and resolution of security incidents.

Customer responsibilities for configuration and vulnerability scans

Customers are responsible for configuring IAM policies, access controls, and encryption settings, and conducting vulnerability scans to ensure the security and compliance of their IAM-enabled resources:

- **Configuration of IAM policies**: Customers are responsible for configuring IAM policies, ensuring they follow the principle of least privilege and are tailored to specific roles and users within the organization.

- **Access control settings**: Customers must configure access control settings within IAM, including user permissions, roles, and group memberships, to align with their security policies and requirements.

- **Encryption settings**: Customers are responsible for configuring encryption settings for IAM data, such as enabling encryption at rest for IAM user data stored in Amazon S3 buckets.

- **Vulnerability scans and patch management**: Customers are responsible for conducting vulnerability scans and implementing patch management processes for their IAM-enabled resources, ensuring that AWS IAM configurations are secure and up to date.

AWS IAM compliance validation

AWS supports IAM compliance through regular assessments, certifications, and audit tools, while customers are responsible for validating their configurations and ensuring compliance with relevant regulations:

- **Compliance assessments**: AWS conducts regular assessments and audits of its infrastructure, including IAM services, to validate compliance with industry standards and regulations.

- **Customer compliance responsibilities**: Customers are responsible for validating their IAM configurations and policies to ensure compliance with industry-specific regulations and internal security standards.

- **Audit trails and compliance reporting**: AWS provides tools like AWS CloudTrail to enable customers to create audit trails for their IAM activities. Customers are responsible for using these tools to generate compliance reports and monitor user activities.

- **Compliance certifications**: AWS maintains a comprehensive list of certifications, such as *SOC 2, ISO 27001*, and *PCI DSS*, for its services. Customers can reference these certifications to ensure that AWS meets specific compliance requirements.

In conclusion, AWS guarantees the security and reliability of the underlying infrastructure for IAM services. Customers, in turn, are responsible for configuring IAM settings securely, conducting vulnerability scans, and validating compliance based on their specific requirements and industry standards. This division of responsibilities ensures a collaborative approach to security and compliance in the AWS environment.

Administrator responsibilities in AWS IAM security

While AWS ensures the security of its infrastructure, administrators have several crucial responsibilities within the IAM service:

- **User management**: Administrators are responsible for creating, managing, and deleting user accounts within IAM. Proper user management includes assigning appropriate permissions, enabling MFA, and regularly reviewing and updating user access.

- **Policy configuration**: IAM policies define permissions for users, groups, and roles. Administrators must craft these policies carefully, following the principle of least privilege, to ensure users have only the necessary permissions to perform their tasks without granting excessive privileges.

- **Access key management**: Administrators need to manage access keys securely. This involves rotating access keys regularly, deleting unused keys, and ensuring that keys are not hard-coded within applications or scripts.

- **Monitoring and auditing**: IAM provides various tools and features for monitoring user activity, such as AWS CloudTrail. Administrators should enable logging and regularly review these logs for any suspicious activities, ensuring the security of user accounts and sensitive resources.

Security level of AWS IAM

AWS IAM offers several security features to safeguard user identities and access to AWS resources:

- **MFA**: IAM supports MFA, adding an extra layer of security to user accounts. Administrators should enforce MFA, especially for privileged accounts, to prevent unauthorized access.

- **Fine-grained access control**: IAM allows administrators to define fine-grained permissions through policies, ensuring that users have access only to specific actions and resources necessary for their tasks.

- **Identity federation (SSO)**: IAM supports identity federation, allowing users to access AWS resources using existing credentials from corporate directories. This enhances security by integrating with existing identity systems.

- **IAM best practices for enhanced security**: To enhance IAM security, administrators should follow these best practices:

  - **Regular security assessments**: Periodic security assessments and audits help administrators identify security gaps and ensure compliance with organizational policies and industry standards.

  - **Continuous training and awareness**: Educating users and administrators about security best practices and the latest threats ensures that security measures remain effective over time.

AWS operates on a shared responsibility model where AWS guarantees the security and availability of its infrastructure, including IAM services. However, administrators play a critical role in ensuring the secure configuration and management of IAM resources. By following best practices, regularly assessing security measures, and staying informed about the latest security threats and solutions, administrators can enhance the security of their AWS IAM environment, thereby safeguarding their organization's data and resources in the cloud.

Conclusion

The chapter highlights how AWS IAM serves as the main set of services AWS offers to ensure that only authorized entities access resources, thereby mitigating potential security breaches and data vulnerabilities. As organizations increasingly migrate their operations to the cloud, understanding IAM's nuances emerges as indispensable. The chapter underlines the imperative for businesses to craft meticulous IAM policies, encompassing user permissions, roles, and groups, aligning them intricately with their unique operational structures. We also introduced AWS CLI and SDK, Access keys and best security practices to handle AWS IAM users like MFA and strong password policies. Readers are left with a profound awareness of IAM's pivotal role in safeguarding digital assets, empowering them to navigate the complex cloud landscape with confidence and resilience. In the next chapter we will cover AWS compute services, navigating the vast space of the different solutions we could use to run our applications on AWS.

Points to remember

- **Users**: mapped to a physical user, has a password and can access AWS Console (main UI).

- **Groups**: contains users only.

- **Policies**: JSON documents that outline permissions for users or groups.

- **Roles**: sets of permissions that define what actions users, services, or resources can perform, allowing temporary secure access to AWS resources without the need for long-term credentials like access keys.

- **Security**: MFA + strong password policy enforcement for the best possible security.

- **Access keys**: access AWS using AWS CLI or AWS SDK. They are long-term credentials. For the best practices on security, they should be checked and rotated after some time.

- **Audit**: IAM credential reports and IAM access advisor. Using those 2 tools we can check and audit all aspects of our IAM configurations and interactions.

- **AWS CLI**: Manage your AWS resources using the command line.

- **AWS SDK**: Manage your AWS resources using a programming language.

Exercises

Here are a few quiz questions related to AWS IAM with single-answer choices:

1. **What does AWS IAM stand for?**

    a.　AWS internet access management

    b.　Advanced web security identity access management

    c.　AWS IAM

    d.　Automated web security and identity management

2. **Which of the following is NOT a component of AWS IAM?**

    a.　Policies

    b.　Roles

    c.　Databases

    d.　Users

3. **What is the primary purpose of AWS IAM?**

    a.　Managing internet connections

    b.　Managing cloud infrastructure

    c.　Managing user permissions and access control

    d.　Managing data storage

4. **In AWS IAM, what is a policy document?**

    a.　A set of rules defining permissions

    b.　A document outlining AWS pricing details

    c.　A document specifying server configurations

    d.　A document containing software development guidelines

5. **Which AWS IAM component allows you to delegate access to AWS resources without sharing your security credentials?**

    a. Users

    b. Policies

    c. Roles

    d. Groups

Answers

1. c

2. c

3. c

4. a

5. c

Key terms

- AWS IAM
- IAM users
- IAM groups
- IAM roles
- IAM policies
- IAM access keys
- AWS CLI
- AWS SDK
- AWS shared responsibility model for IAM
- MFA
- Password policies
- AWS CloudShell
- IAM credential reports
- IAM access advisor

CHAPTER 4

AWS Compute Services

Introduction

In today's rapidly evolving digital world, businesses and organizations are increasingly relying on cloud computing to meet their computational needs efficiently and cost-effectively. One of the key players in this domain is **Amazon Web Services** (**AWS**), a leading cloud service provider offering a plethora of services to businesses of all sizes. At the center of AWS lies its powerful and versatile computing services, which form the backbone of countless applications and services across the globe.

In this chapter, we embark on a comprehensive exploration of AWS compute services, exploring the core concepts, architectures, and best practices that underpin modern cloud-based computing. We begin by unravelling the fundamental building blocks of AWS compute, including virtual servers **Elastic Compute Cloud** (**EC2**) instances, serverless computing (AWS Lambda), and containerization services like Amazon **Elastic Container Service** (**ECS**) and **Elastic Kubernetes Service** (**EKS**).

Structure

In this chapter, we will cover the following topics:

- AWS Elastic Compute Cloud
- AWS Elastic Container Service

- CI/CD
- Serverless Computing on AWS
- Other compute services

Objectives

Through detailed explanations and real-world examples, readers will grasp the AWS compute offerings and learn how to choose the most suitable compute service for various use cases. This chapter will explain the significance of auto scaling, load balancing, and security considerations within the field of AWS computing, equipping readers with the knowledge needed to design resilient and secure cloud architectures. By the end of this chapter, readers will not only have a profound understanding of AWS compute services but also the expertise to harness the full potential of these services, driving innovation and efficiency within their organizations.

AWS Elastic Compute Cloud

Amazon EC2 stands as the cornerstone of AWS, offering businesses unparalleled flexibility and scalability in their computational endeavors. EC2 revolutionizes the way companies approach computing by providing virtual servers in the cloud, allowing users to run applications and workloads of various sizes. Let us explore the intricacies of Amazon EC2, starting with an in-depth examination of its fundamental concepts, including EC2 instances and their diverse types. Operating systems are supported by an EC2-rich array, catering to the diverse needs of users. Additionally, the different pricing models available for EC2, from on-demand instances ensuring instant computing power to reserved instances, offer cost-effectiveness for long-term workloads, and spot instances, enabling users to bid for spare computing capacity at lower costs.

EC2 instance types

At the center of Amazon EC2 lies the concept of instances, virtual servers in the cloud tailored to specific computational needs. EC2 instances come in a variety of types, each optimized to support different workloads. General purpose instances, such as the T series, strike a balance between compute, memory, and network resources, making them ideal for diverse applications. Compute-optimized instances, such as the C series, focus on delivering high-performance processing power, catering to compute-intensive tasks like gaming and scientific modelling. Memory-optimized instances, represented by the R and X series, offer substantial memory for tasks like in-memory databases and real-time big data analytics. Storage-optimized instances, like the I and D series, are designed to handle data-intensive workloads, ensuring rapid data access and processing.

By understanding the difference between these instance types, users can optimize their computing resources, enhance performance, and control costs effectively, thus ensuring a seamless experience for their applications.

You can check out different EC2 instance types here on the AWS official site: **https://aws. amazon.com/EC2/instance-types/**.

Supported operating systems: Flexibility in the cloud

One of the distinctive features of Amazon EC2 is its wide range of supported operating systems, empowering users to choose an environment that aligns with their specific requirements. EC2 supports various Linux distributions, including *Amazon Linux*, *Ubuntu*, and *CentOS*, providing users with the flexibility to leverage open-source solutions for their applications.

Moreover, EC2 seamlessly integrates with *Microsoft* technologies, supporting Windows Server instances for businesses reliant on Microsoft ecosystems. The compatibility with Windows Server enables enterprises to migrate their existing applications to the cloud effortlessly, fostering innovation and scalability.

Additionally, AWS offers a plethora of **Amazon Machine Images (AMIs)**, and pre-configured virtual machines with specific software stacks, facilitating rapid deployment and eliminating the hassle of manual configuration. This diverse array of supported operating systems and AMIs underscores EC2's adaptability, ensuring that users can create environments tailored to their unique needs and preferences.

Types of EC2

Amazon EC2 provides users with multiple options for renting computing capacity, allowing them to optimize costs and performance based on their usage patterns. On demand instances offer instant and scalable computing power, enabling users to pay for the capacity they consume without any long-term commitments.

Reserved instances provide significant cost savings for steady-state workloads with a one or a 3-year commitment. By reserving instances for a specific duration, users can benefit from lower hourly rates, making it an economical choice for predictable workloads.

Spot instances introduce a dynamic element, enabling users to bid for spare Amazon EC2 capacity. They provide substantial cost savings, making them ideal for tasks that can be interrupted and resumed, such as batch processing and data analysis.

By offering these diverse renting models, Amazon EC2 grants users the freedom to choose an approach that aligns with their budget constraints, workload flexibility, and business objectives, ultimately empowering them to optimize their cloud computing experience.

Understanding AWS EC2 and security groups

Amazon EC2 lies at the heart of AWS, offering scalable computing capacity in the cloud. When setting up EC2 instances, security is important. Security groups serve as virtual firewalls for your instances, controlling inbound and outbound traffic where you can specify protocols such as **Transmission Control Protocol (TCP)**, **User Datagram Protocol (UDP)**, etc. **Internet Protocol (IP)** addresses and **Classless Inter-Domain Routing (CIDR)** blocks and ports like 22 **Secure Shell (SSH)**, etc.

By meticulously defining rules within these security groups, you can regulate the flow of data, ensuring that only authorized communication occurs.

Given in the following is a how you can leverage security groups to fortify your EC2 instances:

- **Fine-grained control**: Security groups enable you to define precise rules for inbound and outbound traffic based on IP protocol, port number, and source/ destination IP address or CIDR block. This fine-grained control allows you to restrict access to only necessary ports and IP addresses, reducing the attack surface significantly. For instance, you can configure a security group to permit inbound traffic on port 22 SSH only from your specific IP address, enhancing the security of your SSH access.

- **Dynamic adaptability**: One of the compelling features of security groups is their dynamic adaptability. You can modify the rules of a security group at any time, instantly applying the changes to all instances associated with the group. This agility allows you to respond swiftly to security threats or changing requirements without disrupting your services. For instance, if you need to grant temporary access to a developer for troubleshooting, you can quickly update the security group rules, granting access for a specific period and then revoke it when the task is complete.

- **Layered security**: Security groups operate in conjunction with **network access control lists (NACLs)**, providing a layered approach to security. While NACLs act as network-level firewalls for controlling traffic at the subnet level, security groups offer host-level protection. By strategically combining security groups and NACLs, you can create a robust security architecture that safeguards your EC2 instances from various types of attacks, ensuring both network and host-level security.

- **Logging and monitoring**: AWS provides comprehensive logging and monitoring capabilities for security groups. By leveraging Amazon CloudWatch and AWS CloudTrail, you can gain insights into traffic patterns, identify unauthorized access attempts, and monitor changes made to security group configurations. This visibility allows you to proactively detect and mitigate potential security threats, enhancing your overall security posture.

SSH access to EC2 Linux instances

SSH provides a secure way to access your EC2 instances remotely. To access your instance remotely from your personal computer, use the command line tool SSH on your computer and follow these steps:

1. **Generate SSH key pair**: If you do not have one, generate an SSH key pair by using the **ssh-keygen** command on your local machine.

2. **Launch EC2 instance**: Log in to your AWS Management Console, navigate to EC2, and launch a new instance. During the launch, specify your SSH key pair.

3. **Get public IP**: Once the instance is running, note down its public IP address.

4. **SSH command**: Open your terminal and use the following command to SSH into your instance:

   ```
   ssh -i /path/to/your-key.pem EC2-user@your-instance-public-ip
   ```

5. Here, replace **/path/to/your-key.pem** with the path to your private key file and **your-instance-public-ip** with your instance's public IP address.

EC2 Instance Connect

Amazon EC2 instance connect is a streamlined and secure method for establishing SSH connections to your EC2 instances. Designed to simplify the process of accessing instances securely, EC2 instance connect eliminates the complexities associated with managing SSH keys, allowing users to connect to their instances seamlessly.

Some key features and benefits of EC2 instance connect are mentioned in the following:

- **Eliminating key management hassles**: Traditionally, managing SSH keys for secure access can be a cumbersome task. EC2 Instance Connect is a simpler way to connect to your EC2 instance. leveraging AWS **Identity and Access Management (IAM)** roles and policies. Instead of dealing with SSH key pairs, users can rely on IAM policies to control who can connect to instances. This simplifies the access management process significantly, reducing the potential security risks associated with managing and distributing private keys.

- **Fine-grained access control**: EC2 Instance Connect provides fine-grained access control by allowing you to specify IAM policies that define which users or roles can connect to instances. You can limit access to specific users, groups, or even temporary credentials, ensuring that only authorized personnel can establish SSH connections. This level of granularity enhances security and compliance, enabling organizations to adhere to strict access control policies.

- **Secure connection establishment**: When using EC2 Instance Connect, the entire connection process is secure. The service encrypts the data transmission, safeguarding sensitive information from potential eavesdropping or interception. It ensures end-to-end encryption, maintaining the confidentiality and integrity of the data exchanged between the client and the EC2 instance.

- **Simplified user experience**: From a user perspective, EC2 instance connect offers a seamless experience. Users can initiate SSH connections directly from the AWS Management Console, AWS **Command Line Interface** (**CLI**). There is no need to handle key pairs or manage SSH agents. This simplicity reduces the barrier to entry for users, allowing even those less familiar with SSH configurations to connect securely to instances.

- **Enhanced auditability**: EC2 Instance Connect transactions are logged, providing detailed audit trails for every connection attempt. These logs can be integrated with AWS CloudTrail, allowing organizations to maintain comprehensive records of who accessed which instances and when. This auditability is crucial for compliance, security analysis, and troubleshooting purposes, enabling organizations to maintain visibility into their infrastructure.

Using EC2 Instance Connect simplifies the process of securely connecting to your EC2 instances without the hassle of managing SSH keys.

A step-by-step guide on how to use EC2 instance connect is mentioned in the following:

1. **Ensure IAM configuration**: First, ensure that your AWS IAM user or role has the necessary permissions to establish SSH connections by using EC2 Instance Connect. You need `EC2-instance-connect:SendSSHPublicKey` permission to use this service.

2. **Access the AWS Management Console**: Log in to your AWS Management Console with your browser.

3. **Locate your instance**: Navigate to the EC2 dashboard and locate the instance to which you want to connect. Select the instance you want to access.

4. **Initiate connection**: Click on the **Connect** button in the instance detail's view. If you are using the AWS CLI or an SDK, you can also initiate the connection via the appropriate command (see documentation on AWS on how to use EC2 Instance Connect with AWS CLI/SDK).

5. **Specify user and key**: In the connection dialog, specify the operating system user account you want to connect to (for example, EC2-user for Amazon Linux, ubuntu for Ubuntu instances, or admin for Windows instances). EC2 Instance Connect does not require a separate key pair. You will use your existing IAM user's public key.

6. **Authorize connection**: Click on **Connect** or use the appropriate command if you are using AWS CLI. EC2 Instance Connect will authorize the connection by using your IAM role and will establish a secure SSH session for your instance.

7. **Start working**: Once the connection is established, you will find yourself logged into your EC2 instance. You can now execute commands, manage files, and perform any necessary tasks on your instance directly from your terminal.

AWS Amazon Machine Images

AMIs are pre-configured templates used to create instances within AWS. They encapsulate the information required to launch a fully functional instance, including the root volume, launch permissions, and block device mapping.

Creating a custom AMI involves several steps:

1. **Prepare your instance**: Ensure your instance is configured the way you want. Install necessary software, configure settings, and clean up unnecessary files.

2. **Create an image**: In the AWS Management Console, select your instance, click on **Actions**, then **Create Image**. Provide a name and description for your image and click **Create Image**. This process creates a snapshot of your instance.

3. **Customize the image (Optional)**: Once the image is created, you can customize it by adding additional software, modifying configurations, or making any necessary changes.

4. **Launch instances from custom AMI**: Once your custom AMI is ready, you can launch new instances from it. Specify the custom AMI during the instance launch process, and your new instances will inherit the configurations and software settings from the custom image.

Understanding the AWS shared responsibility model for EC2

AWS operates under a unique paradigm known as the **shared responsibility model**. This model defines the division of responsibilities between AWS as the cloud service provider and the customers who use AWS services.

In the context of Amazon EC2, this model delineates the specific areas of security and compliance that AWS manages and those that fall under the customer's purview.

AWS's responsibilities

At the foundational level, AWS takes responsibility for the security of the cloud. This encompasses the physical infrastructure, data centers, networking, and the hypervisor. AWS ensures that the hardware and software components underpinning EC2 instances are protected from unauthorized access, environmental threats, and other physical vulnerabilities. Furthermore, AWS manages the virtualization layer and the overall infrastructure, ensuring the seamless operation of EC2 instances. This includes patch management, ensuring the latest security updates are applied, and protecting against hardware and software failures.

In order to list all AWS responsibilities for EC2 in the shared responsibility model, refer to the following points:

- Infrastructure and global network security
- Isolation on physical hosts
- Replacing faulty hardware
- Compliance validation

Customer's responsibilities

On the other hand, customers are responsible for the security of the cloud. This entails securing their data, managing access control, configuring their EC2 instances, and implementing network security measures. Customers are expected to apply security best practices, such as regularly updating and patching their operating systems and applications, blocking unused ports on the host system, using NACL along with security groups, configuring firewall rules by using Security Groups, and employing encryption to protect data both in transit and at rest.

In order to recap all customer responsibilities for EC2 in the shared responsibility model, refer to the following points:

- **Security group rules**: Correct setup of the rules to not enable unsecured access to your instances.

- **Operating system patches and updates**: Operating system updates and security fixes are up to you after you rent an EC2 instance.

- **Software and utilities installed in EC2 instances**: What you install should not have backdoors, bugs, security holes, etc.

- **IAM roles assigned to EC2 and IAM user access management**: Handling the security of IAM rules correctly and users that access your EC2 instances, following the rule of least privilege security when possible.

Following are customer responsibilities in detail:

- **EC2 security groups and network configuration**: One of the central aspects of customer responsibility within the AWS shared responsibility model is the configuration of EC2 security groups. They act as virtual firewalls that control inbound and outbound traffic to EC2 instances. Customers are tasked with setting up these security groups to ensure that only authorized traffic is allowed. Properly configuring security groups, including specifying which ports are open and from which IP addresses, is crucial in preventing unauthorized access.

- **IAM**: Customers are responsible for managing user access through AWS IAM. It allows customers to control who can access AWS resources and what actions they can perform. By configuring IAM policies, customers can define granular permissions, ensuring that only authorized individuals can create, modify, or terminate EC2 instances. Proper IAM configuration is vital for safeguarding against insider threats and unauthorized access.

- **Data encryption**: Customers are responsible for encrypting sensitive data. AWS provides various encryption options, including encrypting data at rest using services like AWS **Key Management Service** (**KMS**) and encrypting data in transit by using protocols like **Secure Socket Layer (SSL)/Transport Layer Security (TLS)**. Customers must implement encryption mechanisms to protect their data, especially when dealing with sensitive information, ensuring that even if unauthorized access occurs, the data remains unreadable and secure.

- **Continuous monitoring and compliance**: Beyond initial setup, customers must continuously monitor their EC2 instances and associated configurations. Regular security audits, vulnerability assessments, and compliance checks are essential to ensuring that the security posture remains robust over time. Customers should use AWS services like AWS Config, AWS CloudTrail, and AWS Inspector to automate security checks and monitor changes in their AWS environments.

- **Disaster recovery and backup**: While AWS ensures high availability and redundancy of its infrastructure, customers are responsible for their data backups and disaster recovery plans. This includes regularly backing up data, creating snapshots of EC2 volumes, and devising disaster recovery strategies to ensure business continuity in the event of unexpected incidents.

In summary, the AWS shared responsibility model for EC2 underscores the collaborative effort between AWS and its customers to maintain a secure cloud environment. By understanding and fulfilling their specific responsibilities within this model, customers can leverage the full potential of EC2 while adhering to industry-leading security practices, thus ensuring the confidentiality, integrity, and availability of their data and applications in the AWS Cloud.

AWS Elastic Container Service

Amazon ECS is a highly scalable and efficient container orchestration service provided by AWS. Designed to simplify the deployment and management of containerized applications, ECS allows developers to focus on building applications without worrying about the underlying infrastructure complexities. At its core, ECS enables the deployment of Docker containers as tasks, which are grouped into services for easy management.

ECS provides developers with the flexibility to run containers across a cluster of Amazon EC2 instances or leverage AWS Fargate, a serverless compute engine for containers. With the EC2 launch type, users have complete control over the underlying EC2 instances, allowing them to optimize the environment for specific workloads. On the other hand, Fargate abstracts the underlying infrastructure, enabling developers to focus solely on defining their containerized applications without managing the servers. This flexibility caters to a wide range of use cases, from traditional monolithic applications to modern microservices architectures, providing developers with the freedom to choose the most suitable deployment option for their applications.

ECS seamlessly integrates with other AWS services, such as Amazon **Virtual Private Cloud** (**VPC**) for networking, AWS IAM for access control, and Amazon CloudWatch for monitoring and logging. This integration simplifies the configuration and management of containerized applications within the AWS ecosystem. ECS also offers features like load balancing, auto scaling, and service discovery, allowing developers to build highly available and resilient applications. Overall, ECS empowers developers to deploy, manage, and scale containerized applications effortlessly, making it a fundamental component in AWS's extensive suite of cloud services.

Software packaging and deployment

Docker has emerged as a revolutionary technology in the last years, transforming the way projects are packaged and deployed. Docker is an open-source platform that automates the deployment of applications inside lightweight, portable containers. These containers encapsulate everything an application needs to run, including the code, runtime, libraries, and system tools, ensuring consistency and reliability across different environments.

Understanding Docker

Docker utilizes containerization, a technology that enables developers to isolate applications and their dependencies into self-contained units called **containers**. Unlike traditional virtualization, which runs multiple operating systems on a single host, Docker containers share the host system's OS kernel, making them lightweight and efficient. Each containerized application operates in its isolated environment, ensuring that it runs consistently on any machine, from development to testing and production. This consistency is pivotal in modern software development, where applications must function seamlessly across various environments and platforms.

Docker is the standard way to deploy projects

Let us explore some key aspects of Docker and why it is one of the best tools used by most of the companies worldwide:

- **Portability and consistency**: One of the primary reasons Docker has gained immense popularity is its portability. Docker containers can run on any machine that supports Docker, regardless of the underlying infrastructure. This portability eliminates the infamous it works on my machine problem, ensuring that applications behave consistently across different environments. Developers can build and test applications on their local machines and be confident that the same application will run identically in production, streamlining the development and deployment process.

- **Efficiency and resource optimization**: Docker's lightweight nature and efficient resource utilization make it an attractive choice for developers and system administrators. Unlike the traditional way of deploying the application on the virtual machines, Docker containers do not require a full operating system for each instance, leading to significant resource savings. Multiple containers can run on a single host system without the overhead associated with running multiple virtual machines, enhancing overall system efficiency and reducing infrastructure costs.

- **Scalability and orchestration**: Docker simplifies the process of scaling applications. By leveraging container orchestration tools like AWS ECS, Kubernetes, and Docker Swarm, developers can automate the deployment, scaling, and management of containerized applications. These tools enable the seamless distribution of containerized workloads across clusters of machines, ensuring high availability, Fault-tolerance, and effortless scalability. Docker's integration with orchestration platforms has become instrumental in managing large-scale, complex applications in modern enterprises.

- **Rapid deployment and rollback**: Docker facilitates rapid deployment and rollback of applications, allowing organizations to respond quickly to changing market demands and customer feedback. With Docker, deploying a new version of an application is as simple as stopping the existing container and starting a new one with the updated codebase. If issues arise, rolling back to the previous version is equally straightforward. This agility empowers development teams to release new features and bug fixes faster, enhancing the overall user experience.

Impact on modern software development

Docker's impact on modern software development practices is profound. It has ushered in a new era of agility, enabling **continuous integration/continuous deployment (CI/CD)**, and DevOps practices. CI/CD pipelines, which automate the building, testing, and deployment of applications, are now widely adopted due to Docker's consistency and portability. DevOps teams leverage Docker to bridge the gap between development and operations, fostering collaboration and accelerating the software delivery lifecycle.

Docker has become the cornerstone of modern software development and deployment. Its portability, efficiency, scalability, and agility have made it the preferred choice for developers and organizations worldwide, by providing a standardized and reliable way to package and deploy applications. Docker has not only simplified the complexities of software development but has also paved the way for a more efficient, collaborative, and innovative software industry. As technology continues to advance, Docker's influence is expected to grow, further shaping the future of software development and deployment.

Main use cases of AWS ECS

Amazon ECS, part of AWS's extensive cloud computing platform, has become a cornerstone for businesses aiming to deploy, manage, and scale containerized applications. Its versatility and integration capabilities make it indispensable for a wide array of use cases, transforming the way companies architect their applications and infrastructure. Let us see the main use cases where AWS ECS shines, illustrating its impact on modern software development and deployment strategies.

Microservices architecture

Microservices architecture has gained prominence due to its ability to enhance agility, scalability, and Fault-tolerance. ECS offers a robust environment for deploying microservices-based applications. By breaking down applications into smaller, manageable services, developers can deploy each microservice as a containerized task within ECS. It facilitates the independent deployment, scaling, and management of these microservices. Additionally, ECS integrates seamlessly with AWS features like **Elastic Load Balancing** (**ELB**) and Auto Scaling groups, ensuring that microservices are distributed efficiently and can handle varying workloads. This modular approach enables developers to update and scale specific services without affecting the entire application, enhancing flexibility, and accelerating development cycles.

CI/CD

ECS plays a pivotal role in modern CI/CD pipelines, automating the process of building, testing, and deploying applications. Integrating ECS with CI/CD tools like AWS CodePipeline and AWS CodeBuild streamlines the release process. Developers can push code changes to a version control system, triggering automated builds and tests. Once the code passes these tests, ECS can deploy the updated containerized application. This automation not only ensures faster time-to-market but also enhances the overall reliability of the deployment process. ECS allows developers to define task definitions, specifying the container image, CPU, memory, and networking requirements. These definitions ensure consistent deployments across different environments, eliminating the it works on my machine problem and enhancing collaboration between development and operations teams.

Hybrid and multi-cloud deployments

Hybrid and multi-cloud strategies have become prevalent as businesses seek to optimize costs, improve reliability, and mitigate vendor lock-in. ECS supports these strategies by providing a unified platform for managing containers across on-premises data centers and multiple cloud environments. With ECS anywhere, developers can run ECS tasks on their own infrastructure, extending the ECS experience beyond AWS-managed resources. ECS also integrates with AWS Outposts, enabling the deployment of ECS tasks on-premises within the same hardware used for other AWS services. Furthermore, ECS supports AWS App Runner, which simplifies the deployment of containerized applications directly from source code, allowing developers to focus on building features rather than managing infrastructure. These capabilities empower businesses to choose the most suitable deployment environment for their applications, whether it is on-premises, in the cloud, or across multiple cloud providers, maximizing flexibility and ensuring high availability.

AWS ECS for web services and workers and batch jobs

Amazon ECS is a versatile container orchestration service that can be used for various purposes, including hosting web services and managing background tasks, also known as **worker tasks**.

Here is an overview of how ECS is commonly used in these two scenarios.

Following are the ECS for web services:

- **Load balancing and scaling**: One of the primary use cases of ECS for web services is hosting scalable and highly available web applications. ECS integrates seamlessly with ELB, which enables the distribution of incoming traffic across multiple ECS containers. This load balancing capability ensures that the web service can handle varying levels of traffic efficiently. ECS also supports auto scaling, allowing the service to automatically adjust the number of running tasks based on demand. This ensures that the application remains responsive and available, even during traffic spikes.

- **Service discovery and microservices**: ECS is well-suited for microservices architectures where applications are broken down into smaller, loosely coupled services. ECS allows developers to define service tasks, each representing a specific microservice. These tasks can communicate with each other and with external services. ECS integrates with AWS Cloud Map and Route 53 for service discovery, making it easier for services to locate and communicate with one another. This seamless communication between microservices enables the development of complex applications while maintaining a high level of modularity and scalability.

- **Blue/green deployments and CD**: ECS facilitates blue/green deployments, a technique used to minimize downtime and risk during software releases. In a blue/green deployment, a new version of the application (green) is deployed alongside the existing version (blue). ECS allows developers to achieve this by creating separate task definitions for the blue and green versions. Traffic can then be gradually shifted from the blue tasks to the green tasks, allowing for seamless updates without disrupting the user experience. Additionally, ECS integrates with CI/CD pipelines, enabling CD workflows. Developers can automate the process of building, testing, and deploying new versions of their web services, ensuring rapid and reliable releases.

- **ECS for worker tasks**: ECS is commonly used for running worker tasks that handle background processing and batch jobs. These tasks perform various tasks such as data processing, file conversion, or generating reports. ECS allows developers to define worker tasks that can be scheduled to run periodically or triggered by specific events. This capability ensures efficient utilization of resources, as tasks are only executed when there is work to be done. ECS also supports task scheduling through integration with AWS CloudWatch Events and AWS Step Functions, enabling developers to automate and coordinate complex workflows.

- **Asynchronous processing and queue workers**: ECS is ideal for implementing asynchronous processing systems where tasks are queued for later execution. Services like Amazon **Simple Queue Service** (**SQS**) can be integrated with ECS, allowing tasks to be triggered by messages in the queue. This decouples the components of the system, ensuring that tasks are executed independently and asynchronously. ECS worker tasks can listen to the SQS queue and process messages, enabling the system to handle tasks that do not require immediate user interaction. This architecture enhances the responsiveness of applications by offloading time-consuming tasks to background workers.

- **Data processing and extract, transform, and load (ETL) pipelines**: ECS is well-suited for running data processing tasks, including ETL pipelines. ETL processes involve extracting data from various sources, transforming it into a desired format, and loading it into a data store for analysis. ECS can execute containerized ETL tasks, allowing developers to parallelize data processing tasks and scale resources based on the volume of data to be processed. By containerizing ETL workflows, developers can ensure consistency and reproducibility, making it easier to manage and scale data processing tasks efficiently.

AWS Elastic Container Registry

Amazon **Elastic Container Registry** (**ECR**) is a fully managed Docker container registry provided by AWS. It serves as a secure and scalable repository for storing, managing, and deploying Docker container images. ECR is tightly integrated with other AWS services, particularly Amazon ECS, simplifying the process of storing and deploying containerized applications in the cloud.

Following are the key features and concepts:

- **Secure and private repositories**: ECR allows users to create private Docker repositories to securely store their container images. These repositories are accessible only to authorized AWS users and services, ensuring that sensitive application images remain confidential.

- **Scalability and high availability**: ECR is designed to scale with your containerized applications. It automatically handles the scaling of the underlying infrastructure, ensuring the high availability and reliability of container images. Images are stored across multiple AWS Availability Zones, providing Fault-tolerance and redundancy.

- **Integration with AWS IAM**: ECR integrates seamlessly with AWS IAM, allowing fine-grained control over user access permissions. Users can define who can push or pull images, ensuring that only authorized individuals and services can interact with the stored container images.

- **Lifecycle policies**: ECR supports lifecycle policies, enabling users to define rules for cleaning up outdated or unused images. These policies help optimize storage costs by automatically removing images that are no longer in use, based on specified criteria such as image age or tag.

Following are the main use cases of ECR:

- **Secure storage and versioning**: ECR is used as a centralized repository for storing Docker images securely. Development teams can version their application images, ensuring that specific versions of an application can be rolled back to if issues arise. This versioning capability is crucial for maintaining consistency across various environments, from development and testing to staging and production.

- **CI/CD**: In CI/CD pipelines, ECR acts as a reliable source for Docker images. As part of the deployment process, CI/CD tools build, test, and push container images to ECR. These images can then be seamlessly deployed onto Amazon ECS clusters or other container orchestration platforms, ensuring a smooth and automated release process.

- **Collaboration and distribution**: ECR facilitates collaboration among development teams by providing a centralized location to share container images. Teams working on different parts of an application can push their images to ECR, allowing other teams to pull and integrate them into their respective services. This collaborative approach streamlines the development workflow and ensures consistency across interconnected microservices.

- **Integration with ECS**: ECR integrates seamlessly with Amazon ECS, enhancing the container deployment process:

  o **Simplified deployment**: ECS tasks and services can directly use images stored in ECR repositories. When defining ECS task definitions or services, developers specify the ECR repository and image tag, allowing ECS to pull the correct image during deployment. This integration simplifies the deployment workflow, ensuring that the latest version of the application is always deployed.

  o **Immutable infrastructure**: By coupling ECS with ECR, organizations can implement the concept of immutable infrastructure. Once a container image is stored in ECR, it remains unchanged. When deploying a new version of the application, developers create a new image with an updated tag and push it to ECR. ECS then deploys the new version, ensuring consistency and reducing the risk of configuration drift or unauthorized changes.

o **Secure image distribution**: ECR ensures secure image distribution within ECS clusters. Images stored in private repositories can only be accessed by ECS instances and tasks with the appropriate IAM permissions. This secure distribution mechanism is crucial, especially in multi-tenant environments, where different teams or applications share the same ECS cluster.

In summary, Amazon ECR serves as a robust and secure solution for managing Docker container images. Its seamless integration with ECS streamlines the deployment process, enabling developers to focus on building scalable and reliable containerized applications without worrying about the complexities of image management and distribution.

AWS Fargate

Amazon ECS with AWS Fargate is a powerful combination that simplifies the deployment and management of containerized applications. Traditionally, managing containers required developers to handle the underlying infrastructure, such as servers and clusters, even when utilizing ECS. However, Fargate abstracts this complexity, allowing developers to focus solely on their applications without the need to manage the underlying infrastructure.

Fargate is integrated and can use ECS or other container orchestrators like AWS EKS to run your Docker containers.

Given in the following are the reasons why Fargate exists:

- **Serverless container orchestration**: Fargate embodies the serverless paradigm within the container orchestration space. It enables developers to run containers without managing the servers or clusters, which aligns with the serverless computing model. With Fargate, developers do not need to provision or scale virtual machines; they can focus purely on defining tasks and services, allowing AWS to handle the underlying infrastructure, including server provisioning, scaling, and maintenance.

- **Simplified resource management**: Fargate simplifies resource management by abstracting the compute resources, such as CPU and memory, away from developers. In traditional ECS setups, developers need to specify and manage these resources, ensuring that the right amount is allocated to each container. It eliminates this complexity by automatically provisioning the necessary resources based on the task definition, ensuring optimal performance without manual intervention.

- **Enhanced security and isolation**: Fargate provides enhanced security and isolation by running each task in its dedicated kernel runtime environment. This isolation ensures that tasks are completely isolated from one another, enhancing security and stability. Traditional ECS setups require careful configuration to achieve a similar level of isolation, whereas Fargate offers it out of the box, reducing the complexity associated with securing containerized applications.

Given in the following is how Fargate simplifies the process of:

- **No infrastructure management**: The primary advantage of Fargate is its serverless nature, eliminating the need for developers to manage the underlying infrastructure. Developers can define their tasks and services, specify the desired CPU and memory requirements, and Fargate takes care of launching and scaling tasks based on demand. This abstraction simplifies the entire deployment process, allowing developers to focus on writing code rather than managing servers or clusters.

- **Easy scaling and load balancing**: Fargate seamlessly integrates with ECS and AWS load balancing services. Developers can define auto scaling policies, allowing Fargate to automatically scale the number of tasks based on the workload. Load balancing is simplified, as Fargate tasks can be automatically registered with AWS load balancers, distributing incoming traffic across tasks without manual configuration, making it easier to build highly available and scalable applications.

- **Pay-as-you-go pricing**: Fargate follows a pay-as-you-go pricing model, where users are billed based on the vCPU and memory resources allocated to their tasks. This pricing model eliminates the need to manage reserved instances or calculate complex pricing structures. Developers can focus on optimizing their applications without worrying about the financial intricacies associated with the underlying infrastructure.

Fargate simplifies ECS by abstracting away the complexities of managing infrastructure, enabling developers to deploy, and run containerized applications without the burden of server management. Its serverless approach aligns with modern development practices, emphasizing simplicity, scalability, and efficiency, making it an attractive choice for businesses seeking a hassle-free container orchestration solution within the AWS ecosystem.

Serverless computing on AWS

In the world of cloud computing, the term serverless does not imply the absence of servers but rather a revolutionary way of handling server management. Serverless computing allows developers to build and run applications without managing servers. Instead of worrying about server provisioning, scaling, or maintenance, developers can focus on writing code and deploying functions or applications directly into the cloud, where the underlying infrastructure is abstracted and managed by the cloud provider.

AWS Lambda and its significance

AWS Lambda, a pivotal service in the AWS serverless computing platform, embodies this serverless paradigm. Launched in 2014, AWS Lambda revolutionized how developers approach application development and deployment.

With AWS Lambda, developers can upload their code (written in languages like Node.js, Python, Java, or others) and create functions triggered by events.

These events can come from various sources, such as HTTP requests via *Amazon API Gateway*, modifications to data in Amazon **Simple Storage Service** (**S3**), updates to DynamoDB tables, or even custom events within applications. When an event occurs, Lambda automatically executes the corresponding function, scaling transparently with the number of incoming events. This automatic scaling ensures that applications can handle any workload, from a few requests per day to thousands of **requests per second** (**RPS**), without manual intervention.

AWS Lambda key features and benefits:

- **Cost-effective**: AWS Lambda follows a pay-as-you-go model, where you are charged based on the number of requests for your functions and the time your code executes. This granular pricing means you only pay for the compute time consumed during code execution, making it highly cost-effective, especially for sporadically used or event-driven applications.

- **Seamless scaling**: Lambda functions scale effortlessly in response to incoming events. Whether your application experiences a sudden surge in traffic or remains idle for extended periods, Lambda automatically adjusts the number of instances to handle the load. This scaling flexibility ensures optimal performance and responsiveness without the need for manual intervention or capacity planning.

- **Focus on code, not infrastructure**: Serverless computing, epitomized by AWS Lambda, enables developers to concentrate solely on writing application logic. Without the overhead of server management, developers can innovate faster, iterate more frequently, and focus on delivering business value. The abstracted infrastructure allows developers to build applications without worrying about provisioning, scaling, patching, or monitoring servers.

- **Versatile integrations**: AWS Lambda seamlessly integrates with various AWS services, enabling developers to create powerful, event-driven applications. Whether you are building web applications, data processing pipelines, chatbots, **Internet of Things** (**IoT**) applications, or real-time analytics solutions, Lambda can be triggered by a wide array of events and seamlessly interact with other AWS services.

- **Enhanced developer productivity**: Lambda fosters developer productivity by simplifying the development lifecycle. Developers can deploy code instantly, monitor performance through AWS CloudWatch, and troubleshoot issues efficiently. This streamlined workflow accelerates development cycles, allowing teams to focus on building features and responding to customer needs.

Common properties and use cases

AWS Lambda service has become a linchpin in the world of serverless computing, providing developers with a powerful and scalable platform to build and deploy applications without the hassle of managing servers. Its versatility is reflected in a myriad of common use cases, robust settings, transparent pricing, and the enticing always Free Tier option. Let us explore the facets that make AWS Lambda a go-to choice for developers and businesses alike.

Common use cases

AWS Lambda's adaptability makes it applicable across a wide array of scenarios. Refer to the following points for a better understanding:

- **APIs and web applications**: Lambda functions are often used to power APIs and dynamic web applications. When coupled with Amazon API Gateway, Lambda enables developers to build serverless backends for web and mobile applications, handling HTTP requests and seamlessly scaling to meet varying traffic demands.

- **Event-driven data processing and transformation**: Lambda functions can process and transform data in real-time. From cleaning and enriching streaming data to processing data stored in Amazon S3 or Amazon DynamoDB, Lambda functions simplify data workflows, making them more responsive and efficient. AWS Lambda also tightly integrates with real-time streaming services like AWS Kinesis, so you could process and transform data in real-time as they arrive.

- **Automation and workflow orchestration**: Lambda is instrumental in automating tasks and orchestrating workflows. Developers can create functions triggered by events, like file uploads, database changes, or scheduled events, automating processes such as image resizing, report generation, and database backups.

- **IoT applications**: For IoT solutions, Lambda functions handle data streams from connected devices. They process and analyze sensor data, respond to device triggers, and integrate seamlessly with other AWS services to create robust, real-time IoT applications.

- **Chatbots and AI integrations**: Lambda powers chatbots and AI integrations, enabling **natural language processing (NLP)**, sentiment analysis, and interactive conversational experiences. Integrating with services like Amazon Lex, Lambda facilitates intelligent interactions between applications and users.

AWS Lambda

- **AWS Lambda timeouts**: Lambda functions have a default timeout of 3 seconds, meaning they must complete execution within this timeframe. Developers can configure timeouts based on the expected runtime of the function, ensuring it does not get terminated prematurely. Proper timeout settings are crucial for functions handling time-intensive operations. The maximum timeout limit for a single AWS Lambda at the time of writing this book is 15 minutes, so a single lambda could run for a maximum of 15 minutes, then it will be suspended with a timeout error.

- **Environment variables**: Lambda functions can utilize environment variables, allowing developers to inject configuration values without hard coding them into the code. This flexibility enhances security and simplifies deployments, enabling easy customization of functions for different environments (for example, development, testing, and production).

- **Max memory limit**: Lambda functions can specify the maximum memory allocation, ranging from 128 MB to 3008 MB. Memory settings affect the function's CPU allocation, providing developers with fine-grained control over performance and cost. Optimizing memory allocation ensures efficient resource utilization and cost-effectiveness.

- **Pricing model**: AWS Lambda operates on a pay-as-you-go model, charging users based on the number of requests and the compute time consumed by their functions. Users are billed for the total number of requests, rounded up to the nearest 100ms, and the memory allocation for the function, measured in GB-seconds. This granular billing approach ensures cost efficiency, as users only pay for the exact compute resources utilized by their functions.

- **Always Free Tier**: AWS offers an enticing always Free Tier for Lambda, allowing users to enjoy a specific amount of free compute time and requests per month. As of the current AWS offering, the Free Tier includes 1 million free requests per month and 400,000 GB-seconds of compute time per month. This generous allocation empowers developers to explore and experiment with Lambda without incurring costs, making it an ideal platform for learning and small-scale applications.

There are also some cons when using AWS Lambda that should be known when choosing to use this specific service:

- **Cold start latency**: Lambda functions might experience a latency known as **cold start** when triggered for the first time or after being idle for a while. During cold start, AWS provisions resources for the function, causing a slight delay in response time. While efforts have been made to mitigate this, it can impact applications with strict latency requirements. Usually, companies use scripting languages to mitigate the cold start times, like Python and Node.js, as it is less instead of the cold start of managed languages like Java/C#.

- **Execution time limits**: Lambda functions have a maximum execution time limit (default three seconds, configurable up to 15 minutes). Tasks that exceed this limit must be divided into smaller units, potentially complicating the design of long-running processes. For example, when in need to run a batch job for more than 15 minutes, it can be better to use another AWS service instead of AWS Lambda.

- **Limited state management**: Lambda functions are stateless by design. While they can access external storage solutions like databases, managing and persisting state across multiple invocations might require additional considerations and integrations.

- **Dependency management**: Managing dependencies, especially for functions written in languages like Node.js or Python, can be complex. Lambda packages require only the necessary dependencies, but managing the package size and ensuring compatibility can be challenging, particularly for large applications.

- **Debugging and monitoring complexity**: Debugging serverless applications, especially those with complex event-driven architectures, can be challenging. Tools and techniques for debugging and monitoring distributed, event-driven systems might require additional effort and integration with AWS services like CloudWatch for effective monitoring and logging.

- **Vendor lock-in**: Serverless architectures, including Lambda, might lead to vendor lock-in. While Lambda provides tremendous benefits, transitioning to a different serverless platform or back to traditional infrastructure can be complex and time-consuming, necessitating careful consideration of long-term implications.

- **Local development challenges**: Developing and testing Lambda functions locally can be challenging due to the differences between local development environments and the AWS Lambda runtime. While AWS provides tools like the AWS **Serverless Application Model** (**SAM**) and local testing options, developers might encounter discrepancies between local and production environments.

In summary, AWS Lambda's common use cases, customizable settings, transparent pricing model, and the enticing always-Free Tier make it an indispensable tool for developers. Its ability to abstract infrastructure complexities, coupled with a flexible pricing structure and a Free Tier for exploration, underscores AWS Lambda's position as a catalyst for innovation and a driving force behind the serverless computing revolution. Whether you are building APIs, automating workflows, processing data, or developing IoT applications, AWS Lambda provides the foundation for scalable, efficient, and cost-effective solutions.

AWS Lambda offers significant advantages in terms of scalability, cost-efficiency, and ease of integration. However, developers need to carefully consider its limitations, such as cold start latency and execution time constraints, and plan their architecture accordingly. Proper design, monitoring, and testing practices can mitigate many challenges associated with serverless applications, allowing developers to harness the power of Lambda effectively.

Other compute services

Here, we explore other compute services offered by AWS. In addition to its flagship EC2 service, AWS offers a range of other compute services to meet diverse workload requirements. One such service is AWS Lambda, a serverless computing platform that allows developers to run code without provisioning or managing servers. Lambda automatically scales based on the incoming workload, making it ideal for event-driven applications and microservices architectures. For containerized workloads, AWS provides Amazon ECS and Amazon EKS, which enable customers to easily deploy, manage, and scale containerized applications using Docker and Kubernetes, respectively. These services offer flexibility and control over containerized environments while abstracting away the underlying infrastructure complexities. Additionally, AWS Batch simplifies the execution of batch computing workloads by dynamically provisioning the optimal compute resources based on workload requirements, allowing customers to focus on their applications rather than infrastructure management. With these compute services, AWS provides a comprehensive suite of options to support a wide range of computing needs, from traditional virtual machines to modern serverless and containerized architectures.

API Gateway

AWS API Gateway is a fully managed service that makes it easy for developers to create, publish, monitor, and secure APIs at any scale. APIs are essential for modern applications, allowing different software systems to communicate and interact with each other.

AWS API Gateway acts as a front door for applications to access data, business logic, or functionality from backend services.

AWS API Gateway enables developers to create robust and scalable APIs effortlessly. It supports RESTful APIs and WebSocket APIs, allowing real-time two-way communication between applications. With API Gateway, developers can decouple the frontend and backend systems, making it easier to iterate on both components independently.

API Gateway provides a range of features, including request and response transformations, traffic management, authorization and access control, caching, monitoring, and analytics. These features empower developers to build secure, high-performance APIs that can handle varying levels of traffic and adapt to changing business requirements.

Use cases

API Gateway is versatile and can be applied to various use cases. It is commonly used for building microservices architectures, create a proxy to backend services, request transformation and validation, serverless applications, mobile backends, and IoT applications. Organizations also leverage API Gateway for building partner APIs, enabling third-party developers to access specific functionalities securely.

Key Features of API Gateway:

- **Security**: API Gateway allows developers to implement robust security measures such as authentication and authorization using AWS IAM, OAuth, and custom authorizers. It also supports SSL/TLS encryption for data in transit, ensuring data integrity and confidentiality.

- **Scalability**: API Gateway automatically scales to handle any amount of traffic, from a few requests per day to thousands of RPS It can handle sudden and massive traffic spikes without any manual intervention, ensuring a seamless experience for users.

- **Monitoring and analytics**: AWS API Gateway provides detailed metrics, logs, and tracing capabilities. Developers can monitor API usage, track performance, and gain insights into API behavior, helping them optimize and troubleshoot their APIs effectively.

- **Integration**: API Gateway integrates seamlessly with other AWS services, including AWS Lambda, AWS Elastic Beanstalk, AWS S3, and more. This integration simplifies the development process and allows developers to build powerful serverless applications.

- **Throttling**: Controls the number of RPS that can be sent to an API. It prevents overloading by limiting traffic to a specified threshold.

- **Rate limiting**: Sets quotas on the total number of requests allowed within a specified time frame (for example, per day or per month) to manage API usage and prevent abuse.

Benefits:

- **Cost-effective**: API Gateway follows a pay-as-you-go pricing model, allowing organizations to pay only for the API calls they receive, and the amount of data transferred. This cost-effective approach makes it suitable for businesses of all sizes.

- **Developer productivity**: By handling tasks such as authorization, access control, and traffic management, API Gateway frees developers from managing the underlying infrastructure, enabling them to focus on building and improving the actual APIs and applications.

- **Agility and innovation**: API Gateway accelerates the development cycle by providing a robust platform for building and deploying APIs quickly. This agility fosters innovation, allowing businesses to respond rapidly to market demands and changes in customer preferences.

Best practices:

- **Design API with care**: Careful API design is crucial. Well-designed APIs are intuitive, consistent, and easy to understand, ensuring a positive developer and user experience.

- **Implement security measures**: Use authentication and authorization mechanisms to secure your APIs. Regularly update security policies and access controls to protect against unauthorized access and potential attacks.

- **Monitor and optimize**: Continuously monitor API performance and usage metrics. Use this data to optimize API configurations, identify bottlenecks, and improve overall efficiency.

- **Plan for scale**: Design APIs with scalability in mind. Consider potential traffic spikes and design your API to handle increased loads. Utilize features like caching and request/response transformations to optimize performance.

AWS API Gateway is a powerful tool that simplifies API management, allowing developers to focus on building innovative applications. Its scalability, security features, and integration capabilities make it a preferred choice for businesses aiming to create robust, high-performing APIs. By following best practices and leveraging the extensive features provided by API Gateway, organizations can create reliable, secure, and efficient APIs that drive digital transformation and business success.

AWS EKS Managed Kubernetes service

Amazon EKS is a managed Kubernetes service offered by AWS that simplifies the deployment, management, and scaling of containerized applications by using Kubernetes. Kubernetes is an open-source container orchestration platform that automates the deployment, scaling, and management of containerized applications.

We will explore the key features and benefits of Amazon EKS, its architecture, and how it fits into the broader ecosystem of AWS services:

- **Managed Kubernetes control plane**: Amazon EKS provides a managed Kubernetes control plane, eliminating the operational overhead of managing the control plane components. AWS takes care of high availability, ensuring a highly available and secure cluster control plane.

- **Simplified cluster management**: EKS simplifies cluster management tasks such as upgrades, scaling, and monitoring. It integrates with other AWS services like Amazon CloudWatch and AWS IAM for centralized logging, monitoring, and access control.

- **Security and compliance**: EKS offers a robust security model, integrating with AWS IAM and Amazon VPC for secure networking. It also supports pod and cluster-level isolation through network policies, ensuring compliance with organizational security policies.

- **Integration with AWS services**: EKS seamlessly integrates with other AWS services, allowing you to leverage services like Amazon **Relational Database Service (RDS)**, Amazon S3, and AWS IAM within your Kubernetes applications.

- **Automatic scaling**: EKS supports automatic scaling of worker nodes by using Auto Scaling groups. It allows you to add or remove worker nodes based on the demand, ensuring your applications are highly available and scalable.

Architecture of Amazon EKS

Amazon EKS architecture consists of the following components:

- **Control plane**: It is managed by AWS and consists of Amazon EKS API server and etcd, a distributed key-value store used to store the cluster state. AWS handles the operational aspects of the control plane, including patching, scaling, and upgrades.

- **Worker nodes**: They are instances in your AWS environment that run the Kubernetes pods and other resources like deployments, services, daemon sets, etc. These nodes can be managed using Amazon EC2 instances or AWS Fargate, a serverless compute engine for containers. Worker nodes communicate with the control plane to orchestrate the deployment and management of pods.

- **VPC and networking**: Use EKS integrates with Amazon VPC to provide network isolation for your Kubernetes cluster. Each EKS cluster operates within its own VPC, allowing you to define network policies and securely connect your cluster to other AWS services and resources.

- **IAM integration**: EKS integrates with AWS IAM to manage authentication and authorization for cluster resources. Using RBAC and admin could control access to EKS API operations and other AWS services.

Ecosystem integration

EKS seamlessly integrates with various AWS services, enabling you to build end-to-end solutions within the AWS ecosystem. For example:

- **Amazon ECR**: EKS can pull container images from Amazon ECR, a fully managed Docker container registry that makes it easy for developers to store, manage, and deploy Docker container images.

- **Amazon RDS**: EKS applications can connect to Amazon RDS databases, providing a scalable and managed relational database solution for your applications.

- **Amazon CloudWatch**: EKS integrates with Amazon CloudWatch for monitoring and logging. You can monitor cluster performance, setup alarms, and gain insights into your cluster's behavior by using CloudWatch metrics and logs.

- **AWS App Mesh**: EKS can be integrated with AWS App Mesh, a service mesh that provides application-level networking to make it easy to monitor, control, and debug services across your application.

In summary, Amazon EKS is a powerful and fully managed Kubernetes service that simplifies the deployment, management, and scaling of containerized applications. Its integration with various AWS services, security features, and simplified cluster management make it a popular choice for organizations looking to run Kubernetes workloads in the cloud.

AWS Amazon Elastic Load Balancer

Amazon ELB is an AWS service that automatically distributes incoming application traffic across multiple targets, such as Amazon EC2 instances, containers, and IP addresses, within one or more availability zones. ELB serves as a single point of contact for clients, enhancing Fault-tolerance and enabling high availability and reliability for applications.

Some types of ELB are mentioned in the following:

- **Application Load Balancer (ALB)**: It operates at the application layer (Layer 7) and allows routing decisions based on content. It is ideal for microservices and container-based applications.

- **Network Load Balancer (NLB)**: It operates at the transport layer (Layer 4) and is capable of handling TCP, UDP, and TLS traffic. It is designed for ultra-high-performance, handling millions of requests per second.

Key features:

- **Automatic scaling**: The ELB scales are automatically based on incoming traffic, ensuring that the application can handle varying workloads.

- **High availability**: It distributes traffic across Multiple Availability Zones to ensure the application remains available even if one or more instances fail.

- **Security**: It supports SSL/TLS encryption, ensuring secure communication between clients and the load balancer.

- **Health checks**: It periodically checks the health of registered instances and routes traffic only to healthy instances.

- **Monitoring and logging**: It provides detailed monitoring and logging capabilities, allowing users to gain insights into traffic patterns and troubleshoot issues effectively.

Some benefits of ELB are mentioned in the following:

- **Improved availability**: ELB ensures that applications are highly available by distributing traffic across healthy instances in different Availability Zones.

- **Enhanced performance**: ELB optimizes application performance by distributing traffic efficiently, reducing latency, and ensuring a seamless user experience.

- **Simplified management**: ELB handles the complexities of load balancing, allowing developers to focus on building and scaling applications without worrying about infrastructure management.

- **Cost-effectiveness**: ELB helps in optimizing costs by automatically scaling resources based on demand, preventing over-provisioning and underutilization.

Use cases:

- **Web applications**: ELB is commonly used to distribute traffic among web servers, ensuring that web applications are responsive and reliable.

- **Microservices architecture**: ELB plays a vital role in microservices-based applications, routing traffic to various microservices-based on specific criteria, such as URL paths or headers.

- **Containerized applications**: ELB integrates seamlessly with container services like Amazon ECS and Kubernetes, enabling efficient load balancing for containerized workloads.

- **Hybrid deployments**: ELB can distribute traffic across on-premises servers and AWS resources, facilitating hybrid cloud architectures.

- **IoT**: ELB can handle traffic from IoT devices, ensuring that data from these devices is efficiently processed and routed to the appropriate backend services.

Amazon ELB is a powerful AWS service that enhances the availability, performance, and security of applications by efficiently distributing traffic across multiple targets. Proper configuration and management, following best practices, are essential to maximizing the benefits of ELB for various use cases and application architectures.

AWS Beanstalk

AWS Elastic Beanstalk is a fully managed service provided by AWS that simplifies the deployment and management of applications. It allows developers to focus on writing code without worrying about the underlying infrastructure.

Elastic Beanstalk automates the process of provisioning resources, deploying applications, monitoring application health, and scaling capacity based on demand. This service supports a variety of programming languages, platforms, and frameworks, making it versatile and suitable for a wide range of applications.

Key features:

- **Easy application deployment**: Developers can easily upload their application code, and Elastic Beanstalk automatically handles the deployment, from capacity provisioning to load balancing and application health monitoring.

- **Managed environment**: Elastic Beanstalk automatically manages the underlying infrastructure, including Amazon EC2 instances, networking configurations, load balancing, auto scaling, and security.

- **Multi-language support**: Elastic Beanstalk supports popular programming languages such as Java, .NET, Node.js, Python, Ruby, Go, and PHP, allowing developers to choose their preferred language and framework.

- **Integration with AWS services**: It seamlessly integrates with other AWS services, allowing developers to utilize services like Amazon RDS, Amazon S3, and Amazon DynamoDB for their applications.

- **Scalability**: Elastic Beanstalk can automatically scale the application based on traffic, ensuring that it can handle varying workloads without manual intervention.

Application deployment:

- Developers create a package of their application code and necessary configurations, which can include web servers, application servers, and database systems.

- The application package is uploaded to Elastic Beanstalk using the AWS Management Console, AWS CLI, or an **integrated development environment (IDE)**.

- Elastic Beanstalk automatically handles the deployment process, including provisioning the necessary resources and configuring the environment to run the application.

Managed environments:

- Elastic Beanstalk provides pre-defined configurations, called **environments**, for various platforms and services. Developers can choose an environment that matches their application requirements.

- Each environment includes a set of AWS resources, such as Amazon EC2 instances, load balancers, and databases, configured to work together seamlessly.

- Elastic Beanstalk monitors the health of the environment and automatically replaces unhealthy instances, ensuring high availability and reliability.

Configuration and customization:

- Developers have the flexibility to customize the environment settings, including instance types, security settings, scaling options, and environment variables.

- Elastic Beanstalk allows the use of configuration files to define custom settings and packages for the application environment, enabling fine-grained control over the deployment process.

- Continuous deployment can be setup using integration with popular version control systems like GitHub and AWS CodeCommit, allowing automatic deployment whenever changes are pushed to the repository.

Benefits:

- **Simplicity**: Elastic Beanstalk simplifies the process of deploying and managing applications, reducing the complexity and time required for infrastructure setup.

- **Rapid development**: Developers can focus on writing code and quickly deploy applications, accelerating the development cycle and time-to-market.

- **Scalability**: Elastic Beanstalk automatically scales the application based on demand, ensuring that it can handle high traffic loads without manual intervention.

- **Cost-effectiveness**: By automating infrastructure management, Elastic Beanstalk helps optimize costs, allowing developers to pay attention to application development rather than worrying about infrastructure costs.

- **Monitoring and insights**: Elastic Beanstalk provides monitoring and logging capabilities, allowing developers to gain insights into application performance and troubleshoot issues effectively.

Use cases:

- **Web applications**: Elastic Beanstalk is ideal for web applications, whether they are simple websites or complex, multi-tier applications. It supports various web frameworks and languages.

- **API services**: Developers can deploy **Representational State Transfer (REST)** APIs and other web services easily, allowing them to build scalable and reliable backend services for web and mobile applications.

- **Microservices architecture**: Elastic Beanstalk supports microservices-based applications, enabling developers to deploy and manage multiple microservices independently while ensuring seamless communication between services.

- **Content management systems (CMS)**: These platforms along with content-heavy applications benefit from Elastic Beanstalk's ease of deployment and scaling, ensuring a smooth user experience even during traffic spikes.

- **Development and testing**: Developers can use Elastic Beanstalk to quickly deploy applications for development and testing purposes, facilitating collaboration and efficient testing cycles.

AWS Elastic Beanstalk offers developers a hassle-free way to deploy, manage, and scale applications, allowing them to focus on writing code and building innovative solutions. Its simplicity, flexibility, and seamless integration with other AWS services make it a valuable choice for a wide range of applications and use cases.

Lightsail

Amazon Lightsail is a simplified cloud service provided by AWS that enables users to launch and manage **virtual private servers** (**VPSs**) also known as **instances**, storage, databases, and networking features with ease with a flat monthly price.

Designed for developers, startups, and small to medium-sized businesses, Lightsail offers a user-friendly interface and straightforward pricing, making it an excellent choice for users who are new to cloud computing or require a hassle-free hosting solution.

Also, there is an option for Docker container hosting, with a flat monthly price.

Some key features of Lightsail are mentioned in the following:

- **Docker hosting**: You can host your containers in Lightsail without worrying about managing servers with a flat fee per month.

- **Virtual private servers (instances)**: Lightsail provides pre-configured virtual machines (instances) that are easy to launch and manage, catering to a variety of applications and workloads. It offers predefined images to use, for all the mainstream applications like Django, Node.js, Drupal, WordPress, PrestaShop, Joomla, etc.

- **Storage**: Users can attach scalable and high-performance block storage to their instances, ensuring reliable data storage for applications and websites.

- **Databases**: Lightsail offers managed database services, including Amazon RDS and Amazon Aurora, allowing users to setup, operate, and scale databases effortlessly.

- **Networking**: Lightsail provides features like static IP addresses, load balancers, DNS management, and firewall configurations, enabling users to build secure and highly available applications.

Use cases:

- **Website hosting**: Lightsail is an excellent choice for hosting websites and web applications, offering various CMS options and one-click application installations.

- **Development and testing**: Developers can use Lightsail instances for development, testing, and staging environments, allowing them to prototype and experiment without the complexity of traditional cloud services.

- **E-commerce stores**: Lightsail provides a suitable environment for hosting e-commerce platforms and online stores, ensuring reliable performance and scalability for online businesses.

- **App hosting**: Whether it is a mobile applicaiton backend or a web application, Lightsail offers a straightforward solution for hosting applications, allowing developers to focus on building features rather than managing infrastructure.

- **Blogs and content management**: Lightsail is popular among bloggers and content creators due to its simplicity and ease of use. It supports popular CMS platforms like WordPress, making it effortless to setup and maintain blogs.

Some benefits of Lightsail are mentioned in the following:

- **Simplicity**: Lightsail's intuitive user interface and simplified workflows make it easy for users to deploy and manage instances, databases, and other services without requiring in-depth cloud expertise.

- **Predictable pricing**: Lightsail offers flat-rate pricing, providing users with a clear understanding of their monthly expenses. There are no hidden fees, ensuring predictable costs for hosting services.

- **Scalability**: While Lightsail is designed for simplicity, it still allows users to scale their resources vertically by upgrading instances or horizontally by adding more instances to meet growing demands.

- **Integrated services**: Lightsail integrates seamlessly with other AWS services, allowing users to expand their infrastructure easily by connecting Lightsail instances with services like Amazon S3, AWS Lambda, and more.

- **Global availability**: Lightsail is available in multiple AWS Regions worldwide, ensuring users can deploy their applications close to their target audience for low-latency and improved performance.

Amazon Lightsail is an accessible and user-friendly cloud service that simplifies the process of launching, managing, and scaling virtual servers and other resources. With its straightforward interface, predictable pricing, and integration with other AWS services, Lightsail empowers users to focus on their applications and businesses without getting bogged down by complex infrastructure management.

Conclusion

The chapter highlights AWS compute services and all the main products AWS offers to handle compute use cases. This chapter has explored the diverse range of AWS compute services, each tailored to meet specific business needs. From the flexibility of Amazon EC2 instances to the serverless computing paradigm offered by AWS Lambda, the chapter has highlighted the versatility and scalability that AWS compute services bring to the table.

As businesses continue to navigate the digital world, understanding these powerful tools becomes imperative. AWS compute not only empowers organizations to scale their operations seamlessly but also fosters innovation by enabling developers to focus on building great applications without being burdened by the complexities of infrastructure management. With AWS compute, businesses are not just embracing technology; they are embracing a transformative approach that paves the way for efficiency, agility, and endless possibilities in the ever-evolving world of cloud computing.

In the next chapter, we will discuss AWS storage solutions, used to store our data as files as a virtual disk and object storage by using one of the most famous AWS services S3.

Points to remember

- EC2 provides scalable computing capacity in the cloud, allowing users to launch virtual servers as per their requirements.

- Users can choose different instance types optimized for various use cases such as general computing, memory-intensive applications, or GPU-intensive tasks.

- ECS is a fully managed container orchestration service that supports Docker containers.

- It simplifies the deployment, management, and scaling of containerized applications.

- Lambda is a serverless computing service that lets you run code without provisioning or managing servers.

- It automatically scales based on the incoming traffic and executes code in response to events.

- API Gateway allows developers to create, publish, monitor, and secure APIs for applications. It supports REST APIs and WebSocket connections.

- It acts as a front door for applications to access data, business logic, or functionality from backend services.

- EKS is a managed Kubernetes service that simplifies the deployment, management, and scaling of containerized applications using Kubernetes.

- It allows users to run Kubernetes without the complexity of managing the underlying infrastructure.

- ECR is a fully managed Docker container registry that makes it easy to store, manage, and deploy Docker container images.

- It integrates seamlessly with ECS and simplifies the container deployment process.

- ELB automatically distributes incoming application traffic across multiple targets, such as EC2 instances, containers, and IP addresses, within one or more availability zones.

- It enhances Fault-tolerance of your applications and ensures high availability.

- Elastic Beanstalk is an easy-to-use service for deploying and scaling applications quickly.

- It supports multiple platforms and languages, abstracting the underlying infrastructure complexities.

- Lightsail is designed to simplify the process of launching and managing VPS for small-scale applications.

- It provides a straightforward interface and pre-configured server options for developers new to cloud computing.

Exercises

1. **What does AWS IAM stand for?**

   a. AWS Internet Access Management

   b. Advanced Web Security Identity Access Management

   c. AWS Identity and Access Management

   d. Automated Web Security and Identity Management

2. **What AWS service allows users to launch virtual servers in the cloud and offers different instance types for various use cases?**

   a. Amazon ECS

   b. AWS Lambda

   c. Amazon EC2

   d. AWS Elastic Beanstalk

3. **Which AWS service is a managed container orchestration service that supports Docker containers?**

   a. Amazon ECR

   b. Elastic Load Balancing (ELB)

   c. Amazon ECS

   d. API Gateway

4. **What is the serverless computing service provided by AWS that allows you to run code without provisioning or managing servers?**

   a. Amazon ECR

   b. AWS Lambda

   c. Amazon Lightsail

   d. Elastic Beanstalk

5. **Which AWS service acts as a front door for applications to access data, business logic, or functionality from backend services?**

    a. AWS Elastic Beanstalk

    b. Amazon ECR

    c. API Gateway

    d. Amazon ELB

6. **What AWS service provides a managed Kubernetes environment, allowing users to run Kubernetes without managing the underlying infrastructure?**

    a. Amazon EKS

    b. Amazon ECS

    c. AWS Lambda

    d. Amazon Lightsail

7. **Which AWS service automatically distributes incoming application traffic across multiple targets within one or more availability zones?**

    a. Elastic Load Balancing (ELB)

    b. Amazon EC2

    c. AWS Elastic Beanstalk

    d. API Gateway

8. **Which AWS service simplifies the deployment and management of applications by providing pre-configured environments for various platforms and languages?**

    a. Amazon ECR

    b. Amazon Lightsail

    c. AWS Lambda

    d. Amazon ECS

9. **What AWS service provides a fully managed Docker container registry for storing, managing, and deploying Docker container images?**

    a. Amazon ECR

    b. Elastic Load Balancing (ELB)

    c. Amazon ECS

    d. API Gateway

Answers

1. c
2. c
3. c
4. c
5. c
6. a
7. a
8. b
9. a

Key terms

- AWS EC2
- AWS ECS
- AWS Lambda
- AWS ELB
- AWS ECR
- AWS EKS
- AWS API Gateway
- AWS Beanstalk
- AWS Lightsail

Join our book's Discord space

Join the book's Discord Workspace for Latest updates, Offers, Tech happenings around the world, New Release and Sessions with the Authors:

https://discord.bpbonline.com

CHAPTER 5
AWS Storage Services

Introduction

Amazon Web Services (**AWS**) offers a comprehensive suite of storage services tailored to meet the diverse needs of modern businesses and applications. These storage services play a pivotal role in the AWS ecosystem, providing scalable, durable, and highly available solutions for storing, managing, and retrieving data in the cloud. AWS recognizes that different workloads demand different storage architectures, and as a result, it offers a range of storage options designed to address specific performance, cost, and durability requirements.

At the heart of AWS's storage offerings is Amazon **Simple Storage Service** (**S3**), a versatile object storage service that excels in handling unstructured data with exceptional scalability and durability. S3 is widely adopted for its ease of use and integration with other AWS services. Beyond S3, AWS provides a spectrum of storage solutions, including block storage with Amazon **Elastic Block Store** (**EBS**) for supporting **Elastic Compute Cloud** (**EC2**) instances, file storage with Amazon **Elastic File System** (**EFS**) for scalable file systems in the cloud, and AWS Glacier for cost-effective long-term archival.

This diverse portfolio ensures that businesses can select the most suitable storage service or combination of services to align with their specific use cases and performance requirements. In this exploration, we will explore the various storage services offered by AWS, highlighting their unique features, use cases, and the flexibility they provide for crafting robust and efficient cloud storage solutions.

Structure

The chapter covers the following topics:

- Amazon Simple Storage Service
- Scheduled rules for S3 Storage classes
- Shared responsibility model for AWS S3
- Amazon Elastic Block Store
- Shared responsibility model for AWS EBS
- Amazon Elastic File System

Objectives

In the upcoming chapter on AWS storage services, readers will learn about the diverse field of storage options offered by AWS. The chapter will explore various storage solutions, ranging from the highly scalable and versatile Amazon S3 for object storage to the block-level storage provided by Amazon EBS designed for EC2 instances, and show Amazon EFS for networked file system storage. Readers will gain insights into the unique features, use cases, and best practices associated with each storage service, empowering them to make informed decisions based on their specific application requirements. Whether it is understanding the durability and availability aspects of Amazon S3, the performance characteristics of Amazon EBS, or the archival capabilities of Amazon Glacier, this chapter aims to provide a comprehensive overview of AWS storage services, equipping readers with the knowledge to optimize their storage strategies in the cloud.

Amazon Simple Storage Service

Amazon S3 is a highly scalable, durable, and secure object storage service offered by AWS. It is designed to store and retrieve any amount of data from anywhere on the web. S3 is a key component of AWS's cloud computing services, providing businesses and developers with a versatile and reliable storage solution.

Object storage concept

At its core, Amazon S3 is an object storage service, which is a data storage architecture that manages data as objects rather than as blocks or files. Unlike traditional file storage systems, object storage does not organize data in a hierarchical file structure. Instead, each object is a standalone entity that consists of data, metadata, and a unique identifier. This approach enables seamless scalability, efficient data retrieval, and easier management of vast amounts of unstructured data.

AWS S3 uses the concept of buckets, which are containers for storing objects on AWS. Each bucket must have a globally unique name in the AWS namespace, and buckets are region-specific. When you create a bucket, you select a region to store your data. S3 automatically replicates the data across multiple facilities within the chosen region to ensure durability and availability.

An object in AWS S3 is the fundamental entity stored in Amazon S3. It consists of data, a key, and metadata. These objects can range in size from a few bytes to terabytes.

A key is a unique identifier for an object within a bucket. The combination of bucket name and key uniquely identifies each object. The key plays a crucial role in organizing and categorizing objects within a bucket. For example, if you have a bucket for storing images, you might have keys like **images/cat.jpg** and **images/dog.jpg** to represent different image files.

Each object in S3 can have associated metadata, which is a set of key-value pairs that provide additional information about the object. It can be used for various purposes, such as specifying the content type of the object, defining custom tags, or storing information relevant to your application.

The main features of Amazon S3 are mentioned in the following:

- **Versioning**: Amazon S3 provides a versioning feature that allows users to preserve, retrieve, and restore every version of an object stored in a bucket. This capability is crucial for scenarios where accidental deletion or modification of objects may occur. By enabling versioning, users can track changes, revert to previous versions, and maintain data integrity over time. This feature is particularly valuable for compliance, audit, and backup purposes.

- **Storage classes and life cycle**: Amazon S3 provides different storage classes that offer different access speeds and costs associated with storing and retrieving objects from frequent access to an **infrequent access** (**IA**) storage type. S3 also can transition objects between storage classes based on access patterns and retention policies and we can Setup some life cycle policies on buckets to manage object lifetime and auto-deletion. For example, we can configure to auto-delete objects older than one year from the first save in the bucket, or we can configure to move objects after one month from the standard storage class to a more cost-effective and infrequent storage class for archiving.

- **Replication**: To enhance data durability and availability, Amazon S3 offers **Cross-Region Replication** (**CRR**) and **Same-Region Replication** (**SRR**). CRR allows users to replicate objects across different AWS Regions, providing disaster recovery capabilities. SRR, on the other hand, replicates objects within the same region for Fault-tolerance and high availability. Replication ensures that data is stored redundantly, reducing the risk of data loss due to hardware failures or regional outages.

- **Encryption at rest**: Security is a top priority for AWS, and Amazon S3 offers robust encryption mechanisms to protect data at rest. Users can choose from multiple encryption options, including **server-side encryption (SSE) with Amazon S3 managed keys (SSE-S3)**, **SSE with AWS Key Management Service (SSE-KMS)**, and **SSE with customer-provided keys (SSE-C)**. These encryption methods ensure that data stored in S3 buckets remains confidential and secure, meeting compliance requirements and addressing privacy concerns.

- **Access control**: Amazon S3 provides fine-grained access control mechanisms to regulate who can access and manipulate data stored in S3 buckets. **Access control lists (ACLs)**, **Identity and Access Management (IAM)** policies, and bucket policies enable users to define granular permissions, ensuring that only authorized individuals or systems can interact with specific objects. This level of control is essential for maintaining data privacy, complying with regulatory requirements, and preventing unauthorized access.

- **Scalability and performance**: Amazon S3 is built to scale horizontally, allowing users to seamlessly store and retrieve any amount of data. The service automatically scales to accommodate growing storage needs, making it suitable for a wide range of use cases, from small applications to large-scale enterprise systems. Additionally, S3's low-latency performance ensures fast and reliable access to data, making it ideal for applications with demanding performance requirements.

- **Event notification**: Amazon S3 supports event notifications, allowing you to trigger AWS Lambda functions or **Simple Queue Service (SQS)** queues when certain events (for example, object creation, and deletion) occur in your S3 bucket. Due to this feature, we could build event-driven workloads automatically triggered from an object event such as creation of a new object, and automate some processing.

- **High availability**: Amazon S3 is designed for continuous availability, ensuring that your data can be accessed whenever needed, with multiple copies stored across different physical locations, minimizing downtime.

- **Durability**: S3 provides 99.999999999% (11 9's) durability by replicating data across multiple facilities, ensuring that even in the event of failures or disasters, the risk of data loss is extremely low.

Amazon S3 storage classes

S3 offers a range of storage classes, each designed to meet different performance, durability, and cost requirements. Understanding these storage classes is crucial for optimizing costs and meeting specific use case needs.

The Standard S3 storage classes are:

- **S3 Standard**: This is the default storage class that offers high durability, availability, and low-latency access to frequently accessed data. It is suitable for a wide range of use cases, including big data analytics, mobile and gaming applications, content distribution, and backups.

- **S3 intelligent-tiering**: This storage class is designed to optimize costs for data with unknown or changing access patterns. It automatically moves objects between two access tiers—frequent and IA, based on changing usage patterns.

- **S3 Standard-IA**: This is ideal for data that is accessed less frequently but requires rapid access when needed. It offers lower storage costs compared to the S3 Standard and is suitable for backup and long-term storage.

- **S3 One Zone-IA**: This is Similar to S3 Standard-IA but stores data in a single **Availability Zone** (**AZ**), making it a cost-effective option for infrequently accessed data that can be easily recreated if lost.

The S3 Glacier storage classes are:

- **Amazon S3 Glacier**: Suitable for archiving data with long retrieval times, ranging from minutes to hours. It is a cost-effective solution for data archiving and backup.

- **Amazon S3 Glacier deep archive**: The lowest-cost storage class, designed for long-term retention of data that is rarely accessed. It has the longest retrieval time, ranging from hours to 12 hours.

Now, we will discuss factors affecting the cost of AWS S3. Understanding the costs associated with each storage class is essential for optimizing AWS expenses. The following factors influence the cost of using Amazon S3:

- **Storage volume**: The amount of data stored in S3 directly impacts costs As storage requirements increase, so does the overall expenditure.

- **Data transfer**: These costs are applied when moving data into and out of S3. For example, transferring data between AWS Regions or out to the internet incurs additional charges.

- **Request and operation costs**: S3 charges for various requests and operations, such as GET, PUT, COPY, LIST, and DELETE requests. The frequency and type of these operations contribute to overall costs.

- **Storage class transition costs**: If you configure lifecycle policies to transition objects between storage classes, there may be costs associated with these transitions.

- **Data retrieval costs (For Glacier storage classes)**: For Glacier and Glacier Deep Archive, costs are incurred when retrieving data. Retrieval times vary, and expedited retrievals come with higher costs.

Pricing details for each storage class

Amazon S3 pricing is based on several factors, including storage volume, data transfer, and request rates. The pricing model is designed to be flexible and accommodate a variety of use cases. A brief overview of the pricing structure for each storage class is mentioned in the following:

- **S3 Standard, S3 Intelligent-Tiering, and S3 Standard-IA**:
  - **Storage costs**: Charged per GB-month.
  - **Data transfer costs**: Vary based on the amount of data transferred.
- **S3 One Zone-IA**:
  - **Storage costs**: Similar to S3 Standard-IA but lower due to single-zone redundancy.
  - **Data transfer costs**: Same as S3 Standard-IA.
- **Amazon S3 Glacier and Glacier Deep Archive**:
  - **Storage costs**: Charged per GB-month.
  - **Data retrieval costs**: Incurred when retrieving data. Costs vary based on retrieval speed.

It is important to use the AWS Pricing Calculator and stay updated with the AWS Documentation for the latest pricing details and any changes to the pricing model.

Scheduled rules for S3 Storage classes

Let us see how to create a lifecycle policy for a S3 bucket:

- **Access the S3 management console**: Navigate to the S3 console and select the bucket containing the objects you want to transition.

- **Configure a lifecycle policy**: In the management tab, choose Lifecycle and then click Add lifecycle rule.

- **Define rule scope**: Specify the objects affected by the rule based on prefixes, tags, or the entire bucket.

- **Define transition actions**: Set the conditions triggering the transition, such as the age of the objects or a specific date. Specify the destination storage class (for example, from Standard to Standard-IA).

- **Review and create**: Confirm the rule settings and create the lifecycle policy.

- **Scheduled transition**: By configuring the lifecycle rule with appropriate conditions, you can schedule the transition of objects from one storage class to another. For example, you might choose to transition objects older than 30 days from S3 Standard to S3 Standard-IA.

- **Monitoring and verification**: S3 provides monitoring tools, including CloudWatch metrics and S3 access logs, to track the progress of storage class transitions. This visibility ensures that the scheduled rules are functioning as expected.

Considerations

Check those points before and after creating a Lifecycle policy for your S3 bucket:

- **Impact on access patterns**: Before implementing lifecycle policies, it is crucial to understand the access patterns of your data. Transitioning data to a lower-cost storage class may lead to increased retrieval times.

- **Review and adjust rules**: Periodically review and adjust lifecycle rules based on evolving data access patterns and business requirements.

Implementing scheduled rules for S3 storage class transitions through lifecycle policies empowers users to manage their data efficiently, optimize costs, and ensure that data is stored in the most appropriate storage class throughout its lifecycle. Regular monitoring and adjustment of rules contribute to an effective and responsive data management strategy within the AWS S3 environment.

S3 asset and site hosting

Amazon S3 is not only a powerful storage service but also serves as a reliable solution for hosting static assets, websites, and **Single Page Applications** (SPAs). By leveraging S3 for hosting, users can deploy scalable and cost-effective solutions for modern frontends. To ensure seamless interactions between the frontend and backend, **cross-origin resource sharing** (CORS) plays a crucial role in managing security policies.

Hosting capabilities and use cases on S3:

- **Static assets**: S3 is an excellent choice for hosting static assets like images, stylesheets, and client-side scripts. These assets can be stored in S3 buckets and easily accessed over the web through unique URLs.

- **Website hosting**: S3 allows users to host entire static websites directly from S3 buckets. This feature simplifies website deployment, reduces infrastructure complexity, and takes advantage of S3's high availability and low-latency performance.

- **SPAs**: They rely heavily on client-side rendering and dynamic updates and can benefit from S3 hosting. The simplicity of hosting SPAs on S3 aligns with the serverless architecture and microservices paradigm.

CORS configuration

CORS is a security feature implemented by web browsers to control access to resources on a web page from different origins. For modern frontends and SPAs hosted on S3 to interact with APIs or resources on other domains, a well-configured CORS setup is essential.

Enabling CORS on S3

CORS can be configured at the S3 bucket level. By specifying CORS rules, you define which origins are allowed to access resources in your S3 bucket. This involves setting HTTP headers like Access-Control-Allow-Origin, Access-Control-Allow-Methods, and others.

Example CORS configuration for S3

Here is a basic example of a CORS configuration in XML for an S3 bucket that allows requests from a specific domain:

```
<CORSConfiguration>
 <CORSRule>
 <AllowedOrigin>https://your-frontend-domain.com</AllowedOrigin>
 <AllowedMethod>GET</AllowedMethod>
 <AllowedHeader>*</AllowedHeader>
 </CORSRule>
</CORSConfiguration>
```

This example permits GET requests from the specified frontend domain and allows any headers to be included in the request.

Handling preflight requests

For certain types of requests, browsers may send a preflight request (OPTIONS) to check the permissions before sending the actual request. Proper CORS configuration should handle these preflight requests.

The benefits of S3 Hosting and CORS for modern frontends are mentioned in the following:

- **Scalability and performance**: S3 provides scalable and reliable hosting, ensuring low-latency access to assets globally. This is crucial for delivering a seamless user experience.

- **Cost-effectiveness**: S3 hosting is cost-effective, particularly for static assets and SPAs. Users only pay for the storage and data transfer, without the need for maintaining traditional server infrastructure.

- **Simplified deployment**: Hosting assets and SPAs on S3 simplifies deployment processes. AWS tools like AWS **Command Line Interface (CLI)**, AWS **Software Development Kit (SDK)**, and CI/CD pipelines can automate deployment workflows.

- **Security and CORS compliance**: Proper CORS configuration enhances security by controlling access to resources. It ensures that only specified domains are allowed to interact with your S3-hosted assets.

In conclusion, leveraging Amazon S3 for hosting assets and SPAs, combined with a well-configured CORS setup, provides a robust foundation for building and deploying modern frontends. This approach aligns with principles of scalability, cost-effectiveness, and security, making S3 a versatile solution for a wide range of web applications.

Shared responsibility model for AWS S3

AWS operates on a shared responsibility model, emphasizing the collaborative effort between AWS as the cloud service provider and customers who utilize AWS services. The shared responsibility model delineates the responsibilities for security and compliance, ensuring a comprehensive approach to safeguarding data and resources. When it comes to Amazon S3, the shared responsibility model is a critical framework for understanding the distribution of responsibilities between AWS and the customer.

Refer to the following information about AWS's responsibilities:

- **Infrastructure security**: AWS is responsible for the security of the underlying infrastructure that supports Amazon S3. This includes the physical security of data centers, networking, and hardware.

- **Hardware maintenance**: The maintenance and upkeep of hardware components, such as servers and storage devices, fall under AWS's purview. This ensures the reliability and availability of the S3 service.

- **Software patching**: AWS is responsible for applying patches and updates to the software and systems that constitute the S3 service. This helps mitigate vulnerabilities and ensures the latest security features are in place.

- **Global compliance**: AWS is committed to adhering to various global compliance standards and certifications. This includes implementing and maintaining security controls to meet industry-specific and regulatory requirements.

Some customer responsibilities are mentioned in the following:

- **Data security and encryption**: Customers are responsible for encrypting their data, both in transit and at rest. AWS provides tools and features like SSE and AWS KMS to facilitate secure data handling.

- **Access management**: Controlling access to S3 buckets and objects is the responsibility of the customer. AWS IAM allows customers to define and manage access policies, roles, and permissions.

- **Configuration management**: Customers must configure their S3 buckets securely. This includes setting proper access controls, versioning, logging, and monitoring to align with their security and compliance requirements.

- **Data lifecycle management**: Defining and implementing data lifecycle policies, including archiving and deletion, is the customer's responsibility. AWS S3 provides lifecycle policies to automate these processes based on business needs.

The best practices for customers are mentioned in the following:

- **Regular audits and monitoring**: Conduct regular audits of S3 configurations and implement robust monitoring to detect any unauthorized access or suspicious activities.

- **Versioning and logging**: Enable versioning for S3 buckets to maintain historical versions of objects and enable detailed logging to track access and changes.

- **Data classification**: Classify data based on sensitivity and apply appropriate security measures. Leverage features like S3 object Tags for improved data organization.

- **Training and awareness**: Train personnel to follow security best practices, emphasizing the importance of data protection, access controls, and secure configurations.

The shared responsibility model for AWS S3 underscores the collaborative effort required to maintain a secure and compliant cloud environment. By understanding and adhering to their respective responsibilities, both AWS and customers contribute to a robust security posture, fostering trust and reliability in the use of Amazon S3 for storing and managing data.

AWS Snow Family

AWS Snow Family devices are particularly useful in scenarios where high-speed data transfer, security, and compliance are critical considerations. Each member of the Snow Family serves a specific use case, and AWS Snow Family members are equipped with physical hardware that customers can use to transport data to AWS data centers from their local data centers/servers. So, a customer can migrate a massive amount of data without latencies from an internet connection using different physical devices offered by AWS.

Some details about AWS Snowcone are mentioned in the following:

- **Overview**: AWS Snowcone is the smallest and most portable device in the Snow Family.

- **Use cases**: It is suitable for edge computing, remote or harsh environments, and scenarios where portability is essential.

- **Key features**: It has a rugged design, supports offline data transfer, and includes compute capabilities for lightweight processing on the edge.

Let us take a look at a few details of AWS Snowball:

- **Overview**: AWS Snowball is a larger device designed for more significant data transfer requirements.

- **Use cases**: It is ideal for scenarios where data volumes are substantial, and a physical device is preferable over internet-based transfers.

- **Key features**: It is secure and durable hardware, built-in E Ink shipping label, and multiple capacity options (Snowball Edge has additional compute capabilities).

Learn about AWS Snowmobile by referring to the following points:

- **Overview**: AWS Snowmobile is an exabyte-scale data transfer solution designed for massive data migration.

- **Use cases**: It is suited for enterprises dealing with extremely large datasets, such as large-scale data center migrations.

- **Key features**: It is a shipping container-sized device with high storage capacity, designed to be transported to the customer's location for direct data transfer.

Some common features of the AWS Snow family are mentioned in the following:

- **Security**: All Snow Family devices incorporate security features such as encryption, tamper-evident seals, and secure erasure of data to ensure the confidentiality and integrity of transferred data.

- **Data transfer acceleration**: The Snow Family devices leverage high-speed connections to AWS to accelerate data transfer, providing a more efficient alternative to traditional internet-based methods.

- **Integration with AWS services**: The data transferred using Snow Family devices can be seamlessly integrated into various AWS services, allowing for easy further processing and analysis in the cloud.

- **Offline data transfer**: Snow Family devices support offline data transfer, making them suitable for scenarios where internet connectivity is limited or unreliable.

AWS Storage Gateway

AWS Storage Gateway is a hybrid cloud storage service provided by AWS that enables seamless integration between on-premises environments and AWS Cloud storage. It acts as a bridge, extending on-premises applications to the cloud and allowing businesses to take advantage of scalable, cost-effective, and durable storage options offered by AWS. Storage Gateway supports various use cases, including backup and archive, disaster recovery, tiered storage, and cloud-based applications.

Key features and components of AWS Storage Gateway types:

- **File Gateway (NFS and SMB)**: Enables on-premises file-based applications to store and retrieve objects in Amazon S3 using standard file protocols.

- **Volume Gateway (iSCSI)**: Presents cloud-based volumes as **Internet Small Computer Systems Interface (iSCSI)** devices to on-premises applications, with data stored in Amazon S3 or Amazon EBS.

- **Tape Gateway (VTL)**: Provides a **virtual tape library** (**VTL**) interface for archiving data to Amazon S3 and Glacier.

Local caching

- Storage Gateway includes a local cache that retains frequently accessed data on-premises, optimizing performance and reducing latency for applications.

- All data transferred between on-premises environments and AWS is encrypted in transit using SSL, and data stored in the cloud is encrypted at rest using AWS KMS.

- Storage Gateway seamlessly integrates with various AWS services, allowing data stored on-premises to be accessed, managed, and processed using services like S3, Glacier, and EBS.

Use casesBackup and archive

Storage Gateway enables businesses to create cost-effective and scalable backup solutions by seamlessly integrating on-premises backup applications with cloud storage.

Disaster recovery

Businesses can use Storage Gateway to implement disaster recovery strategies by replicating on-premises data to AWS for quick recovery in case of local infrastructure failures.

Tiered storage

Storage Gateway allows organizations to tier their data, storing frequently accessed data locally for low-latency access while archiving less frequently accessed data to the AWS Cloud for cost savings.

Cloud-based applications

Storage Gateway facilitates the extension of on-premises applications to the cloud, enabling the development of hybrid cloud architectures and leveraging AWS Cloud services.

Following are the benefits:

- **Seamless integration**: Storage Gateway provides a smooth and transparent integration between on-premises environments and AWS, allowing existing applications to leverage cloud storage without significant modifications.

- **Cost-effective storage:** By utilizing the scalable and cost-effective storage options in AWS, businesses can optimize costs associated with on-premises storage infrastructure.

- **Scalability**: Storage Gateway scales with the needs of the business, accommodating growing data volumes and ensuring consistent performance.

- **Flexibility and choice**: With multiple gateway types, organizations have the flexibility to choose the most suitable model based on their specific use case and requirements.

AWS Storage Gateway provides a versatile solution for organizations looking to bridge the gap between on-premises environments and the AWS Cloud. Its ability to seamlessly integrate with existing applications, support various storage protocols, and offer flexible deployment options makes it a valuable tool for hybrid cloud storage scenarios. For the latest information and updates, it is recommended to refer to the official AWS Documentation on Storage Gateway.

Amazon Elastic Block Store

Amazon EBS is a scalable block storage service provided by AWS for use with Amazon EC2 instances. It serves as the primary persistent storage solution for EC2 instances, offering high-performance, low-latency block-level storage volumes. EBS volumes are designed to be highly available and durable, providing the necessary storage infrastructure to meet the requirements of a wide range of workloads.

Following are the key characteristics of Amazon EBS:

- **Block-level storage**: EBS provides block-level storage, allowing EC2 instances to access raw storage volumes, similar to traditional hard drives. This enables greater flexibility in terms of formatting and managing the file system on the EBS volumes.

- **Persistent and durable**: EBS volumes persist independently of the lifespan of an EC2 instance. This persistence makes EBS suitable for applications that require data durability, such as databases and file systems.

- **High-performance**: EBS volumes offer various performance options, allowing users to choose the storage type that meets the performance requirements of their applications.

- **Snapshots and backups**: EBS supports the creation of point-in-time snapshots, providing a mechanism for data backup and disaster recovery. Snapshots can be used to create new volumes or migrate data across AWS Regions.

Following are the use cases of Amazon EBS:

- **Database storage**: EBS is commonly used to store databases, providing reliable and high-performance block storage for database applications. AWS RDS, for example, uses under the hood io1/2 storage classes EBS to store your managed relational database.

- **Enterprise applications**: Business-critical applications, such as **enterprise resource planning** (**ERP**) systems, benefit from the persistent and scalable nature of EBS volumes.

- **Big data analytics**: EBS is often used in conjunction with EC2 instances for storing and processing large datasets in big data analytics applications.

- **Development and testing**: EBS volumes are valuable for development and testing environments, offering a scalable and on-demand storage solution for temporary or long-term storage needs.

Classes of EBS disks

Amazon EBS provides several classes of storage to cater to different performance and cost requirements. As of my last knowledge update in September 2024, the common classes are:

- **General Purpose (SSD)–gp2**:
  o **Type**: gp2
  o **Use case**: Balanced performance for a wide range of workloads, including development, testing, and production.
  o **Properties**:
    ▪ **Volume size**: 1 GB-16 TB
    ▪ **Durability**: 99.8%-99.9% durability
    ▪ **Max IOPS/volume**: 16,000
    ▪ **Max throughput/volume**: 250 MB/s
    ▪ **Max IOPS/instance**: 260,000
    ▪ **Max throughput/instance**: 7,500 MB/s
    ▪ **Latency**: single digit millisecond

- **General Purpose (SSD)–gp3:**
  - ○ **Type:** gp3
  - ○ **Use case:** Virtual desktop, small databases instances, balanced performance for a wide range of workloads, including development, testing, and production.
  - ○ **Properties:**
    - ▪ **Volume size:** 1 GB-16 TB
    - ▪ **Durability:** 99.8%-99.9% durability
    - ▪ **Max IOPS/volume:** 16,000
    - ▪ **Max throughput/volume:** 1000 MB/s
    - ▪ **Max IOPS/instance:** 260,000
    - ▪ **Max throughput/instance:** 12,500 MB/s
    - ▪ **Latency:** single digit millisecond

- **Provisioned IOPS (SSD)–io2:**
  - ○ **Type:** io2 Block Express
  - ○ **Use case:** High-performance storage with consistent and predictable I/O for I/O-intensive applications. such as databases.
  - ○ **Properties:**
    - ▪ **Volume size:** 4 GB-64 TB
    - ▪ **Durability:** 99.999%
    - ▪ **Latency:** sub-millisecond
    - ▪ **Max IOPS/volume:** 256,000
    - ▪ **Max throughput/volume:** 4,000 MB/s
    - ▪ **Max IOPS/instance:** 420,000
    - ▪ **Max IOPS/GB:** 1,000 IOPS/GB
    - ▪ **Max throughput/instance:** 12,500 MB/s

- **Provisioned IOPS (SSD)–io1:**
  - ○ **Type:** io1
  - ○ **Use case:** High-performance storage with consistent and predictable I/O for I/O-intensive applications, such as databases.
  - ○ **Properties:**
    - ▪ **Volume size:** 4 GB-16 TB
    - ▪ **Durability:** 99.8%-99.9%

- **Max IOPS/volume**: 64,000
- **Max throughput/volume**: 1,000 MB/s
- **Max IOPS/instance**: 420,000
- **Max IOPS/GB**: 50 IOPS/GB
- **Max Throughput/instance**: 12,500 MB/s
- **Latency**: single digit millisecond

- **Throughput Optimized (HDD)–st1:**
  - **Type**: st1
  - **Use case**: High throughput, low-cost storage optimized for frequently accessed, throughput-intensive workloads, such as big data processing.
  - **Properties**:
    - **Volume size**: 125 GB-16 TB
    - **Durability**: 99.8%-99.9% durability
    - **Max IOPS/volume**: 500 GB
    - **Max throughput/volume**: 500 MB/s
    - **Max throughput/instance**: 12,500 MB/s

- **Cold HDD–sc1:**
  - **Type**: sc1
  - **Use case**: Lowest-cost HDD storage optimized for infrequently accessed.
  - **Properties**:
    - **Volume size**: 125 GB-16 TB
    - **Durability**: 99.8%-99.9% durability
    - **Max IOPS/volume**: 250 GB
    - **Max throughput/volume**: 250 MB/s
    - **Max throughput/instance**: 7,500 MB/s

Best practices

Following are the best practices for Amazon EBS:

- **Optimizing for performance**: Choose the appropriate EBS volume type based on the performance requirements of your application.

- **Snapshots and backups**: Regularly create snapshots of your EBS volumes to facilitate data backup and recovery.

- **Monitoring and optimization**: Utilize AWS CloudWatch metrics and logs to monitor the performance of your EBS volumes and adjust configurations as needed.

- **Availability and reliability**: Distribute EBS volumes across multiple AZs to enhance availability and reliability.

Advanced features

Following are the advanced features

- **Multi-attach for io2 volumes**: Allows multiple EC2 instances to attach to a single io2 EBS volume, enabling scenarios like clustering and high availability configurations.

- **Elastic volumes:** Enables dynamic adjustment of EBS volume size, IOPS, and throughput without detaching the volume from the EC2 instance.

- **EBS encryption**: Supports encryption of data at rest using AWS KMS, providing an additional layer of security.

- **Fast snapshot restore (FSR):** Allows for faster restoration of EBS volumes from snapshots, reducing the time required to create new volumes.

Shared responsibility model for AWS EBS

Amazon EBS is a key component of AWS, providing scalable and high-performance block storage for EC2 instances. Understanding the shared responsibility model for AWS EBS is crucial for ensuring the security and integrity of data stored on these volumes

AWS responsibilities

- **Infrastructure security**: AWS is responsible for securing the underlying infrastructure, including data centers, networking, and hardware that supports EBS.

- **Data center security**: AWS ensures the physical security of data centers where EBS volumes are stored, implementing measures such as access controls, surveillance, and environmental controls.

- **Service availability**: AWS maintains the availability and durability of EBS volumes, with redundant systems to ensure data integrity and accessibility.

Customer's responsibilities

- **Data encryption**: Customers are responsible for encrypting data at rest on EBS volumes. AWS provides tools like AWS KMS for managing encryption keys.

- **Access control**: Customers are responsible for managing access to EBS volumes by configuring IAM roles and policies, ensuring that only authorized users and services can interact with the data.

- **Data backups**: Implementing regular backups and snapshots of EBS volumes is the customer's responsibility. This ensures data recovery in case of accidental deletions or data corruption.

- **Security best practices**: Customers are encouraged to follow security best practices, such as regularly updating software, monitoring for suspicious activities, and configuring network access controls.

Understanding this shared responsibility model helps organizations adopt a holistic approach to security and compliance when utilizing AWS EBS. By delineating responsibilities between AWS and the customer, it ensures a comprehensive strategy for protecting data and maintaining the integrity of storage solutions in the cloud.

Amazon EBS plays a crucial role in providing scalable and performant block storage for EC2 instances in AWS and it is a fundamental part of the solutions you could use to build very specific workloads for your different use cases.

Amazon Elastic File System

Amazon EFS is a networked, shared, scalable, and fully managed cloud-based file storage service provided by AWS. EFS is designed to provide scalable and elastic shared file storage for EC2 instances and is suitable for a wide range of use cases, from simple file sharing to complex, high-performance workloads. In this overview, we will delve into what EFS is the concept of network storage, and the fundamental characteristics of EFS.

Following are the working of Amazon EFS:

- **Scalable storage**: Amazon EFS provides a scalable file system that can grow or shrink in size as data is added or removed. It supports a virtually unlimited number of concurrent connections.

- **Managed service**: EFS is a fully managed service, eliminating the need for users to manage the underlying infrastructure. AWS takes care of the operational aspects, such as patching, maintenance, and backups.

- **Compatibility**: EFS is compatible with the **Network File System** (**NFS**) protocol, making it easy to integrate with existing applications and services.

Understanding network storage

Network storage is a storage system that provides access to data through a network. Instead of being directly attached to a server or computer, the storage is accessed over a network, allowing multiple systems to connect and share the same data. Network storage provides a centralized and scalable solution for storing and sharing data across multiple servers or instances.

Pricing model

Amazon EFS follows a pay-as-you-go pricing model, and the costs are based on the following factors:

- **Storage usage**: Users are billed based on the amount of storage (in GB-months) used by their file systems.

- **Data transfer**: Data transfer costs apply when data is transferred between an EFS file system and other AWS Region or the internet.

- **Lifecycle management**: EFS offers lifecycle management features that automatically move files to a lower-cost storage class, helping to optimize costs.

Classes of storage

EFS supports different storage classes:

- **Standard storage**: Suitable for frequently accessed files and provides low-latency performance.

- **IA storage**: Designed for files that are infrequently accessed but need to be stored cost-effectively.

- **One Zone and One Zone-IA (One Zone-IA Storage)**: EFS One Zone and One Zone–IA storage classes are designed to provide continuous availability to data within a single AZ. The EFS One Zone storage classes store file system data and metadata redundantly within a single AZ in an AWS Region. Because they store data in a single AWS AZ, data that is stored in these storage classes might be lost in the event of a disaster or other fault that affects all copies of the data within the AZ, or in the event of AZ destruction. EFS One Zone–Standard is used for frequently accessed files. It is the storage class to which customer data is initially written for One Zone storage classes.

The EFS One Zone–IA storage class reduces storage costs for files that are not accessed every day. It is recommended to use EFS One Zone–IA storage if you need your full dataset to be readily accessible and want to automatically save on storage costs for files that are less frequently accessed.

Key features

Following are the key features:

- **Elasticity**: EFS can automatically scale its capacity up or down, allowing users to grow or shrink their storage needs dynamically.

- **High availability**: EFS is designed for high availability with data stored redundantly across multiple AZs within a region.

- **Performance modes**: EFS offers two performance modes—General Purpose and Max I/O. General Purpose is suitable for most workloads, while Max I/O is designed for latency-sensitive applications.

- **Encryption**: EFS supports encryption of data at rest and in transit, ensuring the security of stored data.

Integration with AWS services

Following are the ways of integration with AWS services:

- **Integration with EC2 instances**: EFS can be mounted on multiple EC2 instances, allowing them to share data and collaborate in real-time.

- **AWS IAM integration**: EFS integrates with IAM, allowing users to control access to file systems and directories using IAM policies.

Use cases

Following are the use cases:

- **Content management systems (CMS)**: EFS is well-suited for hosting CMS platforms where multiple instances need access to the same set of files.

- **Development and build environments**: Developers can share code and build artifacts seamlessly across multiple instances using EFS.

- **Big data and analytics**: EFS provides a scalable and shared file system for storing and processing big data and analytics datasets.

- **Database backups:** EFS can be used to store database backups, allowing for easy access and recovery.

Usage Amazon EFS

Following are when to use Amazon EFS:

- **Shared workloads**: When multiple instances need to access shared data concurrently, EFS is an ideal choice.

- **Dynamic workloads**: EFS is well-suited for workloads that require dynamic scaling and storage capacity adjustments.

- **Compatibility with NFS**: If your applications or services are built to work with NFS, EFS provides a seamless integration.

- **High availability requirements**: When high availability and reliability are crucial, EFS, with its Multi-AZ architecture, is a suitable option.

Best practices

Following are the best practices:

- **Optimize performance mode**: Choose the appropriate performance mode (General Purpose or Max I/O) based on the characteristics of your workload.

- **Implement encryption**: Enable encryption to protect data at rest and in transit, enhancing the security of your file systems.

- **Use IAM for access control**: Leverage IAM policies to control access to your file systems and directories, following the principle of least privilege.

- **Monitor and optimize**: Regularly monitor your EFS file systems using AWS CloudWatch metrics and optimize configurations based on usage patterns.

In conclusion, Amazon EFS offers a scalable and managed shared networked file storage solution with a pay-as-you-go pricing model, making it suitable for a variety of use cases. Understanding its features, pricing, and use cases is essential for effectively leveraging EFS in your AWS infrastructure.

Conclusion

This chapter has provided a comprehensive overview of AWS's diverse array of storage services, showcasing the platform's commitment to meeting the varied and evolving needs of businesses and developers. From the highly scalable and versatile Amazon S3, functioning as a secure object storage solution, to the high-performance block-level storage of Amazon EBS, and the archival and data retrieval capabilities of Amazon Glacier, AWS offers a spectrum of storage services tailored to different use cases. The chapter has highlighted the importance of understanding the distinct features and advantages of each service to make informed decisions when architecting storage solutions in the AWS Cloud. As we navigate the ever-expanding landscape of cloud storage, AWS continues to innovate and enhance its storage offerings, positioning itself as a leader in the industry and empowering users to build robust, scalable, and secure storage infrastructures.

In the next chapter, we will delve into AWS databases and analytics solutions, which are used to store our important application data in relational databases or in NoSQL databases, plus we will explore some data analytics solutions available in AWS.

Points to remember

To summarize this chapter, we saw those main concepts and AWS services useful to understand AWS Storage services and its usage:

- **Amazon S3**:
  - **Object storage**: S3 is a scalable and durable object storage service designed for storing and retrieving any amount of data.
  - **Versatility**: Suited for a wide range of use cases, from simple storage and backup to complex data analytics and application hosting.
  - **Versioning**: Provides versioning capabilities to track changes, revert to previous versions, and ensure data integrity.
  - **Replication**: Supports CRR and SRR for enhanced data durability and availability.
  - **Encryption at rest**: Offers various encryption options, including SSE with S3 managed keys, AWS KMS, and customer-provided keys.
  - **Access control**: Implements fine-grained access control using ACLs and bucket policies to regulate who can access and manipulate stored data.
- **Amazon EBS**:
  - **Block storage**: EBS provides scalable block-level storage volumes that can be attached to Amazon EC2 instances.
  - **Performance optimization**: Allows users to select the right type of volume (for example, General Purpose SSD, Provisioned IOPS SSD, etc.) based on performance requirements.
  - **Snapshots**: Enables the creation of point-in-time snapshots for backup, replication, and data recovery purposes.
  - **Data persistence**: EBS volumes persist independently from the life of an EC2 instance, making it suitable for databases and applications that require consistent storage.
  - **High availability**: Supports features like multi-attach for certain volume types, providing high availability and redundancy.
- **Amazon EFS**:
  - **Managed file storage**: EFS provides scalable file storage for use with AWS Cloud services and on-premises resources.
  - **Shared file system**: Allows multiple EC2 instances to access the same file system simultaneously, facilitating collaboration and shared data access.
  - **Fully managed**: EFS is fully managed, eliminating the need for manual capacity planning and administration.
  - **Automatic scaling**: Scales capacity up or down automatically as files are added or removed, ensuring optimal performance.

o **Performance modes**: Offers two performance modes, General Purpose and Max I/O, to accommodate various workloads.

Exercises

Here are a few quiz questions related to AWS Storage with single answer choices:

1. **What is the primary use case for Amazon S3?**

    a. Block-level storage

    b. File storage

    c. Object storage

    d. Network-attached storage

2. **Which AWS storage service is suitable for hosting a scalable and durable data lake?**

    a. Amazon EBS

    b. Amazon S3

    c. Amazon EFS

    d. Amazon Glacier

3. **What does S3 stand for in Amazon S3?**

    a. Simple Storage Service

    b. Secure Storage System

    c. Structured Storage Solution

    d. Storage Support System

4. **Which AWS storage service provides block-level storage volumes that can be attached to EC2 instances?**

    a. Amazon S3

    b. Amazon EBS

    c. Amazon EFS

    d. Amazon Glacier

5. **Which AWS storage service is designed for scalable and elastic file storage for use with EC2 instances?**

    a. Amazon S3

    b. Amazon EBS

    c. Amazon EFS

    d. Amazon Glacier

6. **In which storage service can you enable versioning to maintain different versions of your objects?**

    a. Amazon S3

    b. Amazon EBS

    c. Amazon EFS

    d. Amazon Glacier

7. **What AWS storage service is optimized for low-latency access to frequently accessed data?**

    a. Amazon S3

    b. Amazon EBS

    c. Amazon EFS

    d. Amazon Glacier

8. **Which AWS storage service supports the creation of snapshots for point-in-time backups?**

    a. Amazon S3

    b. Amazon EBS

    c. Amazon EFS

    d. Amazon Glacier

9. **Which storage service is well-suited for storing and retrieving large amounts of infrequently accessed data at a lower-cost?**

    a. Amazon S3

    b. Amazon EBS

    c. Amazon EFS

    d. Amazon Glacier

10. **In which AWS storage service can you create a scalable file system that can be shared across multiple EC2 instances?**

    a. Amazon S3

    b. Amazon EBS

    c. Amazon EFS

    d. Amazon Glacier

Answers

1. c
2. b
3. a
4. b
5. c
6. a
7. a
8. b
9. d
10. c

Key terms

- AWS S3
- AWS Glacier
- AWS EBS
- AWS EFS

Join our book's Discord space

Join the book's Discord Workspace for Latest updates, Offers, Tech happenings around the world, New Release and Sessions with the Authors:

https://discord.bpbonline.com

CHAPTER 6

AWS Database Services

Introduction

As we explore **Amazon Web Services (AWS)** further, we study data management and analytics in detail. In this chapter, we study AWS database services and analytical tools that form the backbone of modern data architectures. From relational databases to NoSQL stores and managed services to analytical engines, AWS offers a comprehensive suite of solutions catering to the diverse needs of businesses and applications.

We begin with Amazon **Relational Database Service (RDS)**. This fully managed database service supports multiple database engines, providing a hassle-free experience for deploying, operating, and scaling relational databases in the cloud. We will study the nuances of configuring and optimizing databases using RDS, gaining insights into best reliability, security, and performance practices.

We will also study Amazon DynamoDB, a NoSQL database service designed for high-performance applications with seamless scalability. Schema-less design, flexibility of indexing, and dynamic scaling capabilities make DynamoDB an integral part of modern, agile application development.

In Amazon Redshift, AWS's managed data warehouse service, we will read about **massively parallel processing (MPP)** for high-performance analytics. Redshift's ability to handle large datasets and complex queries makes it a cornerstone for organizations seeking actionable insights from their data.

In analytical services for **extract, transform, and load (ETL)**, we study Amazon **Elastic MapReduce (EMR)**, AWS Glue, and Athena. EMR provides a scalable, cost-effective solution for processing vast amounts of data using popular frameworks like Apache Spark and Hadoop. AWS Glue simplifies the ETL process with serverless data integration, while Athena empowers users to analyze data directly from **Amazon Simple Storage Service (S3)** using SQL queries without the need for complex ETL jobs.

We will read about the intricacies of AWS mainstay databases like Amazon Neptune, a fully managed graph database, and Amazon ElastiCache, a caching service for enhancing the performance of web applications. We will also learn about Amazon OpenSearch, a managed Elasticsearch Service, designed for search and log analytics.

Finally, we will see what AWS offer us to migrate data from external sources to Amazon cloud. AWS Cloud Data Migration Services offer a comprehensive suite of tools and solutions designed to facilitate the seamless transfer of data from on-premises infrastructure, legacy systems, or other cloud environments to the AWS Cloud.

Structure

In this chapter, we will cover the following topics:

- Amazon Relational Database Service
- NoSQL databases in AWS
- Amazon DynamoDB
- Introduction to AWS Redshift
- Other databases in AWS
- Big data processing in Amazon
- AWS Cloud Data Migration Services

Objectives

This chapter aims to enable a comprehensive understanding of AWS database services, focusing on relational, NoSQL, and analytical databases. The chapter studies the capabilities and features of Amazon RDS, DynamoDB, and Redshift. Readers will gain insights into the management, scalability, and performance optimization of these databases. It also discusses their suitability for various use cases.

The discussion also extends to analytical services for ETL processes, examining AWS EMR, AWS Glue, and Athena. By the end of this chapter, readers will have a solid foundation in leveraging AWS database and analytical services to build robust, scalable, and efficient data solutions.

The chapter also explores other key databases in the AWS ecosystem, including Neptune for graph databases, Elasticache for in-memory caching, and OpenSearch for full-text search capabilities. Each database is studied in detail with its unique features, use cases, and integration possibilities within AWS architectures.

Finally in this chapter, we will explore the key services and tools provided by AWS for efficient cloud data migration. These include AWS Direct Connect, which offers a dedicated network connection to AWS; the AWS Snow Family, which facilitates the physical transfer of large data volumes; AWS Storage Gateway, enabling seamless hybrid cloud storage integration; Amazon **S3 Transfer Acceleration** (**S3TA**) for faster data uploads to Amazon S3; AWS Firehose for real-time data streaming; AWS Transfer Family, which supports secure file transfers to AWS; and third-party connectors that enhance integration with other tools. Additionally, we will cover AWS **Schema Conversion Tool** (**SCT**) for migrating and transforming database schemas.

This comprehensive overview aims to equip readers with the knowledge to make informed decisions when selecting and implementing AWS database services tailored to their business requirements. Whether optimizing for performance, ensuring data durability, or enabling real-time data access, this chapter is a valuable guide to navigating the diverse concepts of AWS databases and analytical tools.

Whether you are a seasoned cloud architect or a data enthusiast, this chapter aims to equip you with the knowledge and skills to harness the full potential of AWS for managing, analyzing, and deriving value from your data.

AWS Relational Database Service

AWS has been a pioneering force in cloud computing, revolutionizing the way organizations manage their IT infrastructure. Among the myriad services offered by AWS, Amazon RDS stands out as a pivotal solution for businesses seeking to streamline their database management in the cloud. Amazon RDS **https://aws.amazon.com/rds/** redefines the traditional approach to relational databases, providing a fully managed service that alleviates the operational burdens of database administration.

As organizations increasingly migrate their applications to the cloud, Amazon RDS emerges as a catalyst for enhanced efficiency, scalability, and reliability in handling critical data.

At its core, Amazon RDS simplifies the complexities associated with traditional relational databases, offering a comprehensive suite of features to automate routine tasks. From automated backups and software patching to robust security measures, RDS allows developers and businesses to focus on innovation and application development rather than the intricacies of database maintenance.

This managed service extends support for various database engines, empowering users to choose from options like Amazon Aurora, MySQL, PostgreSQL, Microsoft SQL Server, Oracle, and MariaDB. This flexibility enables organizations to tailor their database solutions to specific needs, ensuring optimal performance and alignment with existing technology stacks.

The pros of using Amazon RDS lie in its technical prowess and being a strategic enabler for businesses navigating the complexities of a dynamic digital landscape. As we proceed in this section of Amazon RDS, we will study its key features, advantages, and the array of database engines it supports. Through this journey, we aim to illuminate how Amazon RDS is reshaping the database management paradigm, empowering organizations to harness the full potential of their data in the cloud.

Introduction to relational databases

Relational databases have been the cornerstone of data management for decades, providing a structured and efficient way to store, organize, and retrieve data. The relational model, introduced by *E.F. Codd* in 1970, revolves around tables with rows and columns, forming relationships between different pieces of information. This model has proven highly effective for handling complex data relationships, making it the preferred choice for various applications.

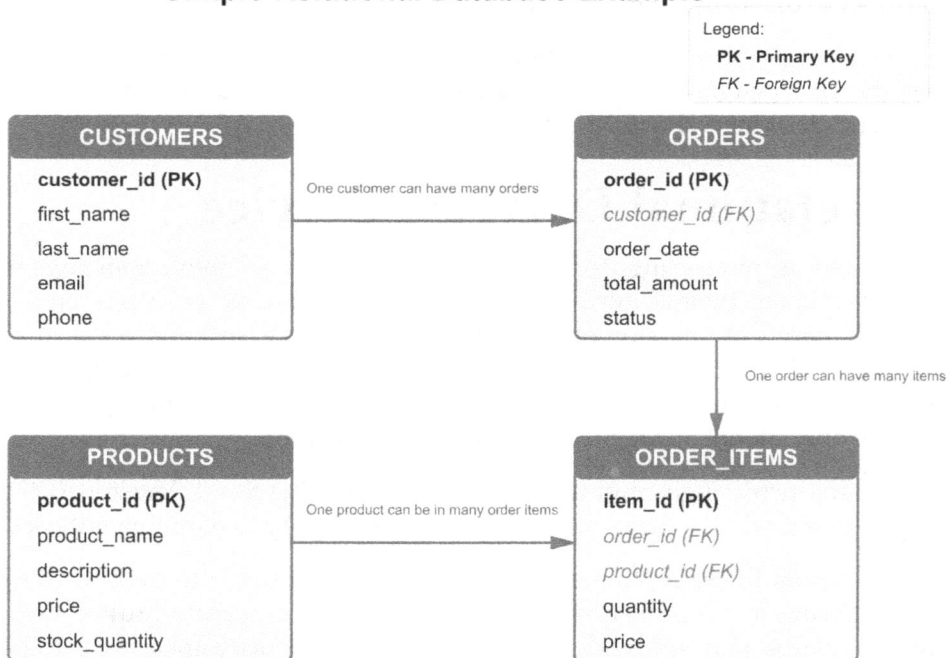

Figure 6.1: Example of a relational database schema

The fundamental idea behind relational databases is to provide a systematic approach to managing and querying data, ensuring consistency, integrity, and ease of retrieval. The structured nature of relational databases facilitates the efficient representation of real-world relationships between entities, making them particularly adept at handling data with intricate connections. Enforcing the principles of normalization and integrity constraints, relational databases not only organize data logically, they also contribute to the maintenance of data accuracy and reliability over time.

In technology, relational databases have continuously evolved to meet the demands of diverse applications, from small-scale projects to large enterprise solutions. As the backbone of countless information systems, these databases have played a pivotal role in shaping how businesses manage, analyze, and derive insights from their data. its diverse range of supported database engines.

ACID in relational databases

Atomicity, Consistency, Isolation, and Durability (**ACID**), represent a set of principles that define the key properties ensuring the reliability and integrity of transactions in a database system. The following is how these principles collectively form the bedrock of the relational database model, providing a robust framework for managing data that guarantees consistency and reliability:

- **Atomicity**: It ensures that a transaction is treated as a single, indivisible unit of work. In the context of a relational database, a transaction might involve multiple operations, such as inserting, updating, or deleting records. Atomicity dictates that either all or none of these operations are completed. If any part fails, the entire transaction is rolled back to its initial state, preventing the database from an inconsistent state.

- **Consistency**: It guarantees that a database transitions from one valid state to another, maintaining the integrity of the data throughout the transaction process. The database must adhere to predefined rules or constraints, ensuring the data remains accurate and valid. If a transaction violates any of these rules, the entire transaction is rolled back, preserving the consistency of the database.

- **Isolation**: It ensures that multiple transactions can occur concurrently without interfering with each other. Each transaction operates in isolation, preventing concurrent transactions from affecting each other's intermediate states, maintaining the integrity of the data, and avoiding conflicts that could arise from simultaneous access to shared resources.

- **Durability**: It guarantees that once a transaction is committed, its effects are permanent and survive any subsequent failures, such as system crashes or power outages. The committed changes are stored in a durable storage medium, such as a disk, ensuring that they can be recovered even with a system failure. This property ensures the long-term reliability and persistence of data in the database.

Relational databases based on ACID provide a solid foundation for data management in various domains, ranging from finance and healthcare to e-commerce and beyond. These principles collectively ensure that transactions are processed reliably, maintaining the integrity and consistency of the database even in the face of system failures or concurrent access. The ACID properties make relational databases a trusted choice for applications where data accuracy and reliability are paramount.

Choosing a relational database

Despite the appeal of NoSQL databases in specific use cases, relational databases remain the preferred choice in several scenarios:

- **ACID transactions are critical**: In applications where maintaining consistency and reliability of transactions is paramount, such as financial systems or applications dealing with sensitive data, relational databases with their ACID guarantees are indispensable.

- **Structured data and complex relationships**: Relational databases excel in managing structured data and complex relationships between entities. When the application data model is well-defined, and relationships between entities are intricate, the relational database is most suitable.

- **Consistency across the board**: In applications, maintaining a high level of consistency across the entire dataset, relational databases provide rigor and assurance that is challenging to match.

- **Mature ecosystem and tooling**: Relational databases have a mature ecosystem with a wide array of tools, libraries, and frameworks developed over decades. If your application can benefit from this extensive support, particularly in terms of reporting, analytics, and **business intelligence** (**BI**), a relational database may be the pragmatic choice.

The choice between a relational database and a NoSQL database depends on the specific requirements and characteristics of the application. While NoSQL databases offer unprecedented scalability and flexibility, relational databases, with their ACID guarantees, continue to be the go-to solution for applications where data consistency, integrity, and well-defined relationships are paramount. The decision should be guided by a careful consideration of the application's use case, data model, and scalability requirements.

Key challenges faced by relational databases

RDS bridges the traditional strengths of relational databases and the scalability demands of modern applications, often addressed by NoSQL databases. Amazon RDS provides a managed service that addresses key challenges faced by relational databases, making them more competitive in the dynamic landscape of cloud computing.

- **Scalability**: One of the primary concerns with traditional relational databases has been their perceived difficulty in scaling horizontally to handle increased workloads. Amazon RDS tackles this challenge by offering multi **Availability Zone** (**AZ**) deployments and read replicas. Multi-AZ deployments involve replicating the database to a standby instance in a different AZ, providing high availability and automatic failover. Read replicas, on the other hand, enable horizontal scaling by creating copies of the database that can handle read traffic, distribute the load, and improve performance. This makes Amazon RDS an attractive solution for applications that demand the reliability of ACID transactions and the ability to scale horizontally.

- **Backups and point-in-time recovery**: Amazon RDS automates the backup process, ensuring the relational database is regularly backed up to Amazon S3. This feature addresses concerns related to data loss by providing a **point-in-time recovery (PITR)** mechanism. In the event of accidental data deletion or corruption, you can restore your database to any specific point within the retention period This level of automation and flexibility simplifies the backup and recovery process, reducing the administrative overhead traditionally associated with relational databases.

- **High availability**: Amazon RDS enhances the high availability of relational databases through Multi-AZ deployments. In a Multi-AZ configuration, Amazon RDS maintains a synchronous standby replica in a different AZ. If the primary database instance fails, Amazon RDS automatically promotes the standby replica to the primary instance, minimizing downtime and ensuring continuous availability. This feature addresses concerns related to system failures, providing a robust and fault tolerant architecture for critical applications.

- **Automated software patching**: Keeping database software up-to-date is crucial for security and performance. Amazon RDS automates the process of applying patches to the database engine, ensuring that your database remains current with the latest security fixes and performance enhancements. This automation simplifies the maintenance tasks associated with relational databases, allowing developers to focus on building and improving their applications.

Amazon RDS acts as a game-changer for relational databases by providing a managed service that addresses the scalability, high availability, and backup challenges traditionally associated with this model. Combining the reliability of ACID transactions with the benefits of automated management and scaling features, RDS makes relational databases a competitive and compelling choice for a wide range of applications, even in the face of the scalability demands posed by NoSQL databases.

Key features of Amazon RDS

RDS stands as a cornerstone in managed database solutions, offering a comprehensive suite of features that streamline database administration, enhance performance, and ensure high availability.

The following are the key features that make Amazon RDS a versatile and powerful solution for handling relational databases in the cloud:

- **Automated database administration**: One of the standouts feature of Amazon RDS is its commitment to automating routine database administration tasks. From backups to software patching, RDS takes the burden off developers and administrators, allowing them to focus on building and optimizing applications. The automated backup feature ensures that regular snapshots of the database, are securely stored in Amazon S3, providing PITR capabilities. This safeguards against data loss and also simplifies the process of restoring databases to specific points in time. Amazon RDS goes further by automating software patching for the supported database engines. Keeping database engines up-to-date is critical for security and performance, and RDS ensures that the latest patches are applied seamlessly. This feature not only enhances the security posture of your databases but also eliminates the challenges associated with manually managing software updates in a traditional database environment.

- **High availability with Multi-AZ deployments**: Ensuring high availability is a non-negotiable requirement for mission-critical applications. Amazon RDS addresses this need through Multi-AZ deployments. In a Multi-AZ configuration, RDS maintains a synchronous standby replica of the primary database instance in a different AZ. This standby replica is continuously updated, providing a failover solution in the event of a primary instance failure. The failover process is automatic, minimizing downtime and ensuring that applications can seamlessly transition to the standby replica without manual intervention. Multi-AZ deployments not only enhance availability but also contribute to the overall durability of the database. By storing copies of data in different physical locations, RDS reduces the risk of data loss due to hardware failures or disasters in a specific region. This robust architecture aligns with best practices for building resilient and fault tolerant systems in the cloud.

- **Scalability**: Scalability is a pivotal consideration in the design of modern applications, and Amazon RDS provides a flexible approach to meet varying scalability requirements. For vertical scaling, RDS allows us to easily resize the database instance to accommodate changes in computational and memory requirements. Whether we need more processing power or additional memory, RDS facilitates seamless adjustments without impacting the application. In addition to vertical scaling, Amazon RDS supports horizontal scaling through the use of read replicas. Read replicas are copies of the primary database instance that can handle read-only workloads, distributing the read traffic and improving overall performance. This feature is particularly beneficial for applications with a high volume of read operations, such as reporting or analytics. By creating read replicas, RDS enables horizontal scaling without compromising the consistency and integrity of the data.

- **Encryption and IAM integration**: Security is paramount in any database environment, and Amazon RDS offers a robust set of features to safeguard your data. Encryption is a key component of RDS security, and it operates on multiple levels. At rest, RDS supports encryption of the entire database instance, ensuring that data stored on disk is protected. In transit, data is encrypted using industry-standard SSL/TLS protocols, securing communication between the database instance and client applications **Identity and Access Management (IAM)** integration adds a layer of security to RDS. By leveraging IAM roles, we can control access to RDS resources at a fine-grained level. IAM integration allows you to define who can manage databases, who can modify security groups, and who can perform other administrative tasks. This integration aligns with AWS's best practices for access control and contributes to a secure and well-managed database environment.

Database engine support

Amazon RDS supports a diverse ecosystem of relational database engines, allowing us to choose the engine that best suits our application's requirements. The following are some of the key database engines supported by RDS:

- **Amazon Aurora**: Amazon Aurora is a MySQL and PostgreSQL-compatible relational database engine designed for the cloud. It offers performance and availability comparable to commercial databases at a fraction of the cost. Aurora is known for its high-throughput and low-latency, making it a compelling choice for mission-critical applications.

- **MySQL**: RDS supports the MySQL database engine, a widely used open-source relational database known for its speed, reliability, and ease of use. Whether you are running a small-scale application or a large enterprise solution, MySQL on RDS provides a familiar and scalable platform.

- **PostgreSQL**: PostgreSQL, with its robust support for complex queries and transactions, is another database engine available on RDS. It is a versatile choice for applications that require advanced data management capabilities, such as those dealing with geospatial data or JSON data types.

- **Microsoft SQL Server**: For organizations entrenched in Microsoft technologies, RDS supports Microsoft SQL Server. This allows seamless migration of SQL Server-based applications to the cloud, leveraging the benefits of Amazon RDS for managed database services.

- **Oracle**: Amazon RDS provides support for Oracle Database, a powerful and feature-rich relational database engine. Organizations with existing investments in Oracle technologies can leverage RDS for Oracle to benefit from the scalability and managed services of the AWS Cloud.

- **MariaDB**: MariaDB, a fork of MySQL, is an open-source database engine supported by RDS. It is known for its performance optimizations and enhanced features, making it suitable for applications requiring high-throughput and reliability.

- **IBM Db2**: Amazon RDS provides support for IBM Db2 through its managed database offering, allowing users to deploy, manage, and scale Db2 databases in the cloud. With RDS for Db2, users can focus on application development without worrying about the underlying infrastructure, while benefiting from scalable resources, easy management, and integration with other AWS services.

  This diversity of supported database engines underlines the flexibility of Amazon RDS, allowing you to choose the engine that aligns with your application's specific needs and your team's expertise.

- **Transforming relational database management**: Amazon RDS stands as a transformative solution for managing relational databases in the cloud. By automating administrative tasks, ensuring high availability through Multi-AZ deployments, offering flexible scalability options, incorporating robust security features, and supporting a variety of database engines, RDS addresses the challenges associated with traditional relational databases.

  The features of Amazon RDS not only simplify database management but also contribute to building resilient, secure, and high-performance applications. As organizations continue to migrate their operations to the cloud, RDS emerges as a strategic choice for those seeking the reliability of relational databases with the added benefits of cloud-native scalability and managed services. Whether developing a small-scale application or managing enterprise-level databases, RDS provides a versatile and powerful platform for relational database needs.

- **Amazon Aurora and standard relational database instances**: AWS offers a range of relational database services to cater to diverse application needs. Amazon RDS provides both standard relational database instances and Amazon Aurora, a MySQL and PostgreSQL-compatible cloud-native database engine. In this comparison, we explore the key differences and advantages of RDS Aurora over standard RDS instances.

- **Basis architecture and performance**:
  - **Amazon RDS standard**:
    - RDS standard instances use traditional database engines such as MySQL, PostgreSQL, Microsoft SQL Server, or Oracle.
    - The architecture follows a master-replica model for high availability, with read replicas available for read scalability.
    - While read replicas can enhance read performance, write operations are primarily handled by the master instance.
    - Scaling read operations might require manual sharding or partitioning of data across multiple read replicas.

- o **Amazon RDS Aurora**:
  - Aurora is a fully managed, cloud-native database engine designed for high-performance and availability.
  - Aurora employs a distributed, fault tolerant architecture with a cluster of instances that share the same storage volume.
  - Both read and write operations are distributed across Aurora instances, enabling better horizontal scaling for both read and write workloads.
  - Aurora Replicas provide additional read capacity, and the storage is automatically and continuously replicated across multiple AZs for durability.

- o **Advantages of Aurora's architecture**:
  - Aurora's distributed architecture allows for seamless horizontal scaling of both read and write operations.
  - Aurora Replicas can be added to the cluster to handle read traffic, enhancing overall performance.
  - The underlying storage architecture in Aurora enables consistent, high-throughput performance for various workloads.

- **Basis high availability and fault-tolerance**:
  - o **Amazon RDS standard**:
    - Multi-AZ deployments are available for standard RDS instances to enhance availability by replicating the primary database to a standby instance in a different AZ.
    - Failover from the primary to the standby instance is automated in the event of a failure, minimizing downtime.

  - o **Amazon RDS Aurora**:
    - Aurora takes high availability to the next level with a distributed and fault tolerant architecture.
    - Aurora Replicas provide not only read scalability but also contribute to fault-tolerance; if the primary instance fails, an Aurora Replica can be promoted to become the new primary instance.
    - Aurora continuously backs up data to Amazon S3, and automated, continuous replication across Multi-AZs enhances durability.

  - o **Advantages of Aurora's high availability**:
    - Aurora's distributed nature and automatic failover mechanisms contribute to enhanced Fault-tolerance.

- The combination of automated backups and replication across AZs ensures data durability and minimizes the risk of data loss.

- **Basis performance and scalability**:

  o **Amazon RDS standard**:

    - Scaling write operations for standard RDS instances might involve vertical scaling, such as upgrading to a larger instance type.

    - Read scalability is achieved through read replicas, but managing and scaling these replicas require additional configuration.

  o **Amazon RDS Aurora**:

    - Aurora's architecture allows for seamless scaling of both read and write operations.

    - Aurora Replicas can be easily added to the cluster to handle read traffic, and the storage scales automatically as needed.

    - Write scalability is inherent in Aurora's design, and it can handle large numbers of concurrent read and write operations.

  o **Advantages of Aurora's scalability**:

    - Aurora simplifies the process of scaling both read and write operations with its distributed architecture.

    - The ability to add Aurora Replicas and distribute read and write workloads across instances enhances scalability for changing application demands.

While both Amazon RDS standard and RDS Aurora serve as robust managed database solutions, the choice between them depends on specific requirements. RDS standard is suitable for traditional database workloads, while RDS Aurora excels in scenarios where high-performance, scalability, and Fault-tolerance are paramount. Aurora's cloud-native architecture, with its distributed nature and automatic scaling capabilities, makes it particularly well-suited for modern, high-performance applications in the AWS Cloud.

- **Single and Multi-AZ configurations**: RDS offers versatile deployment options to meet the availability and Fault-tolerance requirements of diverse applications. In this section we will study both Single-AZ and Multi-AZ configurations, understanding how each deployment option caters to specific needs and challenges in the realm of relational databases.

  o **Single-AZ deployments**: A Single-AZ deployment in Amazon RDS involves running the primary database instance in a Single-AZ. While it may not provide the same level of Fault-tolerance as Multi-AZ configurations, Single-AZ deployments are valuable for scenarios where high availability is not the primary concern and cost-effectiveness and simplicity take precedence. Key characteristics of Single-AZ deployments include:

- **Cost-effective**: Single-AZ deployments are generally more cost-effective than Multi-AZ configurations. For applications with lower availability requirements or where data replication to a standby instance is not critical, Single-AZ can be a budget-friendly choice.

- **Simplicity in management**: With fewer components to manage, Single-AZ deployments are simpler to setup and maintain. This makes them suitable for smaller applications or scenarios where the overhead of managing a standby replica is not justified.

- **Use cases**: Single-AZ configurations are often suitable for development and testing environments, non-critical workloads, or applications where the impact of a temporary outage is acceptable.

While Single-AZ deployments offer simplicity and cost advantages, they come with limitations in terms of Fault-tolerance. In the event of a hardware failure, maintenance, or other disruptions in the chosen AZ, the lack of a standby instance may result in downtime until the primary instance is restored.

○ **Multi-AZ deployments**: In contrast to Single-AZ deployments, Multi-AZ configurations in Amazon RDS are designed to enhance availability and Fault-tolerance. In a Multi-AZ deployment, a synchronous standby replica of the primary database instance is maintained in a different AZ. This standby replica serves as a failover target, ensuring continuity of operations in the face of failures. Key characteristics of Multi-AZ deployments include:

- **Automatic failover**: Multi-AZ configurations provide automatic failover in the event of a primary instance failure. If the primary instance becomes unavailable, RDS automatically promotes the standby replica to the primary instance, minimizing downtime.

- **Enhanced Fault-tolerance**: Replicating data synchronously to a standby instance in a different AZ, Multi-AZ deployments mitigate the impact of hardware failures, maintenance activities, or other disruptions. This enhances the overall Fault-tolerance of the database environment.

- **Use cases**: Multi-AZ configurations are recommended for production environments and applications where downtime is unacceptable. Critical workloads, such as those in finance, healthcare, or e-commerce, benefit from the added resilience and availability provided by Multi-AZ deployments.

While Multi-AZ configurations excel in providing high availability, they come with increased costs compared to Single-AZ deployments. The additional resources required for maintaining a standby replica and the data transfer costs between AZs contribute to a higher overall cost.

- **Considerations while choosing between single or Multi-AZ deployments**:
  - ○ **Application criticality**:
    - ▪ **Single-AZ**: Suitable for non-critical applications or development environments where occasional downtime is acceptable.
    - ▪ **Multi-AZ**: Essential for mission-critical applications where high availability and automatic failover are imperative.
  - ○ **Cost considerations**:
    - ▪ **Single-AZ**: More cost-effective for scenarios where high availability is not a top priority.
    - ▪ **Multi-AZ**: Higher cost due to additional resources required for maintaining standby instances and data replication between AZs.
  - ○ **Complexity and management overhead**:
    - ▪ **Single-AZ**: Simpler to setup and manage, making it preferable for scenarios with fewer availability requirements.
    - ▪ **Multi-AZ**: Involves additional complexity, but the trade-off is increased Fault-tolerance and automatic failover capabilities.
  - ○ **Use case scenarios**:
    - ▪ **Single-AZ**: Ideal for applications with predictable workloads, where occasional downtime is acceptable, such as development and testing environments.
    - ▪ **Multi-AZ**: Essential for applications with dynamic or unpredictable workloads, where maintaining continuous availability is critical, such as in production environments.

The choice between Single-AZ and Multi-AZ deployments in Amazon RDS is driven by specific requirements and priorities. Single-AZ configurations offer simplicity and cost-effectiveness, making them suitable for less critical workloads, while Multi-AZ configurations prioritize high availability and Fault-tolerance, making them essential for mission-critical applications. Understanding the nuances of each deployment option, organizations can tailor their RDS configurations to align with the availability, cost, and management considerations unique to their applications.

- **Read replicas and write replicas**: Amazon RDS provides the capability to create read replicas and write replicas, offering flexibility in managing workloads and enhancing the performance and availability of relational databases. The following are the characteristics and use cases of both types of replicas.

- o **Read replicas**: The following are the characteristics of read replicas:

  - **Read scaling**: Read replicas are primarily used to distribute read workloads and offload read operations from the primary database instance. This helps improve overall performance by allowing multiple instances to handle concurrent read requests.

  - **Asynchronous replication**: Read replicas operate through asynchronous replication. Changes made to the primary instance are eventually replicated to the read replicas, introducing a slight delay in data consistency between the primary and replicas.

  - **Same region, Cross-AZ**: Read replicas can be created within the same AWS Region or in a different AZ (Cross-AZ). Deploying replicas in different AZs enhances Fault-tolerance.

  - **Automatic backups**: Read replicas support automated backups and can be used for PITR, providing a degree of data protection.

  The following are the use cases of read replicas:

  - **Scaling read operations**: Read replicas are ideal for scenarios where there is a high volume of read operations, such as reporting, analytics, or read-heavy workloads. By distributing read traffic across replicas, the primary instance is relieved of the burden of handling all read requests.

  - **Reporting and analytics**: Read replicas are commonly used to run reporting and analytical queries without impacting the performance of the primary instance. This allows for better separation of read and write workloads.

  - **Enhancing Fault-tolerance**: In cases where Fault-tolerance is critical, having read replicas in different AZs ensures continued availability in the event of a failure in one zone.

- o **Write Replicas for Amazon Aurora**: The following are the characteristics of write replicas:

  - **Horizontal scaling for writes**: Write replicas in Amazon Aurora allow for horizontal scaling of write operations. Multiple replicas can handle write traffic simultaneously, providing improved write throughput.

  - **Parallel replication**: Aurora supports parallel replication, enabling write replicas to receive and apply updates in parallel. This contributes to reduced replication lag and improved consistency.

  - **Automatic load balancing**: Aurora write replicas come with automatic load balancing, distributing write traffic evenly across all available replicas. This helps in optimizing resource utilization and ensuring efficient performance.

- **Global databases**: Aurora global databases allow for the creation of cross-region replicas, facilitating low-latency access to the database from different geographic locations.

The following are the use cases for write replicas:

- **Scaling writes operations**: Write replicas in Amazon Aurora are particularly beneficial in scenarios where there is a need to scale write operations horizontally. This is advantageous for applications with heavy write workloads.

- **High-throughput requirements**: Applications that demand high write throughput can leverage write replicas to distribute the load and prevent bottlenecks on the primary instance.

- **Global access**: For applications with a global user base, Aurora global databases allow for the creation of replicas in different regions, improving access speed and responsiveness for users across the globe.

Read replicas and write replicas in Amazon RDS, and specifically in Amazon Aurora, serve distinct purposes in optimizing database performance, scalability, and Fault-tolerance. Read replicas are focused on distributing read traffic and enhancing read performance, while write replicas in Aurora extend the scaling capabilities to write operations, providing a comprehensive solution for both read and write workloads. The choice between read and write replicas depends on the specific requirements and characteristics of the application architecture and workload patterns.

- **Amazon RDS pricing**: Amazon RDS pricing is designed to be flexible, allowing users to pay for the resources they consume based on their database instance type, storage requirements, and additional features. Key aspects of Amazon RDS pricing include:

  - **Instance type**:
    - The type and size of the database instance (for example, db.t3.micro, db.m5.large) influence the pricing.
    - Different instance types offer varying levels of compute power, memory, and network performance.

  - **Storage**:
    - Pricing is based on the amount of provisioned storage for the database.
    - Amazon RDS provides options for General Purpose (SSD), Provisioned IOPS (SSD), and magnetic storage types.

- o **Multi-AZ deployments**:

  - Multi-AZ deployments, which provide high availability, may incur additional costs.

  - Charges apply for the standby instance in a different AZ.

- o **Data transfer**:

  - Data transfer in and out of Amazon RDS instances is subject to pricing.

  - Transfer costs depend on the amount of data transferred over the network.

- o **Additional features**:

  - Features such as automated backups, database snapshots, and encrypted storage may have associated costs.

  - Enhanced monitoring, database events, and additional options increase the overall pricing.

Amazon RDS pricing details can be found on the official AWS pricing page, where users can use the pricing calculator to estimate costs based on their specific usage patterns.

- **Shared responsibility model**: This model outlines the division of security and compliance responsibilities between AWS (the cloud service provider) and the customer.

  - o **AWS responsibilities**:

    - **Infrastructure security**: AWS is responsible for the security of the underlying infrastructure, including data centers, networking, and hardware.

    - **Database software patching**: AWS manages the patching of the database engine software for RDS instances.

  - o **Customer responsibilities**:

    - **Data security**: Customers are responsible for securing their data, managing access controls, and implementing encryption mechanisms.

    - **Database configuration and management**: Customers are responsible for configuring and managing the database instance settings, including security groups, parameter groups, and backups.

    - **Application security**: Securing the application layer, including authentication and authorization mechanisms, is the customer's responsibility.

Users can implement a secure and compliant environment on Amazon RDS by understanding and adhering to the shared responsibility model.

Common patterns and use cases of the shared responsibility model include:

- **High availability**:
  - o **Use case**: Ensuring continuous availability and automatic failover in case of a primary instance failure.
  - o **Pattern**: Deploying Amazon RDS in a Multi-AZ configuration with a standby instance in a different AZ.

- **Read scaling**:
  - o **Use case**: Distributing read traffic to improve performance in read-heavy applications.
  - o **Pattern**: Creating read replicas to offload read operations and enhance overall database performance.

- **Horizontal scaling**:
  - o **Use case**: Scaling write operations horizontally to handle large write workloads.
  - o **Pattern**: Leveraging Aurora write replicas to distribute write traffic and improve write throughput.

- **Cost optimization**:
  - o **Use case**: Minimizing costs during periods of inactivity.
  - o **Pattern**: Using the pause and resume feature to temporarily stop and restart an Amazon RDS instance to save costs when the database is not in use.

- **Global databases**:
  - o **Use case**: Providing low-latency access to databases for a global user base.
  - o **Pattern**: Creating Aurora global databases with replicas in multiple regions to serve users with low-latency access.

These common usage patterns showcase how Amazon RDS can be tailored to meet specific requirements: enhancing availability, improving performance, optimizing costs, or providing global accessibility. The flexibility of RDS allows users to adapt their database configurations to best suit the needs of their applications.

NoSQL Databases in AWS

NoSQL databases have gained significant popularity due to their ability to handle large volumes of unstructured or semi-structured data with ease. Unlike traditional relational databases, which store data in tables with predefined schemas, NoSQL databases are more flexible and scalable, making them ideal for applications that require high availability and low-latency performance. In the context of AWS, NoSQL solutions provide developers with powerful cloud-native options to build, manage, and scale their data layers effectively.

AWS offers a variety of managed NoSQL database services designed to meet diverse application needs. Amazon DynamoDB is the primary NoSQL offering from AWS, providing a fully managed key-value and document database. It automatically scales to handle large amounts of data and offers low-latency read and write performance, making it a suitable choice for real-time applications. Additionally, AWS supports other NoSQL options like Amazon Neptune (for graph databases) and Amazon Keyspaces (for Apache Cassandra), catering to specific use cases in cloud environments.

The flexibility and scalability of NoSQL databases on AWS, combined with the platform's fully managed services, allow businesses to focus on their applications rather than infrastructure management. By leveraging AWS's NoSQL solutions, developers can ensure high availability, automatic scaling, and strong security features while taking advantage of the vast ecosystem of AWS services for integrating data-driven applications.

In this section we will explore NoSQL use-cases in the industry and what AWS offers checking out the most used services in this cloud.

The advent of NoSQL

The rise of NoSQL databases in the late 2000s, marked a paradigm shift in the world of data management, challenging the traditional ACID guarantees of relational databases and giving users more scalable and highly available databases, most of the times having schema-less databases and without ACID guarantees all the IT community granted for solved. NoSQL, encompasses diverse database technologies designed to address specific challenges posed by modern, large-scale, and dynamic applications. While relational databases excel in providing strong consistency and transactional support through ACID, NoSQL databases prioritize scalability, flexibility, and performance, often at the expense of some of these ACID properties.

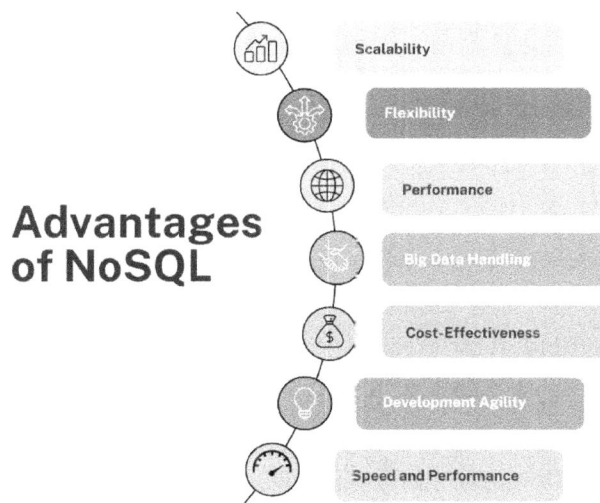

Figure 6.2: *Benefits of adopting NoSQL databases*

In the late 2000s relational databases tried to answer the NoSQL databases challenge and issues found in common relational databases, trying to please the demand for more scalability, more features granting large-scale applications, and trying to catch up in features related to having a more usable database under big load and massive scale users. Some relational databases added features to overcome the initial hurdles, and others tried to catch up with the speed of other NoSQL solutions. The following are the major reasons for the adoption of NoSQL databases:

- **Scalability and flexibility**: One of the primary motivations behind the adoption of NoSQL databases is their ability to scale horizontally, accommodating the massive amounts of data generated in today's digital landscape. NoSQL databases, such as MongoDB and Cassandra, are designed to distribute data across multiple nodes, enabling seamless scalability to handle growing workloads. This contrasts with traditional relational databases, which often face challenges in scaling horizontally due to the rigid structure imposed by the relational model.

- **Schema flexibility**: NoSQL databases often provide a schema-less or schema-flexible data model, allowing developers to store and retrieve data without the need for a predefined schema. This flexibility is particularly advantageous in scenarios where data structures evolve rapidly or exhibit considerable variability. In contrast, relational databases demand a predefined schema, which can be cumbersome to modify, especially in environments where the data schema is subject to frequent changes.

- **High-performance for read and write operations**: Many NoSQL databases prioritize performance, especially speed optimizations for read and write operations. These databases often use techniques like sharding and partitioning to enhance performance, making them well-suited for use cases with high-throughput requirements. Relational databases, while providing strong transactional support, may face performance bottlenecks in certain read and write-intensive scenarios.

Examples of NoSQL databases

NoSQL databases are a category of databases designed to handle a variety of data models and are particularly well-suited for large-scale and complex datasets.

The following are brief descriptions of some common types of NoSQL databases, along with examples of open-source and AWS services for each type:

- **Document-oriented databases**:
  - **Description**: Store and retrieve data in the form of documents, typically using formats like JSON or BSON.
  - **Example (Open-source)**: MongoDB
  - **Example (AWS service)**: Amazon DocumentDB

- **Key-value stores**:

  o **Description**: The simplest form of NoSQL databases, where data is stored as key-value pairs.

  o **Example (Open-source)**: Redis

  o **Example (AWS service)**: Amazon DynamoDB, Amazon ElastiCache

- **Column-family stores**:

  o **Description**: Organize data into columns rather than rows, making them well-suited for analyzing and processing large amounts of data.

  o **Example (Open-source)**: Apache Cassandra

  o **Example (AWS service)**: Amazon Keyspaces (for Apache Cassandra)

- **Graph databases**:

  o **Description**: Designed for data whose relationships are well represented as a graph, with nodes and edges connecting them.

  o **Example (Open-source)**: Neo4j

  o **Example (AWS service)**: Amazon Neptune

- **Wide-column stores**:

  o **Description**: Similar to column-family stores, these databases are optimized for querying large datasets across distributed infrastructure.

  o **Example (Open-source)**: Apache HBase

  o **Example (AWS service)**: Amazon SimpleDB

Examples of AWS NoSQL services include Amazon DynamoDB, Amazon DocumentDB, Amazon Neptune, and Amazon Keyspaces. These services provide scalable, managed solutions for various NoSQL database types, allowing users to focus on their applications rather than the underlying infrastructure. Open-source alternatives, offer flexibility and customization but often require more manual management and scaling.

Amazon DynamoDB

Amazon DynamoDB **https://aws.amazon.com/dynamodb/** is a fully managed NoSQL database service provided by AWS. Its origins can be traced back to the famous Dynamo paper published by Amazon in 2007. The paper, titled *Dynamo: Amazon's highly available key-value store*, was authored by *Giuseppe DeCandia, Deniz Hastorun, Madan Jampani, Gunavardhan Kakulapati, Avinash Lakshman, Alex Pilchin, Swaminathan Sivasubramanian, Peter Vosshall*, and *Werner Vogels* and could be read here **https://www.amazon.science/ publications/dynamo-amazons-highly-available-key-value-store**. This publication laid the foundation for the development of DynamoDB, outlining the principles and architectural choices that form the basis of this robust and scalable NoSQL database.

DynamoDB was conceived to address the challenges of providing a highly available and fault tolerant key-value storage system that could scale horizontally. Leveraging the principles from the Dynamo paper, Amazon engineers built a service that could seamlessly handle the demands of their rapidly growing infrastructure, ensuring low-latency access to data and the ability to scale horizontally in response to changing workloads.

DynamoDB as a NoSQL key-value store

DynamoDB is a NoSQL database under the category of key-value stores. In a key-value store, data is stored as pairs of keys and values, allowing for efficient retrieval and storage of information. DynamoDB's key-value model is designed for simplicity and high-performance, making it suitable for various applications, from small-scale projects to large enterprise solutions. One key feature of DynamoDB is its fully managed nature. AWS takes care of the operational aspects, such as hardware provisioning, setup, and configuration, enabling developers to focus on building applications without the burden of managing the underlying infrastructure. This managed approach extends to automatic scaling, where DynamoDB can dynamically adjust its capacity to handle varying workloads, ensuring consistent performance without manual intervention.

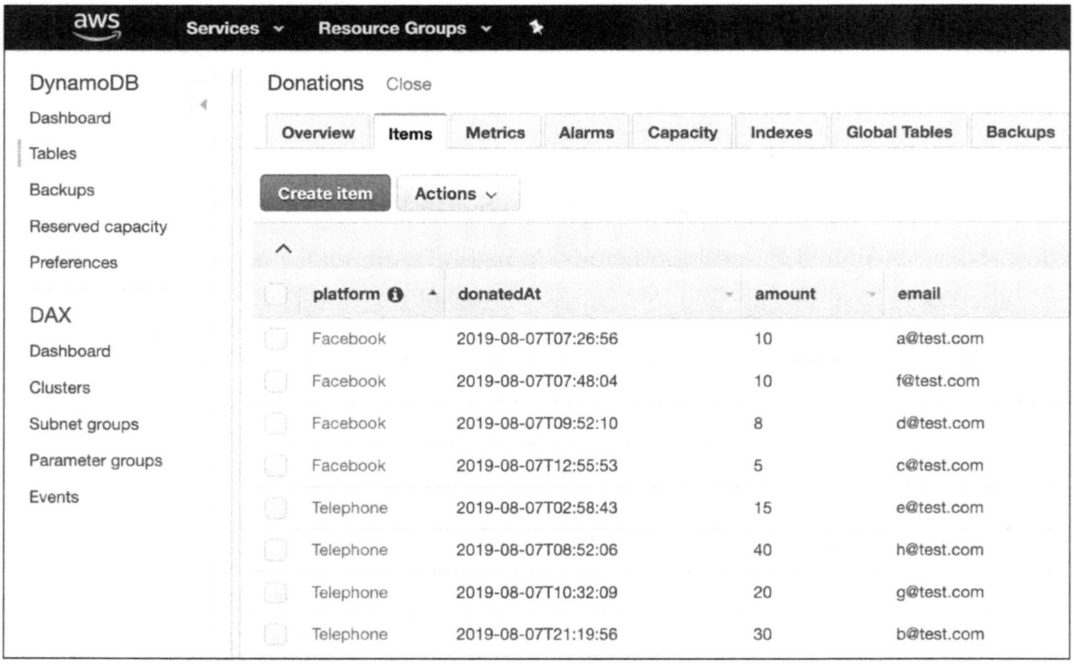

Figure 6.3: Example of a DynamoDB table and data

DynamoDB's data model allows for flexible schema design, accommodating a variety of data types and structures. Each item in DynamoDB is uniquely identified by a primary key, which can consist of a single attribute (for a simple key) or a combination of two attributes (for a composite key). This flexibility in key design enables developers to tailor the database schema to match the specific requirements of their applications.

Features of DynamoDB

The following is a list of common features of DynamoDB:

- **Scalability**: DynamoDB is designed to scale horizontally, allowing applications to seamlessly handle growing workloads. Through partitions, data is distributed across multiple servers, ensuring that the system can handle increased read and write throughput as demands increase.

- **High availability and durability**: DynamoDB maintains multiple copies of data across different AZs to ensure high availability and durability. This design choice, in line with the principles outlined in the Dynamo paper, enhances Fault-tolerance and minimizes the risk of data loss.

- **Consistent performance**: DynamoDB offers predictable and low-latency performance for read and write operations. Developers can specify the desired level of read and write capacity units, and the system automatically adjusts to meet these requirements, ensuring consistent performance even during traffic spikes.

- **Security and access control**: DynamoDB provides robust security features, including fine-grained access control through AWS IAM encryption at rest and in transit further enhances the security posture of the database, meeting stringent compliance requirements.

Use cases of DynamoDB

DynamoDB has been adopted across various industries and use cases. Its ability to handle high-throughput workloads, coupled with features like automatic scaling and flexible schema design, makes it suitable for a diverse range of applications.

Common use cases include real-time bidding platforms, gaming leaderboards, user authentication systems, and IoT data storage.

Amazon DynamoDB stands as a testament to the principles outlined in the Dynamo paper, providing a highly available, scalable, and performant NoSQL key-value store. Its evolution from a research paper **https://www.amazon.science/publications/dynamo-amazons-highly-available-key-value-store** to a fully managed AWS service reflects the commitment to innovation and customer-centric design that characterizes Amazon's approach to cloud computing. As DynamoDB continues to evolve, it remains a powerful tool for developers seeking a robust and hassle-free NoSQL database solution.

On-demand and provisioned throughput

DynamoDB offers two main throughput models: On-demand and provisioned throughput:

- **On-demand throughput**: It eliminates the need for capacity planning and management. With this model, we pay for the read and write capacity our application consumes. DynamoDB automatically scales resources to accommodate the traffic, ensuring consistent, low-latency performance regardless of demand fluctuations. On-demand throughput is ideal for unpredictable workloads or applications with varying traffic patterns.

- **Provisioned throughput**: It allows us to specify the desired read and write capacity for DynamoDB tables. This model is suitable for applications with steady, predictable workloads. It provides cost savings for applications with consistent traffic, as we pay for a predefined amount of capacity rather than for the actual consumed resources. However, it requires manual capacity planning and adjustments to accommodate changes in traffic.

Pricing models and auto scaling options

DynamoDB pricing is based on several factors, including provisioned throughput capacity (for provisioned throughput), on-demand throughput consumption (for on-demand throughput), and additional features like global tables and data transfer. Understanding the pricing structure is crucial for optimizing costs and ensuring efficient resource utilization.

- **Provisioned throughput pricing**: We pay for the provisioned read and write capacity, measured in **read capacity units** (**RCUs**) and **write capacity units** (**WCUs**). Additional charges may apply for features such as global tables and streams.

- **On-demand throughput pricing**: With on-demand throughput, we pay per request, and additional charges may apply for features like global tables and streams. It is important to monitor usage and adjust capacity if necessary.

DynamoDB provides auto scaling capabilities to manage throughput automatically based on actual demand. Auto scaling for DynamoDB helps ensure the tables can handle varying traffic patterns without manual intervention.

- **Provisioned throughput auto scaling**: You can enable auto scaling for tables with provisioned throughput to automatically adjust capacity based on traffic patterns. This helps maintain optimal performance and cost-efficiency.

- **On-demand throughput auto scaling**: On-demand throughput is designed to handle varying workloads without the need for manual adjustments. DynamoDB automatically scales resources up or down based on the application's request patterns, providing a seamless experience for developers.

- **Global distribution**: DynamoDB supports global tables, enabling users to deploy a multi-region, multi-master database architecture for high availability and low-latency access worldwide. Global tables allow the creation of fully replicated, multi-region tables for low-latency access.

  Global tables can be configured with multiple replicas in different AWS Regions. Changes to data in any region are automatically replicated to all other regions, providing a globally distributed, highly available database. Global tables are beneficial for applications requiring active-active configurations, disaster recovery, and ensuring low-latency access for users located in different geographic regions.

DynamoDB Streams

DynamoDB Streams is a feature that captures and records any changes made to the data in a DynamoDB table. It provides a time-ordered sequence of item-level modifications, including inserts, updates, and deletes. This change data capture mechanism enables developers to build applications that respond to changes in the DynamoDB data in real-time.

The following are the key concepts and components of DynamoDB Streams:

- **Stream records**: These are representations of a modification to a DynamoDB item within a stream. Each record contains information about the type of modification, the item itself before and after the change, and a sequence number.

- **Shards**: DynamoDB Streams are divided into shards, independent and ordered sequences of stream records. Each shard has its sequence of records and can be processed in parallel.

The following are the popular use cases of DynamoDB Streams:

- **Real-time analytics**: DynamoDB Streams enable developers to perform real-time analytics on changes happening in the database. This is crucial for businesses that require up-to-the-moment insights into their data.

- **Event-driven architectures**: By leveraging DynamoDB Streams, developers can create event-driven architectures. For example, if a new record is added to a DynamoDB table, a stream can trigger an AWS Lambda function to process the data and take appropriate actions.

- **Data synchronization**: DynamoDB Streams can be used to keep multiple DynamoDB tables in sync. Changes made to one table can be propagated to other tables, ensuring consistency across distributed systems.

- **Audit logs**: Organizations can use DynamoDB Streams to create audit logs by capturing every change made to the data. This is crucial for compliance and security purposes.

Backups in Amazon DynamoDB

Amazon DynamoDB provides a robust backup and restore mechanism to ensure data durability and availability. Backups are continuous and incremental, allowing PITR.

Some key concepts of backups are as follows:

- **On-demand backups**: Users can create on-demand backups of their DynamoDB tables. These backups capture the entire table, including all its indexes.

- **PITR**: DynamoDB supports PITR, enabling the restoration of a table to any specific point-in-time within the last 35 days.

- **Backup retention**: Users can define the retention period for backups, and DynamoDB automatically manages the storage and deletion of old backups.

- **Use cases of backups**:

  o **Data protection**: Backups provide a crucial layer of protection against accidental data deletion or corruption. Users can restore their tables to a specific point-in-time, minimizing the impact of data loss.

  o **Compliance and auditing**: Organizations with strict compliance requirements often need to retain historical data. DynamoDB backups support these requirements by allowing users to recover data as it existed at any point.

  o **Development and testing**: Backups facilitate creating snapshots of production data for use in development and testing environments, ensuring that these environments mirror the production environment closely.

Secondary indexes in Amazon DynamoDB

DynamoDB provides the ability to create secondary indexes on tables, allowing for more flexible querying and improved performance for various access patterns.

- **Key concepts of secondary indexes**:

  o **Global secondary index (GSI)**: A secondary index with a partition key and optional sort key that is different from those on the table.

  o **Local secondary index (LSI)**: A secondary index that has the same partition key as the table but a different sort key.

- **Use cases of secondary indexes**:

  o **Query flexibility**: Secondary indexes enable querying the data based on attributes other than the primary key. This is particularly useful when the primary key alone does not cover the required query patterns.

o **Optimizing query performance**: Using secondary indexes, developers can optimize query performance for specific access patterns. This is especially beneficial in cases where certain queries need to be executed quickly and efficiently.

o **Sorting and filtering**: Secondary indexes facilitate sorting and filtering of data based on attributes that are different from the primary key. This is essential for scenarios where data needs to be retrieved in a specific order or filtered based on certain criteria.

Introduction to AWS Redshift

Amazon Redshift **https://aws.amazon.com/redshift/** is a fully managed, petabyte-scale data warehouse service in the cloud, provided by AWS. It is designed for high-performance analysis using SQL queries on large datasets. Redshift makes it easy to setup, operate, and scale a data warehouse, allowing businesses to gain valuable insights from their data without the complexities associated with traditional on-premises data warehouses.

A data warehouse is a specialized database optimized for the analysis and reporting of large volumes of data. Unlike transactional databases designed for quick read-and-write operations, data warehouses are tailored to support complex queries and aggregations across vast datasets. The need for data warehouses arises from the increasing volume, variety, and velocity of data.

Data warehouses provide a centralized repository for structured and often historical data, enabling businesses to make informed decisions based on comprehensive insights. They play a crucial role in consolidating data from various sources, cleaning and transforming it, and making it accessible for analysis.

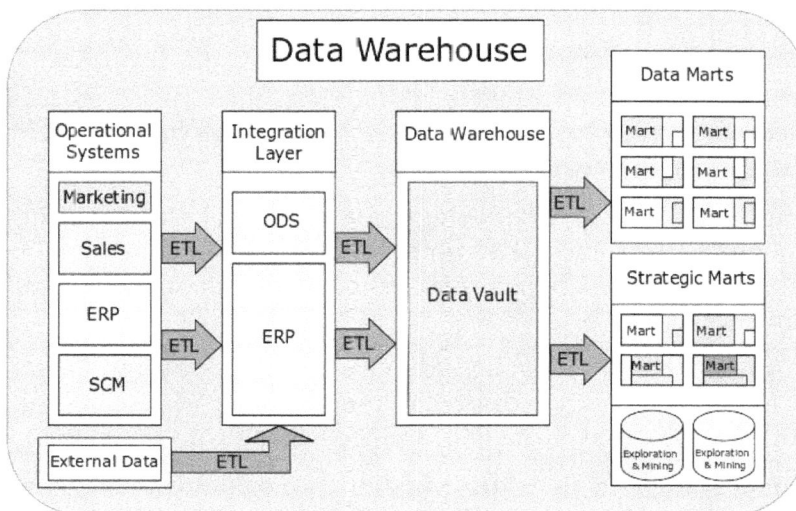

Figure 6.4: Data warehouse example

With the rise of big data and the demand for real-time analytics, the importance of efficient data warehousing solutions has grown significantly.

Amazon Redshift is a fully managed data warehousing service that enables organizations to analyze vast amounts of data quickly and cost-effectively. Positioned as an **online analytical processing (OLAP)** database, Redshift plays a crucial role in BI, analytics, and reporting. This section studies the distinctions between OLAP and **online transactional processing (OLTP)**, explores the main use cases of Redshift, examines its data-handling capabilities, and introduces the concept of Redshift Serverless.

OLAP versus OLTP

In the database workloads, the typical use cases are related to OLTP and OLAP. The following are the differences between the two:

- OLAP databases are optimized for complex queries and reporting, making them suitable for analytical workloads. They are designed to support read-heavy operations and aggregate large volumes of data to provide insights into historical trends and business performance. Redshift excels in OLAP scenarios, allowing users to run complex queries across massive datasets efficiently.

- In contrast, OLTP databases are geared towards transactional processing, handling high volumes of short, simple transactions. These systems are optimized for write-heavy workloads, ensuring fast and reliable transactional capabilities. Examples of OLTP databases include Amazon Aurora and Amazon RDS. Redshift is not intended for OLTP workloads, as its architecture and optimizations align with the demands of analytics rather than transactional processing.

Features of Amazon Redshift

Key features of Amazon Redshift include:

- **Performance**: Redshift delivers high-performance query processing through parallel execution and optimization techniques. It uses columnar storage to reduce I/O and improve query speed.

- **Scalability**: Redshift is fully managed and can easily scale up or down based on the volume of data and the complexity of queries. This scalability ensures that organizations can handle increasing amounts of data without compromising on performance.

- **Ease of use**: Redshift integrates seamlessly with popular BI tools, and its SQL-based interface makes it accessible to users familiar with relational databases. It supports a wide range of analytics and reporting tools.

- **Columnar storage in Redshift**: Redshift uses columnar storage, which is well-suited for analytics workloads. This storage format allows for efficient compression and speeds up query performance by reading only the necessary columns.

- **Automatic compression**: Redshift automatically chooses the most appropriate compression encoding for each column, minimizing storage space requirements and improving query performance.

- **Advanced security**: Redshift provides robust security features, including encryption of data in transit and at rest, **virtual private cloud** (**VPC**) support, and IAM integration.

- **Integration with other AWS services**: Redshift seamlessly integrates with other AWS services, such as Amazon S3 for data storage, AWS IAM for access control, and AWS **Key Management Service** (**KMS**) for encryption key management.

- **Main use cases of AWS Redshift**:

  o **BI and reporting**: Redshift is commonly used for BI and reporting purposes, allowing organizations to analyze large datasets to derive meaningful insights and make data-driven decisions.

  o **Data warehousing**: As a data warehousing solution, Redshift is ideal for consolidating and analyzing data from various sources, providing a centralized platform for analytics and reporting.

  o **Data lakes integration**: Redshift can seamlessly integrate with data lakes stored in Amazon S3, enabling organizations to combine structured and unstructured data for a more comprehensive analysis.

  o **Real-time analytics**: With its ability to handle large datasets and scale dynamically, Redshift is well-suited for organizations requiring real-time analytics capabilities, allowing them to respond quickly to changing business conditions.

Amazon Redshift offers a powerful, scalable, and cost-effective solution for organizations seeking to harness the full potential of their data through advanced analytics and reporting. Its features, scalability, and integration with other AWS services make it a versatile choice for a wide range of use cases in the ever-evolving landscape of data management and analysis.

- **Data handled by Amazon Redshift**: Amazon Redshift is designed to scale effortlessly as data volumes grow. Its architecture allows for the distribution of data across multiple nodes, and the introduction of Amazon Redshift RA3 instances further enhances scalability as those type of instances decouple storage and compute, allowing users to scale storage independently of compute resources. This helps size easily your cluster and pay only for the managed storage you use. It uses high-performance SSD for hot data, and use S3 for infrequent accessed data, providing a cost-effective way to handle your storage needs.

The amount of data that Redshift can handle depends on factors such as the chosen node type, the distribution key design, and data compression techniques.

For instance, a dense compute node with high-performance storage can handle large datasets efficiently. Additionally, Redshift Spectrum enables organizations to analyze vast amounts of data stored in Amazon S3 directly, further extending its analytical capabilities.

Redshift's ability to handle petabytes of data positions it as a powerful solution for enterprises with ever-growing data requirements. Its performance optimizations ensure that queries on massive datasets are executed with minimal latency, providing users with timely and actionable insights.

- **Redshift Serverless**: Amazon Redshift introduced the concept of serverless in response to the evolving needs of modern data analytics. Redshift Serverless allows users to run analytics queries without the need to manage clusters or allocate resources manually. This pay-as-you-go model eliminates the need for upfront commitments, providing a cost-effective solution for sporadic or unpredictable workloads.

Redshift Serverless is particularly beneficial for scenarios where the demand for analytics varies over time. Users can leverage the advantages of Redshift's analytical capabilities without the overhead of managing and provisioning clusters continuously. This flexibility aligns with the cloud's core principles, allowing organizations to optimize costs and resources based on their actual usage patterns.

AWS Redshift pricing model

Amazon Redshift has different pricing models listed here:

- **On-demand pricing**: Amazon Redshift offers on-demand pricing, allowing users to pay for the compute and storage resources they consume. The pricing includes separate charges for compute node hours and per **terabyte** (**TB**) of storage provisioned. This model is suitable for organizations with fluctuating workloads, as it provides flexibility without the need for upfront commitments.

- **Reserved Instances**: For more predictable workloads, organizations can opt for Reserved Instances, which offer significant cost savings compared to on-demand pricing. Reserved Instances involve a one-time upfront payment and a reduced hourly rate for a 1 or 3-year term. This pricing model is ideal for stable workloads with known resource requirements over an extended period.

- **Concurrency scaling pricing**: Concurrency scaling is a feature that automatically adds and removes capacity to handle unpredictable query workloads. It comes with its pricing, separate from the main cluster pricing. Users pay for the total number of clusters and the number of seconds the clusters are active. This ensures cost-effectiveness for sporadic bursts of queries.

- **Spectrum pricing**: Amazon Redshift Spectrum allows users to query data in Amazon S3 directly, extending the data warehouse's reach to unstructured and semi-structured data. Spectrum has its pricing based on the amount of data scanned from Amazon S3. This model enables cost-effective analysis of vast datasets without loading them into the main Redshift cluster.

- **Amazon Redshift Serverless pricing**: Amazon Redshift Serverless is a new pricing model introduced to provide greater flexibility and cost-efficiency. With serverless, users pay for the actual query processing rather than provisioning and maintaining a fixed cluster. Key aspects of the serverless pricing model include:

  o **On-demand query pricing**: Users pay for the amount of data processed by their queries. This allows for cost savings when the workload is sporadic or varies in intensity.

  o **Concurrency scaling**: If additional capacity is needed to handle concurrent queries, users are billed based on the amount of additional capacity provisioned for the duration of the query.

  o **Data storage**: Similar to the traditional Redshift pricing model, users are charged based on the amount of data stored in the serverless data lake.

- **Additional costs**: It is important to consider additional costs, such as data transfer fees for moving data into and out of Redshift, and costs associated with features like backup storage, main Redshift storage, cross-region snapshots, and enhanced VPC routing. Organizations should carefully analyze their usage patterns to estimate and optimize costs effectively.

- **Shared responsibility model for Amazon Redshift**: AWS follows a shared responsibility model, delineating the responsibilities of AWS and its customers in terms of security and management. For Amazon Redshift, this model applies to aspects such as infrastructure security, data protection, and access control:

  o **AWS responsibilities**: These responsibilities include:

    ▪ **Infrastructure security**: AWS manages the security of the physical infrastructure and underlying compute resources that power Amazon Redshift. This includes network, hardware, and facility security.

    ▪ **Data center compliance**: AWS ensures that its data centers comply with various industry-standards and certifications, providing a secure environment for hosting Amazon Redshift clusters.

    ▪ **Service availability**: Ensuring the availability and durability of Amazon Redshift falls under AWS's responsibility. This includes measures to minimize downtime and data loss.

    ▪ **Managed service updates**: AWS takes care of the operational aspects, including patching and updating the Redshift service. This ensures that customers benefit from the latest features and security patches without manual intervention.

o **Customer responsibilities**: The customer responsibilities include:

- **Data security and encryption**: Customers are responsible for securing their data within Amazon Redshift. This involves implementing encryption for data at rest and in transit, using mechanisms like AWS KMS.

- **Access control and authentication**: Defining and managing access controls, user authentication, and authorization within Amazon Redshift is the responsibility of the customer. This includes configuring user roles, permissions, and network access.

- **Data backups and retention**: While AWS manages the operational aspects of data backup and retention, customers must define and implement their backup and retention policies. This ensures data recovery in case of accidental deletion or corruption.

- **Performance optimization**: Optimizing the performance of Amazon Redshift for specific workloads is the responsibility of the customer. This involves designing efficient queries, selecting appropriate data distribution keys, and monitoring and tuning the cluster as needed.

Amazon Redshift has become indispensable in data analytics and warehousing. Positioned as an OLAP database, it excels in handling large-scale analytical workloads, making it indispensable for organizations seeking powerful insights from their data. Whether used for BI, data warehousing, reporting, or advanced analytics, Redshift's scalability, performance, and now, serverless capabilities, position it as a versatile solution in the AWS ecosystem. Understanding the distinctions between OLAP and OLTP, exploring Redshift's use cases, and appreciating its data-handling capabilities is key to harnessing the full potential of this robust data warehousing service.

Other databases in AWS

AWS offers a variety of database services beyond RDS, DynamoDB, and Redshift, catering to different needs within the cloud ecosystem.

Amazon ElastiCache is an in-memory data store, typically used to accelerate application performance by caching frequently accessed data. It supports Redis and Memcached, offering fast data retrieval for scenarios like session management, real-time analytics, and caching web pages or API responses. ElastiCache is ideal for workloads requiring low-latency, high-throughput access to data.

Amazon OpenSearch Service (formerly Elasticsearch) is a search and analytics engine used for managing and analyzing large amounts of log, event, and time-series data. It is a highly scalable, distributed service that supports full-text search, filtering, and data visualization. OpenSearch is widely used for log analytics, monitoring applications, and enabling search functionality in websites and applications, allowing organizations to derive insights from vast datasets.

Amazon Neptune is a fully managed graph database service optimized for applications that need to store and query highly connected data. It supports both property graph and RDF graph models, making it suitable for social networking, fraud detection, recommendation engines, and knowledge graphs. Neptune's ability to handle complex relationships between entities allows it to power use cases such as social media analytics, financial fraud detection, and network security.

Amazon DocumentDB is a fully managed NoSQL database service designed for handling document-based data models, typically JSON. It is compatible with MongoDB, offering features like scalability, high availability, and security. DocumentDB is ideal for applications requiring flexible data schemas, such as content management systems, customer profiles, and mobile apps, where structured and semi-structured data are common. It enables developers to focus on application logic while AWS handles infrastructure management.

A different kind of databases

An in-memory database (like Amazon ElastiCache) is a type of database that primarily stores data in the system's main memory (RAM) rather than on disk. This allows for much faster data retrieval and processing, as accessing data in-memory is orders of magnitude faster than reading from disk. In-memory databases are ideal for use cases that require low-latency, high-throughput access, such as caching frequently used data, session storage, and real-time analytics. Their speed makes them suitable for applications where performance is critical, such as e-commerce websites or gaming backends.

A search and analytics engine, like Amazon OpenSearch, is a specialized database designed to index and search large volumes of unstructured or semi-structured data quickly. These engines provide powerful search capabilities, such as full-text search, filtering, and aggregations, making them well-suited for analyzing logs, event data, and time-series data. Search engines allow users to search and derive insights from vast amounts of data, making them essential for use cases like website search functionalities, log analysis, and data monitoring.

A graph database, such as Amazon Neptune, is a database designed to handle highly interconnected data using graph structures like nodes (entities) and edges (relationships). This type of database excels at representing complex relationships between entities, allowing for efficient querying of interconnected data. Graph databases are commonly used in social networks, recommendation engines, fraud detection, and network analysis because they can model relationships more naturally and flexibly than traditional relational databases, which use tables to represent data.

A document database like Amazon DocumentDB is a NoSQL database that stores data in document formats (usually JSON or BSON), where each document can have a flexible, semi-structured schema. Unlike relational databases that use tables with fixed columns, document databases allow developers to store data in a more natural, flexible way. They are particularly useful when dealing with varied or rapidly changing data structures, such as in content management systems, user profiles, and mobile applications where data does not fit nearly into rows and columns.

Let us see each of those type of alternative databases and how they could be used, exploring the main managed services AWS offers us.

In-memory database in AWS

Amazon ElastiCache **https://aws.amazon.com/elasticache/** it is a fully managed, in-memory caching service that can be used to improve the performance of web applications by enabling them to retrieve information from fast, managed, in-memory caches instead of slower disk-based databases. ElastiCache supports two widely used open-source in-memory caching engines: Redis and Memcached.

- **Redis**: Redis is an open-source, in-memory key-value data store. It is known for its versatility, supporting a variety of data structures such as strings, hashes, lists, sets, and more. Redis is often used as a caching layer to store frequently accessed data in-memory, reducing the load on databases and improving application performance. With ElastiCache for Redis, AWS provides a fully managed Redis service, handling tasks like hardware provisioning, setup, and patching.

- **Memcached**: Memcached is another open-source, distributed memory caching system. It is simple and effective, providing a key-value store for caching arbitrary data. ElastiCache for Memcached on AWS allows users to deploy and manage Memcached clusters, helping improve the performance of web applications by caching frequently accessed data.

Search database in AWS

Amazon OpenSearch **https://aws.amazon.com/opensearch-service/** formerly known as **Amazon Elasticsearch**, is a managed service that makes it easy to deploy, secure, and scale Elasticsearch clusters. Elasticsearch is an open-source search and analytics engine that is widely used for full-text search, log analytics, and other use cases where large amounts of data need to be quickly and efficiently searched. Amazon OpenSearch provides features such as real-time indexing, support for complex queries, and integration with various data sources. It is highly scalable, allowing users to easily add or remove nodes to accommodate changing workloads. The service also offers built-in security features, including encryption and access controls, to ensure data protection.

Graph database in AWS

Amazon Neptune **https://aws.amazon.com/neptune/** it is a fully managed graph database service that supports two popular graph models: Property graph and **Resource Description**

Framework (RDF). It is designed for applications that require highly connected data, such as social networking, fraud detection, and recommendation engines. The following popular graph models are supported by Amazon Neptune:

- **Property graph**: Represents data as vertices and edges with associated properties. This model is suitable for scenarios where relationships between entities have attributes.

- **RDF graph**: This represents data as subject-predicate-object triples, making it ideal for scenarios where relationships need to be expressed in a standard, interoperable way.

Amazon Neptune provides features like high availability, durability, and automatic backups, making it easier for developers to focus on building applications rather than managing infrastructure.

Document database in AWS

- **Amazon DocumentDB**: DocumentDB **https://aws.amazon.com/it/documentdb/** it is a fully managed document database service designed to work with MongoDB applications. It is compatible with MongoDB 3.6 and provides a scalable, highly available, and secure platform for storing, querying, and indexing JSON-like documents. The following are its key advantages:

  o **Compatibility**: It is compatible with existing MongoDB applications. This allows users to migrate their MongoDB workloads to DocumentDB seamlessly without making changes to their application code.

  o **Performance and scalability**: It is designed for high performance and low latency, making it suitable for a wide range of applications, from content management systems to e-commerce platforms. It offers features such as automatic backups, PITR, and continuous monitoring to ensure the availability and durability of data.

Pricing models of alternative AWS databases

Understanding the pricing models of AWS databases is crucial for optimizing costs and selecting the right service for specific use cases. The following is a brief overview of the pricing models for ElastiCache, OpenSearch, Neptune, and DocumentDB:

- **Amazon ElastiCache**: Pricing is based on the type and size of the cache nodes used. Users pay for the compute capacity of the nodes and any additional features, such as Multi-AZ deployments for high availability.

- **Amazon OpenSearch**: Pricing is based on instance type, storage, and data transfer. Users pay for the compute capacity of the instances, storage volume, and data transfer in and out of the service.

- **Amazon Neptune**: Pricing is based on the instance type and the amount of storage used. Users pay for the compute capacity of the instances and the storage volume provisioned.

- **Amazon DocumentDB**: Pricing is based on the instance type and the amount of storage used. Users pay for the compute capacity of the instances and the storage volume provisioned.

These AWS database services collectively contribute to a comprehensive ecosystem, empowering developers to choose the right tool for their specific use cases. Whether optimizing for speed with ElasticCache, enabling advanced search with OpenSearch, managing graph data with Neptune, or leveraging document-oriented databases with DocumentDB, AWS caters to diverse application requirements. The managed nature of these services further allows developers to focus on innovation and application development rather than the operational aspects of database management. Overall, AWS's database offerings play a crucial role in facilitating scalable, performant, and resilient data solutions for a wide array of applications.

Big data processing in Amazon

Big data has become a driving force in modern business, providing organizations with valuable insights, actionable intelligence, and a competitive edge. The sheer volume, velocity, and variety of data generated require sophisticated processing solutions. AWS stands at the forefront, offering a comprehensive suite of tools and services for efficient big data processing.

Big data processing involves collecting, storing, and analyzing large and complex datasets to extract meaningful patterns and insights. The scale and complexity of big data require a flexible, cost-effective platform for organizations to harness the power of their data.

Concept of data lakes

A data lake is a centralized repository that allows organizations to store structured and unstructured data at any scale. Unlike traditional data warehouses, data lakes accommodate diverse data types without the need for extensive preprocessing. This flexibility makes data lakes a crucial component of big data processing, enabling organizations to consolidate data from various sources, such as logs, clickstreams, and social media, into a single, accessible repository.

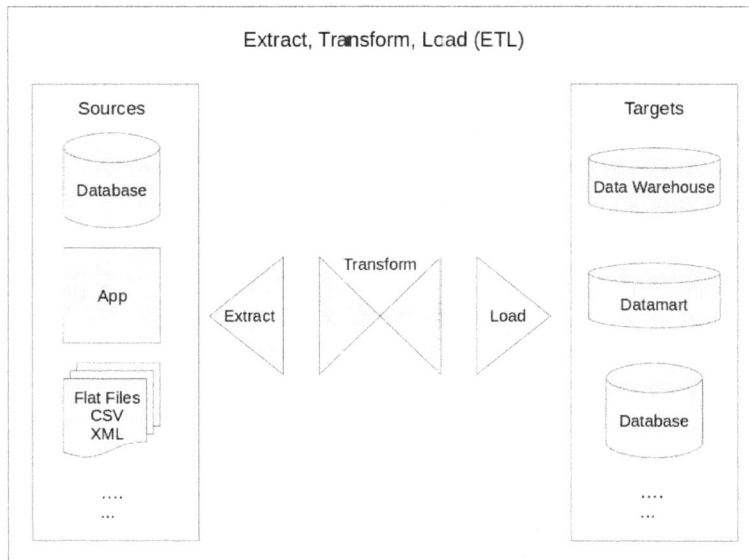

Figure 6.5: *ETL architecture for big data processing*

AWS offers several services to build and manage data lakes:

- **Amazon S3**: It is an important part of AWS data lakes. It provides scalable, secure, and durable object storage, allowing organizations to store and retrieve any amount of data. S3 is highly versatile, supporting data in various formats, including CSV, JSON, and Parquet.

- **AWS Lake Formation**: It simplifies setting up, securing, and managing a data lake. It provides tools for defining and enforcing data access policies, making it easier to control who can access and analyze the data within the lake.

- **AWS Glue**: It is a fully managed ETL service that makes it easy to prepare and load data for analysis. Glue automatically discovers, catalogs, and transforms data stored in Amazon S3, simplifying the ETL process.

- **Amazon Athena**: It enables ad-hoc querying of data in S3 using standard SQL. It eliminates the need for complex ETL processes by allowing users to directly analyze data in its raw form. This makes it an excellent tool for exploratory data analysis within the data lake.

- **ETL and its services**: ETL is a critical process in big data workflows, that involves extraction of data from source systems, transformation into a suitable format, and loading it into a target data store. AWS provides several services to streamline and automate the ETL process:

  - **AWS Glue**: As mentioned earlier, AWS Glue simplifies ETL tasks by automating the discovery, cataloging, and transformation of data. It supports multiple data sources, including on-premises databases, Amazon RDS, and Amazon Redshift.

o **Amazon EMR**: It is a cloud-based big data platform that supports popular frameworks such as Apache Spark and Apache Hadoop. EMR facilitates ETL tasks by providing a scalable and cost-effective environment for processing large datasets.

o **AWS Data Pipeline**: It is a web service for orchestrating and automating the movement and transformation of data between different AWS services and on-premises data sources. It allows users to define data-driven workflows, making it easier to schedule and monitor ETL jobs.

- **AWS analytical services**: These services include:

  o **Amazon EMR**: Amazon EMR is a cloud-based big data platform designed to simplify processing large amounts of data using popular frameworks such as Apache Spark and Apache Hadoop. It enables users to provision and scale clusters dynamically, allowing them to focus on processing tasks rather than infrastructure management.

  Its key features include:

    ▪ **Managed clusters**: EMR provides pre-configured clusters with popular frameworks, reducing setup time and effort.

    ▪ **Flexibility**: Users can choose from a variety of applications and frameworks based on their specific needs.

    ▪ **Integration**: Seamlessly integrates with other AWS services, including Amazon S3 for data storage and AWS Glue for ETL tasks.

    ▪ **Security**: EMR ensures data security through features like encryption and IAM controls.

  The following are the use cases of Amazon EMR:

    ▪ **Log analysis**: Process and analyze server logs or clickstream data for insights.

    ▪ **Data warehousing**: Query large datasets interactively with tools like Presto and Hive for BI.

    ▪ **Big data processing**: Process massive datasets using distributed frameworks like Apache Hadoop, Apache Spark, and Presto.

    ▪ **Data analytics**: Perform data transformation, ETL, and advanced analytics.

    ▪ **Stream processing**: Analyze real-time data streams using Apache Kafka and Apache Flink.

- **Batch processing**: Automate recurring data workflows like nightly batch jobs.

- **Machine learning**: Train, tune, and deploy **machine learning (ML)** models using Spark MLlib or integrated ML tools.

For example, a retail company can utilize EMR to analyze customer purchase patterns, running Apache Spark jobs on a dynamically scalable cluster to gain insights into buying behavior.

o **Amazon Athena**: Amazon Athena is a serverless query service that enables users to analyze data directly in Amazon S3 using SQL queries. It eliminates the need for complex ETL processes and data loading, making it particularly useful for ad-hoc analysis of large datasets.

Its key features include:

- **Serverless architecture**: Users only pay for the queries they run, with no infrastructure to manage.

- **Presto engine**: Athena uses the Presto query engine, providing fast and interactive query performance.

- **Integration**: Seamlessly integrates with various data formats in Amazon S3, such as CSV, JSON, and Parquet.

- **Security**: Supports AWS IAM for fine-grained access control.

The following are the use cases of Amazon Athena:

- **Ad-hoc analysis**: Execute SQL queries on structured, semi-structured, or unstructured data without needing complex ETL processes.

- **Log analysis**: Parse and query logs (for example, AWS CloudTrail, application logs) for troubleshooting, monitoring, or security insights.

- **Data lake analytics**: Analyze large datasets stored in S3, often as part of a modern data lake architecture.

- **Integrate with BI tools**: Connect Athena with BI tools (for example, Tableau, Power BI) for advanced visualization and analysis.

- **Data exploration and reporting**: Quickly explore and generate reports on data stored in S3 using SQL-compatible tools.

An e-commerce company can use Athena to run SQL queries on its customer data stored in Amazon S3, extracting valuable insights without a traditional database setup.

o **AWS Glue**: AWS Glue is a fully managed ETL service that makes it easy to prepare and load data for analysis. It automates the process of discovering, cataloging, and transforming data, simplifying the preparation of data for analytics.

Its key features include:

- **Data catalog**: Glue automatically creates a centralized metadata repository (data catalog) for all data sources, providing a unified view.

- **ETL automation**: Glue automatically generates ETL code, reducing the need for manual coding and speeding up the transformation process.

- **Serverless execution**: Users can focus on defining transformations, while Glue takes care of the underlying infrastructure.

- **Integration**: Works seamlessly with other AWS services, including S3, Redshift, and EMR.

The following are the use cases of AWS Glue:

- **Data integration**: Combine data from multiple structured and unstructured sources for unified analysis.

- **ETL workflow automation**: Automate the ETL of data from various sources into data lakes or warehouses.

- **Serverless data pipelines**: Build scalable, serverless data pipelines without managing infrastructure.

- **Data transformation**: Perform data cleansing, normalization, and transformation for analytics or application use.

- **Data preparation for analytics**: Automatically discover, catalog, and maintain metadata about datasets, making them searchable and easy to manage.

- **Schema evolution**: Handle changes in data schemas dynamically to ensure data compatibility over time.

- **Data migration**: Move and transform data between on-premises systems and cloud-based solutions.

A media streaming service can use Glue to transform and aggregate viewer interaction data from multiple sources into a format suitable for analysis, facilitating better content recommendations.

o **AWS Glue DataBrew**: AWS Glue DataBrew is a visual data preparation tool built on the AWS Glue platform. It provides a visual interface to clean, normalize, and transform data without the need for coding, making data preparation accessible to a broader audience.

Its key features include:

- **Visual data transformation**: Users can visually explore, clean, and transform data using a point-and-click interface.

- **Data profiling**: DataBrew automatically profiles data, identifying quality issues and suggesting transformations.

- **Recipe automation**: Allows users to save and reuse transformation steps as recipes, improving workflow efficiency.

- **Integration**: Seamlessly integrates with AWS Glue, providing a unified data preparation and transformation experience.

The following are the use cases of AWS Glue DataBrew:

- **Data cleaning and normalization**: Remove duplicates, fill missing values, correct data formats, and standardize inconsistent data.

- **Data enrichment**: Add calculated fields, combine datasets, and enrich data using custom transformations.

- **Exploratory data analysis**: Visualize distributions, outliers, and correlations to understand data quality and structure.

- **Data quality assessment**: Profile datasets to identify data quality issues with detailed statistics and insights.

- **ETL simplification**: Automate repeatable data preparation tasks and integrate them into ETL pipelines.

- **Data preparation for ML**: Normalize, scale, and encode data to make it ready for ML workflows.

A healthcare organization can use Glue DataBrew to visually clean and prepare patient data from various sources before feeding it into a machine-learning model for predictive analytics.

Pricing model for EMR, Athena, and Glue

AWS offers a flexible and pay-as-you-go pricing model, allowing users to scale their infrastructure based on actual usage. This model is particularly beneficial for services like Amazon EMR, Athena, and Glue, each designed to address specific needs in the realm of big data processing, querying, and ETL tasks.

- **Amazon EMR**: It is a cloud-based big data platform that simplifies the processing of large datasets using popular frameworks such as Apache Spark and Apache Hadoop. The AWS pricing model for EMR is based on several factors:

- o **Instance types and EC2 pricing**: EMR clusters run on Amazon EC2 instances. Users can choose different instance types based on their processing needs. Pricing is based on the chosen instance type, with different costs for On-Demand and Reserved Instances.

- o **EMR software pricing**: Users pay for the Amazon EMR software stack that includes popular big data frameworks. Pricing varies based on the selected applications and versions.

- o **Additional data storage**: Costs are associated with additional data storage, whether using Amazon S3 or **Hadoop Distributed File System (HDFS)**.

- o **Spot Instances**: Users can take advantage of Spot Instances to reduce costs. Spot Instances are spare EC2 capacity available at lower prices.

- o **Data transfer costs**: Data transfer costs apply when moving data between different AWS Regions or out of the AWS network.

- o **Reserved capacity**: Users can save costs by purchasing Reserved Instances for predictable workloads with a 1 or 3-year commitment.

- o **Additional services**: Any additional AWS services used in conjunction with EMR, such as Amazon S3 or Amazon CloudWatch, will incur separate charges.

- **Amazon Athena**: It is a serverless query service that allows users to analyze data in Amazon S3 using standard SQL. The pricing model for Athena is straightforward and revolves around the amount of data scanned during queries:

  - o **Data scanned**: Users are billed based on the amount of data scanned by their queries. Pricing is per TB scanned, with a minimum charge per query.

  - o **Query performance**: Athena offers different performance options, and users can choose between standard and fast query performance. Fast queries are priced at a higher rate but provide faster results.

  - o **Output data**: Charges also apply to the amount of data written to Amazon S3 as query output.

  - o **Encryption**: Athena supports encrypted query results, and there are additional charges for storing these encrypted results in Amazon S3.

- **AWS Glue**: It is a fully managed ETL service that simplifies the process of preparing and loading data for analysis. The pricing model for Glue is based on the following components:

  - o **Data catalog**: Users pay for the storage used by the AWS Glue Data Catalog, which stores metadata about data sources, targets, transformations, and targets.

o **Crawling**: Glue uses crawlers to discover and catalog metadata from different data sources. Users are billed based on the number of objects crawled.

o **Data processing units**: Users pay for **data processing units (DPUs)** consumed by ETL jobs and development endpoints. DPUs represent a measure of computing capacity, and users can choose the number of DPUs for their jobs.

o **Development endpoints**: Charges apply for the use of development endpoints, where users can author, test, and debug Glue ETL scripts.

o **Job execution time**: Users are billed for the time their ETL jobs take to run, measured in seconds.

o **Data transfer costs**: Data transfer costs apply when moving data between AWS Glue and other AWS services.

o **Additional services**: Any additional AWS services used in conjunction with AWS Glue may incur separate charges.

In summary, AWS offers a granular and flexible pricing model for EMR, Athena, and Glue, enabling users to optimize costs based on their specific usage patterns and requirements. It is essential for users to carefully assess their needs and leverage the available pricing options to ensure cost-effectiveness in their big data processing workflows.

AWS Cloud Data Migration Services

Migrating data to the cloud is a critical step for organizations aiming to modernize their infrastructure and take full advantage of AWS scalable and secure services. AWS offers a suite of tools designed to simplify and accelerate the migration process, ensuring that data can be transferred seamlessly from on-premises environments to the cloud. These services provide flexibility, cost-effectiveness, and high-performance, allowing businesses to move data securely while minimizing disruption.

Among the most widely used services are AWS Direct Connect, which establishes a dedicated network connection for faster, more reliable transfers, and the AWS Snow Family, offering physical devices for large-scale data migration when network conditions are not optimal. Other tools such as AWS Storage Gateway and Amazon S3TA make it easier to integrate on-premises data with cloud storage, while AWS Firehose and AWS Transfer Family provide real-time streaming and managed file transfer capabilities.

For comprehensive migrations, AWS provides additional solutions like AWS **Database Migration Service (DMS)**, third-party connectors and the AWS SCT These tools help automate the migration of databases, adapt schemas, and integrate legacy systems with cloud-native environments, ensuring a smooth transition to the AWS ecosystem. Together, these services enable organizations to move their data securely, quickly, and efficiently to the cloud while meeting the specific needs of their infrastructure.

For each of those managed services described in this section, you could find more information here: **https://docs.aws.amazon.com/whitepapers/latest/overview-aws-cloud-data-migration-services/aws-managed-migration-tools.html**.

AWS Direct Connect

AWS Direct Connect is a dedicated network connection that allows businesses to securely transfer data between their on-premises environments and AWS services. Unlike traditional internet connections, which can be affected by network congestion, Direct Connect offers a consistent, high-bandwidth connection that improves performance and reliability. It is particularly beneficial for applications requiring large data transfers, such as disaster recovery, backup, and big data analytics, as it bypasses the public internet and ensures lower latency and higher throughput.

One of the key use cases for AWS Direct Connect is hybrid cloud environments. It enables seamless integration between on-premises data centers and AWS services, ensuring data consistency and faster access to cloud resources. Direct Connect is also useful for organizations that require compliance with strict data governance and security policies, as the private network connection helps protect sensitive data during transmission. Additionally, industries such as finance and healthcare benefit from Direct Connect's enhanced security features, reducing the risk of data breaches.

In terms of pricing, AWS Direct Connect operates on a pay-as-you-go model, with costs based on the port hours and data transfer out of AWS. There are different pricing tiers for port speeds, ranging from 1 Gbps to 100 Gbps, depending on the chosen connection capacity. Customers are charged for the port usage and the data transfer that occurs over the connection. AWS also offers data transfer pricing based on the destination, which includes charges for traffic to and from AWS Regions. To optimize costs, customers can choose between a dedicated connection or a hosted connection depending on their network needs and budget.

Overall, AWS Direct Connect is a powerful tool for enterprises seeking to optimize their cloud data migration strategy. By offering a dedicated, private connection to AWS, it helps organizations enhance network performance, improve security, and reduce the complexities associated with transferring large amounts of data over the public internet.

AWS Snow Family

The AWS Snow Family consists of a set of physical and virtual appliances designed to simplify large-scale data migrations to the AWS Cloud. This family includes several products: AWS Snowcone, Snowball, and Snowmobile, each tailored for different use cases, data volumes, and security needs. Snowcone is the smallest, designed for edge computing and data transfer on a smaller scale, while Snowball is better suited for medium-sized data transfers, with Snowmobile being the largest offering, capable of moving petabytes of data through a physical truck-based appliance.

Use cases for the AWS Snow Family are broad and versatile. Companies with limited internet bandwidth or facing bandwidth throttling often use Snowcone or Snowball to move large datasets efficiently. Snowmobile is ideal for enterprises that need to migrate massive amounts of data, such as video archives, scientific data, or datasets from data centers that need to be decommissioned. Additionally, the Snow Family can be used for edge computing scenarios, where processing data locally before sending it to the cloud can reduce latency and improve performance.

The pricing model for the AWS Snow Family is based on the size of the appliance and the duration of the rental. For example, AWS Snowcone has a lower cost, as it is smaller and meant for smaller data migrations, while Snowball and Snowmobile are priced according to their data capacity and transportation requirements. The pricing typically includes the cost of the physical device, shipping, and data transfer, with some variations depending on geographic location and additional services. AWS also provides support for data encryption and secure deletion, ensuring that sensitive data is protected throughout the migration process.

Overall, the AWS Snow Family provides a robust solution for businesses looking to migrate data securely, reliably, and efficiently. Whether it's moving a few TBs or several petabytes, AWS offers scalable options that can meet the demands of diverse industries, from healthcare to media and entertainment.

AWS Storage Gateway

AWS Storage Gateway is a hybrid cloud storage service designed to seamlessly connect on-premises environments with AWS Cloud storage. It enables businesses to securely store, manage, and process data in the cloud while retaining the flexibility to manage part of the data on-premises. The service supports various configurations, including file, volume, and tape gateways, allowing users to integrate on-premises systems with cloud-based solutions like Amazon S3, Amazon EBS, and Amazon Glacier. With AWS Storage Gateway, companies can transition to the cloud while maintaining their existing infrastructure and workflows.

Key use cases for AWS Storage Gateway include disaster recovery, backup, and archiving solutions, where businesses can replicate critical on-premises data to the cloud to ensure business continuity. It is also valuable in environments that need low-latency access to data while benefiting from cloud scalability and cost savings. For instance, a company can use a file gateway to create a local cache of frequently accessed data, while storing the bulk of the data in S3 for cost-effective long-term retention. This configuration makes it ideal for enterprises seeking a balance between cloud flexibility and on-premises control.

The pricing model for AWS Storage Gateway is based on a pay-as-you-go structure, with costs incurred for both the storage and data transfer used. For file gateway and volume gateway services, customers are charged for the amount of data stored in AWS and for data retrieval and upload activities. The pricing also varies depending on the specific AWS Storage solutions leveraged, such as Amazon S3 or Amazon Glacier. Additionally, tape gateway pricing is based on the number of virtual tapes created and the storage used in the cloud. AWS offers a Free Tier for Storage Gateway, allowing customers to explore its capabilities at no cost for the first 12 months, with a limited amount of usage.

AWS Storage Gateway enables organizations to bridge the gap between on-premises infrastructure and the cloud, supporting a wide range of use cases while maintaining high-performance and cost-efficiency. By integrating seamlessly with other AWS services, it provides a flexible and scalable solution to address complex data management and storage requirements. Its hybrid approach ensures that businesses can modernize their data storage infrastructure without sacrificing control or accessibility.

AWS S3 Transfer Acceleration

Amazon S3TA is a feature of Amazon S3 designed to speed up the transfer of files to and from S3 buckets, particularly for large files or long-distance transfers. This service leverages Amazon's globally distributed edge locations to accelerate the upload and download of data by routing it through the optimal path across the AWS global network. S3TA is particularly useful for organizations with dispersed teams, large datasets, or operations spread across different geographic regions, making data movement more efficient and less time-consuming.

One common use case for S3TA is the rapid upload of large media files, such as video and image assets, to S3 for content delivery or storage. Another use case involves backup and disaster recovery scenarios where data needs to be transferred quickly from remote locations to AWS for safekeeping. S3TA can also benefit enterprises migrating large volumes of data to the cloud or facilitating ML workflows that require large datasets to be accessed from various locations.

In terms of pricing, S3TA is charged based on the amount of data transferred and the distance between the source and the AWS edge location used for the transfer. The pricing is tiered, with rates varying by region and the volume of data moved. There is also a cost associated with the data retrieval from S3 buckets using the accelerated transfer, and it is important to monitor usage to optimize the cost-effectiveness of the service. The service provides customers with an easy way to estimate costs through the AWS Pricing Calculator.

Overall, Amazon S3TA is a powerful tool for businesses that require faster, more efficient cloud data migration and transfer capabilities. Its scalability and flexibility make it a valuable asset for a variety of industries, including media and entertainment, healthcare, and large-scale enterprise operations. By reducing transfer times and improving the user experience, S3TA helps organizations optimize their cloud workflows and reduce latency.

AWS Firehose

AWS Firehose is a fully managed service that simplifies the process of loading real-time streaming data into AWS data stores, such as Amazon S3, Amazon Redshift, and Amazon Elasticsearch. With Firehose, users can easily collect, transform, and load vast amounts of streaming data without the need for managing any infrastructure. It supports multiple data sources and is ideal for scenarios that involve high-throughput, low-latency data transfer. Firehose can be used for logging, monitoring, analytics, and building data lakes. Its integration with other AWS services makes it a powerful tool for businesses seeking to migrate or handle large-scale data streams effectively.

AWS Firehose is ideal for applications that generate high volumes of real-time data such as IoT devices, web applications, and log data from servers. For example, it is commonly used to stream log data from applications and servers into Amazon S3 for storage, or to load user activity data into Amazon Redshift for analytics. Additionally, AWS Firehose supports integration with Amazon Elasticsearch for real-time data search and visualization, making it a popular choice for businesses that need to perform live data analysis or monitoring. Its scalability makes it a suitable solution for industries such as e-commerce, gaming, financial services, and healthcare.

AWS Firehose follows a pay-as-you-go pricing model, where customers are charged based on the volume of data ingested and delivered to destinations. The pricing includes fees for data transfer, data transformation, and optional storage features like buffering. Costs are also affected by the frequency of data delivery and the type of destination used (for example, Amazon S3 or Redshift). There are no upfront fees or long-term commitments, allowing businesses to scale their data streaming capabilities as needed. Additionally, there are minimal costs for data transformation when using the service's built-in capabilities.

One of the key advantages of AWS Firehose is its ability to scale effortlessly based on the volume of data. Firehose automatically adjusts to handle the increased load without requiring manual intervention or infrastructure management. This makes it an attractive option for businesses with fluctuating data streams. Furthermore, its seamless integration with other AWS services allows it to fit into existing cloud architectures and workflows, making the migration process smoother. Whether you are consolidating logs, real-time application data, or sensor data, AWS Firehose provides an efficient, reliable, and cost-effective solution for cloud data migration.

AWS Transfer Family

AWS Transfer Family is a fully managed service that enables seamless and secure data migration to and from AWS using widely adopted file transfer protocols like SFTP, FTPS, and FTP. It facilitates moving large datasets, including files, application data, and backups, to Amazon S3 or Amazon EFS without the need for complex infrastructure management. Whether migrating data from legacy systems or enabling secure file sharing between organizations, AWS Transfer Family simplifies the migration process by supporting both on-premises-to-cloud and cloud-to-cloud transfers. It is particularly useful for industries that require secure, efficient data migration, such as healthcare, finance, and media.

One of the primary use cases of AWS Transfer Family is the migration of on-premises data to the cloud, enabling businesses to take advantage of the scalability, durability, and security offered by AWS storage solutions like Amazon S3 and EFS. It also supports hybrid architectures where organizations need to synchronize or migrate data between on-premises systems and AWS. Another key use case is secure file exchange, where businesses can provide external parties with access to specific data stored in AWS without exposing the entire storage environment, helping to maintain security and compliance.

In terms of pricing, AWS Transfer Family operates on a pay-as-you-go model, where customers are charged based on the number of hours their file transfer protocol endpoints are running, as well as the volume of data transferred. There are no upfront fees, and the service is designed to scale with customer usage, making it cost-effective for both small-scale and enterprise-level data migration projects. Additionally, customers only pay for the storage and transfer activities they actually use, which allows for a high degree of flexibility and cost control, especially when dealing with variable data transfer workloads.

Overall, AWS Transfer Family provides a scalable, secure, and cost-efficient solution for data migration and file transfer needs. With built-in integration with AWS storage services and support for industry-standard protocols, it enables businesses to streamline their data management workflows, improve security, and ensure compliance with regulatory requirements, all while reducing the complexity of managing custom transfer infrastructure.

Third-party connectors

AWS Cloud Data Migration Services leverage third-party connectors to streamline the process of integrating and transferring data between disparate environments, including on-premises systems and cloud infrastructure. These connectors offer specialized tools designed to bridge gaps between AWS services and external data sources, such as databases, applications, and enterprise systems. Use cases for third-party connectors include migrating legacy applications, consolidating multi-cloud environments, and enhancing hybrid cloud architectures. By utilizing these connectors, organizations can ensure seamless data flow and maintain application continuity during the migration process.

The pricing model for third-party connectors varies depending on the specific service and vendor. AWS typically charges based on the amount of data transferred, the number of connectors used, or the duration of the migration process. For example, some third-party connectors are priced on a subscription basis, while others may include usage-based fees, such as per-hour or per-Gb charges. This flexibility allows organizations to choose a model that best fits their budget and usage patterns. Additionally, some connectors come with tiered pricing, offering discounts for larger volumes or longer-term commitments.

Use cases for third-party connectors include enabling data transfers from legacy systems that are not natively compatible with AWS, simplifying database migrations, and integrating complex **enterprise resource planning** (ERP) solutions. For instance, a financial services company may use third-party connectors to migrate data from on-premises SQL databases to Amazon RDS while maintaining compliance with regulatory requirements. In another scenario, connectors can be used to migrate customer data from various CRM systems into AWS, enabling more powerful analytics and reporting through AWS-native tools.

The integration of third-party connectors into AWS Cloud Data Migration Services also plays a crucial role in reducing the migration timeline and ensuring minimal downtime. By leveraging pre-built connectors for commonly used platforms such as SAP, Oracle, and Salesforce, businesses can avoid the need for custom development. This allows organizations to migrate data faster and with reduced complexity, ultimately ensuring a smoother transition to the cloud with lower risks and costs.

AWS Database Migration Service

AWS DMS is a managed service designed to help users migrate databases to AWS quickly and securely. DMS supports a wide variety of databases, including both on-premises and cloud databases, allowing for seamless migration to Amazon RDS, Amazon Aurora, Amazon Redshift, and other AWS database services. Common use cases include migrating databases from on-premises data centers to AWS, consolidating databases into a central data warehouse, and upgrading to modern database versions. It can also be used for real-time replication of data across different environments, which is critical for maintaining data availability and consistency during migration.

When it comes to pricing, AWS DMS follows a pay-as-you-go model, where users are charged based on the resources they use during the migration process. The pricing factors include the type and size of the database instance, data transfer rates, and the duration of the migration. There are no upfront costs, and users only pay for the compute resources, storage, and any data transfer involved in the migration. Additionally, there are charges for ongoing replication if you choose to keep the data synchronized across multiple environments after the migration is complete.

The flexibility and cost-efficiency of AWS DMS make it a valuable tool for organizations of all sizes looking to transition their databases to the cloud. It minimizes downtime, reduces migration risks, and simplifies the process of moving large volumes of data. With features like automatic failover and monitoring, DMS ensures that your data migration is both reliable and cost-effective.

Schema Conversion Tool

AWS SCT is a key service for migrating databases to AWS Cloud environments. SCT simplifies the migration of database schemas from various source databases (such as Oracle, SQL Server, and MySQL) to Amazon Aurora, Amazon RDS, or other AWS-compatible databases. It converts database schema, including tables, indexes, views, and stored procedures, into a format compatible with the target AWS database. SCT also helps reduce manual effort in database migration by automating the schema conversion process, ensuring that applications using the database continue functioning post-migration with minimal changes.

SCT is ideal for organizations looking to migrate their on-premises or legacy databases to the cloud with minimal downtime and disruption. It supports migrations for both homogeneous (same database engines) and heterogeneous (different database engines) environments, such as moving from Oracle to Amazon Aurora or MySQL. Some common use cases include modernizing legacy applications, reducing operational costs by moving to the cloud, or increasing scalability and performance by adopting AWS-managed databases. It also supports migration projects that involve database upgrades or the consolidation of data sources.

AWS SCT is offered at no additional charge for the tool itself. The pricing is based on the usage of the underlying AWS resources that are involved in the migration process. This includes costs associated with the target database (such as Amazon RDS or Aurora), data transfer fees, and storage for the converted schema. AWS recommends considering the cost of the source and target database instances during the migration process, as well as the ongoing operational costs in the AWS environment after migration. The tool's use is typically free, but the migration project will incur costs based on resource consumption during the process.

One of the key benefits of using SCT is its ability to automate much of the schema conversion, minimizing manual intervention and the risk of errors. This significantly reduces the time and effort involved in complex database migrations. However, some limitations exist, such as SCT's support for only certain database engines and the potential need for custom tuning and optimization of the converted schema. Additionally, users may need to combine SCT with other AWS services, such as AWS DMS, to fully migrate and synchronize data.

Conclusion

This chapter provides a comprehensive overview of AWS database services, showcasing the versatility and scalability they offer for various data management needs. Amazon RDS, with its managed relational databases, provides a seamless and efficient solution for organizations seeking reliable and easily scalable databases. DynamoDB, on the other hand, caters to the demands of NoSQL databases, delivering high-performance and flexibility for applications requiring low-latency access to vast amounts of unstructured data. Redshift, AWS's managed data warehouse service, stands out for its exceptional analytical capabilities, making it an ideal choice for businesses dealing with large-scale data analytics and complex queries.

It also studies the analytical services for ETL processes, exploring the capabilities of EMR, AWS Glue, and Athena. Amazon EMR enables the processing of vast amounts of data quickly and cost-effectively, while AWS Glue simplifies the ETL process with its fully managed, serverless approach. Athena, a serverless query service, empowers users to analyze data directly in Amazon S3 using SQL queries without the need for complex data transformations. Additionally, the chapter highlights other key database services in AWS, such as Neptune for graph databases, ElastiCache for in-memory caching, and OpenSearch for powerful search and analytics. Together, these services form a robust ecosystem that caters to the diverse needs of businesses, ensuring optimal performance, scalability, and flexibility in managing and analyzing data on the AWS Cloud.

AWS Cloud Data Migration Services provide a robust suite of tools to ensure seamless and efficient migration of data to the cloud. Services like AWS Direct Connect enable high-performance, low-latency connections to AWS, while the AWS Snow Family facilitates the secure and physical transfer of large datasets. AWS Storage Gateway bridges on-premises environments with cloud storage, and Amazon S3TA ensures fast and secure uploads to Amazon S3, even from remote locations. For real-time data ingestion, AWS Firehose streamlines the process, and the AWS Transfer Family provides fully managed FTP, SFTP, and FTPS solutions, simplifying file transfers. Third-party connectors and the AWS SCT further enhance compatibility, offering a more customizable and efficient migration process.

In the next chapter, we will study AWS networking services, used to configure secure and reliable VPCs, subnets, and handling of firewalls and VPNs to better understand what AWS offers to handle all networking-related jobs.

Points to remember

- **Amazon RDS**: It is a managed relational database service, it:
  - Supports popular database engines like MySQL, PostgreSQL, Oracle, SQL Server, and MariaDB.
  - Automates backups, software patching, and scaling capabilities.
  - Provides high availability options with Multi-AZ deployments.
  - Read replicas for read scalability.

- **Amazon DynamoDB**: It is a fully managed NoSQL database service that:
  - Provides seamless and consistent performance at any scale.
  - Provides automatic scaling with on-demand and provisioned capacity modes.
  - Supports key-value and document data models.
  - Has global tables for multi-region, multi-master deployments.

- **Amazon Redshift**: It is a fully managed data warehouse service that:
  - Is designed for high-performance analysis using SQL queries.
  - Has columnar storage for efficient data compression and retrieval.
  - Has MPP architecture.

o Is integrated with various BI tools for analytics.

- **Analytical services for ETL include**:
  - o **Amazon EMR**: It is a managed Hadoop framework for big data processing that:
    - ▪ Supports Apache Spark, Hadoop, and other frameworks.
    - ▪ Has scalable clusters for processing large datasets.
  - o **AWS Glue**: It is a fully managed ETL service that:
    - ▪ Has serverless data integration with automatic schema discovery.
    - ▪ Supports various data sources and destinations.
  - o **Amazon Athena**: It is a serverless query service for analyzing data in Amazon S3 that:
    - ▪ Uses standard SQL for querying data.
    - ▪ Does not need pre-defined schema; schema-on-read approach.

- **Other main databases in AWS**:
  - o **Amazon Neptune**: It is a fully managed graph database service that:
    - ▪ Supports both property graph and RDF graph models.
    - ▪ Is used for building applications that work with highly connected data.
  - o **Amazon ElastiCache**: It is a fully managed in-memory caching service that:
    - ▪ Supports Redis and Memcached for caching and session management.
    - ▪ Improves application performance by storing frequently accessed data.
  - o **Amazon OpenSearch**: It is a fully managed, open-source search and analytics engine that:
    - ▪ Is derived from Elasticsearch, supporting various search and analytics use cases.
    - ▪ Provides real-time insights into large datasets.

- **AWS Data migration services**:
  - o **AWS Direct Connect**: Dedicated, high-speed connection between on-premises data centers and AWS that:
    - ▪ Reduces latency and improves bandwidth for data migration.
    - ▪ Secure and private transfer of large datasets to the cloud.

- o **AWS Storage Gateway**: Hybrid cloud storage solution connecting on-premises environments to AWS that:
  - Offers file, volume, and tape-based storage options.
  - Useful for backup, archiving, and disaster recovery.

- o **AWS S3TA**: Speeds up the upload and download of data to/from Amazon S3 that:
  - Uses AWS global edge locations to reduce latency and increase throughput.
  - Optimized for large file transfers.

- o **AWS Firehose**: Real-time streaming data transfer service that:
  - Simplifies delivery of streaming data to destinations like Amazon S3, Redshift, and Elasticsearch.
  - Supports continuous data flow with near real-time analytics.

- o **AWS Transfer Family**: Managed service for securely transferring files via SFTP, FTPS, and FTP that:
  - Facilitates data migration to Amazon S3 without requiring modifications to workflows.
  - Ensures encryption and scalability.

- **Third-party connections**: Integration with external tools like CRM, ERP, etc. that:
  - o Helps with replicating and migrating on-premises data to AWS.
  - o Useful for specialized needs, including lift-and-shift migrations.

- **AWS SCT**: Automates database migration by converting database schema from one platform to another that:
  - o Supports heterogeneous migrations (for example, Oracle to PostgreSQL).
  - o Reduces manual effort in schema conversion during database migrations

Exercises

1. **Which AWS service is a managed relational database service?**

   a. Amazon DynamoDB

   b. Amazon RDS

   c. Amazon Redshift

   d. AWS Glue

2. **What type of NoSQL database does Amazon DynamoDB belong to?**

   a. Document store

   b. Key-value store

   c. Graph database

   d. Column-family store

3. **Which AWS service is designed for analytical query processing of large datasets?**

   a. Amazon RDS

   b. Amazon DynamoDB

   c. Amazon Redshift

   d. AWS Glue

4. **Which service is suitable for running distributed data processing frameworks like Apache Spark or Apache Hadoop?**

   a. Amazon EMR

   b. AWS Glue

   c. Amazon Athena

   d. Amazon Redshift

5. **What AWS service is fully managed, serverless, and used for ETL tasks?**

   a. Amazon RDS

   b. AWS Glue

   c. Amazon Neptune

   d. Amazon DynamoDB

6. **Which AWS service allows you to run SQL queries directly on data stored in Amazon S3 without the need for ETL?**

   a. Amazon Redshift

   b. Amazon Athena

   c. Amazon RDS

   d. AWS Glue

7. **What type of database is Amazon Neptune primarily designed for?**

   a. Relational database

   b. Key-value store

    c.   Graph database

    d.   Document store

8.   **Which AWS service is a fully managed in-memory data store service?**

    a.   Amazon ElastiCache

    b.   Amazon RDS

    c.   Amazon DynamoDB

    d.   AWS Glue

9.   **What is the primary use case for Amazon OpenSearch (formerly Amazon Elasticsearch)?**

    a.   Graph database

    b.   Full-text search and analytics

    c.   Key-value store

    d.   Relational database

10.   **Which AWS service provides a fully managed graph database?**

    a.   Amazon DynamoDB

    b.   Amazon Neptune

    c.   Amazon RDS

    d.   AWS Glue

11.   **Which AWS service is designed for high-speed, low-latency connections to AWS?**

    a.   AWS Snow Family

    b.   AWS Direct Connect

    c.   AWS Storage Gateway

    d.   Amazon S3 Transfer Acceleration

12.   **Which AWS service provides a fully managed service to automatically ingest and load streaming data?**

    a.   AWS Snow Family

    b.   AWS Firehose

    c.   AWS Transfer Family

    d.   AWS Storage Gateway

13. **Which AWS service facilitates hybrid cloud environments by connecting on-premises storage to AWS Cloud storage?**

    a. Amazon S3 Transfer Acceleration

    b. AWS Transfer Family

    c. AWS Storage Gateway

    d. Third-Party Connectors

14. **Which AWS service is used to convert database schemas from one database engine to another during migration?**

    a. AWS Snow Family

    b. AWS SCT

    c. AWS Firehose

    d. AWS Direct Connect

Answers

1. b
2. b
3. c
4. a
5. b
6. b
7. c
8. a
9. b
10. b
11. b
12. b
13. c
14. b

Key terms

- Amazon RDS
- AWS DynamoDB
- AWS Redshift
- AWS Glue
- AWS EMR
- AWS Athena
- AWS Neptune
- AWS ElasticCache
- AWS OpenSearch
- AWS DocumentDB
- AWS Direct Connect
- AWS Snow Family
- AWS Storage Gateway
- Amazon S3 Transfer Acceleration
- AWS Firehose
- AWS Transfer Family
- Third-Party Connectors
- Schema Conversion Tool

Join our book's Discord space

Join the book's Discord Workspace for Latest updates, Offers, Tech happenings around the world, New Release and Sessions with the Authors:

https://discord.bpbonline.com

CHAPTER 7
AWS Networking

Introduction

In this chapter, we will explore the **Amazon Web Services** (**AWS**) Cloud, where the threads of connectivity weave together to create a tapestry of possibilities. AWS networking and **virtual private clouds** (**VPCs**) are the cornerstone of building robust, isolated, and interconnected infrastructures, allowing businesses to harness the power of the cloud while maintaining control over their resources.

We will unravel the layers of AWS networking, exploring the fundamental concepts that underpin the seamless flow of data within and beyond the cloud. Each section unveils a new facet of the AWS network architecture, from the basics of VPC creation to the intricacies of subnetting, security groups, and route tables.

Prepare to navigate through elastic IP addresses, peering connections, and virtual private gateways as we explore the complexities that ensure your cloud infrastructure not only meets but exceeds the demands of modern digital enterprises. This chapter explores AWS networking, empowering you to chart your course in the vast cloud possibilities.

Structure

In this chapter, we will discuss the following topics:

- Amazon Virtual Private Cloud introduction
- IP addresses in AWS VPC
- Elastic IPs in AWS VPC
- Default VPC in AWS
- Subnets in AWS VPC
- AWS route tables
- Internet gateway and NAT gateway in AWS VPC
- AWS Elastic Balancer types
- Network access control lists in AWS VPC
- Understanding VPC peering
- Unlocking VPC endpoints
- AWS networking and other services

Objectives

In the initial part of this chapter, our primary objective is to establish a solid understanding of the foundational concepts that constitute AWS networking. We will explore the core principles of VPCs, elucidating how they serve as the building blocks for creating isolated and customizable cloud environments. By exploring key elements such as subnets, security groups, and route tables, readers will gain insights into the architecture that governs data flow within their AWS infrastructure. The aim is to equip the audience with a comprehensive grasp of the essential components, fostering a solid foundation for more advanced topics later in the chapter.

Building upon the foundational knowledge, the chapter then transitions into a detailed exploration of the expansive AWS networking landscape. Readers will navigate through elastic IP addresses, peering connections, and virtual private gateways, unraveling the intricacies that contribute to a robust and interconnected cloud environment. The objective is to empower readers with the skills to design and manage their AWS network effectively. By understanding the role of each component and their interactions, users will be better equipped to optimize their network architecture for scalability, performance, and security.

Amazon Virtual Private Cloud introduction

At the center of AWS infrastructure lies the VPC, a fundamental building block that encapsulates the essence of cloud networking. A VPC is a logically isolated section of the AWS Cloud where you can launch resources in a virtual network defined by your specifications. This virtual network closely mirrors a traditional data center environment but provides the agility, scalability, and efficiency that the cloud promises.

AWS VPC enables users to design and customize their network architecture, creating a virtual environment that mirrors their on-premises infrastructure. From its humble beginnings as a solution to provide secure and isolated cloud environments, AWS VPC has evolved into a powerful tool for architects and developers, providing the flexibility to define and control their virtual networks with precision.

As an overview of what a VPC in AWS is let us dissect his main components:

- **VPC encapsulating the whole structure**:
    - **Subnets (Divided into public and private)**:
        - Public subnet(s)
        - Private subnet(s)
- **Internet gateway (IGW) connected to public subnet**:
    - Provides public internet access to instances in the public subnet.
    - **Network Address Translation (NAT)** gateway, in the public subnet, enabling private subnets to access the internet securely.
    - Private subnet instances use the NAT gateway for outbound internet traffic.
- **Route tables**:
    - Public route table associated with public subnet, routes to IGW.
    - Private route table associated with private subnet, routes through NAT gateway.
- **EC2 instances**:
    - Public subnet EC2 directly accessible from the internet via the IGW.
    - Private subnet EC2 accessible through bastion host or NAT gateway for outbound internet.
- **Security groups and network access control lists (NACLs)**:
    - Security groups attached to instances, controlling inbound/outbound traffic.
    - NACLs providing subnet level traffic control.
- **VPN/Direct Connect (Optional)**:
    - Securely connects the VPC to an on-premises data center.

Here is a diagram of AWS VPC and main components:

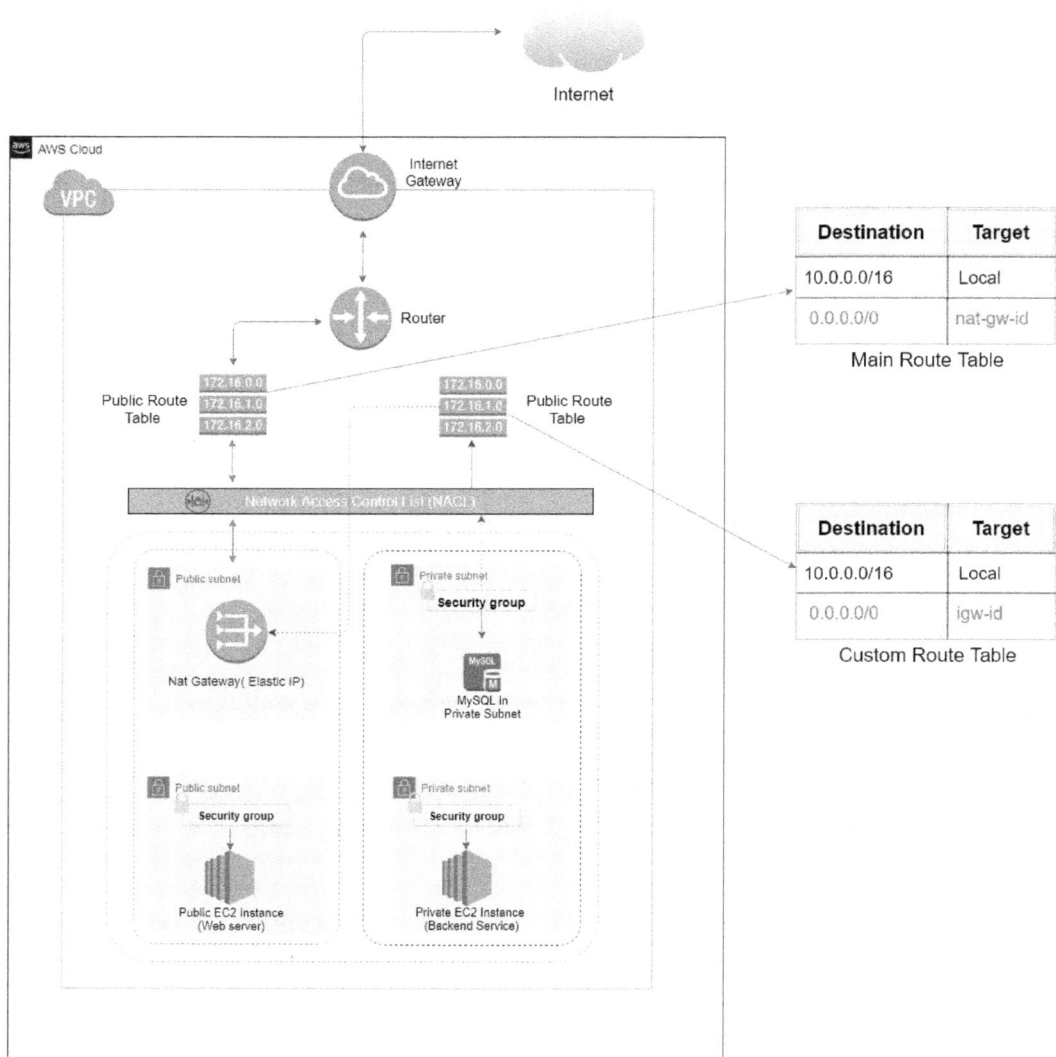

Figure 7.1: AWS VPC diagram

Definition of VPC

A VPC is a virtual network dedicated to your AWS account. Think of it as your slice of the AWS Cloud, where you have complete control over the network environment, including IP address ranges, subnets, routing tables, and security groups and NACLs.

With AWS VPC, users can launch AWS resources, such as Amazon EC2 instances, into a virtual network that they have defined. This virtual network is a secure bridge between the isolated components, providing a controlled and private space within the vast AWS Cloud.

VPCs enable users to partition a single AWS account into multiple virtual networks, ensuring that resources within one VPC are isolated from resources in another. This isolation is crucial for security and compliance, allowing organizations to maintain strict control over their data and applications. Each VPC can be further divided into subnets, providing additional layers of segmentation to accommodate different application and workload requirements.

Importance of VPCs

The utility of AWS VPC is multifaceted. It addresses key concerns and challenges faced by organizations transitioning to the cloud.

Here we list the main utilities a VPC provides:

- **Isolation and security**: VPCs enable users to create a logically isolated environment, providing a secure space for deploying resources. This isolation ensures that instances within one VPC cannot communicate directly with instances in another unless explicitly configured.

- **Customization and control**: VPCs offer a high degree of customization, allowing users to define their IP address range, create subnets, and configure routing tables. This level of control empowers organizations to design a network that aligns with specific project requirements.

- **Scalability**: As organizations grow, so do their infrastructure needs. VPCs provide the scalability required to meet increasing demands. Users can easily scale their virtual network by adding or removing subnets, adjusting routing tables, and deploying resources across multiple **Availability Zones (AZ)**.

- **Enhanced networking capabilities**: Beyond the fundamental advantages, AWS VPC brings forth advanced networking capabilities that elevate its significance in the cloud ecosystem. VPC peering allows for seamless communication between VPCs, expanding connectivity possibilities. **Elastic Load Balancing (ELB)** and NAT gateways further enhance the network's performance and reliability.

IP addresses in AWS VPC

IP addresses form the backbone of network communication, and in an AWS VPC, understanding how they are allocated and managed is fundamental to designing a robust and scalable architecture.

In the AWS VPC environment, IP addresses are assigned to resources such as instances, load balancers, and network interfaces. Amazon VPC supports both IPv4 and IPv6 addresses, allowing for a wide range of addressing options.

The main differences between IPv4 and IPv6 are:

- **Internet Protocol Version 4 (IPv4)**:

  o **Address format**: IPv4 addresses are 32-bit numbers represented in decimal format. They are written as four sets of numbers, separated by periods called **dotted decimal notation**. Each number or octet ranges from 0 to 255.

    Example: 192.168.1.1

  o **Number of addresses**: IPv4 provides about 4.3 billion unique addresses (2^{32}), but due to the growth of the internet, IPv4 addresses are running out.

  o **Address space**: Limited address space; this has led to techniques like NAT to extend its lifespan by allowing private IPs within networks.

  o **Routing efficiency**: Generally, less efficient because of the need for address conservation techniques like NAT.

- **Internet Protocol Version 6 (IPv6)**:

  o **Address format**: IPv6 addresses are 128-bit numbers represented in hexadecimal format. They are written as eight groups of four hexadecimal digits, separated by colons. Each group is a 16-bit block.

    Example: 2001:0db8:85a3:0000:0000:8a2e:0370:7334

  o **Number of addresses**: IPv6 provides a vastly larger pool of addresses, about 340 undecillions (2^{128}). This is enough to assign unique IP addresses to virtually every device on the planet.

  o **Address space**: Vast and capable of handling the exponential growth of devices connected to the internet, including **Internet of Things (IoT)**.

  o **Routing efficiency**: IPv6 offers better routing efficiency and network performance without needing NAT, simplifying network configurations.

- **Key differences**:

  o **Size**: IPv4 uses 32-bit addresses; IPv6 uses 128-bit addresses.

  o **Notation**: IPv4 is written in decimal, IPv6 in hexadecimal.

  o **Availability**: IPv4 is running out of space, IPv6 has nearly limitless addresses.

  o **Complexity**: IPv4 often requires workarounds like NAT; IPv6 is designed to be simpler and more scalable.

IPv6 is the long term solution to the limitations of IPv4, though both protocols are still in use today.

IPv4 addressing in AWS VPC

By default, when you create a VPC, you can specify the IPv4 address range for the VPC in **Classless Inter-Domain Routing** (**CIDR**) notation. This range determines the pool of available addresses for instances and other resources within the VPC. It is essential to choose an address range that is large enough to accommodate the anticipated number of resources while adhering to best practices for efficient IP address allocation.

IPv6 addressing in AWS VPC

For organizations requiring IPv6 support, AWS VPCs offer seamless integration. IPv6 addresses provide a vast address space, enabling the connection of many devices. When creating a VPC, you can associate an IPv6 CIDR block to ensure that your VPC can handle both IPv4 and IPv6 traffic.

Elastic network interfaces and private IP addresses

Each Amazon EC2 instance in a VPC is associated with an **Elastic Network Interface** (**ENI**), which, in turn, has one or more private IP addresses. This IP address is used for communication within the VPC, while the public IP address if associated, allows communication with the internet.

Understanding the allocation of private and public IP addresses is critical for designing secure and well-performing VPC architectures. Whether using default VPC configurations or creating custom VPCs, managing IP addresses effectively is a key aspect of AWS VPC administration.

Elastic IPs in AWS VPC

Amazon **Elastic IP** (**EIP**) addresses play a crucial role in the flexibility and reliability of your AWS VPC. An EIP is a static IPv4 address that can be associated with an instance in your VPC, providing a consistent and unchanging address for dynamic cloud environments.

EIPs are particularly useful for scenarios where instances need to have a constant point of access, such as web applications or databases. Unlike traditional static IPs, EIPs can be easily reassigned to different instances within your VPC. This capability is beneficial for scenarios where you need to replace or upgrade instances without changing the IP address associated with your services.

One notable characteristic of EIPs is their ability to be disassociated and re-associated with different instances, making them a valuable tool for high availability configurations. Additionally, EIPs can be moved between different AZs within the same region, facilitating seamless failover strategies.

It is important to note that while EIPs provide a level of persistence, they are not a limitless resource. AWS imposes some restrictions and charges for EIPs not associated with a running instance, encouraging users to manage and utilize these addresses efficiently.

In summary, EIPs in AWS VPCs offer a dynamic and flexible approach to IP addressing, providing a stable point of access for your instances while accommodating changes and upgrades within your cloud infrastructure.

Default VPC in AWS

When you create an AWS account, a default VPC is automatically provisioned in each AWS Region. The default VPC is designed to provide a hassle-free environment for users who are just starting with AWS services, offering a ready-made network configuration with sensible defaults.

Characteristics of the default VPC

Here are some of the main properties of the default VPC:

- **Automatic creation**: The default VPC is created in each region without user intervention. It includes default subnets, route tables, and security groups.

- **Internet connectivity**: The default VPC is configured to allow instances to connect to the internet. Instances launched in the default VPC receive both public and private IP addresses.

- **Default security group**: Instances in the default VPC are associated with a default security group. This security group allows inbound traffic from other instances within the same group.

- **Default subnets**: The default VPC includes a default subnet in each region's AZ. These subnets are configured with specific IP address ranges.

- **Default DHCP options set**: **Dynamic Host Configuration Protocol (DHCP)** options, such as domain name servers and domain name, are configured by default for instances launched in the default VPC.

While the default VPC provides a quick start for users, it is important to note that its characteristics might not align with specific security or architectural requirements. As organizations evolve and deploy more complex infrastructures, they often opt for custom VPC configurations to have greater control over network design, security, and resource allocation.

Subnets in AWS VPC

Subnets are a fundamental building block of a VPC. They allow you to divide your VPC's IP address range into smaller, manageable segments. Understanding subnets is crucial for creating a well-architected and secure network within AWS.

Key characteristics of subnets are mentioned in the following:

- **CIDR notation**: Each subnet is associated with a specific CIDR block, which defines the range of IP addresses available within that subnet. The CIDR block is specified when creating the subnet.

- **AZs**: Subnets are linked to a specific AZ within a region. This ensures that resources deployed in a subnet are distributed across multiple data centers for high availability.

- **Public and private subnets**: Subnets can be classified as public or private based on their accessibility to the internet. Public subnets typically host resources like web servers that require Internet access, while private subnets contain resources that should not be directly accessible from the internet.

- **Route tables**: Each subnet is associated with a route table, which determines traffic routing within the subnet. By configuring route tables, you can control how traffic flows between subnets and to the internet.

- **NACLs**: Subnets are protected by NACLs, which act as stateless firewalls. NACLs define rules for inbound and outbound traffic at the subnet level, adding a layer of security.

Use cases for subnets are mentioned in the following:

- **High availability**: Distributing resources across multiple subnets in different AZs ensures high availability and Fault-tolerance.

- **Security isolation**: You can control access to sensitive data and applications by strategically placing resources in public and private subnets.

- **Scalability**: Subnets provide a scalable way to organize and manage resources, accommodating growth and changes in your architecture.

- **Compliance**: To meet regulatory compliance requirements, organizations can implement subnet configurations that align with specific security and data protection requirements.

In practice, subnetting involves careful planning to allocate IP address ranges effectively and ensure that the network architecture meets performance and security standards. By mastering the intricacies of subnets, AWS users can design and implement resilient and scalable VPC architectures.

AWS route tables

AWS route tables are a fundamental component of the AWS networking infrastructure. They are crucial in managing and directing traffic within VPCs. A route table is a set of rules, called **routes**, that are used to determine where network traffic is directed. These tables define the paths that network packets take from their source to their destination.

VPC integration

Route tables are closely integrated with VPCs, which are isolated network environments within the AWS Cloud. Each VPC has a default main route table, and additional custom route tables can be created to meet specific networking requirements. Subnets within a VPC are associated with these route tables to govern traffic flow in and out.

Routes and propagation

A route in AWS route tables specifies a destination and a target. The destination can be a specific IP address or a range of IP addresses, and the target is where the traffic should be directed. Targets can include IGWs, virtual private gateways, NAT gateways, or instances within the AWS account EC2 fleet.

Those are the key features and main capabilities of route tables in AWS:

- **Route priority**: Routes in a route table are prioritized based on the specificity of the destination. More specific routes take precedence over less specific ones, allowing for fine-grained control over traffic routing. For any given destination IP address, the route with the longest matching prefix is chosen.

- **Association and disassociation**: Route tables are associated with subnets within a VPC. Each subnet must be associated with a route table. This association determines how traffic is routed within the VPC. Subnets can be easily moved from one route table to another, providing flexibility in network design.

- **Propagation of routes**: AWS route tables support route propagation, enabling dynamic route updates. This is particularly useful when working with virtual private gateways and VPN connections. Propagation allows learned routes from connected networks to be automatically added to the route table, simplifying the management of dynamic networking scenarios.

- **Internet and VPN connectivity**: Internet-bound traffic from private subnets typically flows through a NAT gateway or instance. AWS route tables facilitate this by defining routes to the NAT gateway for outbound traffic. In contrast, public subnets associated with an IGW have routes that direct traffic to the internet.

- **Multi-region connectivity**: AWS route tables are not confined to a single region. Network connectivity can be established across multiple regions through VPC peering, VPN connections, or Direct Connect. Route tables are crucial in configuring and managing these complex, cross-region networking setups.

- **Security considerations**: Careful design of route tables is essential for ensuring the security of a VPC. Controlling traffic flow at the network level is a key aspect of AWS security. Administrators can enforce security policies and segment different parts of their infrastructure by appropriately configuring routes and associating them with the right subnets.

The best practices of AWS route tables are mentioned in the following:

- Regularly review and update route tables to accommodate changes in network architecture.

- Leverage route propagation for dynamic routing scenarios.

- Use VPC peering for interconnecting VPCs securely.

- Implement route table logging and monitoring for enhanced visibility into network traffic patterns.

- Ensure proper segmentation and isolation of resources using route tables.

In conclusion, AWS route tables are critical components in the design and management of VPCs. Their flexibility and integration with other AWS services make them powerful tools for architects and administrators tasked with building and maintaining robust, secure, and scalable cloud infrastructures. Understanding and effectively utilizing AWS route tables is essential for anyone working with AWS networking.

Internet gateway and NAT gateway in AWS VPC

In the intricate tapestry of AWS VPC, the IGW is a pivotal architectural component. It facilitates seamless communication between VPC instances and the vast expanse of the internet. The IGW serves as the gateway for outbound and inbound traffic, enabling instances within the VPC to connect with the Internet and vice versa.

Internet gateway

At its core, an IGW is a horizontally scaled, redundant, and highly available component that allows communication between instances in your VPC and the internet. When an instance within the VPC needs to access the internet, the traffic flows through the IGW. Similarly, for inbound traffic from the Internet to reach instances within the VPC, the IGW acts as the entry point.

Configuring an IGW involves associating it with a VPC and updating the VPC route table to direct internet-bound traffic through the gateway. This seamless connectivity to the internet empowers applications hosted in the VPC to fetch updates, patches, or external resources, ensuring they remain current and responsive.

NAT gateway

While the IGW is crucial for instances within a VPC to communicate directly with the internet, scenarios arise where instances within the VPC need outbound internet access. Still, direct connectivity is not desired or feasible. This is where NAT gateways come into play.

A NAT gateway allows instances within a private subnet to initiate outbound traffic to the internet while preventing inbound traffic initiated by external sources. This additional layer of security enhances the isolation of resources within private subnets, mitigating potential security risks. By associating a NAT gateway with a private subnet and configuring the route tables accordingly, instances can leverage the NAT gateway to access the internet indirectly, enhancing security without compromising functionality.

Load balancers in AWS VPC

In the dynamic landscape of AWS VPC, load balancers emerge as a linchpin for ensuring high availability, Fault-tolerance, and efficient distribution of incoming traffic across multiple instances. AWS offers three types of load balancers: The **Application Load Balancer (ALB)**, **Network Load Balancer (NLB)** and the **Gateway Load Balancer (GLB)**.

ALBs, NLBs, and GLBs operate at different layers of your network communication. An ALB operates on **Open Systems Interconnection (OSI)** layer 7 and allows for application level traffic manipulation and routing. An NLB operates on layer 4 for network level traffic management based on ports and IP addresses. A GLB works across layers 3 and 7, providing balancing and routing services at the network level along with gateway functionality.

The OSI model is a conceptual framework used to understand and implement network communications between diverse systems. It consists of seven layers, each serving a specific purpose:

- **Physical layer**: Deals with the transmission of raw data bits over a physical medium.

- **Data link layer**: Ensures error-free transmission between adjacent network nodes through framing and error detection.

- **Network layer**: Manages packet forwarding, including routing through different networks.

- **Transport layer**: Provides reliable or unreliable delivery of data, including segmentation and flow control.

- **Session layer**: Manages sessions between applications, handling the opening, closing, and managing of connections.

- **Presentation layer**: Translates data between the application layer and the network, handling encryption and data compression.

- **Application layer**: Interfaces directly with end-user applications, providing services such as email, file transfer, and web browsing.

By standardizing these layers, the OSI model facilitates interoperability and communication across different network devices and technologies.

AWS Elastic Balancer types

Now, let us see the key differences and purposes of all AWS Elastic Balancers:

Following are the types of AWS Elastic Balacer:

- **Application Load Balancer (ALB):**
  - **Layer**: Operates at layer 7 (Application layer) of the OSI model.
  - **Use cases**: Ideal for web applications, microservices, and HTTP/HTTPS traffic.
  - **Features**:
    - **Content-Based Routing**: Routes requests based on URL, HTTP headers, or query strings.
    - **WebSocket support**: Supports WebSocket connections.
    - **Path-based and host-based routing**: Allows routing to different services based on the request path or host.
    - **Health checks**: Monitors the health of registered targets.
    - **Integration with AWS WAF**: Provides enhanced security features through integration with AWS **Web Application Firewall (WAF)**.

- **Network Load Balancer (NLB):**
  - **Layer**: Operates at layer 4 (Transport layer) of the OSI model.
  - **Use cases**: Suitable for handling TCP and UDP traffic, especially for applications requiring ultra-low latency.
  - **Features**:
    - **High performance**: Capable of handling millions of requests per second.
    - **Static IP addresses**: Allows the assignment of a static IP to the load balancer.
    - **TLS termination**: Supports TLS termination, offloading the encryption and decryption process from the backend.
    - **Health checks**: Performs health checks on targets to ensure they can handle traffic.
    - **IP address targeting**: Can direct traffic to instances in a VPC using IP addresses directly.

- **Gateway Load Balancer (GLB):**
  - **Layer**: Operates at Layer 3 (Network layer) of the OSI model.

- o **Use cases**: Designed for deploying and managing virtual appliances, such as firewalls and intrusion detection systems.

- o **Features**:

  - ▪ **Transparent network gateway**: Allows you to deploy, scale, and manage third-party appliances while maintaining the same IP address for the target.

  - ▪ **Traffic distribution**: Distributes traffic across a fleet of virtual appliances seamlessly.

  - ▪ **Health checks**: Regularly checks the health of virtual appliances to ensure they are available for handling traffic.

  - ▪ **Integration with VPC**: Integrates with Amazon VPC to ensure secure connectivity between your load balancer and targets.

In summary:

- ALB is best for HTTP/HTTPS traffic with advanced routing needs.

- NLB is suitable for TCP/UDP traffic requiring high throughput and low latency.

- GLB is ideal for managing third-party network appliances efficiently.

Each load balancer type has its own strengths and is suited to different use cases, allowing users to choose the right one based on their specific application requirements.

Understanding DHCP in AWS VPC

In the dynamic field of AWS VPCs, implementing DHCP plays a pivotal role in simplifying the management of IP addresses.

DHCP automates the assignment of IP addresses to instances within a VPC, streamlining network configuration and reducing administrative overhead.

In a VPC, DHCP operates by assigning private IP addresses to instances upon launch. This alleviates manual IP address assignment and allows for a more flexible and scalable infrastructure. The DHCP options set within a VPC define crucial parameters such as domain name servers, domain names, and the default lease time for IP addresses, offering administrators fine-grained control over the network environment.

One of the key advantages of DHCP in AWS VPC is its ability to dynamically allocate IP addresses based on the defined address range, ensuring efficient resource utilization. Additionally, DHCP supports reservation, allowing specific IP addresses to be assigned consistently to instances. This flexibility is instrumental in managing complex network architectures and ensures a seamless experience for administrators and end-users within the VPC.

Security groups in AWS VPC

Security is important in AWS VPC, and security groups are at the forefront of defense mechanisms. Functioning as virtual firewalls, for instance, security groups enable administrators to control inbound and outbound traffic at the instance level, enhancing the overall security posture of the VPC.

Security groups operate on a simple yet effective principle: instances are associated with one or more security groups, each containing a set of rules governing traffic. These rules specify the allowed communication patterns, including protocols, ports, and source or destination IP ranges. By leveraging security groups, administrators can enforce the principle of least privilege, restricting access only to necessary resources and minimizing the attack surface.

The dynamic nature of security groups allows for real-time adjustments to security policies. This adaptability is particularly valuable in cloud environments where instances may be added or removed on demand. Moreover, the stateful nature of security groups ensures that responses to allowed inbound traffic are automatically permitted, simplifying rule configuration and reducing the likelihood of misconfigurations compromising security.

Network access control lists in AWS VPC

Complementing security groups in the AWS VPC security architecture, NACLs provide an additional layer of control at the subnet level. While Security Groups operate at the instance level, NACLs operate at the subnet level, allowing administrators to define rules that apply to all instances within a subnet.

NACLs serve as stateless packet filters, inspecting inbound and outbound traffic based on user-defined rules. Each rule specifies a range of allowed IP addresses, protocols, and ports, affording administrators the flexibility to craft comprehensive network access policies. Unlike security groups, NACLs do not have the inherent statefulness, requiring explicit rules for both inbound and outbound traffic.

The hierarchical nature of AWS VPC security means that NACLs are evaluated before security groups. This order of evaluation allows NACLs to function as an initial layer of defense, filtering traffic before it reaches the instances. While security groups provide granular control at the instance level, NACLs offer broader, subnet level control, creating a robust security framework within the AWS VPC.

VPC Flow Logs

VPC Flow Logs are an indispensable tool for understanding and monitoring traffic within a VPC. This feature provides a detailed, real-time view of the flow of network traffic, offering insights crucial for troubleshooting, security analysis, and compliance.

Anatomy of VPC Flow Logs

At its core, VPC Flow Logs captures information about the traffic flowing through network interfaces in your VPC. These logs include data about source and destination IP addresses, ports, protocols, and actions taken on the traffic (for example, accepted or rejected). By comprehensively recording this information, VPC Flow Logs empower administrators with a forensic lens into their network activities. Configurable at the VPC, subnet, or network interface level, the granularity of flow logs allows for tailored monitoring to meet specific needs.

Use cases and benefits

VPC Flow Logs prove invaluable in various scenarios. From troubleshooting connectivity issues to analyzing traffic patterns to optimize network performance, administrators gain a holistic view of their VPC. Additionally, the logs play a pivotal role in enhancing security measures by enabling anomaly detection and identifying potential threats.

Understanding VPC peering

Amazon VPC peering is a service AWS provides that enables the connection of multiple VPCs within the same or different AWS Regions. VPC peering allows these VPCs to communicate with each other as if they were on the same network. This feature is crucial for organizations with complex cloud architectures, as it facilitates seamless communication and resource sharing between different VPCs.

The key concepts of VPC are mentioned in the following:

- **VPC**: It is a logically isolated section of the AWS Cloud where you can launch AWS resources. It acts as a private, virtual network in the cloud.

- **VPC peering**: It establishes a network connection between two VPCs, enabling them to communicate securely. This connection is established over the AWS backbone, ensuring low latency and high performance communication.

- **Peer VPCs**: It can occur between VPCs in the same AWS account or different AWS accounts. It allows for creating a direct, private connection between the peer VPCs.

The benefits of VPC peering are mentioned in the following:

- **Simplified network architecture**: VPC peering simplifies network architecture by allowing VPCs to communicate directly without needing gateways or VPN connections. This streamlines data transfer and reduces latency.

- **Resource sharing**: Peered VPCs can share resources like Amazon EC2 instances, databases, and other services, creating a cohesive and integrated application environment.

- **Cost savings**: VPC peering can reduce data transfer and network infrastructure costs by avoiding the need for additional VPN connections or transit gateways.

Keep the following facts in mind for setting up VPC peering:

- **Prerequisites**:
  - o Each VPC must have a unique CIDR block.
  - o The VPCs must not have overlapping CIDR blocks.
  - o The AWS accounts owning the VPCs must accept the peering connection.
- **Configuration**:
  - o **Sender VPC**:
    - In the AWS Management Console, you can navigate to the VPC dashboard.
    - After selecting the sender VPC, choose **Create peering connection**.
    - Specify the peering connection details and send a peering request.
  - o **Receiver VPC**:
    - In the AWS Management Console, accept the incoming peering request.
    - Update route tables to enable traffic between the peered VPCs.

Managing VPC peering connections

Monitor the status of VPC peering connections through the AWS Management Console or AWS **Command Line Interface** (**CLI**). Ensure the connections are in the active state for proper functionality.

For modifying or deleting peering connections, refer to the following points:

- Modify peering connection settings, such as enabling DNS resolution or modifying security group rules.
- Delete peering connections when they are no longer needed to stop resource sharing.

The best practices of VPC peering connections are mentioned in the following:

- **Security considerations**:
  - o Implement proper security group and NACL configurations to control traffic between peered VPCs.
  - o Use VPC peering across AWS accounts cautiously, considering security implications.
- **Routing**:
  - o Update route tables to ensure proper routing between peered VPCs.
  - o Avoid overlapping IP addresses to prevent routing conflicts.

- **Performance optimization**:
  - o Leverage AWS Direct Connect or AWS Global Accelerator for improved performance in low latency communication scenarios.

- **Documentation**:
  - o Maintain thorough documentation of VPC peering configurations, including CIDR blocks, routing, and security configurations.

By adhering to these guidelines and best practices, organizations can effectively utilize AWS VPC peering to build scalable, interconnected, and secure cloud environments tailored to their needs.

Unlocking VPC endpoints

AWS VPC endpoints are crucial in enhancing the security and efficiency of communication between resources within an AWS VPC. They are instrumental in reducing exposure to the public internet, providing a direct and private connection to AWS services. In this overview, we will discuss the types of VPC endpoints, their functionality, and the benefits they bring to AWS users.

AWS offers the following two primary types of VPC endpoints: Gateway endpoints and interface endpoints:

- **Gateway endpoints**: These are associated with Amazon S3 and DynamoDB. Gateway endpoints allow direct and secure access to these services from within a VPC without needing a NAT gateway or public IP address. This ensures that traffic stays within the AWS network, enhancing security and reducing data transfer costs.

- **Interface endpoints**: These endpoints provide private connectivity to supported AWS services, such as Amazon **Simple Notification Service** (**SNS**), **Simple Queue Service** (**SQS**), and others. Unlike gateway endpoints, interface endpoints use ENIs and private IP addresses, making them more versatile and suitable for various services.

Functionality of VPC endpoints

The primary function of VPC endpoints is to facilitate private communication between resources within a VPC and AWS services, minimizing exposure to the public internet. This is achieved through the following mechanisms:

- **Routing**: VPC endpoints utilize route tables to direct traffic destined for AWS services through the appropriate endpoint, ensuring a private and efficient connection.

- **Secure connectivity**: By leveraging the Amazon backbone network, VPC endpoints establish secure and reliable connections to AWS services without traversing the public internet. This enhances data security and reduces latency.

The benefits of VPC endpoints are mentioned in the following:

- **Enhanced security**: VPC endpoints allow resources within a VPC to communicate with AWS services in a secure and private manner, mitigating the risks associated with internet exposure.

- **Cost savings**: Direct connections to AWS services through VPC endpoints eliminate the need for NAT gateways and reduce data transfer costs by keeping traffic within the AWS network.

- **Improved performance**: The private connectivity provided by VPC endpoints, along with the Amazon high-speed backbone network, results in improved performance and lower latency than accessing services over the public internet.

Use cases

VPC endpoints find application in various scenarios, including:

- **Data processing**: When accessing and processing data stored in Amazon S3 or DynamoDB within a VPC.

- **Messaging**: This is for secure communication with Amazon SNS or SQS services.

- **Serverless computing**: Supporting serverless architectures by facilitating private connections to AWS Lambda.

Configuring and managing VPC endpoints

Setting up VPC endpoints involves defining the endpoint type, associating it with a specific VPC, and configuring the necessary security settings. Users can manage VPC endpoints through the AWS Management Console, AWS CLI, or AWS SDKs.

In order to maximize the benefits of VPC endpoints, users should consider the following best practices:

- **Fine-grained access control**: It utilizes IAM policies to define fine-grained access controls for resources accessing AWS services through VPC endpoints.

- **Monitoring and logging**: It implements comprehensive monitoring and logging to track endpoint usage, detect anomalies, and troubleshoot issues effectively.

- **Cost optimization**: It regularly reviews and optimizes endpoint configurations to ensure cost-effective usage of resources.

- **Security groups and NACLs**: It leverages security groups and NACLs to control inbound and outbound traffic to and from VPC endpoints.

AWS VPC endpoints are a critical component for organizations seeking to enhance their AWS infrastructure's security, efficiency, and cost-effectiveness. By providing private connectivity to AWS services, VPC endpoints empower users to build robust and secure architectures, supporting various applications and use cases. As organizations continue to leverage AWS for their computing needs, understanding and effectively implementing VPC endpoints becomes essential for optimizing performance and ensuring the integrity of their cloud-based operations.

AWS networking and other services

Here, we will describe the remaining AWS networking services that are important for your certification exam. Those services are sometimes less known and used than the previous services described in this chapter, but it is fundamental to have at least a basic understanding of their main responsibility and functionality in the AWS ecosystem as for all the main AWS networking services we have already seen before, so you can reach a complete view of the AWS offering, and also because you could find them during your exam certification.

AWS PrivateLink

AWS PrivateLink is a service that enables private connectivity between VPCs and supported AWS services. It allows you to access these services directly from your VPC without traversing the public internet, ensuring enhanced security, reduced latency, and improved performance.

With AWS PrivateLink, you can create endpoints within your VPC that act as entry points to various AWS services, such as Amazon S3, Amazon DynamoDB, and more. These endpoints are assigned private IP addresses, establishing a secure communication channel between your VPC and the AWS service. This approach is particularly beneficial for organizations prioritizing data privacy and security, as it eliminates exposure to the public internet and minimizes the attack surface.

AWS Direct Connect

AWS Direct Connect is a dedicated network connection service that links an on-premises data center or office network directly to an AWS Region. This establishes a private, high-bandwidth, and low latency connection, providing a more reliable and consistent network experience than internet-based connections.

AWS Direct Connect suits organizations requiring a dedicated and predictable network connection to AWS resources. By establishing a direct physical link, users can benefit from reduced data transfer costs, increased network performance, and improved security. AWS Direct Connect can be especially advantageous for large-scale data migrations, hybrid cloud architectures, and applications with stringent performance requirements.

Site-to-site VPN, Client VPN, and Transit Gateway

Refer to the following details for a better understanding of this topic:

- **Site-to-site VPN**: It allows organizations to establish encrypted connections between their on-premises networks and AWS VPCs. This enables secure communication over the public internet, extending the on-premises network into the AWS Cloud. It is a versatile solution suitable for various use cases, such as remote office connectivity, disaster recovery, and hybrid cloud setups.

- **Client VPN**: It extends the concept of VPN connectivity to individual users and devices. It enables remote users to securely access AWS resources and services online. Client VPN is a user-friendly solution that provides remote workers with secure access to the AWS Cloud, enabling them to connect to VPCs with encryption and authentication measures.

- **Transit Gateway**: It simplifies network architecture by acting as a hub that connects multiple VPCs and on-premises networks. It streamlines the management of network connectivity, making it easier to scale and control the flow of traffic between different networks. Transit Gateway enhances the scalability, performance, and simplicity of network architectures, making it an ideal solution for organizations with complex and dynamic workloads spread across multiple VPCs and on-premises environments.

Conclusion

In conclusion, the VPC is a foundational and powerful service that is critical in designing and deploying scalable, secure, and isolated cloud environments. Throughout this chapter, we discussed the key components, features, and best practices associated with AWS VPC. We explored the concept of VPCs as logically isolated sections of the AWS Cloud, allowing users to customize their network configurations, control traffic flow, and securely connect to on-premises data centers. Understanding the anatomy of a VPC, including subnets, route tables, and security groups, is essential for creating a robust and well-architected cloud infrastructure.

The flexibility of AWS VPC is evident in its support for IPv4 and IPv6 addressing, enabling organizations to adapt to evolving networking standards. Additionally, the concept of peering connections and VPN connections expands the reach of VPCs, facilitating seamless communication between cloud resources and on-premises environments. Security is an important concern in the cloud, and AWS VPC provides a robust set of tools for implementing network security measures. Leveraging NACLs and security groups, users can define fine-grained access controls, ensuring that only authorized traffic reaches their resources.

In the next chapter, we will explore AWS security in more detail, all aspects of the AWS shared responsibility model. We will also provide more information on VPC security, encryption, security best practices, compliance, and auditing, following standards such as GDPR, HIPAA, etc.

Points to remember

- AWS VPC is a logically isolated section of the AWS Cloud where you can launch AWS resources in a defined virtual network.

- Subnets are divisions of IP address ranges in your VPC.

- Route tables control traffic between subnets.

- IGW enables communication between your VPC and the internet.

- ELB distributes incoming traffic across multiple instances.

- NACLs control inbound and outbound traffic at the instance and subnet levels.

- CIDR notation is used to specify IP address ranges for your VPC and subnets.

- AWS provides a default VPC for each region, but you can also create custom VPCs to meet specific requirements.

- VPCs can be connected to the internet using an IGW or to your corporate data center through a VPN connection.

- ELB distributes incoming traffic across multiple targets (instances) within your VPC for improved availability and Fault-tolerance. It allows you to connect one VPC with another, enabling the resources in the peering VPCs to communicate as if they are on the same network.

- NAT enables instances in a private subnet to initiate outbound traffic to the internet while preventing inbound traffic.

- Use security groups to control inbound and outbound traffic to instances.

- NACLs provide an additional layer of security at the subnet level. They capture information about the IP traffic going to and from network interfaces in your VPC, providing visibility into network activity.

- NACLs allow you to privately connect your VPC to supported AWS services without requiring an IGW, VPN, or NAT device. It provides dedicated network connections from your on-premises data center to AWS, enhancing the performance and reliability of your VPC.

- Be aware of the default limits and quotas associated with VPC resources, and request increases when needed.

- Regularly monitor VPC performance using AWS CloudWatch and troubleshoot issues using VPC Flow Logs and other diagnostic tools.

Exercises

1. **Which AWS service is a managed relational database service?**

   a. Amazon DynamoDB

   b. Amazon RDS

   c.   Amazon Redshift

   d. AWS Glue

2. **What does VPC stand for in AWS?**

   a. Virtual Private Cloud

   b. Very Private Connection

   c. Virtual Public Cloud

   d.   Variable Private Configuration

3. **What is the primary purpose of a VPC in AWS?**

   a. To store data in the cloud

   b. To create virtual machines

   c. To isolate and securely connect AWS resources

   d. To manage billing information

4. **Which of the following is NOT a valid VPC component in AWS?**

   a. Subnet

   b. Elastic Load Balancer

   c. Internet gateway

   d. Route table

5. **How are IP addresses assigned within a VPC?**

   a. Automatically assigned by AWS

   b. Manually configured by the user

   c. Imported from on-premises networks

   d. Assigned by the Internet Service Provider

6. **What is the purpose of a subnet in a VPC?**

   a. To define security groups

   b. To isolate instances within the VPC

    c.   To connect to external networks

    d.   To manage billing information

7. **Which AWS service connects a VPC to an on-premises network?**

    a.   AWS Direct Connect

    b.   AWS VPN Gateway

    c.   AWS Elastic Beanstalk

    d.   AWS Lambda

8. **What is the function of a NACL in a VPC?**

    a.   To manage IAM roles

    b.   To control access to instances

    c.   To configure routing tables

    d.   To define security groups

9. **Which of the following is a valid VPC peering configuration?**

    a.   One-to-many

    b.   Many-to-many

    c.   One-to-one

    d.   None of the above

10. **In a VPC, what does a security group control?**

    a.   Inbound and outbound traffic at the instance level

    b.   Subnet level access permissions

    c.   Route tables for internet access

    d.   VPC-wide encryption settings

Answers

1. b
2. a
3. c
4. b
5. a
6. b

7. a

8. b

9. c

10. a

Key terms

- AWS Virtual Private Cloud
- VPC subnets
- VPC route tables
- VPC security groups
- DHCP
- CIDR
- NACL
- Internet gateway
- NAT gateway
- VPC endpoints
- VPC peering
- VPC Flow Logs
- AWS PrivateLink
- AWS Direct Connect
- AWS Transit Gateway

Join our book's Discord space

Join the book's Discord Workspace for Latest updates, Offers, Tech happenings around the world, New Release and Sessions with the Authors:

https://discord.bpbonline.com

CHAPTER 8

AWS Security

Introduction

Welcome to the world of **Amazon Web Services** (**AWS**) security, where safeguarding your digital assets is a priority and a shared responsibility between you and AWS. In this chapter, we embark on a comprehensive exploration of the intricate tapestry that forms the foundation of AWS security. As organizations increasingly migrate their infrastructure to the cloud, understanding the shared responsibility model becomes paramount. We will explore the nuanced collaboration between AWS and its users, demystifying the roles and responsibilities in securing the cloud environment.

Within **virtual private clouds** (**VPCs**), **access control lists** (**ACLs**) and security groups serve as the frontline defenders, fortifying your network against unauthorized access and potential threats. We will unravel the intricacies of these components, understanding how they work synergistically to create a secure enclave for your applications and data.

Encryption, a cornerstone of modern security, takes center stage as we navigate through the AWS landscape. From data in transit to data at rest, we will explore the robust encryption mechanisms available and discuss the art of key management, ensuring that your sensitive information remains confidential and protected.

In a world governed by regulatory frameworks and compliance standards, AWS provides a compliant and audit-ready environment. We will unravel the layers of compliance, understanding how AWS aligns with various industry standards and the tools at your disposal to facilitate audits and assessments.

Whether you are a seasoned cloud professional or a newcomer to the AWS ecosystem, this chapter promises to deepen your understanding of the security principles that underpin the cloud infrastructure, enabling you to architect and maintain a robust, secure environment for your applications and data.

Structure

In this chapter, we will cover the following topics:

- AWS encryption and key management
- AWS shared responsibility model
- ACL and security groups in VCPs
- AWS Network Firewall
- AWS Shield
- AWS compliance and auditing

Objectives

In this chapter, our primary objective is to elucidate the shared responsibility model and the security and compliance best practices offered by AWS, shedding light on the collaborative effort required to secure your AWS environment effectively. By understanding the distinct responsibilities of both AWS and the user, you will gain clarity on how to implement best practices for securing applications, data, and infrastructure. We will emphasize the crucial role each stakeholder plays in this shared responsibility, empowering you with the knowledge to make informed decisions and optimize security configurations within your AWS ecosystem.

Furthermore, we aim to provide a comprehensive guide to AWS security features within a VPC. Focusing on the intricacies of ACLs and security groups, our goal is to equip you with the skills to architect a robust network security posture. Through practical insights and examples, you will learn how to craft effective network access controls, mitigating risks and ensuring the confidentiality and integrity of your resources in the AWS Cloud.

Then the reader will gain insights into compliance and audit features of AWS to handle regulatory standards such as *General Data Protection Regulation (GDPR)*, *Health Insurance Portability and Accountability Act (HIPAA)*, and so on.

AWS encryption and key management

Welcome to the realm of AWS encryption and key management, where the protection of sensitive data takes center stage in the dynamic field of cloud security. As organizations entrust an increasing volume of critical information to cloud environments, the imperative to safeguard data has never been more paramount. In this exploration, we will unravel the intricacies of encryption techniques employed by AWS to secure data both in transit and at rest. From understanding the fundamental principles of encryption to exploring sophisticated key management strategies, this chapter aims to demystify the art and science of fortifying your digital assets within the AWS ecosystem.

Encryption stands as a formidable pillar in the defense against unauthorized access and potential breaches. As we continue, we will discuss the cryptographic foundations that underpin AWS encryption capabilities, demystifying algorithms, protocols, and best practices. Moreover, we will navigate the terrain of key management, exploring how AWS facilitates the secure generation, storage, and rotation of cryptographic keys. Through practical insights and real-world examples, this chapter aims to empower you with the knowledge and skills needed to implement a robust encryption strategy, ensuring the confidentiality and integrity of your data in the cloud.

The meaning of encryption at rest in AWS

Encryption at rest refers to the practice of securing data stored in persistent storage mediums, such as databases, file systems, and object storage, by transforming it into an unreadable format without the appropriate decryption key. In the context of AWS, this security measure is pivotal in mitigating the risk of unauthorized access and data breaches. AWS offers a variety of encryption options, ranging from service-managed encryption to customer-managed key encryption, providing users with the flexibility to tailor their security postures based on their specific needs.

AWS encryption at rest operates on the principle of defense-in-depth, ensuring that even if an unauthorized entity gains access to the physical storage infrastructure, the encrypted data remains indecipherable. This approach safeguards sensitive information from potential threats, internal or external, and reinforces the overall resilience of an organization's data ecosystem.

Key components of encryption at rest in AWS are mentioned in the following:

- **Service-managed encryption**: AWS offers several managed services that inherently provide encryption at rest. For instance, Amazon **Simple Storage Service** (**S3**) automatically encrypts objects at rest using **server-side encryption** (**SSE**). This approach simplifies the encryption process for users, as the encryption and key management are handled seamlessly by the AWS service.

- **Customer-managed key encryption**: For those organizations with stringent security requirements or regulatory compliance needs, AWS provides the option for customer-managed key encryption. This empowers users to take greater control over their encryption keys, allowing them to create, rotate, and manage keys using AWS **Key Management Service** (**KMS**). This level of control ensures that only authorized entities can access and decrypt the data.

- **Integration with AWS KMS**: It plays a pivotal role in the encryption landscape, serving as a centralized service for managing cryptographic keys used by various AWS services. Users can leverage KMS to create and control encryption keys, audit key usage, and integrate key management seamlessly into their data protection strategies.

As organizations continue to navigate the digital frontier, understanding the nuances of encryption at rest in AWS becomes integral to crafting a robust security posture. On the following page, we will discuss the practical aspects of implementing encryption at rest, exploring use cases, best practices, and the overall impact on data integrity and confidentiality in the AWS ecosystem.

Encryption in AWS S3 and KMS

Amazon S3 stands as a cornerstone in the AWS Cloud infrastructure, offering scalable and durable object storage for a myriad of use cases. As organizations increasingly entrust critical data to the cloud, the need for robust security measures becomes paramount. AWS recognizes this imperative and provides a comprehensive suite of encryption features for S3, ensuring that your data remains confidential and protected throughout its lifecycle.

Encryption in transit and at rest

AWS S3 encryption operates on the dual fronts of data in transit and data at rest. In transit, the use of secure communication protocols, such as HTTPS ensures that data moving to and from S3 buckets is encrypted, thwarting potential eavesdropping attempts. On the other hand, encryption at rest is accomplished through various mechanisms, allowing users to choose the level of security that aligns with their specific encryption level requirements. Refer to the following points for a better understanding:

- **S3 SSE**: AWS S3 offers SSE as a seamless and transparent approach to protect data at rest. SSE encompasses three distinct methods, each with its unique advantages. SSE-S3 employs strong, multi-factor encryption, using encryption keys managed by AWS. SSE-KMS leverages AWS KMS to grant more granular control over encryption keys, enabling key rotation and audit trails. **SSE with customer-provided keys** (**SSE-C**) allows users to bring and manage their encryption keys, offering a heightened level of control over data security.

- **Client-side encryption**: For users who seek to retain control over the entire encryption process, AWS S3 supports **client-side encryption** (**CSE**). This approach involves encrypting data on the client-1side before transmitting it to S3. Clients manage the encryption keys, ensuring that S3 only stores and retrieves the encrypted data. This grants users the highest level of control over their data's security, particularly useful for scenarios where compliance or internal policies necessitate client-side control.

Best practices and considerations in AWS S3 encryption

In the field of AWS S3 encryption, proper access control and permissions play a pivotal role. By utilizing AWS **Identity and Access Management (IAM)**, users can define granular access policies, determining who can access, modify, or delete objects within S3 buckets. This ensures that encryption keys and, by extension, the encrypted data, are only accessible by authorized entities.

AWS shared responsibility model

In the field of cloud computing, security is a concern for businesses and individuals alike. As organizations increasingly leverage the power and flexibility of cloud services, understanding the nuanced concept of the shared responsibility model becomes not just a necessity, but a foundational element of a robust security posture.

AWS, as a leading cloud service provider, has pioneered a paradigm that delineates the responsibilities of both the cloud service provider and the customer in ensuring a secure cloud environment.

Defining the shared responsibility model

The AWS shared responsibility model is a collaborative security framework that articulates the division of responsibilities between AWS and its customers. At its core, this model seeks to establish a clear delineation of tasks related to security, where AWS manages the security of the cloud infrastructure, and customers are responsible for the security in the cloud, encompassing data, applications, and configurations. This distinction is pivotal in fostering a cooperative approach to security, recognizing that both parties play indispensable roles in safeguarding the overall cloud ecosystem.

AWS shoulders the responsibility for the security and resilience of the underlying cloud infrastructure, including the physical data centers, networking hardware, and hypervisors. This foundational layer, known as the security of the cloud, encompasses measures such as data center access controls, network security, and infrastructure patching. AWS invests heavily in state-of-the-art security protocols, continuously updating and fortifying the cloud infrastructure against emerging threats. This ensures that customers can rely on a robust and resilient foundation for their cloud-based operations.

On the flip side, customers are entrusted with the responsibility of securing their data, applications, and configurations within the AWS Cloud, the realm referred to as the security in the cloud. This encompasses tasks like configuring access controls, implementing encryption, and managing user identities. Customers retain control over how their applications are configured, who has access to their data, and the security policies governing their cloud resources. This collaborative model promotes a sense of empowerment, as customers have the flexibility to tailor security measures to align with their specific needs and compliance requirements.

Understanding this shared responsibility is fundamental for organizations navigating the cloud landscape. It not only provides clarity on security but also empowers customers to make informed decisions about their security strategies within the AWS ecosystem. As we explore the layers of this model, subsequent sections will illuminate the specific responsibilities of AWS and customers, providing practical insights and best practices to enhance the security posture of cloud deployments.

In the next sections, we will explore how the shared responsibility model affects the most common AWS services, what the cloud offers, and what the AWS users must implement to make a robust and secure environment.

Shared responsibility model for Amazon EC2

The shared responsibility model in AWS for **Elastic Compute Cloud (EC2)** instances, as the provider, takes responsibility for the security of the cloud infrastructure, including the hardware, software, networking, and facilities that support EC2 instances. This encompasses tasks such as data center security, server hardware maintenance, and the hypervisor that enables virtualization. However, the onus shifts to the user when it comes to securing the data, applications, and operating systems running on EC2 instances.

Users must implement robust security measures within their EC2 instances, considering factors such as operating system patches, application security, and data encryption. Patch management becomes a shared responsibility, requiring users to stay vigilant about updating their instances with the latest security patches and ensuring the overall health of their virtual machines. This collaborative model fosters a secure environment where both AWS and users play integral roles in fortifying the overall security posture of EC2.

Effectively implementing the shared responsibility model for EC2 necessitates a strategic approach to security that spans multiple layers. Firstly, users must meticulously configure security groups and network ACLs to control inbound and outbound traffic to their EC2 instances. By customizing these settings, users can define the communication rules, creating a secure perimeter for their virtual machines within the AWS ecosystem.

Encryption is another pivotal aspect of the shared responsibility model for EC2. Users are responsible for implementing encryption mechanisms to protect data both in transit and at rest. This involves leveraging AWS KMS to manage cryptographic keys securely. By encrypting sensitive data, users fortify their EC2 instances against unauthorized access and potential data breaches.

AWS IAM enables users to manage access to AWS resources securely, defining and controlling permissions for users and applications. Additionally, AWS provides a wealth of documentation and best practice guides to assist users in aligning their EC2 security configurations with industry standards and compliance requirements.

In conclusion, the shared responsibility model for EC2 encapsulates a collaborative effort between AWS and users to create a secure and resilient computing environment.

By comprehending and actively participating in this model, users can harness the full potential of EC2 while ensuring the confidentiality, integrity, and availability of their applications and data in the AWS Cloud.

Securing an application deployed in EC2

Securing an EC2 application requires understanding the AWS shared responsibility model, which divides security responsibilities between AWS and the customer. AWS manages the security of the cloud, which includes the physical infrastructure, hardware, and foundational services. Customers, on the other hand, are responsible for security in the cloud, encompassing how they configure and manage EC2 instances, networks, and data.

To secure your EC2 application, start with instance-level controls. Use IAM roles for EC2 instances to grant minimal necessary permissions for accessing AWS services. Regularly update your instance's operating system and software to patch vulnerabilities. Enable security groups and network ACLs to restrict inbound and outbound traffic. Additionally, consider deploying an **intrusion detection system** (**IDS**) or endpoint protection solutions to monitor and protect against unauthorized access or malware.

At the application and data level, encrypt sensitive data in transit and at rest using AWS services like KMS and **Secure Sockets Layer** (**SSL**)/**Transport Layer Security** (**TLS**) protocols. Regularly review logs and Setup AWS CloudTrail and CloudWatch for monitoring and anomaly detection. Implement backup and disaster recovery strategies, such as EBS snapshots or S3 Versioning, to ensure data integrity. By combining these practices with AWS's foundational security, you can create a robust, multi-layered defense for your EC2 application.

Shared responsibility model for Amazon EBS

The shared responsibility model for Amazon **Elastic Block Store** (**EBS**) stands as a fundamental component, as EBS like EC2, are the fundamental components to host your application in the AWS Cloud. This model delineates the demarcation of security responsibilities between AWS and the customer, establishing a collaborative framework that ensures the integrity and confidentiality of data stored in the cloud. For EBS, the model manifests in a shared commitment to protect against a spectrum of potential threats, from hardware failures to malicious attacks.

At its core, the shared responsibility model for EBS encompasses the operational aspects, infrastructure security, and data protection. AWS takes charge of securing the underlying infrastructure, including the physical data centers, networking components, and the EBS storage infrastructure itself. This spans measures such as environmental controls, access controls, and continuous monitoring to safeguard against physical threats and unauthorized access.

On the customer's side, the responsibilities encapsulate the secure usage and configuration of the EBS service. This involves defining access controls, setting up appropriate encryption, and managing the data lifecycle. Customers are tasked with implementing best practices for data security, including encryption of data at rest and in transit, ensuring proper access controls, and implementing backup and recovery strategies. The customer is also responsible for monitoring their EBS volumes for any unusual activities and promptly responding to security events.

A pivotal element of EBS security within the shared responsibility model is data encryption. AWS provides customers with the tools and mechanisms to encrypt data at rest using industry standard encryption algorithms. Customers, in turn, must decide whether to enable encryption for their EBS volumes, selecting the encryption method that aligns with their security and compliance requirements. This collaborative approach ensures that even in the event of a physical compromise, the data remains encrypted and protected, mitigating the risk of unauthorized access.

Beyond encryption, EBS snapshots are a critical aspect of the data protection strategy. Customers are responsible for managing and securing their snapshots, ensuring that they are appropriately stored and encrypted. This extends to implementing access controls on snapshots to restrict unauthorized access.

In summary, the shared responsibility model for EBS establishes a cooperative framework wherein AWS and customers collaborate to fortify the security posture of data storage in the cloud. AWS shoulders the responsibility of securing the infrastructure, while customers are entrusted with the secure configuration and usage of the EBS service. This symbiotic relationship is fundamental in establishing a robust security foundation for the storage infrastructure, fostering a secure and resilient environment for businesses leveraging EBS within the AWS ecosystem.

Securing your data stored in EBS

Ensuring proper access controls for Amazon EBS involves managing who can access and modify your volumes and snapshots. Start by using AWS IAM policies to grant the least privilege required for users and applications to interact with EBS resources. Encrypt EBS volumes at creation using AWS KMS to protect data at rest and ensure only authorized entities can access the encrypted data. Additionally, secure snapshots by restricting their sharing and ensuring they are not publicly accessible unless explicitly needed. Regularly review permissions, monitor access using AWS CloudTrail, and remove unused or unnecessary volumes to minimize the attack surface. By implementing these controls, you safeguard your EBS resources from unauthorized access and potential data breaches.

Shared responsibility model for Amazon S3

Amazon S3 is a cornerstone of cloud storage solutions, providing scalable and durable object storage. Object storage in AWS S3 is a storage architecture designed to handle and store unstructured data as discrete units called **objects**. Each object consists of the data itself, metadata, and a unique identifier, enabling efficient retrieval without a traditional file hierarchy. Unlike block or file storage, S3 object storage is highly scalable and designed for durability, offering features like versioning, encryption, and lifecycle policies. It is ideal for use cases like storing backups, media files, big data analytics, and static website content, with seamless integration into AWS services for accessibility and management. However, its robust infrastructure does not imply a one-size-fits-all approach to security. AWS employs a shared responsibility model, a paradigm that defines the demarcation between AWS responsibilities for the infrastructure and the customer's responsibilities for data and access management.

AWS responsibilities

In the context of Amazon S3, AWS shoulders the responsibility for securing the underlying infrastructure, ensuring the physical security of data centers, and managing the availability and durability of S3 buckets. AWS employs a multi-tiered approach to physical security, encompassing strict access controls, surveillance, and environmental controls to safeguard the data centers where S3 is hosted. Moreover, AWS guarantees the durability of objects stored in S3, utilizing data redundancy and error-checking mechanisms across multiple devices and facilities.

Additionally, AWS manages the operational aspects of S3, including software patching, network security, and system maintenance. This alleviates customers from the burden of routine infrastructure management tasks, allowing them to focus on utilizing S3 for their specific storage needs. Users must recognize that while AWS provides a secure foundation, the responsibility for securing data and configuring access controls falls squarely on the customer.

Customer responsibilities

Customers leveraging Amazon S3 must address key aspects of security within the shared responsibility model. This includes defining access controls and permissions for S3 buckets, encrypting sensitive data, and monitoring and auditing activities within their S3 environment. The flexibility and configurability of S3 afford users the capability to tailor security measures to their specific requirements.

Managing access control policies is paramount in securing S3 buckets. Through IAM, customers can define granular permissions, ensuring that only authorized entities can interact with S3 resources. Moreover, the implementation of bucket policies and ACLs allows for fine-grained control over who can access, modify, or delete objects within a bucket. To secure S3 using identity-based policies, define granular permissions in AWS IAM policies attached to users, groups, or roles, specifying allowed actions, resources, and conditions (for example, IP address restrictions or **multi-factor authentication** (**MFA**) requirements). For example, limit access to specific S3 buckets or prefixes by using resource ARNs in the policy. Use S3 access grants (bucket policies or ACLs) to control permissions at the bucket and object level, but avoid ACLs unless necessary, as they are less flexible. Implement S3 Access Points to simplify and centralize bucket access for specific use cases, such as data processing workflows, by creating unique endpoints with tailored policies. Combine these tools to enforce least privilege and ensure secure, controlled access to your S3 resources.

Encryption is another critical facet of customer responsibility. AWS offers multiple options for encrypting data in transit and at rest within S3, such as SSL)/TLS for transit encryption and SSE for data at rest. Customers must decide on the appropriate encryption strategy based on their specific security and compliance requirements.

In summary, while AWS shoulders the responsibility for the security of the underlying infrastructure and operational aspects, users must actively engage in securing their data and managing access controls within the Amazon S3 environment.

Best practices and considerations for secure S3

Securing Amazon S3 effectively requires a proactive approach from customers, aligning their practices with industry standards and AWS best practices. Consider the following guidelines to enhance the security of your S3 implementation:

- **Least privilege access**: Adopt the principle of least privilege when defining IAM roles and permissions for S3. Only grant the minimum level of access required for individuals and applications to perform their tasks. Regularly review and audit IAM policies to ensure they align with business needs.

- **Encryption**: Embrace encryption to protect data both in transit and at rest. Leverage SSL/TLS for secure data transfer and consider implementing SSE using AWS KMS for enhanced control over encryption keys. Additionally, implement CSE for an added layer of security.

- **Access logging and monitoring**: Enable S3 access logging to capture details about requests made to your S3 buckets. Integrate these logs with AWS CloudWatch or other monitoring solutions to gain insights into access patterns and detect any anomalous activities. Implement real-time alerts for suspicious events to enable swift responses to potential security incidents.

- **Regular audits and reviews**: Periodically audit and review your S3 configurations, access controls, and encryption settings. Conduct regular security assessments to identify and address vulnerabilities promptly. Utilize AWS Config to continuously monitor and evaluate the compliance of your S3 resources with desired configurations.

- **Versioning and MFA delete**: Enable versioning for S3 buckets to preserve multiple versions of an object, providing an additional layer of protection against accidental deletions or modifications. Consider enabling MFA delete, requiring additional authentication for critical operations to prevent unauthorized access.

- **Secure bucket policies**: Craft and implement secure bucket policies and ACLs to control access to your S3 resources effectively. Regularly review and update these policies to accommodate changes in organizational structure, applications, or data access requirements.

- **Compliance and data governance**: Align your S3 configurations with industry-specific compliance requirements and data governance policies. Leverage AWS services such as AWS KMS to manage encryption keys securely and enforce data retention policies to meet regulatory standards.

By adhering to these best practices, users can fortify their Amazon S3 implementations, ensuring a secure and compliant storage environment. The AWS shared responsibility model provides a foundational framework, but it is the collaboration between AWS and its users that results in a robust and secure cloud storage solution.

Shared responsibility model for Amazon RDS

AWS has revolutionized the way organizations manage their databases through the fully managed **Relational Database Service** (**RDS**). However, the unparalleled convenience and scalability of RDS come with shared responsibilities between AWS and the users, as outlined in the AWS shared responsibility model.

At its core, the shared responsibility model signifies a collaborative approach to security, where AWS manages the security of the cloud infrastructure, while users are responsible for securing their data, applications, and configurations. In the context of RDS, AWS takes charge of the underlying infrastructure, patching the database software, ensuring high availability, and implementing physical security measures. This allows users to focus on optimizing their database configurations and managing access controls to safeguard sensitive data.

For RDS users, the shared responsibility commences with configuring their database instances securely. This involves defining robust access controls, such as setting up database user accounts, managing database roles, and establishing fine-grained permissions. AWS IAM plays a pivotal role in this phase, allowing users to define and manage access policies for their RDS resources.

Additionally, users are responsible for securing data within the database by implementing encryption, both in transit and at rest, to protect against unauthorized access and potential data breaches. As RDS users architect and fine-tune their databases, they contribute significantly to the overall security posture, ensuring that their applications and data are resilient to evolving cyber threats.

Operational aspects of shared responsibility in RDS security

Beyond the initial configuration, ongoing operational aspects of the shared responsibility model for RDS demand continuous attention. AWS handles routine maintenance tasks, updates, and backups to ensure the reliability and availability of the RDS infrastructure. However, users are accountable for implementing secure backup strategies, defining retention policies, and regularly testing the restoration process to guarantee business continuity in the face of unforeseen events.

Monitoring and auditing are integral components of the shared responsibility in RDS security. AWS provides tools like Amazon CloudWatch for monitoring database performance metrics, but users must actively configure and analyze these metrics to identify potential security incidents or performance issues. Moreover, implementing database auditing and logging features is crucial for compliance and forensic purposes. Users need to leverage AWS CloudTrail and database-specific logging mechanisms to capture events, allowing for traceability and visibility into database activities.

In conclusion, the AWS shared responsibility model for RDS encapsulates a dynamic collaboration between AWS and users to ensure the security and resilience of database workloads. As users leverage the benefits of RDS, understanding and actively participating in the shared responsibility framework is important to establishing a robust, secure, and compliant database environment in the AWS Cloud.

Shared responsibility model for Lambda

In the dynamic field of cloud computing, AWS Lambda stands as a pivotal service, offering serverless computing capabilities that allow developers to focus solely on code without the burden of managing servers. As organizations increasingly embrace the serverless paradigm, a fundamental understanding of the AWS shared responsibility model becomes imperative. This model delineates the distribution of security responsibilities between AWS, as the cloud service provider, and the users leveraging Lambda for their applications.

At its core, AWS Lambda simplifies infrastructure management, abstracting away the operational complexities associated with traditional server-based deployments. However, the shared responsibility model underscores that while AWS takes responsibility for the security of the cloud, users are entrusted with securing their data in the cloud. For Lambda, this means AWS manages the security of the underlying infrastructure, ensuring the availability, integrity, and resilience of the serverless environment. AWS oversees the physical security of data centers, network infrastructure, and the maintenance of the Lambda runtime environment.

On the users end, the responsibility lies in crafting secure Lambda functions, defining proper access controls, and safeguarding the data processed within these functions. To secure AWS Lambda functions, start by defining fine-grained access controls using IAM policies to ensure the functions have only the permissions they need to interact with other AWS resources, following the principle of least privilege. Use resource-based policies or VPC-based access to control who can invoke the functions. Safeguard data processed within Lambda by encrypting it both in transit and at rest using AWS KMS and enabling environment variable encryption for sensitive information like API keys or database credentials. Additionally, ensure input validation and sanitize data to prevent injection attacks or other exploits. Monitor and log Lambda activity using AWS CloudTrail and CloudWatch Logs to detect anomalies or unauthorized access promptly. Security aspects such as function code, environmental configurations, and access permissions fall within the user's purview. The granularity of AWS IAM roles allows users to define who can invoke their functions, control access to other AWS resources, and set appropriate execution permissions. This collaborative effort between AWS and users ensures a holistic security posture for Lambda-based applications.

Best practices and implementation strategies

In order to navigate the AWS shared responsibility model effectively in the context of AWS Lambda, adopting best practices is essential. Implementing a robust IAM strategy is paramount. This involves crafting fine-grained policies for Lambda functions, ensuring that only authorized entities can invoke or modify them. By the least privilege principle, users can minimize the attack surface, mitigating potential risks.

Encryption is another crucial facet of Lambda security. Leveraging AWS KMS, users can encrypt data both in transit and at rest, fortifying the confidentiality of sensitive information processed within Lambda functions.

Additionally, continuous monitoring and logging are integral components of Lambda security. CloudWatch Logs and CloudTrail provide insights into function execution, enabling users to detect anomalies and respond promptly to security incidents. To track errors and security incidents in AWS Lambda in real-time, you can use CloudWatch Logs and CloudTrail in tandem with Amazon CloudWatch Alarms and Amazon **Simple Notification Service** (**SNS**). When your Lambda function runs, it automatically sends execution logs, including errors, to CloudWatch Logs. You can setup metric filters in CloudWatch Logs to look for specific patterns, such as error keywords (**ERROR** or **Exception**), and create CloudWatch alarms based on these metrics. For security-specific events, enable CloudTrail to log API activity, such as unauthorized access attempts or changes to permissions, and configure CloudTrail Insights to detect unusual API activity. Integrate these alarms with an SNS topic, which can send real-time notifications via email, SMS, or push alerts to designated responders. This setup ensures that both operational errors and security anomalies are quickly identified and addressed.

Regularly updating dependencies and adhering to AWS Lambda best practices contribute to a resilient and secure serverless architecture. This involves staying informed about the latest security patches, following AWS Lambda security best practices documentation, and engaging in proactive threat modeling.

In conclusion, mastering the shared responsibility model for AWS Lambda entails a dual commitment, AWS ensuring the security of the underlying infrastructure, and users implementing robust security practices within their Lambda functions. By adhering to best practices and staying vigilant, organizations can harness the power of serverless computing while maintaining a strong security posture in the evolving field of cloud.

Shared responsibility model for Redshift

Amazon Redshift, a fully managed data warehouse service by AWS, has revolutionized the way organizations handle and analyze vast amounts of data. As we continue to explore the AWS shared responsibility model specific to Amazon Redshift, it is imperative to grasp the fundamental concept that forms the bedrock of AWS security.

The shared responsibility model delineates the distinct security responsibilities between AWS and its customers. In the context of Amazon Redshift, AWS undertakes the responsibility for the security of the cloud, encompassing the physical infrastructure, networking, and the hypervisor layer. This includes the robust design of the data centers, ensuring redundancy, availability, and compliance with industry standards. AWS also manages the security configuration of the Amazon Redshift infrastructure, ensuring that the underlying environment is resilient to potential threats.

On the other hand, customers are entrusted with security in the cloud, which pertains to the data, access controls, and configurations within their Amazon Redshift clusters. Customers have the autonomy to define and enforce security policies for their data, including encryption and access management. This level of control empowers organizations to align their security measures with specific business needs and compliance requirements.

As we explore the intricacies of the AWS shared responsibility model for Amazon Redshift, a key focus will be on understanding how customers can leverage AWS security features and best practices to fortify their data warehouse against a myriad of potential threats.

Implementing security measures in Amazon Redshift

Implementing a robust security posture in Amazon Redshift requires a comprehensive understanding of the AWS shared responsibility model.

One pivotal aspect within the customer's purview is data encryption. Amazon Redshift provides encryption at-rest and encryption-in-transit capabilities, allowing customers to safeguard their data throughout its lifecycle. It is also important to manage encryption keys securely using AWS KMS.

Access controls within Amazon Redshift are another critical facet of customer responsibility. By discussing the granular details of user roles, privileges, and permissions, we will unravel the strategies for enforcing the principle of least privilege. Understanding the role of IAM in the context of Amazon Redshift is important, as it provides a robust framework for managing access to resources.

Moreover, auditing and monitoring play a pivotal role in maintaining a secure Amazon Redshift environment. Leveraging AWS CloudTrail and Amazon CloudWatch, users gain insights into activities and potential security events within their data warehouse.

Shared responsibility model for DynamoDB

At its core, the shared responsibility model for DynamoDB underscores AWS commitment to managing and securing the underlying infrastructure and foundational components of the DynamoDB service. This encompasses physical data centers, networking, and the DynamoDB control plane. AWS takes charge of ensuring the reliability, availability, and resilience of the DynamoDB infrastructure, allowing users to focus on leveraging the database service for their applications without the burden of managing the underlying infrastructure.

On the user's side of the spectrum, the responsibilities shift towards the configuration and management of the DynamoDB environment. This includes defining access controls, designing appropriate table structures, implementing encryption, and ensuring data integrity. Users are entrusted with configuring fine-grained access permissions through AWS IAM to govern who can interact with DynamoDB resources. Moreover, users are responsible for optimizing DynamoDB tables, selecting appropriate read and write capacities, and implementing data backup and recovery strategies. By understanding and fulfilling these responsibilities, users contribute significantly to the overall security and efficiency of their DynamoDB deployments.

Navigating security best practices and implications

When exploring the AWS shared responsibility model for DynamoDB, it is imperative to consider security best practices to fortify your database environment. DynamoDB offers a range of security features that users can leverage to enhance the confidentiality, integrity, and availability of their data.

Encryption is a pivotal aspect of DynamoDB security, with options to encrypt data at rest and in transit. By implementing encryption mechanisms, users safeguard their sensitive information, rendering it unreadable to unauthorized entities. DynamoDB integrates seamlessly with AWS KMS, providing users with robust key management capabilities to control access to their encrypted data.

Access control in DynamoDB is orchestrated through IAM rules and policies, allowing users to define who can perform specific actions on their DynamoDB tables. Users should adopt the principle of least privilege, ensuring that each IAM entity is granted the minimum permissions required for its tasks. This granular control over access mitigates the risk of unauthorized or malicious activities.

Monitoring and auditing DynamoDB activities through AWS CloudWatch and AWS CloudTrail contributes to a proactive security stance. By analyzing logs and monitoring performance metrics, users can detect and respond to potential security incidents promptly. CloudTrail Logs provide an audit trail of actions performed on DynamoDB tables, offering transparency and accountability.

In conclusion, navigating the AWS shared responsibility model for DynamoDB requires a holistic approach that combines AWS's commitment to infrastructure security with user-driven configurations and best practices. By embracing this shared responsibility, users can harness the power of DynamoDB with confidence, knowing that their data is secure, available, and resilient in the AWS Cloud.

ACL and security groups in VPCs

In the world of AWS security, safeguarding your virtual infrastructure is a multifaceted endeavor. In this section, we will discuss the intricate mechanisms that fortify your AWS VPCs against potential threats. ACLs and security groups emerge as pivotal components in the armory of network defenses, shaping the perimeter of your VPC and determining the flow of traffic. As we unravel the intricacies of these constructs, you will gain a profound understanding of how to architect and implement robust network security policies to shield your applications and data from unauthorized access.

Beyond the VPC boundaries, we explore the broader landscape of defense against cyber threats. Firewalls stand as stalwart guardians, regulating traffic and enforcing security policies. We will also discuss the diverse options available within AWS to fortify your network perimeter, empowering you to make informed decisions about the selection and configuration of firewalls to meet your specific security needs.

Additionally, our journey extends to AWS Shield, a robust shield against **distributed denial of service** (**DDoS**) attacks. By comprehending the functionalities and configurations of AWS Shield, you will be equipped to proactively defend your infrastructure against the evolving landscape of cyber threats. Join us as we navigate through the layers of AWS security, unraveling the complexities to empower you in building resilient, secure, and highly available architectures in the cloud.

Security groups in VPCs

Amazon VPC serves as the backbone of your AWS infrastructure, allowing you to provision a logically isolated section of the AWS Cloud where you can launch AWS resources in a virtual network that you define. Within this field, security groups emerge as powerful guardians, providing a crucial layer of defense for your instances. A security group acts as a virtual firewall, controlling inbound and outbound traffic at the instance level.

Security groups are stateful, meaning that if you allow inbound traffic from a specific IP address, the corresponding outbound traffic is automatically allowed. This simplifies the task of defining rules and reduces the likelihood of misconfigurations. Each security group operates at the instance level, and an instance can be associated with multiple security groups, enabling fine-grained control over network access.

The rule set within a security group is explicit, specifying allowed traffic rather than denied traffic. This design ensures that, by default, all inbound and outbound traffic is denied. Administrators then craft rules to permit necessary traffic explicitly, adhering to the principle of least privilege. This approach enhances security by minimizing the attack surface and reducing the risk of inadvertent exposure.

Security groups can be applied to instances based on tags, making it easier to manage and scale security policies across your environment. As your infrastructure evolves, the dynamic and scalable nature of security groups ensures that security policies can adapt seamlessly, providing a robust foundation for the evolving needs of your applications and services.

Best practices and use cases for AWS security groups

In order to maximize the efficacy of security groups within your VPC, it is essential to adhere to best practices and understand common use cases. First and foremost, embracing the principle of least privilege is paramount. By only allowing necessary traffic, you minimize potential security vulnerabilities. Regularly reviewing and auditing security group rules ensures that your security posture remains aligned with your organizational policies and evolving requirements.

Security groups prove invaluable in the context of microservices architecture, where numerous services communicate across a dynamic and distributed environment. Here, Security groups facilitate secure communication by enabling developers to define and manage communication paths between services with precision. Moreover, security groups play a pivotal role in multi-tier applications, allowing you to segregate and secure different layers of your application stack.

Real-time monitoring and logging of security group activities provide insights into the network traffic patterns, aiding in the identification of potential security incidents. AWS CloudWatch Logs and AWS CloudTrail can be leveraged to gain visibility and respond promptly to security events. Regularly updating security groups based on these insights ensures that your security policies remain adaptive and resilient against emerging threats.

In conclusion, AWS security groups in VPCs embody a fundamental element of AWS security, offering a flexible, scalable, and intuitive approach to network security. By understanding their intricacies, adhering to best practices, and aligning their use with your application architecture, you can fortify your AWS environment and navigate the field of cloud security with confidence.

ACL in VPCs

ACLs serve as the first line of defense in securing traffic at the subnet level within a VPC. Think of them as virtual stateless firewalls that evaluate and control inbound and outbound traffic at the subnet level. Unlike security groups, which operate at the instance level, ACLs are associated with subnets and act as traffic filters for controlling traffic entering or leaving a subnet.

Each subnet in a VPC comes with an associated ACL, acting as a default outbound and inbound rule for all traffic in the absence of any custom rules. These rules are evaluated based on numbered entries, with a lower number indicating a higher priority. It is important to note that ACLs are stateless, meaning they do not keep track of the state of established connections. For every inbound and outbound rule, you must explicitly define the rules for both directions.

Configuring and customizing ACLs

Configuring ACLs involves defining rules that explicitly allow or deny traffic based on criteria such as IP addresses, protocols, and port ranges. When multiple rules exist, AWS evaluates them in order, and the first rule that matches the traffic is applied. This sequential evaluation makes it imperative to design ACLs thoughtfully, ensuring that rules are structured to meet security and operational requirements effectively.

ACLs offer the flexibility to tailor rules for specific scenarios, enabling users to create a customized security posture for their VPC. In addition to specifying IP addresses and port ranges, ACLs can be associated with specific traffic types, allowing for granular control over different types of communication. Whether it is allowing or denying access to specific IP addresses, or regulating traffic based on protocols, ACLs provide the necessary controls to enforce a robust security framework within your VPC.

Best practices for AWS ACLs

In order to leverage the full potential of ACLs in AWS VPCs, it is essential to adhere to best practices. One crucial consideration is to avoid overly permissive rules, as they might inadvertently expose resources to potential security threats. Regular audits of ACL configurations, combined with thorough testing, help ensure that the intended security policies are effectively implemented.

Additionally, AWS provides default outbound rules in ACLs, allowing all outbound traffic by default. This lenient outbound stance underscores the importance of configuring outbound rules to restrict unnecessary communication and prevent data exfiltration. As ACLs are stateless, it is crucial to define rules for both inbound and outbound traffic to facilitate desired communication between resources.

In conclusion, AWS ACLs in VPCs offer a robust mechanism for shaping and securing network traffic at the subnet level. Understanding the intricacies of ACLs empowers users to implement effective security controls, mitigating potential risks and ensuring the confidentiality and integrity of data within their VPCs. By following best practices and leveraging the flexibility of ACL configurations, users can architect a resilient network security posture that aligns with their specific operational and security requirements in the dynamic landscape of the AWS Cloud.

AWS Network Firewall

AWS Network Firewall, a managed service, is designed to protect your applications and data hosted in VPCs by allowing or denying traffic based on a set of predefined rules. At its core, it operates as a virtual barrier, filtering incoming and outgoing traffic to and from resources within the VPC. The AWS Network Firewall supports both stateful and stateless rule evaluations, providing flexibility in defining security policies based on the specific needs of your applications.

Stateful rule evaluations enable the firewall to make decisions based on the context of the traffic, allowing responses to incoming packets without the need for explicit rules. This ensures that established connections are seamlessly monitored and secured. Stateless rule evaluations, on the other hand, evaluate each packet in isolation, making decisions based solely on the defined rules. This combination of stateful and stateless capabilities provides a robust foundation for crafting nuanced security policies tailored to the intricacies of your VPC architecture.

Key features and functionality

AWS Firewall in VPCs comes equipped with a multitude of features that empower users to fortify their network security posture. At the forefront is the ability to define custom rules, allowing organizations to tailor their security policies to specific application requirements. Whether restricting access to certain ports, IP addresses, or protocols, the granularity of these rules provides a fine-tuned control mechanism.

Additionally, AWS Firewall seamlessly integrates with other AWS services, such as AWS **Web Application Firewall** (**WAF**), allowing for a comprehensive security strategy. By leveraging AWS Firewall in conjunction with AWS WAF, users can protect their applications from a wide array of web-based attacks, including SQL injection, **cross-site scripting** (**XSS**), and more. This integrative approach enables a holistic security framework within the VPC, safeguarding against diverse threats.

Furthermore, AWS Firewall offers insightful logging and monitoring capabilities, allowing users to gain visibility into traffic patterns and potential security incidents. By leveraging Amazon CloudWatch, users can create custom metrics and alarms based on firewall logs, enabling proactive responses to security events. This level of visibility is instrumental in maintaining the integrity of your VPC and swiftly addressing any emerging security concerns.

Scalability and automation

As organizations scale their infrastructure, the need for scalable security solutions becomes paramount. AWS Firewall caters to this requirement by seamlessly integrating with AWS CloudFormation and AWS Lambda. Through CloudFormation, users can automate the deployment of firewall rules, ensuring consistency and efficiency across different environments. Integration with Lambda enables the execution of custom scripts and actions based on specific events, offering a dynamic and responsive security architecture.

In conclusion, AWS Firewall in VPCs stands as a pivotal tool in the arsenal of AWS security offerings. Its flexibility, scalability, and integrative capabilities empower organizations to craft robust security policies tailored to their specific needs. By leveraging the features and functionalities of AWS Firewall, users can fortify their VPCs against a constantly evolving threat landscape, ensuring the resilience and security of their cloud-based applications and data. As cloud security continues to be a top priority, AWS Firewall remains a stalwart guardian within the AWS ecosystem.

AWS Shield

At its core, AWS Shield is a managed DDoS protection service that operates in concert with the global AWS network to safeguard against a spectrum of DDoS attacks. DDoS attacks, which aim to overwhelm online services by flooding them with traffic, can have debilitating effects on the availability and performance of applications. AWS Shield employs a multi-layered defense strategy, leveraging machine learning, anomaly detection, and a robust traffic scrubbing infrastructure to identify and mitigate DDoS threats in real-time.

One of the distinctive features of AWS Shield is its seamless integration with AWS's vast global network infrastructure. This integration enables Shield to provide DDoS protection at the edge, mitigating attacks close to their source and preventing them from reaching the targeted AWS resources. This approach not only enhances the effectiveness of DDoS protection but also ensures minimal impact on the performance of the protected applications. AWS Shield is available in two tiers: Standard and Advanced. The Standard tier is automatically included at no extra cost for all AWS customers, providing essential DDoS protection. Meanwhile, the Advanced tier offers an additional layer of security, including more extensive DDoS protection capabilities and access to a team of DDoS experts for personalized guidance during and after an attack.

Key features and benefits of AWS Shield

AWS Shield's robust suite of features extends beyond mere DDoS protection, encompassing a range of capabilities designed to fortify the security posture of AWS-hosted applications. Some features and benefits are mentioned in the following:

- **Global threat environment monitoring**: AWS Shield continuously monitors the global threat landscape, leveraging the vast reach of the AWS network to detect and respond to emerging DDoS threats promptly.

- **Automatic DDoS mitigation**: The service provides automatic DDoS mitigation, leveraging machine learning algorithms and real-time traffic analysis to identify and thwart malicious traffic patterns without requiring user intervention.

- **Anomaly detection and behavioral analysis**: AWS Shield employs sophisticated anomaly detection and behavioral analysis to identify abnormal patterns in traffic, allowing it to adapt and respond to evolving DDoS tactics.

- **WAF integration**: AWS Shield seamlessly integrates with AWS WAF, providing a holistic approach to application security by combining DDoS protection with the capability to filter and control web traffic based on defined rules.

- **Global response team**: AWS Shield Advanced subscribers benefit from the expertise of the AWS **DDoS Response Team** (**DRT**), a group of security experts available 24/7 to provide guidance and support during and after a DDoS attack.

In conclusion, AWS Shield stands as a formidable guardian against the ever-present threat of DDoS attacks, reinforcing the security foundations of AWS-hosted applications. With its proactive and reactive measures, coupled with global threat intelligence and expert support, AWS Shield empowers organizations to navigate the digital landscape with confidence, ensuring the availability and reliability of their critical online assets.

Versioning and logging

Enabling versioning on S3 buckets can be a crucial aspect of your data protection strategy. Versioning allows you to preserve, retrieve, and restore every version of every object stored in a bucket. This can be invaluable in scenarios where accidental deletion or data corruption occurs, providing a historical record of changes. Additionally, enabling AWS CloudTrail for S3 allows you to capture API events related to bucket access and object manipulations, aiding in security audits and compliance efforts.

Regular key rotation and auditing

A fundamental security best practice in AWS S3 encryption involves the regular rotation of encryption keys. Key rotation is especially pertinent when utilizing AWS KMS (SSE-KMS) for SSE. Rotating keys helps mitigate risks associated with prolonged key exposure. Simultaneously, implementing auditing mechanisms, such as AWS CloudTrail, ensures that all activities related to your S3 buckets are logged and can be reviewed for potential security incidents.

In conclusion, AWS S3 encryption provides a robust framework to safeguard your data in the cloud, offering a blend of SSE and CSE options. By adhering to best practices, managing access controls, and embracing encryption features, users can harness the full power of AWS S3 while maintaining the highest standards of data security and compliance.

CloudHSM

AWS CloudHSM, a dedicated **hardware security module** (**HSM**) service, stands as a cornerstone in AWS's suite of security offerings, providing customers with a robust and scalable solution for managing cryptographic keys and ensuring the security of sensitive data. In the ever-evolving landscape of cloud computing, where data protection is important, AWS CloudHSM emerges as a specialized service designed to meet the high standards of security-conscious organizations.

At its core, AWS CloudHSM offers a secure and tamper-resistant environment for key storage and cryptographic operations. This is achieved using dedicated HSMs, which are hardware devices specifically designed to safeguard cryptographic keys. By utilizing FIPS 140-2 Security Level 3 certified HSMs, AWS CloudHSM ensures that cryptographic operations are performed in a physically secure and verifiable environment, meeting the stringent requirements set by various industry compliance standards.

One of the key advantages of AWS CloudHSM is its ability to enable organizations to maintain full control over their cryptographic keys. This level of control is crucial for regulatory compliance and data governance, allowing businesses to manage their keys securely while leveraging the benefits of the AWS Cloud infrastructure. As organizations migrate sensitive workloads to the cloud, the need for a scalable and secure key management solution becomes increasingly apparent, and AWS CloudHSM rises to meet this demand with its flexible and scalable architecture.

Key features and use cases

AWS CloudHSM boasts a set of compelling features that cater to a diverse range of use cases, making it a versatile solution for organizations with varying security requirements. The service integrates seamlessly with other AWS services, allowing customers to incorporate robust key management into their cloud-based applications. The following key features highlight the capabilities of AWS CloudHSM:

- **Highly secure key storage**: CloudHSM ensures the security of cryptographic keys by storing them within dedicated hardware modules that are tamper-evident and resistant to physical attacks. This provides a level of assurance that is vital for applications requiring the highest standards of security.

- **Comprehensive key management**: Organizations can generate, store, and manage their cryptographic keys within the CloudHSM environment. This includes support for various cryptographic algorithms, allowing flexibility in key management-based on specific security and compliance requirements.

- **Integration with AWS services**: CloudHSM seamlessly integrates with various AWS services, including Amazon RDS, Amazon Redshift, and Amazon S3. This integration allows customers to enhance the security of their data and applications by utilizing CloudHSM to manage encryption keys for these services.

- **Scalability and availability**: CloudHSM is designed to scale with the needs of the organization. Whether handling a few keys or a large-scale key management infrastructure, CloudHSM can be seamlessly integrated and scaled to meet evolving requirements. Additionally, the service provides high availability by distributing HSMs across multiple availability zones.

- **Regulatory compliance**: AWS CloudHSM is designed to help organizations meet stringent regulatory requirements. With FIPS 140-2 Security Level 3 certification, the service aligns with industry standards and is suitable for applications in finance, healthcare, and other sectors with rigorous compliance demands.

Use cases for AWS CloudHSM span a wide spectrum, including securing communication between applications, protecting sensitive data in databases, and ensuring the integrity of cryptographic operations within the AWS Cloud. Whether in finance, healthcare, or any industry with stringent security and compliance requirements, AWS CloudHSM empowers organizations to take control of their cryptographic keys and elevate the security posture of their cloud-based infrastructure.

AWS Certificate Manager

AWS Certificate Manager (**ACM**) stands as a cornerstone in the realm of cloud security, providing a seamless and automated solution for managing SSL/TLS certificates. In an era where online security is important, ACM simplifies the often complex and time-consuming process of obtaining, deploying, and renewing digital certificates. This page offers an exploration of ACM's features, benefits, and its pivotal role in enhancing the security posture of applications hosted on AWS.

At its core, ACM streamlines the certificate management process by offering a centralized and scalable service. One of its standout features is the ability to provision SSL/TLS certificates for use with AWS services like **Elastic Load Balancers** (**ELB**), Amazon CloudFront, and APIs deployed on Amazon API Gateway. ACM takes the hassle out of certificate management by automatically handling the complexities of certificate renewal, eliminating the risk of expired certificates, and ensuring the continuous availability of secure connections.

Moreover, ACM operates with a user-friendly interface, allowing users to easily request, import, and manage certificates through the AWS Management Console or programmatically via the AWS **Command Line Interface** (**CLI**) and SDKs. This accessibility extends to the integration with other AWS services, fostering a cohesive ecosystem for secure and scalable cloud applications. The robust and highly available nature of ACM ensures that your certificates are stored securely and can be quickly deployed, contributing to a seamless and secure user experience.

Key features and benefits of AWS Certificate Manager

ACM encompasses a rich set of features that enhance security, automated certificate management, and streamline the deployment of secure applications. One notable feature is the integration with AWS services, allowing ACM to seamlessly deploy certificates on supported services like Amazon CloudFront, AWS Elastic Beanstalk, and more. This not only simplifies the certificate deployment process but also ensures consistent security across diverse AWS environments.

Automated certificate renewal is a standout capability of ACM. It automates the complex and error-prone task of renewing SSL/TLS certificates, reducing the risk of downtime due to expired certificates. ACM handles the renewal process automatically, relieving users of the burden of manual certificate updates. Additionally, ACM provides visibility into certificate expiration dates, empowering users with proactive insights to manage and update certificates.

ACM operates on a pay-as-you-go pricing model, aligning with AWS's commitment to cost-effectiveness. This means that users only pay for the resources they consume, making ACM an economical choice for organizations of all sizes. The secure and scalable nature of ACM, coupled with its ease of use, positions it as a valuable tool in the arsenal of AWS services, empowering organizations to focus on building and scaling secure applications without the complexities of managing digital certificates.

AWS Secrets Manager

At the heart of AWS's secret storage capabilities lies AWS Secrets Manager, a fully managed service that simplifies the management of sensitive information such as API keys, database passwords, and other credentials. Secrets Manager provides a centralized repository for securely storing and rotating these secrets, offering a seamless solution for handling credentials across various AWS services and applications.

One of the primary advantages of AWS Secrets Manager is its automation capabilities. The service facilitates the automatic rotation of secrets, reducing the risk associated with long-lived credentials. Automated rotation not only enhances security by regularly updating credentials but also minimizes the operational overhead traditionally associated with manual rotation processes. Additionally, Secrets Manager integrates seamlessly with AWS IAM, allowing for fine-grained access control over who can retrieve and manage secrets. This integration ensures that only authorized entities have access to sensitive information, bolstering the overall security of the stored secrets.

Beyond the field of credentials, AWS Secrets Manager extends its functionality to the storage and management of other types of sensitive data. For example, it supports the storage of arbitrary key-value pairs, enabling users to securely store and retrieve configuration settings, API keys, and encryption keys. This versatility makes AWS Secrets Manager a versatile solution for safeguarding a broad spectrum of sensitive information and streamlining security practices across diverse use cases.

Client-side encryption and security best practices

While AWS Secrets Manager provides a robust platform for secret storage, AWS users must also adhere to security best practices to maximize the effectiveness of their secret management strategy. One critical aspect is the implementation of CSE. By encrypting sensitive data before it reaches the cloud, users add a layer of security to their secrets. AWS KMS seamlessly integrates with AWS Secrets Manager, allowing users to manage the encryption keys used to protect their stored secrets. This integration ensures that even if unauthorized access were to occur, the encrypted data remains indecipherable without the appropriate decryption keys.

Furthermore, organizations leveraging AWS secret storage should adopt the principle of least privilege. This involves restricting access to secrets based on the minimum permissions required for a given task or service. AWS IAM plays a pivotal role in enforcing the principle of least privilege, allowing organizations to define precise permissions for users and services accessing secrets.

In conclusion, AWS secret storage, anchored by services such as Secrets Manager, offers a robust and scalable solution for safeguarding sensitive information in the cloud. By embracing automated rotation, CSE, and adhering to security best practices, organizations can fortify their security posture and navigate the cloud landscape with confidence. As cloud computing continues to evolve, AWS remains at the forefront, providing users with the tools and services necessary to secure their most valuable digital assets.

AWS compliance and auditing

Welcome to the realm of AWS compliance and auditing, where the digital landscape meets regulatory standards and governance requirements head-on. As organizations entrust their critical workloads to the secure confines of AWS, the imperative to adhere to stringent compliance frameworks becomes important. In this chapter, we embark on a comprehensive journey into the intricate tapestry of AWS compliance and auditing, illuminating the pathways to achieving and maintaining regulatory alignment within the cloud environment.

As the digital world evolves, so do the compliance challenges that organizations face. AWS has thoughtfully created a framework that meets and often surpasses global standards across various industries. From financial services to healthcare, and from data privacy to information security, we will explore how AWS seamlessly integrates compliance into its services.

This section aims to demystify the compliance landscape, providing you with the insights and tools needed to navigate the intricate regulatory waters confidently. Whether you are a compliance officer ensuring adherence to specific standards or a cloud architect architecting secure environments, this exploration of AWS compliance and auditing promises to equip you with the knowledge and strategies essential for building and maintaining a robust, compliant cloud infrastructure.

Compliance introduction

In the field of cloud computing, where organizations entrust cloud service providers with their data and applications, ensuring compliance with industry regulations and standards becomes important. Compliance in the cloud is a multifaceted endeavor that involves aligning your organization's practices with a myriad of legal, regulatory, and industry-specific requirements. This introduction delves into the fundamental concepts of compliance within the AWS environment, providing a foundational understanding of the mechanisms and frameworks in place to meet diverse compliance needs.

Understanding the compliance landscape in AWS

AWS's commitment to providing a secure and compliant cloud platform is evident through its adherence to a multitude of international, regional, and industry-specific compliance standards. Whether your organization operates in healthcare, finance, or government, AWS offers a comprehensive suite of compliance certifications, including but not limited to ISO 27001, HIPAA, *Payment Card Industry Data Security Standard* (*PCI DSS*), FedRAMP, and *System and Organization Controls* (*SOC*) reports. These certifications signify that AWS meets rigorous security and privacy standards, providing customers with a solid foundation to build upon for their own compliance requirements.

Furthermore, AWS provides customers with the tools and resources needed to navigate the compliance landscape effectively. From well-documented compliance reports to the AWS Artifact service, which centralizes compliance-related documentation, customers have access to a wealth of information to aid in their own compliance efforts. This commitment to transparency empowers organizations to assess the security and compliance posture of the AWS services they leverage, fostering a collaborative approach to meeting regulatory requirements.

Compliance journey

Embarking on a compliance journey in AWS involves a strategic and iterative process. Organizations must first identify the specific compliance requirements relevant to their industry and geography. AWS provides a robust set of resources, including the AWS Compliance Center, to guide customers through this initial phase. Once the compliance requirements are understood, organizations can leverage AWS services and features designed to assist in meeting these obligations.

Throughout this journey, it is crucial to recognize the shared responsibility model and understand the demarcation between the responsibilities of AWS and the customer. While AWS manages the security of the cloud, customers are responsible for the security in the cloud, including the configuration and management of their own applications and data.

In the subsequent sections of this chapter, we will discuss specific compliance certifications and standards, providing insights into how AWS facilitates compliance across various industries. From healthcare to finance, from government to e-commerce, understanding the compliance landscape in AWS is key to building and maintaining a secure and trustworthy cloud environment.

Compliance tools in AWS

AWS operates in a globally distributed environment, serving a diverse clientele spanning industries such as finance, healthcare, and government. AWS has committed itself to achieving and maintaining compliance with an extensive array of international and regional standards. From widely recognized certifications such as ISO 27001 to industry-specific mandates like HIPAA for healthcare or PCI DSS for payment card industry data security, AWS offers a compliance framework that caters to the diverse needs of its customers.

One notable aspect of AWS compliance is the adherence to the shared responsibility model. While AWS is responsible for the security of the cloud, customers are responsible for the security of the cloud. This delineation of responsibilities is crucial in understanding how compliance is a collaborative effort. AWS provides a robust set of tools and features to help customers achieve their compliance goals, but organizations must configure and manage their resources in a manner that aligns with their specific compliance requirements. The transparency and flexibility AWS provide in this regard empower organizations to navigate the intricate web of compliance standards efficiently.

Tools for ensuring compliance

In the pursuit of compliance, AWS offers a suite of tools and services to assist organizations in maintaining a secure and auditable environment. AWS Config, for instance, enables continuous monitoring of resources and their configurations, helping organizations assess their compliance against predefined rules. AWS CloudTrail provides a comprehensive trail of API calls, allowing organizations to track user activity and changes made to resources, a critical component for audit purposes.

Moreover, AWS Artifact provides on-demand access to AWS compliance reports, making it easier for organizations to conduct their assessments and audits. These tools, coupled with AWS commitment to providing a secure and compliant infrastructure, empower organizations to not only meet regulatory requirements but also to proactively manage and monitor their compliance posture in real-time.

Shared responsibility in compliance

One of the distinctive features of AWS is the shared responsibility model, which extends to the field of compliance. While AWS takes responsibility for the security of the cloud infrastructure, customers bear the responsibility of securing their data and applications in the cloud. This shared responsibility is pivotal in achieving and maintaining compliance.

Customers must understand the specific requirements of the regulations that apply to their industry and configure their AWS resources accordingly. This includes implementing encryption, access controls, and regular audits of their AWS environment. AWS provides the necessary building blocks, such as AWS IAM for access control and AWS KMS for encryption, allowing customers to tailor their security controls to meet compliance standards.

AWS CloudTrail

AWS CloudTrail serves as a robust trailblazer in the field of compliance by providing a comprehensive solution for auditing and monitoring AWS account activity. Compliance, a multifaceted concept encompassing regulatory standards and internal policies, is a critical consideration for organizations across diverse industries. CloudTrail, with its ability to record and store AWS API calls, offers organizations the means to maintain an audit trail of actions, enabling them to demonstrate compliance with regulatory frameworks, such as HIPAA, GDPR, SOC 2, and more.

Key features for compliance

AWS CloudTrail achieves compliance by capturing detailed information about API calls, including the identity of the caller, the time of the call, the source IP address, the request parameters, and the response elements returned by AWS. This wealth of data facilitates thorough audits and investigations, allowing organizations to trace back every action performed within their AWS environment. Additionally, CloudTrail enables the creation of trails, which are configurations that specify the types of events to log and the destination to which log files should be delivered, typically an Amazon S3 bucket. By employing trails, organizations can tailor their logging to align with specific compliance requirements and internal security policies.

Integration with AWS Key Management Service

To bolster the security of logged data, AWS CloudTrail seamlessly integrates with the AWS KMS. This integration allows organizations to encrypt CloudTrail log files at rest, ensuring that sensitive information remains confidential and meets encryption-related compliance mandates. By leveraging KMS, CloudTrail provides organizations with control over the encryption keys, reinforcing the principle of data ownership and enhancing overall security.

Automated compliance monitoring

One of the distinctive features of AWS CloudTrail is its ability to facilitate automated compliance monitoring. Through the integration with AWS Config, organizations can establish rules that evaluate CloudTrail events against desired configurations. This automated approach helps organizations promptly identify and rectify any deviations from compliance standards, offering a proactive stance in maintaining a secure and compliant AWS environment.

In essence, AWS CloudTrail serves as a linchpin in achieving and maintaining compliance within the AWS Cloud. As we explore further on the next page, we will discuss specific use cases, implementation strategies, and real-world examples that showcase the efficacy of CloudTrail in meeting the diverse compliance needs of organizations operating in the cloud.

Implementation and use cases of compliance in AWS CloudTrail

Let us explore the compliance in AWS CloudTrail and explore practical implementation strategies and real-world use cases of this service. Whether it is tracking user activity, monitoring changes to resources, or ensuring data integrity, CloudTrail offers a myriad of use cases that align with diverse compliance requirements, such as tracking user activity for reporting and monitoring, ensuring data integrity, and for different implementation strategies, as explained in the following:

- **Tracking user activity**: One fundamental aspect of compliance is the ability to trace user activity within the AWS environment. CloudTrail captures details such as the identity of the user, the actions performed, and the resources affected. This comprehensive visibility into user activity enables organizations to satisfy audit requirements related to accountability and access control.

- **Monitoring changes to resources**: Compliance mandates often necessitate organizations to monitor changes to critical resources. AWS CloudTrail records modifications to resources, including the type of change and the identity of the entity responsible. Whether it is alterations to security groups, changes in IAM policies, or modifications to S3 bucket configurations, CloudTrail offers a granular view of resource-level activity.

- **Ensuring data integrity**: Data integrity is a cornerstone of compliance, especially in regulated industries like healthcare and finance. With CloudTrail, organizations can verify the integrity of their AWS environment by examining the recorded events. This not only ensures that data remains unaltered but also provides a historical record that aids in incident response and forensic analysis.

- **Implementation strategies**: Successful implementation of AWS CloudTrail for compliance requires thoughtful planning and configuration. Organizations can strategically deploy trails based on specific compliance requirements, tailoring the logging of events to meet the standards of regulatory bodies and internal policies.

In conclusion, AWS CloudTrail emerges as an indispensable ally in the pursuit of compliance within the AWS Cloud. By offering a potent combination of detailed logging, encryption, and automated monitoring, CloudTrail empowers organizations to navigate the complex terrain of regulatory frameworks with confidence. As cloud environments continue to evolve, CloudTrail stands as a testament to AWS's commitment to providing robust solutions that not only meet but exceed the expectations of organizations striving for compliance excellence in the digital era.

AWS Config

AWS Config fundamentally transforms the compliance landscape by providing continuous monitoring, assessment, and auditing of AWS resource configurations. Its proactive approach allows organizations to detect and rectify any deviations from the desired configuration, fostering a state of perpetual compliance. The service enables the recording and evaluation of configuration changes over time, affording organizations a historical perspective that aids in auditing and forensic analysis.

One of the foundational elements of compliance in AWS Config is the establishment of Config rules. These rules act as customizable policy definitions, allowing organizations to express their compliance requirements in a granular manner. Whether aligning with industry standards such as HIPAA, PCI DSS, or adhering to internal security policies, Config rules provide a flexible framework to ensure that AWS resources comply with the desired configuration. The ability to create custom rules further empowers organizations to tailor their compliance checks to specific business needs, reflecting the unique nuances of their operational environment. Config rules not only streamline the compliance validation process but also serve as an integral part of an organization's proactive risk management strategy.

Moreover, AWS Config simplifies the complex task of tracking changes across the AWS resource landscape. The configuration history feature captures a detailed record of configuration changes, enabling organizations to understand the evolution of their infrastructure. This historical context is invaluable during compliance audits, as it provides auditors with a comprehensive view of how configurations have evolved. The timeline of changes, coupled with the ability to attribute modifications to specific actions or individuals, enhances transparency and accountability, a critical aspect of maintaining compliance in dynamic cloud environments.

An integral part of the compliance journey facilitated by AWS Config is the automated remediation of non-compliant resources. Config rules not only identify deviations from the desired state but can also trigger automated responses to bring the resources back into compliance. This automated remediation capability significantly reduces the manual effort required to enforce compliance, allowing organizations to maintain a consistent and secure configuration posture without constant human intervention. The combination of continuous monitoring, proactive rule enforcement, and automated remediation establishes AWS Config as a linchpin in the orchestration of a robust compliance strategy within AWS.

Beyond the technical capabilities, AWS Config integrates seamlessly with other AWS services, amplifying its impact on the compliance landscape. Integration with AWS CloudTrail enables a holistic view of configuration changes alongside API activities, offering organizations a comprehensive audit trail. Additionally, AWS Config works in harmony with AWS IAM, allowing organizations to define precise permissions for Config resources, ensuring that compliance monitoring is conducted with the appropriate level of access.

In conclusion, compliance in AWS Config represents a paradigm shift in how organizations approach and maintain compliance in the cloud. Through continuous monitoring, rule-based evaluations, and automated remediation, AWS Config empowers organizations to uphold the highest standards of compliance while navigating the dynamic and ever-expanding AWS ecosystem. As organizations embark on their cloud journey, the integration of AWS Config into their security and compliance frameworks emerges as a strategic imperative, fostering a culture of continuous compliance and risk mitigation in the cloud era.

AWS Artifact

At its core, AWS Artifact serves as a centralized repository for crucial compliance-related documents and resources. It acts as a gateway for organizations seeking to understand, assess, and demonstrate their adherence to various industry standards and regulations. Whether navigating the intricacies of data privacy laws, industry-specific regulations, or international compliance requirements, AWS Artifact offers a curated collection of compliance reports, certifications, and other artifacts that empower users to make informed decisions about their cloud infrastructure.

One of the standouts feature of AWS Artifact is its ability to streamline the compliance process. Organizations can access a wide array of compliance documents, including but not limited to SOC reports, PCI DSS reports, and HIPAA documentation. This centralized repository not only simplifies the often complex and time-consuming task of gathering compliance-related information but also enhances transparency by providing a clear view of the security and operational controls implemented by AWS. This transparency is crucial for organizations as they navigate the intricate landscape of regulatory requirements and work toward building and maintaining the trust of their customers, partners, and regulatory bodies.

AWS Artifact acts as a compass, guiding organizations through the intricate terrain of compliance. The service goes beyond offering documentation and reports, it also provides tools and resources that aid in the assessment and validation of compliance postures. For instance, organizations can leverage AWS Artifact to download compliance reports and use them as part of their risk management and audit processes. This not only facilitates internal assessments but also streamlines the interaction with external auditors, making the compliance validation process more efficient and collaborative.

Moreover, AWS Artifact is dynamic, adapting to the evolving compliance landscape. AWS routinely updates the service to include the latest certifications and compliance artifacts, ensuring that organizations can stay ahead of regulatory changes and industry standards. This proactive approach enables AWS customers to align their cloud infrastructure with the most up-to-date compliance requirements, reducing the risk of non-compliance and potential regulatory penalties.

In conclusion, AWS Artifact emerges as a cornerstone in the foundation of AWS's commitment to security, trust, and compliance. By providing a centralized hub for compliance artifacts, the service not only simplifies the often-intricate process of navigating regulatory landscapes but also empowers organizations to build and maintain a secure cloud infrastructure. As the regulatory environment continues to evolve, AWS Artifact stands as a reliable companion, ensuring that organizations can confidently navigate the compliance landscape, focus on innovation, and build a foundation of trust with their stakeholders.

AWS GuardDuty

As organizations increasingly migrate their workloads to the cloud, the need for robust security and compliance measures becomes more pronounced. AWS GuardDuty emerges as a pivotal service within the AWS security arsenal, designed to proactively identify and thwart potential security threats. This discussion delves into the role of AWS GuardDuty in ensuring compliance with industry standards and regulations, providing a comprehensive overview of its features, benefits, and practical applications.

AWS GuardDuty operates at the intersection of threat detection and compliance, offering a dynamic solution that aligns with diverse regulatory frameworks and security standards. One of its primary strengths lies in its ability to assist organizations in meeting the stringent requirements set forth by regulatory bodies such as GDPR, HIPAA, PCI DSS, and more. By continuously monitoring and analyzing data across AWS accounts, GuardDuty not only identifies malicious activity but also aids in maintaining a secure and compliant environment.

GuardDuty's compliance-centric approach is evident in its support for various log retention policies, allowing organizations to adhere to specific data retention regulations. The service provides detailed findings and alerts related to potential security threats, facilitating the documentation and reporting required for compliance audits. Whether it be monitoring unauthorized access, detecting data exfiltration attempts, or identifying unusual API activities, GuardDuty's threat intelligence and machine learning capabilities contribute significantly to maintaining a compliant posture in the cloud.

Key features and benefits

A cornerstone of AWS GuardDuty's effectiveness in compliance management is its amalgamation of threat intelligence feeds, anomaly detection, and machine learning algorithms. By continuously analyzing VPC Flow Logs, AWS CloudTrail event logs, and DNS logs, GuardDuty identifies patterns indicative of malicious activity. This not only enhances threat detection capabilities but also plays a pivotal role in meeting compliance requirements that mandate proactive security measures.

GuardDuty's automated response mechanisms further contribute to compliance by swiftly containing and mitigating security incidents. Through integration with AWS CloudWatch

Events and AWS Lambda, GuardDuty enables organizations to automate responses to specific findings, ensuring a rapid and well-coordinated reaction to potential threats. This automated response capability aligns with compliance mandates that emphasize not just detection but also swift remediation of security incidents.

In conclusion, AWS GuardDuty stands as a formidable ally in the pursuit of compliance within the cloud environment. Its amalgamation of threat intelligence, machine learning, and automated response mechanisms positions it as a versatile tool for organizations seeking to not only detect but also proactively address security threats. By leveraging GuardDuty, organizations can not only enhance their security posture but also streamline compliance efforts, meeting the evolving demands of regulatory frameworks in the vast field of cloud computing.

Amazon Inspector

Amazon Inspector, a comprehensive security assessment service provided by AWS, plays a pivotal role in enhancing the overall security posture of cloud-based applications. Amazon Inspector is designed to assist users in identifying security vulnerabilities and potential compliance violations within their AWS resources. In this detailed exploration, we will delve into the key features, functionalities, and benefits of Amazon Inspector, shedding light on how this service contributes to the continuous improvement of security measures in the cloud.

At its core, Amazon Inspector automates the often complex and time-consuming task of security assessments, enabling users to proactively identify and address potential security issues. The service employs a robust set of rules packages that encompass common security best practices, ensuring a thorough examination of AWS resources. Amazon Inspector not only simplifies the security assessment process but also provides actionable insights and recommendations for remediation.

The key features are mentioned in the following:

- **Agent-based assessments**: Amazon Inspector utilizes lightweight agents deployed on EC2 instances to gather detailed information about the system configurations and installed software. This agent-based approach ensures a comprehensive and accurate assessment of the security posture of each individual instance.

- **Rule packages**: Amazon Inspector comes equipped with predefined rule packages, each tailored to evaluate specific aspects of security. These rule packages cover a wide range of criteria, including common vulnerabilities, security best practices, and compliance standards. Users can choose and customize rule packages to align with their specific security requirements.

- **Scalability**: As a cloud-native service, Amazon Inspector seamlessly scales to meet the demands of various deployment scenarios. Whether you have a small number of instances or a sprawling infrastructure, Inspector adapts to your needs, allowing for efficient and effective security assessments at any scale.

- **Integration with AWS Config and CloudWatch**: Amazon Inspector seamlessly integrates with other AWS services, such as AWS Config and Amazon CloudWatch. This integration enhances the overall visibility into the security posture of your AWS environment, providing a holistic view of compliance and potential vulnerabilities.

- **Actionable findings**: One of the standouts feature of Amazon Inspector is its ability to deliver actionable findings. Instead of inundating users with a barrage of data, Inspector prioritizes and presents findings based on their severity, allowing users to focus on addressing the most critical security issues first.

Amazon Macie

Amazon Macie is an intelligent security service designed to discover, classify, and protect sensitive data within AWS. Launched to address the growing challenges associated with data privacy and compliance, Macie utilizes machine learning algorithms and pattern recognition to identify and safeguard sensitive information.

One of the standouts feature of Amazon Macie is its ability to automatically discover and classify sensitive data at scale. Through a combination of content inspection, metadata analysis, and machine learning, Macie can identify a wide range of sensitive data types, including **personally identifiable information** (**PII**), intellectual property, financial data, and more. This automated classification process allows organizations to gain insights into their data landscape, helping them understand where sensitive information resides and take proactive measures to secure it.

Amazon Macie extends its capabilities beyond data discovery and classification by providing actionable insights and automated responses. The service generates detailed reports and alerts, enabling organizations to monitor access patterns and potential security risks associated with their sensitive data. Additionally, Macie can be configured to integrate with other AWS services, allowing for automated remediation actions based on policy violations. This integration not only streamlines security operations but also ensures a swift and effective response to potential threats, bolstering an organization's overall security posture.

Key features and benefits of Amazon Macie

Amazon Macie offers a plethora of features and benefits that make it a valuable addition to any organization's security toolkit. Here are some key aspects of Amazon Macie:

- **Content discovery and classification**: Macie employs advanced content inspection techniques to identify and classify sensitive data. It goes beyond simple keyword matching, utilizing machine learning models to understand the context and meaning of data, ensuring accurate and reliable classification.

- **Automated policy enforcement**: With Macie, organizations can define custom data security policies based on their specific compliance requirements. The service then automatically enforces these policies, providing real-time alerts and responses to any deviations from established security guidelines.

- **Integration with AWS ecosystem**: Macie seamlessly integrates with other AWS services, allowing organizations to leverage its capabilities in conjunction with existing security and compliance tools. Integration with AWS CloudTrail, Amazon S3, and AWS IAM enhances the overall visibility and control over data security.

- **Incident response and reporting**: In the event of a security incident or policy violation, Macie provides detailed incident reports, aiding in forensic analysis and compliance reporting. This facilitates a swift and informed response to security events, reducing the potential impact of data breaches.

- **Scalability and flexibility**: As with many AWS services, Macie is designed to scale with the needs of the organization. Whether dealing with a small dataset or a vast repository of information, Macie can adapt to the scale and complexity of the data environment.

Amazon Macie is a robust and intelligent solution that empowers organizations to take control of their data security and compliance needs. By automating the discovery and protection of sensitive information, Macie not only enhances the overall security posture but also instills confidence in organizations that their data is in safe hands within the AWS Cloud. As data security continues to be a top priority, Amazon Macie stands as a valuable ally in the journey toward a more secure and compliant digital landscape.

AWS Detective

AWS Detective is a powerful security service that plays a pivotal role in bolstering the overall security posture of AWS users. At its core, AWS Detective simplifies and accelerates the process of detecting, investigating, and responding to security incidents within your AWS environment. This service operates seamlessly across multiple AWS accounts and workloads, providing a centralized platform for security analysis.

One of the key features of AWS Detective is its ability to aggregate and analyze data from various AWS services. This includes AWS CloudTrail, VPC Flow Logs, and AWS GuardDuty findings. By consolidating these disparate sources of data, AWS Detective creates a comprehensive and cohesive view of your AWS resources and their activities. This holistic approach allows security teams to gain insights into potential security threats and anomalies, facilitating a more proactive and informed security posture.

AWS Detective employs graph theory to map the relationships and dependencies between different resources and accounts. This graphical representation aids security teams in visualizing and understanding the context of security incidents. The interactive graph not only simplifies the identification of potential security issues but also expedites the investigation process by providing a clear and intuitive interface for navigating through complex relationships.

Key features and benefits

AWS Detective offers a range of features and benefits that contribute to its effectiveness in enhancing security within the AWS ecosystem, some are mentioned in the following:

- **Automated insights**: AWS Detective leverages machine learning and analytics to automatically generate insights and correlations from the collected data. This automation significantly reduces the time and effort required for security teams to identify and respond to security incidents.

- **Collaborative investigation**: Security is a collaborative effort, and AWS Detective acknowledges this by providing a platform that facilitates seamless collaboration among security teams. It allows multiple users to access and contribute to the investigation, ensuring that insights are shared efficiently across the team.

- **Integration with AWS services**: AWS Detective seamlessly integrates with other AWS security services, including AWS GuardDuty and AWS CloudTrail. This integration enhances its capability to detect and analyze security events, providing a comprehensive view of potential threats.

- **Scalability**: As with other AWS services, AWS Detective is designed to scale with the needs of your organization. Whether you are a small startup or a large enterprise, the service accommodates varying workloads and data volumes, ensuring that it remains effective as your AWS footprint expands.

- **Cost-effective security analysis**: By automating much of the security analysis process, AWS Detective optimizes resource utilization and reduces the operational overhead associated with manual investigation. This cost-effective approach allows organizations to allocate resources more efficiently while maintaining a high level of security.

In conclusion, AWS Detective stands as a testament to AWS's commitment to providing robust and innovative solutions for securing cloud environments. By offering a centralized platform for security analytics and investigation, AWS Detective empowers organizations to proactively address security incidents, mitigate risks, and maintain a resilient security posture in the ever-evolving landscape of cloud computing.

Conclusion

In conclusion, this chapter has provided a comprehensive overview of key aspects of AWS security, highlighting the vital principles and practices that form the foundation for a robust and secure cloud infrastructure. The shared responsibility model has been emphasized as a fundamental concept, delineating the distinct responsibilities between AWS and its customers in ensuring the security of their data and applications.

The discussion on ACLs and security groups within VPCs has underscored the significance of implementing granular control over network traffic, thereby fortifying the defense mechanisms against potential threats. Understanding and effectively configuring these network security features are critical steps in creating a secure and well-isolated environment within the AWS Cloud.

Encryption and key management have been explored as pivotal components in safeguarding data both at rest and in transit. By adopting robust encryption protocols and managing cryptographic keys securely, organizations can enhance the confidentiality and integrity of their sensitive information, mitigating the risk of unauthorized access or data breaches.

The examination of compliance and audit processes has shed light on the importance of adhering to industry-specific regulations and best practices. AWS provides a multitude of compliance certifications, offering customers assurance that their cloud infrastructure complies with stringent security standards. Regular audits and assessments play a crucial role in evaluating and maintaining the security posture of an AWS environment, ensuring ongoing adherence to security policies and standards.

In essence, a holistic approach to AWS security encompasses a combination of understanding the shared responsibility model, implementing effective network security through ACL and security groups, employing robust encryption practices, and maintaining compliance through thorough audit processes. By embracing these principles, organizations can establish a secure foundation in the AWS Cloud, fostering trust, and ensuring the confidentiality, integrity, and availability of their critical assets. As the field of cloud evolves, an ongoing commitment to staying abreast of emerging security threats and implementing proactive measures will be important in safeguarding the digital assets entrusted to the AWS platform.

In the next chapter, we will explore AWS **content delivery network (CDN)**, to accelerate globally your assets. We will see CloudFront, Edge functions in AWS, AWS Global Accelerator, and other services used to accelerate the serving of your assets on the internet.

Points to remember

- **Shared responsibility model**:
  - o AWS follows a shared responsibility model, where the responsibilities for security are divided between AWS and the customer.
  - o AWS manages the security of the cloud infrastructure, while customers are responsible for security in the cloud, including data, applications, and identity management.
- **ACL and security groups in VPC**:
  - o ACLs and security groups are crucial components for controlling network access in Amazon VPC.
  - o ACLs operate at the subnet level, providing stateless filtering of traffic, while security groups operate at the instance level, offering stateful filtering based on rules.

- o Careful configuration of these elements is essential for defining and enforcing network access controls within an AWS environment.

- **Encryption and keys management**:

  - o AWS offers various encryption mechanisms to safeguard data at rest, in transit, and during processing.

  - o KMS is a centralized service for creating and controlling encryption keys, providing a secure way to manage cryptographic keys used to encrypt data.

- **Compliance and audit**:

  - o AWS complies with a wide range of global security standards and certifications, ensuring a secure foundation for customers.

  - o Regular audits and assessments, such as SOC 2, HIPAA, and PCI DSS, demonstrate AWS's commitment to maintaining a secure and compliant cloud environment.

  - o Customers can leverage AWS tools and services to implement their own compliance measures, and AWS provides a wealth of resources for audit logging and monitoring.

- **Identity and access management**:

  - o IAM is a fundamental service for controlling access to AWS resources.

  - o Implementing the principle of least privilege is crucial, granting users and systems only the permissions necessary for their specific tasks.

  - o MFA adds an additional layer of security to user accounts, enhancing overall access control.

- **Network security best practices**:

  - o Implementing proper network segmentation using VPCs, subnets, and routing tables enhances security by limiting the blast radius of potential security incidents.

  - o Regularly reviewing and updating security groups and ACLs is essential to adapt to changing security requirements and threats.

- **Incident response and monitoring**:

  - o AWS provides tools like CloudWatch, CloudTrail, and AWS Config to monitor and track activities within the environment.

  - o Establishing an incident response plan, including automated responses and manual intervention steps, is critical for identifying and mitigating security incidents promptly.

- **Continuous security improvement**:
  - ○ Security is an ongoing process, and continuous improvement is necessary to adapt to evolving threats.
  - ○ Regularly review and update security policies, conduct security assessments, and stay informed about AWS security best practices and new features.

Exercises

1. **What is the fundamental concept in AWS security that outlines the division of responsibilities between AWS and the customer?**

    a. Shared collaboration model

    b. Shared responsibility model

    c. Mutual security agreement

2. **In the context of AWS VPC, what is used to control inbound and outbound traffic to instances?**

    a. Network Firewall

    b. Access control lists

    c. Security groups

3. **Which AWS service is commonly used for encrypting data at rest and managing encryption keys?**

    a. AWS KMS

    b. AWS IAM

    c. AWS SSL

4. **What is the primary function of AWS IAM in the context of security?**

    a. Data encryption

    b. User authentication and authorization

    c. Network Firewall management

5. **In AWS, what does the term ACL stand for in the context of network security?**

    a. Amazon cloud logging

    b. Access control list

    c. Advanced cryptographic layer

6. **Which AWS compliance framework helps customers ensure that their workloads comply with industry-specific regulations and standards?**

   a. AWS IAM compliance

   b. AWS HIPAA compliance

   c. AWS security group compliance

7. **How do security groups and ACLs differ in terms of their scope in AWS VPC?**

   a. Security groups are applied at the subnet level, while ACLs are applied at the instance level.

   b. Security groups are stateful, while ACLs are stateless.

   c. Security groups are applied at the instance level, while ACLs are applied at the subnet level.

8. **Which AWS service provides a centralized location to manage, monitor, and audit AWS resources?**

   a. AWS CloudTrail

   b. AWS CloudWatch

   c. Amazon Inspector

9. **In the context of encryption, what is the purpose of the term "key rotation"?**

   a. Changing encryption algorithms

   b. Periodically updating encryption keys

   c. Encrypting data during transmission

10. **Which AWS service allows customers to automate the evaluation of their AWS resource configurations for security vulnerabilities?**

    a. AWS Config

    b. Amazon Inspector

    c. AWS GuardDuty

Answers

1. b

2. c

3. a

4. b

5. b

6. b

7. c

8. a

9. b

10. b

Key terms

- AWS shared responsibility model
- Access control list
- Security groups in VPC
- Encryption
- AWS Key Management Service
- Compliance
- Audit
- AWS CloudTrail
- AWS Config
- AWS Artifact
- AWS GuardDuty
- Amazon Inspector

Join our book's Discord space

Join the book's Discord Workspace for Latest updates, Offers, Tech happenings around the world, New Release and Sessions with the Authors:

https://discord.bpbonline.com

CHAPTER 9

AWS Content Delivery and Global Applications

Introduction

The demand for seamless, high-performance content delivery on a global scale has never been more critical. In this chapter, we study the transformative capabilities of **Amazon Web Services (AWS)** content delivery and its pivotal role in empowering global applications.

AWS content delivery services provide a comprehensive suite of tools and technologies designed to optimize the delivery of digital content, ensuring low latency, high availability, and exceptional user experiences regardless of the end-user's location.

This chapter explores the intricacies of AWS content delivery, shedding light on the fundamental components that make it a cornerstone for global application architectures. From Amazon Route 53, a highly available **Domain Name System (DNS)**, to Amazon CloudFront, a scalable **content delivery network (CDN)**, to the integration with other AWS services like Amazon S3 and Lambda, we navigate the landscape of possibilities that AWS offers for building, deploying, and scaling applications on a global scale.

Structure

In this chapter, we will cover the following topics:

- Amazon Route 53
- Amazon content delivery network

- Introduction to AWS CloudFront
- Other AWS services for global applications

Objectives

This chapter on AWS content delivery and global applications aims to comprehensively understand the key objectives and strategies for optimizing content delivery and supporting global applications on the AWS platform. A primary objective is to explore the fundamentals CDNs and their integration with AWS services, emphasizing the importance of efficient content distribution to enhance user experience and reduce latency. The chapter studies the AWS Global Accelerator and Amazon CloudFront services, elucidating how these tools empower businesses to deliver content seamlessly and scale their applications globally, catering to diverse user bases across different geographic locations.

The chapter also seeks to elucidate strategies for building and deploying global applications effectively on AWS. This includes discussing the utilization of AWS Global Infrastructure and the significance of selecting appropriate AWS Regions to meet specific performance and compliance requirements. Additionally, the chapter aims to guide readers on implementing fault-tolerant architectures and leveraging AWS services such as Amazon Route 53 for intelligent DNS routing. By the end of the chapter, readers should have a comprehensive understanding of how to leverage AWS content delivery and global applications services to optimize their digital content delivery, enhance application performance, and ensure a seamless user experience on a global scale.

Whether a seasoned AWS practitioner or just beginning the cloud journey, this chapter will equip us with the insights needed to harness the full potential of AWS content delivery to create globally resilient and high-performing applications.

Amazon Route 53

Amazon Route 53 is a highly scalable and reliable DNS web service offered by AWS. Launched in 2010, Route 53 plays a critical role in managing domain names and directing internet traffic to the appropriate resources.

This service is designed to ensure seamless and efficient routing of user requests, providing a foundation for a robust and responsive web presence.

AWS Route 53 offers different routing policies to control how DNS queries are handled, directing traffic to resources based on specific conditions. These policies help optimize performance, improve availability, and provide disaster recovery capabilities.

Here is a list of routing policies Route 53 offers:

- **Simple routing**: Directs traffic to a single resource.
- **Weighted routing**: Distributes traffic based on assigned weights.

- **Latency-based routing**: Routes traffic to the resource with the lowest latency.

- **Failover routing**: Directs traffic to a primary resource, switching to a secondary if the primary fails.

- **Geolocation routing**: Routes based on the user's geographic location.

- **Geoproximity routing**: Routes based on proximity and configurable bias.

- **Multivalue answer routing**: Returns multiple healthy resources for better availability.

DNS and its importance

DNS is a fundamental internet component that translates human-readable domain names into **Internet Protocol** (**IP**) addresses that computers use to identify each other on the network. Without DNS, users need to memorize complex IP addresses rather than using easily recognizable domain names.

Navigating the internet using numerical IP addresses instead of familiar domain names like **https://www.example.com/** would be impractical and user-unfriendly. DNS solves this problem by providing a hierarchical and decentralized naming system. It acts as a distributed database, allowing users to access websites using easy-to-remember domain names instead of grappling with complex numerical addresses.

DNS is organized in a hierarchical tree-like structure, resembling an inverted tree with the root at the top. At the root level, authoritative servers manage **top-level domain** (**TLD**) information, such as `.com`, `.org`, `.net`, and country-code TLDs like `.uk` or `.jp`. Beneath each TLD, there are authoritative name servers responsible for specific domain names. This hierarchical structure helps distribute the workload and ensures efficient and reliable name resolution.

When a user enters a domain name in a web browser, the DNS resolution process starts. The local DNS resolver, often provided by the **Internet Service Provider** (**ISP**), checks its cache for the corresponding IP address. If not cached, the resolver queries the root DNS servers. These servers direct it to the authoritative servers for the specific TLD. The process continues until the authoritative server for the requested domain returns the corresponding IP address, which is then cached by the resolver for future use.

DNS functions and challenges

DNS serves several critical functions beyond translating domain names into IP addresses. It also supports email delivery by resolving domain names to mail server IP addresses, enables services like **Voice over IP** (**VoIP**), and plays a crucial role in the security of the internet through mechanisms like **DNS Security Extensions** (**DNSSEC**), which helps prevent domain hijacking and man-in-the-middle attacks.

DNS is a robust and essential system but not without challenges. One significant concern is DNS spoofing or cache poisoning, where malicious actors manipulate DNS responses to redirect users to fraudulent websites. To address these issues, DNSSEC adds an extra layer of security by digitally signing DNS data to ensure its authenticity. Additionally, efforts to improve privacy have led to the development of **DNS over HTTPS (DoH)** and **DNS over TLS (DoT)** protocols, encrypting DNS queries to protect users from eavesdropping and tracking.

The DNS is a cornerstone of the internet, providing a user-friendly way to navigate the vast network of interconnected devices. Its hierarchical structure and efficient resolution process make it a reliable and indispensable tool for internet communication. As the digital landscape evolves, DNS continues to adapt to new challenges, ensuring the integrity and security of online interactions. Understanding the intricacies of DNS is essential for anyone seeking a deeper comprehension of the internet's underlying infrastructure.

Route 53, as a DNS service, simplifies the management of domain names and enhances the overall accessibility and reliability of web applications.

Key qualities of using AWS Route 53

Here are some key qualities of using AWS Route 53:

- **Global coverage**: Route 53 operates on a global scale with a vast network of DNS servers strategically distributed around the world. This global presence ensures low latency and high-performance DNS resolution for end-users, regardless of their geographic location.

- **Scalability**: The service is designed to handle the varying demands of web traffic, making it suitable for small-scale applications and large enterprises with extensive online presence. Route 53 effortlessly scales to accommodate increasing workloads, ensuring optimal performance.

- **High availability**: Route 53 is built with redundancy and high availability in mind. It provides a reliable infrastructure that minimizes downtime and ensures that DNS requests are processed promptly. This is crucial for maintaining an uninterrupted online presence.

Main features of AWS Route 53

Here are some main features of AWS Route 53:

- **Domain registration**: One of the primary features is its ability to register new domain names. Users can search and register domain names directly through the AWS Management Console. This simplifies acquiring and managing domain names, allowing users to consolidate their domain management within the AWS environment.

- **DNS service**: Route 53 is a scalable and highly available DNS service, that translates human-readable domain names into IP addresses that computers use to identify each other. With a global network of DNS servers, Route 53 ensures low latency and high-performance DNS responses, providing a reliable and efficient experience for end-users.

- **Health checks and monitoring**: Route 53 enables users to Setup health checks for their applications and resources. These health checks can be configured to monitor the availability and performance of endpoints, such as web servers or load balancers. If an endpoint fails a health check, Route 53 can automatically reroute traffic to healthy endpoints, enhancing the application's overall resilience.

Use cases of AWS Route 53

Here are some use cases of AWS Route 53:

- **Global server load balancing**: Route 53 supports **global server load balancing** (**GSLB**), allowing users to distribute incoming traffic across multiple AWS Regions or data centers. This ensures optimal performance and availability for applications with a global user base. GSLB also provides failover capabilities, automatically directing traffic away from unhealthy or underperforming regions.

- **Domain management and DNS routing**: Route 53 is a powerful tool for managing domain names and controlling how traffic is routed to different AWS resources. Users can create records, such as A, CNAME, or alias records, to define the routing behavior for their domains. This flexibility is valuable for complex architectures with multiple services and endpoints.

- **Content delivery**: Leveraging Route 53 with other AWS services like Amazon CloudFront, users can create a scalable and globally distributed CDN. Route 53 integrates seamlessly with CloudFront, enabling users to associate their domain names with CloudFront distributions. This results in faster content delivery, reduced latency, and improved user experiences.

Advanced features of AWS Route 53

Here are some advanced features of AWS Route 53:

- **Traffic flow**: Route 53 Traffic Flow is a visual traffic management feature allowing users to control how their DNS traffic is routed globally. Users can create policies to dynamically adjust traffic based on various parameters such as geographic location, health checks, or endpoint weights. This advanced feature enhances flexibility and enables efficient traffic management for applications with varying demands.

- **Integration with AWS services**: Route 53 integrates seamlessly with various AWS services, including **Elastic Load Balancing** (**ELB**), S3, and CloudFront. This integration simplifies associating domain names with different AWS resources, ensuring a smooth and cohesive experience for users managing their infrastructure on AWS.

- **Security and compliance**: Route 53 provides features like DNSSEC to enhance the security of the DNS infrastructure. Additionally, users can configure Route 53 Resolver rules to route DNS queries between on-premises and AWS resources securely. These security features contribute to a robust and compliant DNS environment.

Best practices for AWS Route 53

Here are some best practices while using AWS Route 53:

- **Regular monitoring**: Routinely monitor DNS performance metrics and health checks to identify potential issues before they impact users.

- **Use alias records**: Instead of traditional CNAME records, leverage Alias records to map domain names directly to AWS resources like ELB or S3 buckets.

- **Implement DNS failover**: Configure DNS failover to redirect traffic to healthy endpoints in the event of resource failures, ensuring high availability.

Amazon Route 53 pricing

Route 53's pricing is structured to accommodate various usage scenarios, making it suitable for small startups to large enterprises. The pricing is based on usage metrics, and users are billed separately for each component they use.

Some key aspects of Route 53 pricing include:

- **Domain registration**: Route 53 allows users to register new domain names or transfer existing ones. Domain registration pricing can vary based on the TLDs ranging from common TLDs like **.com** to more specialized ones. Users pay an annual fee for domain registration, and the pricing can differ for different TLDs.

- **DNS queries**: Route 53 charges for the number of DNS queries on the hosted zones. DNS queries include domain name resolution, health checks, and other DNS-related requests. Different types of DNS queries have different associated costs, and Route 53 provides a tiered pricing structure, where the cost per query decreases as the volume of queries increases.

- **Health checks**: Route 53 offers health checks to monitor the health and performance of applications. Users are billed based on the number of health checks performed. The pricing for health checks depends on factors such as the interval between health checks and the number of health checks conducted.

- **Traffic Flow**: Traffic Flow is a feature of Route 53 that allows users to control traffic routing to their applications based on various parameters. Users are billed as per Traffic Flow policies. The pricing for Traffic Flow is based on the number of policies configured and the number of DNS queries evaluated by those policies.

- **Resolver endpoints**: Route 53 Resolver allows users to resolve DNS queries within their VPC. Users are billed on the number of DNS queries resolved using Resolver. The pricing for Resolver depends on the number of DNS queries and the type of queries (forwarding or conditional forwarding).

- **Cost optimization and flexibility**: Route 53 provides users with the ability to optimize costs based on their specific needs. The pay-as-you-go pricing model ensures that users only pay for the resources and services they consume.

  Additionally, users can take advantage of cost-saving measures such as:

  o **Reserved capacity**: Users can commit to a minimum monthly query volume for a specific period, allowing them to receive discounted rates.

  o **Bulk domain registration**: Users managing multiple domains can benefit from bulk registration discounts, streamlining the process and reducing costs.

  o **Free Tier**: AWS offers a Free Tier for Route 53, allowing users to explore and use the service within certain limits without incurring charges.

Amazon Route 53's pricing is transparent, flexible, and tailored to meet the diverse needs of users. Whether it is domain registration, DNS queries, health checks, or Traffic Flow policies, Route 53 provides a scalable and cost-effective solution for managing the critical aspects of a domain's infrastructure on the internet.

AWS Route 53 is a comprehensive DNS web service that offers a wide range of features and use cases, making it an essential tool for managing domain names, routing traffic, and ensuring the reliability and performance of applications hosted on AWS. With its global reach, scalability, and seamless integration with other AWS services, Route 53 continues to be a foundational element for businesses operating in the cloud. The common issues and security concerns of DNS services could be solved using AWS Route53 as it offers all the best practices for using and managing domain names with the best security and compliance in the industry.

Amazon content delivery network

In today's digital age, where online content consumption is ubiquitous, the need for efficient and fast content delivery has become paramount. CDNs have emerged as a critical component in addressing this need, and AWS CloudFront stands out as a leading solution in the realm of CDN services. This introduction aims to provide an overview of CDNs, their significance, and a closer examination of AWS CloudFront as a powerful and versatile CDN platform.

Understanding content delivery networks

CDN is a network of strategically located servers that work collaboratively to minimize the latency and maximize the speed of delivering digital content to users. The primary objective of a CDN is to enhance the user experience by reducing the time it takes for web pages, images, videos, and other digital assets to load.

CDNs achieve this by storing cached copies of content on servers distributed across various geographical locations. CDN delivers user-requested content from the server that is physically closest to the user, reducing the data distance and, decreasing latency. This not only accelerates content delivery but also optimizes bandwidth usage. CDNs play a crucial role in ensuring the scalability and reliability of web applications, especially in increasing global internet traffic and the demand for high-quality, low latency content delivery.

CDN architecture, operation, and benefits

The architecture of a CDN typically involves the following key components:

- **Content servers**: These are the servers strategically placed across the globe. They store cached copies of the website's content, such as images, videos, and scripts.

- **Edge servers: Point of presence (PoP)** servers, or edge servers, are located in various geographical locations. They serve as the frontline in content delivery, delivering cached content to end-users based on their proximity to the nearest edge server.

- **Caching**: CDNs use caching to store static content on edge servers, reducing the load on the origin server. Cached content is readily available to users, enhancing response times and reducing server load.

- **Load balancing**: CDNs use load balancing techniques to distribute user requests across multiple servers. This prevents any single server from being overloaded and improves overall system efficiency.

The following are the benefits of using a CDN for the application:

- **Reduced latency**: CDNs significantly reduce latency by delivering content from servers closer to the end-users. This minimizes the time it takes for data to travel from the server to the user's device.

- **Enhanced scalability**: CDNs enable websites to handle increased traffic and demand without overloading the origin server. The distributed architecture allows for seamless scalability to accommodate growing user bases.

- **Improved reliability and availability**: With content cached on multiple servers, CDNs enhance the reliability and availability of web content. Even if one server experiences issues, others can seamlessly take over, ensuring uninterrupted service.

- **Bandwidth savings**: Offloading the delivery of static content to edge servers, CDNs reduce the load on the origin server, resulting in substantial bandwidth savings and cost optimization.

- **Security**: CDNs often include security features such as DDoS protection and SSL/TLS encryption, safeguarding websites and content from potential threats.

Introduction to AWS CloudFront

AWS CloudFront is a prominent player in the CDN landscape. Launched in 2008, CloudFront has evolved into a comprehensive and globally distributed content delivery service. It seamlessly integrates with other AWS services, providing users with a scalable and secure platform for delivering content to end-users.

CloudFront leverages the AWS infrastructure, utilizing a vast network of edge locations strategically positioned globally. These edge locations serve as points of presence where cached content is stored, ensuring quick and efficient retrieval for users. The integration with AWS's suite of services allows CloudFront to seamlessly work with S3 buckets, EC2 instances, and other AWS resources. A key strength of AWS CloudFront is its ability to deliver dynamic and static content with low latency and high transfer speeds. The service supports popular content delivery features such as **Secure Sockets Layer** (**SSL**) encryption, custom domain support, and caching options to optimize content delivery.

Key features of AWS CloudFront

Here are some key features of AWS Route 53:

- **Global content delivery**: AWS CloudFront operates on a global network of edge locations. This ensures low latency access to content for end-users, irrespective of their geographical location. The ability to distribute content from the edge reduces the load on the origin server, resulting in faster load times and a better user experience.

- **Security and access control**: CloudFront offers various security features to protect content during distribution. It supports HTTPS by encrypting data in transit, ensuring the confidentiality and integrity of the transmitted information. Additionally, AWS CloudFront integrates with AWS **Identity and Access Management** (**IAM**) and Amazon CloudWatch for access control and monitoring.

- **Customization and personalization**: CloudFront enables content customization through features like Lambda@Edge, allowing developers to run serverless functions at the edge locations. This allows real-time content customization and personalization based on user behavior or specific criteria, enhancing the overall user experience.

- **Origin Shield**: AWS CloudFront's Origin Shield acts as a centralized cache layer between the edge locations and the origin server. It reduces the load on the origin server by consolidating requests and responses. The Origin Shield also improves cache efficiency and minimizes the impact of spikes in traffic.

- **Comprehensive caching**: CloudFront supports cache of static and dynamic content, allowing users to configure **time-to-live** (**TTL**) settings and cache behaviors. Intelligently caching content at the edge locations, AWS CloudFront reduces latency and optimizes bandwidth usage.

Best practices for AWS CloudFront implementation

Follow these best practices for AWS CloudFront implementation:

- **Optimized cache settings**: Configure cache settings based on the nature of your content. For static assets, set longer TTLs to take advantage of caching, while for dynamic content, implement proper cache invalidation strategies to ensure users receive the latest data.

- **HTTPS everywhere**: Prioritize HTTPS to encrypt data in transit. AWS CloudFront supports SSL/TLS protocols, enabling secure communication between end-users and the CDN. This is crucial for maintaining the integrity and confidentiality of transmitted information.

- **Origin optimization**: Optimizing the origin server for better performance by leveraging compression and resource minification. Additionally, consider using CloudFront's Origin Shield to reduce the load on the origin and enhance cache efficiency.

- **Content compression**: Enabling content compression to reduce the size of files transmitted over the network. This not only speeds up content delivery but also reduces data transfer costs.

- **CloudFront Functions and Lambda@Edge for customization**: Leveraging CloudFront Function or Lambda@Edge for real-time content customization at the edge. This allows you to tailor content based on user preferences, device characteristics, or any other criteria without additional server infrastructure.

- **Monitoring and logging**: Implementing thorough monitoring and logging using Amazon CloudWatch. Setting up alerts for key metrics to proactively identify and address any issues. Regularly reviewing logs to gain insights into user behavior, traffic patterns, and potential security threats.

AWS CloudFront vs Lambda@Edge functions

In cloud computing, AWS continues to push the boundaries of innovation. AWS Edge functions, specifically CloudFront Functions and Lambda@Edge, have emerged as powerful tools that enable developers to deploy serverless code at the edge of the AWS network. This capability brings unprecedented flexibility and efficiency to content delivery, offering a wide array of use cases for developers and businesses alike:

- **CloudFront function**:
  - CloudFront stores a cache in two different layers the edge location and the regional edge cache. The regional edge cache runs on the 13 AWS Regions available worldwide. Due to the complexity involved in opening and maintaining regional data centers, AWS has also established smaller data centers called **edge locations** to help reduce latency. Edge locations are easier to maintain and only support a few AWS services at a time (ex: CloudFront, Route 53, and AWS Shield). As of writing this book in 2024, there were more than 400 edge locations spread across 48 countries (See: **https://docs.aws. amazon.com/whitepapers/latest/aws-fault-isolation-boundaries/points- of-presence.html**). Edge locations are the actual data centers that users access when requesting content cached in CloudFront.

  - They enable access to requests as they arrive on the edge location through a lightweight JavaScript runtime. CloudFront Function code is executed directly on an edge location and runs at the physical location closest to users. Since CloudFront Functions are executed before the request hits the cache and is invoked for each request, the latency they incur must be minimal. CloudFront Functions is ideal for high-scale and latency-sensitive operations like HTTP header manipulations, URL rewrites/redirects, and cache-key normalizations. These types of short-running, lightweight operations support unpredictable traffic. For example, we can use CloudFront Functions to redirect requests to language-specific versions of your site based on the Accept-Language header of the incoming request. These functions execute at all CloudFront's edge locations, they can scale instantly to millions of requests per second with minimal latency overhead, typically under one millisecond.

  - CloudFront Functions is a serverless compute service that allows developers to run lightweight JavaScript code at the edge locations of the AWS CloudFront CDN This serverless architecture eliminates the need for provisioning or managing servers, enabling developers to focus solely on writing code. The primary goal of CloudFront Functions is to seamlessly execute code closer to the end-users, reducing latency and improving overall application performance.

- **Lambda@Edge function**:
  - Its role is similar to CloudFront Functions. It serves as a middleware service that allows developers to run code with both Python and JavaScript. The main difference is that Lambda@Edge runs on the regional edge cache. Lambda@ Edge functions have fewer limitations and are similar to conventional

AWS Lambda functions. Lambda@Edge is best suited for computationally intensive operations. This could be computations that take longer to complete (several milliseconds to seconds), take dependencies on external thrid-party libraries, require integrations with other AWS services (for example, S3, DynamoDB), or need network calls for data processing. Some popular advanced use cases include HTTP live streaming (**HLS**), streaming manifest manipulation, integrations with thrid-party authorization and bot detection services, **server-side rendering** (**SSR**) of **single-page apps** (**SPA**) at the edge, and more.

o While CloudFront Functions excel at simplicity and quick execution, Lambda@Edge offers a broader set of capabilities and a more mature ecosystem. Lambda@Edge allows developers to deploy serverless functions written in Node.js or Python to AWS's Global network of CloudFront edge locations. This means, Lambda@Edge can be used for various use cases beyond simple request-response handling.

o Lambda@Edge provides greater flexibility for complex workloads, such as dynamic content generation, user authentication, or even implementing custom security measures. With the ability to hook into CloudFront events like viewer requests, origin requests, and responses, Lambda@Edge enables developers to execute code at various stages of the content delivery process. This makes it suitable for scenarios where fine-grained control and customization are paramount.

One key differentiator of CloudFront Functions is its simplicity. Developers can easily integrate their functions with CloudFront distributions using the AWS Management Console or the AWS **Command Line Interface** (**CLI**). The lightweight nature of CloudFront Functions makes them suitable for quick and dynamic tasks such as header manipulation, URL rewrites, or A/B testing. This service is valuable for scenarios where low latency execution is critical, such as personalized content delivery or security-related functions.

Differences and use cases

The primary distinction between CloudFront Functions and Lambda@Edge lies in their scope and complexity. CloudFront Functions are designed for lightweight tasks and ease of use, catering to scenarios where simplicity and rapid deployment are essential. On the other hand, Lambda@Edge provides a more comprehensive set of features, making it suitable for complex and customizable use cases.

- **Use cases for CloudFront Functions**:
  - **Header manipulation**: Easily modify HTTP headers for caching or security purposes.
  - **URL rewrites**: Implement URL transformations without the need for a server.

  o **A/B testing**: Conduct experiments by routing users to different webpage versions.

- **Use cases for Lambda@Edge**:

  o **User authentication**: Enforce authentication and authorization at the edge for improved security.

  o **Dynamic content generation**: Generate personalized content based on user attributes or preferences.

  o **Custom security measures**: Implement custom security policies, such as rate limiting or IP filtering.

  o **Global load balancing**: Distribute traffic intelligently across multiple origins for improved availability.

AWS edge functions, with its components like CloudFront Functions and Lambda@Edge, represent a paradigm shift in serverless computing. The ability to deploy code at the edge of the AWS network brings unparalleled performance benefits and opens a vast array of use cases for developers. Choosing between CloudFront Functions and Lambda@Edge depends on the specific requirements of the task at hand, with CloudFront Functions excelling in simplicity and rapid deployment, and Lambda@Edge offering a more comprehensive set of features for complex scenarios. These services empower developers to build efficient, scalable, and highly responsive applications in the ever-expanding AWS ecosystem.

Amazon CloudFront pricing

Amazon CloudFront plays a crucial role in enhancing the performance and delivery of web content to users across the globe. As businesses increasingly rely on the cloud for their digital infrastructure, comprehending the pricing structure of services like CloudFront becomes essential. In this section, we will study the intricacies of Amazon CloudFront pricing, exploring the factors that influence costs and providing insights to help users make informed decisions. You could see more information about CloudFront pricing here: **https://aws.amazon.com/cloudfront/pricing/** and here **https://docs.aws.amazon.com/whitepapers/latest/how-aws-pricing-works/cloudfront.html**.

Factors influencing pricing are mentioned in the following:

- **Data transfer-out**: One of the primary factors contributing to CloudFront costs is data transfer-out. CloudFront is a global network of edge locations that enable efficient content delivery. The pricing model is based on the volume of data transferred from these edge locations to end users. Costs vary depending on the geographic region and the amount of data transferred, with tiered pricing that offers reduced rates as usage increases.

- **HTTP/HTTPS requests**: CloudFront pricing includes charges for HTTP and HTTPS requests made to the CDN. This encompasses both viewer requests and origin fetches. Viewer requests refer to interactions between end-users and CloudFront, while origin fetches involve content retrieval from the origin server. Different pricing tiers exist for standard and premium content delivery, with associated costs for both request types.

- **Data transfer-in**: While data transfer-out is a key consideration, CloudFront users must also factor in data transfer-in. This pertains to the data transferred from the origin server to the CloudFront edge locations. Pricing for data transfer is generally lower than data transfer-out, but understanding the complete data flow is essential for accurate cost estimation.

- **Edge location storage**: CloudFront provides the option to cache and store content at its edge locations, reducing latency for frequently accessed resources. However, edge location storage incurs additional costs, and users should be aware of storage pricing, which varies depending on the storage class (standard or premium) and the region in which the data is stored.

- **Lambda@Edge charges**: Additional charges apply for users leveraging serverless computing with AWS Lambda@Edge, additional charges apply. This feature enables the execution of serverless functions at CloudFront edge locations, enhancing the flexibility and customization of content delivery. Users should be aware of the associated costs when incorporating Lambda@Edge into their CloudFront setup.

AWS CloudFront provides a robust and scalable solution for optimizing the delivery of content, applications, and APIs on a global scale. By understanding and implementing best practices, businesses can harness the full potential of CloudFront to enhance user experience, improve security, and cost-effectively optimize content delivery. As technology evolves AWS CloudFront remains a critical component for organizations seeking to deliver seamless and performant digital experiences to their users worldwide.

Other AWS services for global applications

Beyond the well-known services like CloudFront and Route 53, AWS offers a suite of advanced solutions designed to cater to the unique needs of global applications, ensuring seamless performance and reliability.

Among these innovative services are **S3 Transfer Acceleration** (**S3TA**), Global Accelerator, Outposts, and Wavelength, each contributing to the creation of a robust and efficient infrastructure for global businesses:

- S3TA is a game-changer for organizations requiring high-speed data transfers. Leveraging Amazon's global network, this service optimizes the transfer of large files or datasets, ensuring swift and secure movement of data across geographical boundaries.

- AWS Global Accelerator takes a step further by providing a fully managed, Anycast-based service that enhances the availability and performance of applications by directing traffic over the AWS Global network to the optimal endpoint.

- AWS Outposts extend AWS Cloud infrastructure to on-premises locations, enabling organizations to seamlessly integrate their existing infrastructure with AWS services for a consistent and unified experience.

- Lastly, AWS Wavelength brings AWS infrastructure to the edge of telecommunication networks, reducing latency and enhancing performance for applications that demand ultra-low latency, such as those powering **augmented reality** (**AR**), **virtual reality** (**VR**), and machine learning at the edge.

Together, these services epitomize AWS commitment to empowering businesses with the tools needed to create resilient, scalable, and high-performing global applications.

S3 Transfer Acceleration

In today's rapidly evolving digital landscape, businesses and individuals alike are generating and consuming massive amounts of data. Efficient and speedy data transfer is crucial for various applications, ranging from backup and restore operations to content distribution and data migration. AWS recognizes the importance of fast and reliable data transfer, and in response, they offer a solution that addresses these needs head-on: Amazon S3TA.

Amazon S3TA is a service provided by AWS that enhances the speed of transferring files to and from Amazon S3 buckets. Leveraging the power of the AWS CloudFront CDN, S3TA employs a network of globally distributed edge locations to optimize the delivery of data. This service is particularly beneficial for scenarios where large files need to be transferred over long distances, reducing latency and improving overall transfer speeds.

- **Key features and benefits**:

  o **Global acceleration**: One of the standout features of Amazon S3TA is its ability to accelerate data transfers on a global scale. Utilizing AWS CloudFront's extensive network of edge locations, data can be transferred quickly and reliably to and from S3 buckets, regardless of the geographical distance between the source and destination.

  o **Optimized for large objects**: This service is designed to excel in cases with large files. Whether dealing with high-definition videos, large datasets, or other sizable objects, S3TA ensures that these files are transferred efficiently and without unnecessary delays.

  o **Simple configuration**: Implementing S3TA is straightforward and requires minimum configuration. Users can enable acceleration for their S3 buckets by updating the endpoint URLs used for data transfers. This simplicity makes it easy for businesses to integrate this acceleration into their existing workflows without a steep learning curve.

o **Secure and reliable**: as with other AWS services, security is a top priority for Amazon S3TA. The service supports SSL encryption for data in transit, ensuring that your files are transferred securely over the internet. Additionally, AWS CloudFront's reliability and scalability contribute to the overall robustness of the solution.

o **Cost-effective**: While performance and reliability are paramount, cost considerations are always crucial. S3TA is designed to be cost-effective, with pricing based on usage. Users can take advantage of the enhanced transfer speeds without incurring exorbitant costs, making it an attractive solution for a wide range of use cases.

- **Use cases for S3TA**:

  o **Content delivery**: S3TA is ideal for content delivery scenarios where large files, such as videos, images, or software updates, need to be distributed globally. The accelerated transfer speeds ensure a seamless and fast user experience for consumers worldwide.

  o **Backup and restore operations**: When dealing with backup and restore operations that involve transferring large volumes of data, S3TA can significantly reduce the time required to complete these processes. This is particularly valuable for businesses with stringent **recovery time objectives (RTOs)**.

  o **Data migration**: Moving large datasets between S3 buckets or from on-premises storage to the cloud can be time-consuming. S3TA expedites these data migration processes, allowing organizations to adopt and leverage the benefits of cloud storage.

  o **Media and entertainment**: In the media and entertainment industry, where large media files are commonplace, S3TA accelerates content distribution to end-users, ensuring that streaming services deliver high-quality experiences with minimal buffering.

Amazon S3TA is a powerful solution for organizations seeking to optimize their data transfer workflows. By harnessing the capabilities of AWS CloudFront, this service enables high-speed, secure, and cost-effective transfer of large files globally. Whether you are a content provider, enterprise, or individual user, the enhanced performance and simplicity of S3TA make it a valuable tool in the AWS ecosystem, propelling data transfer into the fast lane of the digital age.

AWS Global Accelerator

Businesses operating in a digital era require solutions that ensure optimal user experience and guarantee reliability and resilience across diverse geographical locations. AWS Global Accelerator emerges as a game-changer in this context, offering a robust and scalable platform to enhance the performance and availability of applications on a global scale.

AWS Global Accelerator is a fully managed service designed to improve application availability and performance by leveraging the vast AWS Global network infrastructure. It acts as a traffic manager, intelligently routing user requests over the optimal AWS endpoint based on factors like health, geography, and routing policies. With AWS Global Accelerator, organizations can achieve lower latency, improved Fault-tolerance, and a seamless application user experience.

- **Key features of AWS Global Accelerator**:
    - **Anycast IP addresses**: AWS Global Accelerator employs Anycast IP addresses, allowing users to access applications through a consistent set of IP addresses. This ensures simplified DNS configurations and improved Fault-tolerance as traffic is automatically rerouted to healthy endpoints in case of failures.

    - **Global network reach**: Leveraging the extensive AWS Global network, AWS Global Accelerator optimizes the user traffic route to reach applications. This results in lower latency and faster response times. It is crucial for delivering a superior user experience, particularly latency-sensitive applications.

    - **Health checks and failover**: The service continuously monitors the health of application endpoints and directs traffic only to healthy instances. In case of any issues or failures, AWS Global Accelerator automatically reroutes traffic to healthy endpoints, minimizing downtime and ensuring uninterrupted service.

    - **Traffic dials**: AWS Global Accelerator provides granular control over traffic distribution using traffic dials. Organizations can easily adjust the percentage of traffic directed to different endpoints, facilitating A/B testing, canary releases, or gradual deployments without impacting the entire user base.

- **Benefits of AWS Global Accelerator**:
    - **Improved application performance**: Optimizing the route and reducing latency, AWS Global Accelerator significantly enhances application performance This is particularly beneficial for global organizations with users distributed across different regions.

    - **Enhanced availability and Fault-tolerance**: Automatic health checks and failover mechanisms of AWS Global Accelerator contribute to improved application availability and Fault-tolerance. This ensures that users experience minimal disruptions even in the face of potential failures.

- o **Simplified global deployment**: With Anycast IP addresses and simplified DNS configurations, AWS Global Accelerator makes it easier for organizations to deploy and manage global applications. This simplicity leads to operational efficiency and a more streamlined deployment process.

- o **Cost-effective scaling**: Efficiently distributing traffic and automatically scaling resources based on demand, AWS Global Accelerator helps organizations optimize costs. It ensures that resources are utilized effectively, providing a cost-effective solution for handling varying workloads.

AWS Global Accelerator is a powerful solution for organizations seeking to deliver high-performance, globally distributed applications. Its unique features, such as Anycast IP addresses, global network reach, and traffic dials, empower businesses to optimize application delivery, improve user experience, and ensure the availability of their services on a global scale. As organizations continue to embrace the cloud for their critical workloads, AWS Global Accelerator stands out as a crucial tool in their arsenal for achieving optimal performance and reliability.

AWS Outpost

AWS Outpost is a fully managed service that extends AWS infrastructure, services, and APIs to customers' on-premises locations. This hybrid cloud solution provides a consistent and seamless experience across the entire IT environment, allowing organizations to run applications with low latency and data residency requirements on-premises. Whether it is due to regulatory compliance, data sensitivity, or specific performance needs, AWS Outposts caters to a variety of scenarios.

- • **Key features of AWS Outpost**:
    - o **Consistency with AWS services**: AWS Outposts brings the same AWS infrastructure, services, APIs, and tools to on-premises environments. This ensures a consistent operational experience for developers and IT teams, making it easier to manage and deploy applications.

    - o **Configurable options**: Customers can choose from a range of Outposts configurations to meet their specific workload requirements. This includes options for compute and storage capacity, allowing organizations to tailor the solution to their unique needs.

    - o **Local data processing**: AWS Outposts enables local data processing with minimal latency, making it suitable for applications that require real-time responsiveness. This is particularly beneficial for industries such as manufacturing, healthcare, and finance where low latency data processing is critical.

    o **Seamless integration**: Integration with AWS Outposts is seamless, allowing organizations to extend their existing AWS applications to the on-premises environment without significant modifications. This simplifies the migration process and minimizes disruption to ongoing operations.

- **Use cases of AWS Outpost**:
  - o **Data residency and compliance**: For organizations operating in regions with strict data residency regulations, AWS Outposts provides a solution to keep sensitive data on-premises while still leveraging the power of AWS services.

  - o **Low latency applications**: Applications requiring low latency data processing, such as IoT **Internet of Things (IoT)** deployments and real-time analytics, benefit from AWS Outposts by running critical workloads on-premises.

  - o **Hybrid cloud deployments**: AWS Outposts is an ideal choice for organizations adopting a hybrid cloud strategy, allowing them to seamlessly integrate on-premises environments with their AWS infrastructure.

AWS Outposts represents a significant step forward in addressing the diverse needs of organizations seeking a hybrid cloud solution. By bringing AWS services to on-premises locations, AWS Outposts enables businesses to achieve a harmonious balance between the flexibility of the cloud and the control of on-premises infrastructure. As technology continues to evolve, AWS Outposts remains a pivotal tool for organizations navigating the complexities of modern IT environments.

AWS Wavelength

AWS Wavelength is a groundbreaking service offered by AWS that brings ultra-low latency and high-bandwidth connectivity to mobile and edge devices by deploying compute and storage resources at the edge of the 5G networks. This innovative solution is designed to meet the increasing demands of applications requiring real-time processing, such as AR, VR, gaming, and IoT applications. In this section, we will explore key features, benefits, and use cases of AWS Wavelength.

The primary advantage of AWS Wavelength is its ability to significantly reduce latency. Deploying computing resources at the edge of the 5G network, AWS Wavelength enables applications to process data closer to end-users. This proximity minimizes the round-trip time for data to travel between devices and the cloud, resulting in lower latency and improved performance. This is particularly crucial for latency-sensitive applications, where even a fraction of a second can make a difference in user experience.

Moreover, AWS Wavelength provides seamless integration with AWS services, allowing developers to extend their existing applications to the edge without significant modifications. This ensures a smooth transition for developers already familiar with AWS infrastructure and services. The compatibility with popular AWS services simplifies the development and deployment process, enabling organizations to leverage the benefits of edge computing without a steep learning curve.

Another key aspect of AWS Wavelength is its scalability. As the demand for low latency applications grow, AWS Wavelength allows organizations to scale their infrastructure horizontally by deploying instances at multiple edge locations. This scalability ensures that applications can handle increasing workloads while maintaining low latency, providing a flexible and responsive environment for diverse use cases.

AWS Wavelength caters to a wide range of use cases across various industries. In gaming, for instance, real-time multiplayer games can benefit from reduced latency, providing players with a more immersive and responsive experience. Similarly, in AR and VR applications, where responsiveness is critical for user engagement, AWS Wavelength ensures that the processing power is brought closer to the end-user device, enhancing the overall experience.

In the context of IoT, AWS Wavelength enables organizations to process and analyze data at the edge, reducing the need to send large volumes of raw data to the cloud. This not only minimizes bandwidth requirements but also allows for quicker decision-making based on real-time insights. For autonomous vehicles, smart cities, and industrial automation, AWS Wavelength offers a platform to deploy edge computing solutions, enhancing the efficiency and responsiveness of these systems.

- **Key features of AWS Wavelength**:
    - **Ultra-low latency infrastructure**: The core of AWS Wavelength is its ability to deploy compute and storage resources at the edge of telecommunication networks. This proximity minimizes the round-trip time between the end-user device and the application, resulting in ultra-low latency. This is particularly crucial for applications that demand real-time responsiveness, such as AR, VR and gaming.

    - **Seamless integration with AWS services**: AWS Wavelength seamlessly integrates with various AWS services, enabling developers to extend their existing applications to the edge without major architectural changes. This includes popular services like Amazon EC2, AWS Lambda, and Amazon S3, providing a familiar environment for developers to build and deploy applications.

    - **5G network integration**: Wavelength is designed to coordinate with 5G networks, leveraging their high-speed, low latency capabilities. Co-locating AWS infrastructure with 5G networks ensures that data travels the shortest distance possible, reducing latency and enhancing the overall user experience.

    - **Global reach**: AWS Wavelength is strategically deployed in multiple locations worldwide, extending its global reach. This ensures developers can deploy edge applications closer to their end-users, regardless of their geographic location, fostering a consistent and reliable user experience.

- **Use cases of AWS Wavelength**:
    - **Gaming**: Online gaming demands instantaneous response times to provide a seamless and immersive experience. AWS Wavelength allows game developers to deploy compute resources at the edge, ensuring minimal latency and delivering a gaming experience that rivals traditional, on-premises setups.

    - **AR and VR applications**: AR and VR applications rely heavily on low latency to provide users with a realistic and responsive environment. Leveraging AWS Wavelength, developers can deploy the necessary resources at the edge, reducing latency and enhancing the overall quality of AR and VR experiences.

    - **IoT edge computing**: IoT devices generate vast amounts of data that require real-time processing. Wavelength facilitates IoT edge computing deploying compute resources closer to the devices, allowing faster data processing and response times.

    - **Live video streaming**: Latency can significantly impact the viewer's experience of live events or streaming services, AWS Wavelength enables broadcasters to deploy edge resources, reducing the latency of live video streams and enhancing the overall quality of streaming services.

AWS Wavelength represents a pivotal advancement in cloud computing, bringing compute and storage resources closer to end-users to achieve ultra-low latency. Its integration with 5G networks, seamless connection to AWS services, and global reach make it a powerful tool for various latency-sensitive applications. As industries continue to embrace technologies that demand real-time responsiveness, AWS Wavelength stands out as a key enabler, allowing developers to create innovative and immersive experiences for users across the globe. As the digital landscape continues to evolve, AWS Wavelength is poised to play a central role in shaping the future of edge computing and low latency applications.

Conclusion

This chapter has provided a comprehensive exploration of AWS Global applications and CDN, elaborating on their pivotal role in enhancing the performance, reliability, and global reach of modern applications. Leveraging AWS Global Accelerator and AWS CloudFront, businesses can seamlessly deploy and manage applications across a distributed network of edge locations.

The discussion emphasized the significance of low latency, high-throughput, and fault-tolerant solutions in today's digital landscape, where user experience is paramount. AWS

Global applications enable organizations to achieve optimal global routing and traffic management, ensuring that end-users experience minimal latency and enjoy reliable access to applications.

Furthermore, the integration of AWS CloudFront as a robust CDN solution has been explored, highlighting its ability to accelerate the delivery of dynamic and static content. The chapter has underscored the importance of leveraging CloudFront's vast network of edge locations to cache and distribute content closer to end-users, reducing latency and improving load times.

As businesses expand their global footprint, the insights provided in this chapter serve as a valuable guide for architects and developers seeking to optimize their applications for a worldwide audience. By harnessing the power of AWS Global applications and CDN, organizations can enhance their digital presence and ensure a seamless and responsive user experience across diverse geographical regions. The integration of these AWS services emerges as a strategic imperative for those aiming to stay at the forefront of the ever-evolving digital landscape.

In the next chapter, we will study AWS events and message delivery; we will see AWS SQS, SNS, and other messaging services like Kinesis and AWS MQ used to communicate across services and web applications.

Points to remember

- **Global application deployment**:

    o AWS provides services and features that enable the deployment of applications on a global scale.

    o Global applications are designed to deliver low latency, high-performance experiences to users worldwide.

- **Amazon CloudFront**: It is AWS CDN service:

    o It accelerates the delivery of content, such as web pages, images, and videos, by distributing it across a network of edge locations.

    o Edge locations are strategically positioned around the world to reduce latency and improve user experience.

- **Benefits of CDN include**:

    o **Improved latency**: Content is served from the nearest edge location to the user, reducing the time it takes to load.

    o **Scalability**: CDN automatically scales to handle varying levels of traffic and demand.

- o **DDoS protection**: CDN can help mitigate Distributed Denial of Service (DDoS) attacks by distributing traffic across multiple locations.

- **Integration with AWS services**:

  - o CloudFront integrates seamlessly with other AWS services like Amazon S3, EC2, and Lambda.

  - o It can be used to accelerate the delivery of dynamic, static, and streaming content.

  - o The requests and responses could be customized on the edge using CloudFront Functions for short-lived small tasks deployed on all the CDN edge locations (400+ in the world) or using more powerful and long-running Lambda@Edge functions deployed in regional edge locations, able to access some AWS services and the internet to better customize some specific functionality.

- **Route 53 AWS DNS service**:

  - o Amazon Route 53 is a scalable and highly available DNS web service.

  - o It translates friendly domain names into IP addresses, directing traffic to the appropriate resources.

- **Global traffic management with Route 53**:

  - o Route 53 can be configured for global traffic management, directing users to the nearest endpoint based on their geographic location.

  - o It supports routing policies like latency-based routing, geolocation-based routing, and weighted routing.

- **High availability and Fault-tolerance**:

  - o Both CloudFront and Route 53 contribute to the high availability and Fault-tolerance of global applications.

  - o CloudFront distributes content to multiple edge locations, reducing the risk of a single point of failure.

  - o Route 53's global traffic management ensures users are directed to healthy endpoints.

- **Security considerations**:

  - o AWS provides security features such as SSL/TLS support, access controls, and AWS **Web Application Firewall (WAF)** for securing global applications.

  - o It is essential to implement security best practices to protect against various threats and vulnerabilities.

- **Monitoring and performance optimization**:
  - o Utilize AWS CloudWatch and other monitoring tools to keep track of the performance and health of global applications.
  - o Continuously optimize configurations to ensure optimal performance and cost-effectiveness.

- **Cost management**:
  - o Understand the cost implications of deploying a global application using AWS services.
  - o Utilize AWS pricing tools and consider cost optimization strategies to manage expenses effectively.

By understanding and implementing these key points, the readers can enhance the global portability and high availability of their AWS environments and contribute to a fast and always-on cloud infrastructure.

Exercises

1. **What AWS service is commonly used to distribute content globally and reduce latency for end-users?**

    a. Amazon S3

    b. Amazon EC2

    c. Amazon CloudFront

    d. Amazon Route 53

2. **Which AWS service provides a scalable and secure DNS (DNS) web service?**

    a. Amazon S3

    b. Amazon EC2

    c. Amazon CloudFront

    d. Amazon Route 53

3. **In the context of AWS Global applications, what is the primary purpose of a CDN?**

    a. Load balancing

    b. Database management

    c. Distributing content globally

    d. Serverless computing

4. **Which AWS service can be used to route end-user requests to the closest AWS endpoint, thus optimizing global application performance?**

    a. Amazon S3

    b. Amazon EC2

    c. Amazon CloudFront

    d. Amazon Route 53

5. **What is the benefit of using Amazon CloudFront with Amazon S3 for static content delivery?**

    a. Improved security

    b. Faster content delivery

    c. Enhanced database performance

    d. Cost reduction

6. **Which AWS service is suitable for securely storing and retrieving any amount of data at any time?**

    a. Amazon S3

    b. Amazon EC2

    c. Amazon CloudFront

    d. Amazon Route 53

7. **What is the primary function of Amazon Route 53 in a global application architecture?**

    a. Load balancing

    b. DNS web service

    c. Content delivery

    d. Serverless computing

8. **How does Amazon CloudFront help improve a global application's performance?**

    a. By providing serverless computing

    b. By distributing content globally

    c. By managing databases efficiently

    d. By optimizing DNS services

9. **In a global application scenario, what role does latency play, and how can a CDN help mitigate it?**

   a. Latency has no impact on global applications.

   b. Lower latency improves user experience, and CDNs distribute content closer to end-users.

   c. Higher latency is desirable for better security, and CDNs slow down content delivery intentionally.

   d. Latency is only relevant for on-premises applications, not for global cloud-based applications.

Answers

1. c
2. d
3. c
4. d
5. b
6. a
7. b
8. b
9. b

Key terms

- AWS Route 53
- Domain Name System
- AWS CloudFront
- Content delivery network
- Edge locations
- Edge functions
- S3 Transfer Acceleration
- AWS Global Accelerator
- AWS Outpost
- AWS Wavelength

CHAPTER 10
AWS Events and Messages

Introduction

AWS provides a robust set of event-driven messaging services that are pivotal in building scalable and resilient applications. The key components are Amazon **Simple Queue Service** (**SQS**) and Amazon **Simple Notification Service** (**SNS**). SQS is a fully managed message queuing service that allows decoupling components in a distributed system, ensuring reliable and asynchronous communication between them. On the other hand, SNS enables the **publish/subscribe** (**pub/sub**) messaging paradigm and broadcast messages to multiple subscribers, enhancing flexibility and adaptability in distributed architectures.

In addition to SQS and SNS, AWS offers other powerful services to address diverse messaging and event streaming requirements. Amazon Kinesis is designed for real-time streaming data processing, providing the capability to ingest, process, and analyze data in near real-time. Amazon MQ is a managed message broker service based on the popular Apache ActiveMQ that supports industry-standard protocols, making it seamless for migrating existing applications. AWS EventBridge simplifies event-driven application development through the easy integration of various AWS services and third-party applications through a central event bus.

These AWS event and messaging services collectively form a comprehensive ecosystem, offering developers the flexibility to choose the most suitable solution based on the specific needs of their applications. Whether building decoupled microservices, handling real-time data streams, or orchestrating event-driven workflows, AWS provides a diverse set of tools to empower developers in creating scalable, responsive, and resilient systems.

Structure

In this chapter, we will cover the following topics:

- Amazon Simple Queue Service
- Amazon Simple Notification Service
- Other AWS services for event and messaging
- Other AWS event-driven services

Objectives

The primary objective of this chapter is to study the robust event and messaging systems provided by AWS. The chapter aims to provide a comprehensive understanding of key AWS services, focusing on SQS and SNS. Studying these foundational messaging services, readers will gain insights into the core principles of decoupling and scalability in distributed systems. This foundational knowledge sets the stage for a deeper exploration of more advanced messaging solutions within the AWS ecosystem, such as Amazon Kinesis, Amazon MQ, and Amazon EventBridge. The chapter further aims to elucidate the core concepts and functionalities of SQS and SNS. Readers will explore how SQS facilitates the decoupling of components in a distributed architecture, ensuring reliable message delivery and Fault-tolerance. The discussion on SNS will center on its role in enabling pub/sub messaging patterns and providing a flexible and scalable communication channel for various AWS services. By comprehending the intricacies of these services, readers will lay a solid foundation for understanding how different applications can leverage them to enhance reliability, scalability, and flexibility.

Building on the foundational knowledge of SQS and SNS, the chapter will discuss more advanced messaging solutions within the AWS ecosystem. This includes a detailed study of Amazon Kinesis, which empowers users to process and analyze streaming data at scale. Additionally, the chapter will cover Amazon MQ, a managed message broker service supporting multiple protocols. The discussion will conclude with an overview of Amazon EventBridge, emphasizing its role as an event bus that simplifies the integration of various applications and services. By the end of the chapter, readers will have a comprehensive understanding of AWS event and messaging systems, enabling them to make informed decisions when architecting scalable and resilient cloud-based applications.

Amazon Simple Queue Service

Amazon SQS is a fully managed message queuing service provided by AWS that enables the decoupling and scaling of microservices, distributed systems, and serverless applications. It allows different components of an application to communicate and exchange data asynchronously by sending, storing, and receiving messages at scale. By separating message producers and consumers, SQS helps eliminate direct dependencies, reducing system complexity and improving reliability. Its scalable architecture supports high throughput workloads, making it suitable for a wide range of applications, from simple job processing to complex workflows.

SQS offers two types of message queues: Standard queues and **First-In-First-Out** (**FIFO**) queues. Standard queues provide high throughput and best-effort message delivery, with the possibility of message duplication or out-of-order delivery. This makes them ideal for use cases like event logging or batch processing, where strict ordering is not critical. FIFO queues, on the other hand, guarantee exactly once processing and strict message ordering, which is essential for applications that require consistent and predictable behavior, such as financial transactions or inventory management systems. Both queue types ensure that messages are durably stored until they are successfully processed or expire.

SQS also integrates seamlessly with other AWS services, such as Lambda, SNS, and CloudWatch, enabling powerful event-driven architectures and monitoring capabilities. Developers can easily incorporate SQS into workflows using SDKs, CLI, or the AWS Management Console. Additionally, SQS automatically scales based on demand, eliminating the need for manual provisioning or capacity planning. With built-in security features like encryption, **Identity and Access Management** (**IAM**) policies, and access controls, SQS provides a robust and secure foundation for building scalable and decoupled applications.

Definition of a queue

In IT, queues play an important role in managing and optimizing data flow and processes. A queue refers to a data structure that follows the FIFO principle, where the first element added is the first to be removed. This concept is analogous to a real-world queue, such as people waiting in line at a grocery store or a ticket counter. Queues are indispensable in IT systems for their ability to orchestrate tasks, coordinate processes, and ensure efficient communication between different components.

A queue consists of elements or items arranged in a linear order. Each element is enqueued, or added to the end of the queue, and dequeued, or removed from the front of the queue, in a sequential manner. This simple structure enables a variety of applications in IT systems, ranging from task scheduling to managing asynchronous communication.

Queues are implemented using various data structures, with linked lists and arrays being the most common. Linked lists offer dynamic memory allocation and are well-suited for scenarios where the queue size may vary. On the other hand, arrays provide constant-time access to elements but have a fixed size. The choice of the underlying data structure depends on the specific requirements and constraints of the IT system in question.

Use cases of queues in IT

Queues, such as those provided by AWS SQS, are widely used in IT to enable asynchronous communication between different components of an application, ensuring decoupling and scalability. Common use cases include:

- **Task processing**: Queues handle tasks like image resizing, video encoding, or data processing by distributing jobs to worker instances for asynchronous processing.

- **Message buffering**: Smooth out traffic spikes by temporarily storing messages, preventing backend systems from becoming overloaded.

- **Workflow orchestration**: Manage task sequencing in multi-step processes, ensuring reliable execution of workflows.

- **Event-driven architectures**: Relay events to downstream services, such as AWS Lambda or other consumers, for real-time or batch processing.

- **Decoupling microservices**: Enable independent scaling and reduce dependencies between services, improving Fault-tolerance and scalability.

- **Retry mechanisms**: Ensure reliable message delivery by supporting retries in case of temporary processing failures.

Message queues are widely used in enterprise applications, microservices architectures, and event-driven systems. Popular message queue systems like RabbitMQ, Apache Kafka, and AWS SQS provide reliable and scalable solutions for managing communication between disparate components.

Challenges and considerations

While queues offer numerous advantages in IT systems, some challenges and considerations must be addressed to ensure their effective implementation. Following is some of those:

- **Scalability**: In scenarios with rapidly changing workloads, the scalability of queues becomes a crucial factor. Ensuring that the queue system can handle varying levels of demand is essential for maintaining optimal performance. Cloud-based queue services often provide elasticity, automatically scaling resources based on demand.

- **Reliability and durability**: For mission-critical applications, the reliability and durability of queues are paramount. Message queues, in particular, need mechanisms to handle message persistence and ensure that messages are not lost in the event of a system failure. Redundancy and backup strategies are often employed to enhance the durability of queues in such scenarios.

- **Latency and throughput**: The choice of queue implementation can significantly impact the latency and throughput of an IT system. Different types of queues, such as in-memory queues or persistent message queues, have varying characteristics. It is crucial to select the appropriate type of queue based on the specific requirements of the application to achieve the desired balance between low latency and high throughput.

Queues are indispensable in information technology, providing a fundamental mechanism for managing tasks, orchestrating processes, and facilitating communication between different components. Whether it is task scheduling in operating systems, managing communication in distributed systems, or optimizing resource utilization in cloud computing environments, queues play a central role in enhancing the efficiency and reliability of IT systems. As technology continues to evolve, the role of queues is likely to expand, making them a foundational concept for the design and implementation of robust and scalable IT solutions.

Overview of AWS SQS

SQS acts as a mediator between different components of a distributed system, allowing them to communicate asynchronously. It helps in decoupling the sender and receiver components, which promotes fault isolation and improves overall system resilience. SQS supports both standard and FIFO queues, catering to different message processing requirements.

Standard queues provide at least one delivery, meaning each message is delivered at least once. FIFO queues provide exactly one processing, meaning each message is delivered once and remains available until a consumer processes it and deletes it. Duplicates are not introduced into the queue.

Types of SQS queues

AWS SQS supports high throughput standard queues and strictly ordered FIFO queues. SQS simplifies message management for diverse use cases like task processing, workflow orchestration, and microservice decoupling while automatically scaling to meet demand. The following are the various types of queues offered by AWS SQS:

- **Standard queues**: Standard queues in SQS provide a reliable, highly scalable, and fully managed queuing service. They deliver messages at least once and support a nearly unlimited number of transactions per second. Standard queues provide best-effort ordering, meaning that the order of messages is preserved, but occasionally, messages might be delivered out of order. This makes standard queues suitable for use cases where order is not critical, and the system can handle occasional message reordering.

- **FIFO queues**: They ensure that messages are processed exactly once and in the order they are received. They are ideal for applications that require strict ordering, such as financial transactions or ensuring the correctness of data processing. FIFO queues are designed to provide a higher level of message ordering and deduplication compared to standard queues. However, they have a lower throughput than standard queues and may incur a slightly higher cost.

SQS pricing

AWS SQS pricing is designed to be flexible and cost-effective, allowing you to pay only for what you use. Charges are based on the number of requests made and the volume of data transferred, with separate pricing tiers for standard queues and FIFO queues. Additional costs may apply for features like message storage beyond the Free Tier or long polling. AWS also provides a generous Free Tier, offering one million requests per month for free, making SQS accessible for both small-scale and enterprise-level applications. The following is a breakdown of the key pricing components:

- **Request pricing**: SQS charges for the number of requests made to the service. Requests include actions such as sending a message, receiving a message, and deleting a message. Both standard and FIFO queues have request-based pricing.

- **Data transfer pricing**: Data transfer costs are associated only with the data transferred out of SQS. Inbound data transfer (messages sent to SQS) is typically free. However, outbound data transfer (messages retrieved from SQS) incurs charges based on the amount of data transferred.

- **Message retention and dead letter queue charges**: SQS allows configuration of the retention period for messages in a queue. There are additional charges for messages that remain in the queue beyond the Free Tier retention period. **Dead-letter queues (DLQs)**, which capture undeliverable messages for analysis, also have associated charges.

- **Extended retention**: SQS provides a feature called **extended message retention**, allowing you to store messages in Amazon S3 for longer durations. Extended retention incurs additional charges based on the storage used in S3.

Key features of AWS SQS

Amazon SQS offers a range of key features designed to simplify message queuing and enable reliable communication between application components. These include fully managed infrastructure with automatic scaling, support for both standard and FIFO queues to suit different use cases, high message durability, and configurable message retention. SQS ensures secure message transmission with encryption at rest and in transit, integrates seamlessly with other AWS services, and provides advanced features like delay queues, message batching, and DLQs for error handling. These capabilities make SQS a powerful tool for building scalable, decoupled, and fault-tolerant applications. The following are some key features of AWS SQS:

- **Fully managed**: AWS SQS is a fully managed service, which means AWS takes care of the operational overhead such as infrastructure provisioning, maintenance, and scaling.

- **Scalability**: SQS scales seamlessly with the size of the workload, ensuring that applications can handle varying message volumes without any manual intervention.

- **Reliability**: SQS stores messages redundantly across multiple servers and data centers, ensuring high availability and durability of messages.

- **Security**: It integrates with AWS IAM for access control and provides features like encryption in transit and at rest for enhanced security.

Use cases and benefits of AWS SQS

AWS SQS provides a reliable way to transmit, store, and process messages between distributed components, ensuring smooth communication and workflow orchestration. With features like high scalability, secure message delivery, and support for asynchronous processing, SQS is ideal for use cases such as task queues, event-driven systems, and microservice decoupling.

The following are the use cases of AWS SQS:

- **Decoupling applications**: SQS is commonly used in microservices architectures to help decouple different services thanks to his asynchronous messaging. This allows for independent scaling and development of microservices reducing direct dependencies across services and parts of an application. Instead of coupling one application together we can slice different microservices and let them communicate through SQS in an event-driven style.

- **Batch processing**: It facilitates batch processing by allowing messages to be sent in groups, improving efficiency and reducing latency.

- **Event-driven systems**: SQS is well-suited for building event-driven systems where components react to events by processing messages from queues.

- **Reliable workload distribution**: SQS ensures that messages are distributed reliably across multiple consumers, enabling efficient workload distribution.

The benefits of AWS SQS include:

- **Fault-tolerance**: With SQS, components can continue processing messages even if one or more components fail. This Fault-tolerance is crucial for building robust and resilient systems.

- **Scalability**: SQS automatically scales to accommodate changes in message volume, ensuring that applications can handle increased loads without manual intervention.

- **Cost-efficiency**: The pay-as-you-go pricing model of SQS ensures cost-efficiency. Users only pay for the messages they send and receive, without worrying about infrastructure management costs.

AWS SQS usage and best practices

AWS SQS enables secure, decoupled, and scalable communication between application components. It supports use cases like task processing, event-driven workflows, and buffering traffic spikes. Best practices for SQS include choosing the right queue type (Standard or FIFO) based on your requirements, implementing DLQs to handle message processing failures, using encryption for data security, and leveraging message attributes to filter and route messages efficiently.

The following is how to get started with AWS SQS:

- **Create a queue**: To get started with SQS, users can create a queue through the AWS Management Console, AWS SDKs, or AWS **Command Line Interface** (**CLI**).

- **Send and receive messages**: Once a queue is created, components can start sending messages to it, and other components can retrieve and process those messages.

The best practices include:

- **Visibility timeout**: Set an appropriate visibility timeout to ensure that messages are not processed by multiple consumers simultaneously.

- **DLQs**: Use DLQs to capture and analyze messages that could not be processed successfully, aiding in identifying and resolving issues.

- **Monitoring and metrics**: Leverage AWS CloudWatch to monitor SQS queues, Setup alarms for critical metrics, and gain insights into the performance of your message processing.

The following are the advanced features of AWS SQS:

- **Long polling:** It uses long polling to reduce the number of empty responses, making message retrieval more efficient and cost-effective.

- **Message attributes**: It utilizes message attributes to provide additional metadata and context to messages.

SQS dead-letter queue

SQS is designed to be highly available and scalable, ensuring that messages are reliably delivered between producers and consumers, even in varying workloads. One crucial aspect of SQS is its support for DLQs, which enhance the reliability and Fault-tolerance of distributed systems.

DLQ in AWS SQS is a special queue designated to store messages that cannot be processed successfully after a certain number of attempts. When a message in the main queue repeatedly fails to be processed, it is moved to the DLQ, allowing for further analysis and troubleshooting without affecting the main processing flow. Several scenarios may lead to a message being sent to the DLQ. One common situation is when the processing of a message encounters errors or exceptions repeatedly, indicating a potential issue with the consumer or the message content. The DLQ serves as a safety net, preventing messages that might cause a continuous failure loop from blocking the processing of other messages in the main queue.

Configuring a DLQ involves associating it with a standard SQS queue. Each standard SQS queue can be linked to a DLQ, and the system will automatically move messages to the DLQ after a specified number of delivery attempts. This number is customizable based on the specific needs of the application. DLQs also offer visibility into the failed messages by allowing developers to inspect the contents of the problematic messages and understand the reasons behind their failure. This insight is invaluable for diagnosing and addressing issues within the application.

Best practices for AWS SQS DLQs

AWS recommends using DLQs as a best practice for handling message processing failures in SQS. A DLQ is a secondary queue that captures messages that could not be successfully processed after multiple attempts. By configuring DLQs, you can isolate and analyze problematic messages without impacting the flow of your primary queue, ensuring reliable message delivery and system resilience. This approach helps with debugging, monitoring, and improving the overall robustness of message processing workflows by retaining failed messages for further inspection and troubleshooting. Effectively leveraging AWS SQS DLQs requires adhering to best practices to ensure optimal performance and reliability in distributed systems. Following are some of the best practices to use SQS DLQs effectively:

- **Monitoring and logging**: Implement thorough monitoring and logging for both the main queue and the associated DLQ. AWS CloudWatch can be used to setup alarms for specific metrics, providing real-time visibility into the health of the queues.

- **Redrive policies**: Configure redrive policies to specify the maximum number of receive attempts for a message before it is moved to the DLQ. This ensures that problematic messages are promptly identified and addressed without causing prolonged disruptions.

- **DLQ retry mechanism**: Integrate a robust retry mechanism for processing messages retrieved from the DLQ. After addressing the issues that caused the initial failures, messages can be retried and reprocessed to prevent unnecessary message loss.

- **Handling poison messages**: Identify and handle poison messages that consistently fail to process. These may indicate issues with the message content or the processing logic. Analyze and modify the application to handle such messages appropriately.

- **Testing and simulation**: Simulate failure scenarios to validate the DLQ setup and ensure that messages are correctly redirected to the DLQ under various error conditions. This helps in building confidence in the Fault-tolerance mechanisms of the system.

AWS SQS DLQs are a crucial component in building robust and fault-tolerant distributed systems. By providing a mechanism to handle and analyze failed messages, DLQs contribute to the overall reliability and resilience of applications utilizing SQS for message queuing. Implementing best practices ensures that DLQs are effectively utilized, enhancing the overall operational excellence of the AWS infrastructure.

Amazon Simple Notification Service

AWS SNS stands out as a powerful and versatile messaging service that enables seamless communication between distributed components of a cloud-based application.

AWS SNS simplifies the task of sending messages or notifications to a distributed set of subscribers. Whether pushing updates to mobile devices, notifying stakeholders about critical events, or integrating with other AWS services, SNS serves as a flexible and scalable solution.

Notification services in AWS SNS

AWS SNS is a cloud-based messaging service that allows developers to send messages or notifications to a distributed set of subscribers via a variety of transport protocols. These protocols include HTTP/HTTPS, email/SMTP, SQS, AWS Lambda, and more. It enables the creation of topics where messages can be published, and subscribers can receive notifications based on their preferences and subscriptions.

The following are the components of the SNS notification service:

- **Topics**: In the context of SNS, a topic is a communication channel to which messages can be published. Subscribers, or endpoints, can then receive these messages. Topics act as the central hub for message distribution in a pub/sub model.

- **Subscribers**: Subscribers are the entities that receive messages from topics. These can be endpoints such as HTTP endpoints, email addresses, Lambda functions, and more. Subscribers define the transport protocol and endpoint-specific details for receiving notifications.

- **SNS and the notification service**: The notification service in SNS enables the delivery of messages to subscribers in real time. This service is designed to be highly scalable, ensuring that messages are reliably delivered to all subscribed endpoints. The decoupling of publishers and subscribers allows for flexibility and adaptability in the overall system architecture.

The following are the capabilities of the SNS notification service:

- **Multiple protocol support**: SNS supports multiple protocols, allowing messages to be delivered to a wide range of endpoints. This flexibility enables developers to choose the most suitable communication mechanism for their applications. Whether it is a mobile push notification, an email alert, or a call to an AWS Lambda function, SNS accommodates various communication channels seamlessly.

- **Message filtering**: SNS supports message filtering, allowing subscribers to receive only the messages that are relevant to them. This feature is particularly useful in scenarios where a single topic caters to multiple types of events, and subscribers are interested in specific message attributes. Filtering ensures that subscribers receive only messages that match their predefined criteria, reducing unnecessary processing and improving efficiency.

- **Fanout and scalability**: The fanout capability of SNS allows for the distribution of messages to a large number of subscribers in parallel. This ensures that as the number of subscribers grows, the system remains scalable and can handle increased message volume without sacrificing performance. The fanout architecture makes SNS suitable for use cases ranging from small applications to large-scale, global systems.

The following are the use cases and best practices of SNS:

- **Real-time alerts and notifications**: SNS is commonly used to send real-time alerts and notifications to users or systems based on events or changes in the application. Whether it is notifying users about a new message, alerting administrators to a system issue, or triggering automated workflows, SNS plays a vital role in keeping stakeholders informed in real-time.

- **Mobile push notifications**: For mobile applications, SNS can be integrated to send push notifications to devices running on iOS, Android, or other mobile platforms. This is especially valuable for engaging users with timely updates and relevant information.

- **Topic naming conventions**: Adopting a clear and consistent naming convention for topics is crucial for maintaining an organized and easily manageable SNS environment. This becomes especially important as the number of topics and subscribers grows.

- **Monitoring and logging**: Implementing robust monitoring and logging practices helps track the performance and health of SNS. AWS CloudWatch can be utilized to monitor metrics, set alarms, and gain insights into the usage patterns of SNS topics.

The notification service in AWS SNS is a fundamental component for enabling real-time communication and event-driven architectures in cloud-based applications. With its support for multiple protocols, message filtering, and scalable fanout capabilities, SNS provides developers with a powerful tool for building flexible and responsive systems.

Key features of AWS SNS are mentioned in the following:

- **Topics and subscriptions**: The core building blocks of SNS are topics and subscriptions. Topics act as communication channels, and subscribers can receive messages published on these topics. Subscribers can include Amazon SQS queues, AWS Lambda functions, HTTP endpoints, and more.

- **Pub/sub model**: SNS operates on a pub/sub model, allowing decoupling between the sender (publisher) and the receivers (subscribers). This model enhances the scalability and flexibility of applications, making them more resilient to changes and updates.

- **Message filtering**: SNS supports message filtering, enabling subscribers to receive only the messages relevant to their interests. This feature optimizes resource utilization and ensures that recipients receive only the information they require.

- **Delivery protocols**: SNS supports various delivery protocols, including **Short Message Service** (**SMS**), email, HTTP/HTTPS, and more. This diversity facilitates the integration of SNS into a broad range of applications, making it adaptable to different communication requirements.

Use cases of AWS SNS

AWS SNS is a fully managed messaging service that enables the efficient delivery of messages to multiple subscribers, applications, and endpoints. It supports use cases like pub/sub messaging, where one message can be broadcast to many recipients; application alerts, by sending real-time notifications to mobile devices, emails, or SMS; event-driven architectures, where SNS triggers workflows in response to events from other AWS services; and system monitoring, sending notifications to teams or systems based on custom metrics or alarms. SNS simplifies communication between distributed systems and enhances scalability, reliability, and responsiveness in applications. AWS SNS finds application in a multitude of scenarios, enhancing communication and coordination in cloud-based architectures:

- **Mobile app notifications**: SNS is widely used for sending push notifications to mobile devices. Developers can easily integrate SNS into their applications to notify users about updates, messages, or important events.

- **Alerts and monitoring**: SNS plays a crucial role in alerting and monitoring systems. It can be integrated with various AWS services to trigger notifications based on events, ensuring timely responses to critical situations.

- **Application-to-application communication**: SNS facilitates communication between different components of an application, helping achieve asynchronous messaging and event distribution. This is particularly useful in microservices architectures.

- **Fan-out architectures**: With the pub/sub model, SNS is well-suited for fan-out architectures, where a single message can be sent to multiple subscribers concurrently. This is advantageous in scenarios where parallel processing of information is required.

AWS SNS empowers developers to create resilient, scalable, and responsive applications by providing a reliable messaging infrastructure.

Types of SNS messages

AWS SNS supports different types of messages for flexible communication across distributed systems. These include text messages, for sending simple notifications; email notifications, which can be sent to individuals or groups; SMS messages, for delivering alerts directly to mobile phones; and mobile push notifications, for app notifications on iOS or Android devices. SNS also supports messages to HTTP/HTTPS endpoints and AWS Lambda functions, allowing for integration with various applications and services. Each message type can be customized to fit the needs of different use cases, enabling efficient and reliable communication across platforms. The following are the detailed types of SNS messages:

- **Pub/sub messaging**:
  - **Topic-based messaging**: SNS allows the creation of topics to which messages can be published. Subscribers interested in specific topics receive notifications whenever a message is published to the corresponding topic. This pub/sub model facilitates decoupling between the sender and receiver components, enhancing scalability and flexibility.

- **Point-to-point messaging**:
  - **Direct messaging**: SNS also supports direct messaging, where messages are sent to individual endpoints (such as mobile devices or email addresses). This allows for personalized communication tailored to specific recipients.

- **Fanout messaging**:
  - **Broadcast messaging**: With SNS, messages can be broadcast to multiple endpoints simultaneously. This is particularly useful when a message needs to reach a wide audience or when redundancy and Fault-tolerance are essential.

Protocols supported by AWS SNS

AWS SNS supports multiple protocols for message delivery, ensuring compatibility with various devices and services. Some of the supported protocols include:

- HTTP/HTTPS
- Amazon SQS
- Email/Email-JSON
- SMS
- SNS (SNS)
- Application (for mobile push notifications)

Pricing structure

Understanding the pricing structure is crucial for optimizing costs and ensuring efficient use of AWS SNS. The pricing for AWS SNS is primarily based on two components:

- **Requests**: The charges are basis the number of requests made to the SNS service. This includes actions like publishing messages, creating topics, subscribing endpoints, etc. The pricing varies depending on the request type.

- **Data transfer**: Data transfer charges apply when delivering messages to different AWS Regions or when sending SMS messages. The pricing is tiered based on the volume of data transferred.

It is essential to consider the message size and delivery frequency, as they directly impact costs. Additionally, cross-region communication and SMS delivery costs should be factored in when estimating expenses.

Cost optimization tips

AWS SNS offers several cost optimization tips to help users reduce expenses while maintaining efficient messaging. By selecting the appropriate message delivery protocols and optimizing message formats, users can ensure more cost-effective communication. Additionally, managing subscriptions and implementing message filtering can prevent unnecessary charges. With these best practices, AWS SNS users can keep costs low while scaling their messaging infrastructure efficiently. The following tips help with cost optimization:

- **Message compression**: Compress messages before publishing them to reduce data transfer costs.

- **Batching**: Combine multiple messages into a single request to minimize the number of requests and lower costs.

- **Lifecycle policies**: Implement lifecycle policies to automatically delete unused topics and subscriptions, avoiding unnecessary charges.

- **Monitoring and alerts**: Setup monitoring and alerts to track SNS usage and costs, enabling proactive management and optimization.

Amazon SNS plays a vital role in creating flexible and scalable communication systems in the AWS ecosystem. Understanding the types of messages, supported protocols, and the pricing structure is crucial for making informed decisions about its usage. By effectively leveraging AWS SNS and implementing cost optimization strategies, businesses can ensure efficient communication within their distributed systems while managing costs effectively.

Other AWS services for event and messaging

In this section, we study other services that enable us to architect real-time event-driven systems for different use cases, from real-time ingestion of events to coordinated custom events in an event bus that can connect different services in architecture.

Event-driven programming

Event-driven programming is a programming paradigm that revolves around the occurrence of events, such as user actions, sensor outputs, or system notifications, rather than the traditional sequential flow of control. In this conceptual framework, the execution of a program is determined by events that trigger specific actions or responses. Events can be user interactions, like mouse clicks or keyboard inputs, or they can be generated by the system, such as timer expirations or data arriving from external sources.

One key aspect of the event-driven concept is the decoupling of components within a system. Instead of relying on direct method calls or tight dependencies between modules, components communicate through events. This decoupling promotes modularity and flexibility, as changes to one part of the system are less likely to affect other components. This makes event-driven programming particularly suitable for building responsive and scalable applications, as it enables parallel processing of events without blocking the main execution thread.

In an event-driven system, a central component called the **event dispatcher** or **event bus** manages the flow of events. Components interested in particular events register themselves as listeners, and the event dispatcher notifies them when the corresponding events occur. This asynchronous and loosely coupled nature of event-driven programming makes it well-suited for various applications, ranging from graphical user interfaces to distributed systems and real-time processing environments.

Asynchronous programming

In the context of event-driven systems, the concept of asynchronous programming plays a pivotal role in optimizing performance and responsiveness. Asynchronous programming refers to a programming paradigm where tasks can execute independently of the main program flow, allowing for concurrent operations without waiting for each task to complete before moving on to the next. This is particularly valuable in event-driven systems, where events can occur unpredictably and concurrently.

In event-driven architectures, events such as user interactions or external triggers drive the flow of the program. Asynchronous programming enables handling these events efficiently by allowing the system to initiate and process tasks concurrently. Instead of blocking the entire program, asynchronous programming allows the system to continue executing other tasks. This responsiveness enhances the overall user experience and system efficiency, especially in scenarios where events occur asynchronously and may not follow a predetermined order.

One common implementation of asynchronous programming in event-driven systems is through the use of callbacks, promises, or asynchronous functions. These mechanisms enable the initiation of tasks that can run in the background, and once completed, trigger a callback function or handle the resolution of a promise. Asynchronous programming thus promotes scalability and responsiveness in event-driven systems, ensuring that tasks can be efficiently managed in parallel without hindering the overall system performance.

Other AWS event-driven services

AWS offers a range of event-driven computing services designed to enable real-time processing and analytics at scale. Here is a list of some of the most powerful services for building event-driven applications:

- One of these powerful services is Amazon Kinesis. Kinesis provides a platform for building real-time applications that can process streaming data at scale. Streaming data refers to a continuous flow of data that is generated in real-time or near real-time from multiple sources. This data is ingested, processed, and analyzed as it arrives, rather than being stored and processed later in batches. Amazon Kinesis includes multiple components like Kinesis Data Streams for ingesting and processing real-time data streams, Kinesis Data Firehose for loading streaming data into other AWS services, and Kinesis Data Analytics for analyzing streaming data using SQL queries. Kinesis is particularly useful in scenarios such as real-time analytics, machine learning model updates, and monitoring applications where low latency processing of data streams is crucial.

- Amazon MQ is another event system in AWS that manages message-oriented middleware, making it easier to Setup and operate message brokers. Built on the popular Apache ActiveMQ and RabbitMQ messaging engines, Amazon MQ supports industry-standard messaging protocols and provides a managed environment for message brokers. A message broker (for example, RabbitMQ) and a queue system (for example, Amazon SQS) both handle messaging but differ in control and complexity. A message broker is a full-fledged middleware that supports advanced messaging patterns (pub/sub, routing, persistence, transactions) and requires management. It typically follows a push-based model, delivering messages in near real-time. A queue system, like SQS, is a managed service focused on simple, reliable message queuing with less configuration, using a pull-based model where consumers retrieve messages on demand. Brokers offer more flexibility, while queue systems prioritize scalability and ease of use. Amazon MQ service simplifies the process of building decoupled and distributed applications by handling the complexities of message delivery and enabling reliable communication between different components. Amazon MQ is a versatile choice for applications that require reliable and scalable message queuing, such as order processing, task scheduling, and communication between microservices. You should use Amazon MQ over Amazon SQS when you need advanced messaging features, compatibility with traditional message brokers, and real-time message delivery. Amazon MQ supports protocols like AMQP, MQTT, OpenWire, and STOMP, making it ideal for migrating legacy applications that already rely on RabbitMQ or ActiveMQ. It also provides message ordering, transactions, persistent subscriptions, and lower latency, which are essential for complex architectures requiring fine-tuned messaging. In contrast, SQS is better for simple, decoupled, and scalable message queuing without managing brokers, making it ideal for cloud-native applications with unpredictable workloads.

- AWS EventBridge is a serverless event bus service that simplifies the development of event-driven architectures. It enables seamless communication between different AWS services, custom applications, and third-party **software as a service** (**SaaS**) applications. EventBridge allows the building of event-driven workflows, automation, and integrations without the need for complex code. Using event buses and rules, we can route events from one source to multiple targets, making it easier to connect and coordinate various components in applications. EventBridge supports a wide range of event sources, making it a versatile choice for creating loosely coupled and scalable architectures. A real-time scenario for using AWS EventBridge is in an e-commerce platform handling order processing. When a customer places an order, an OrderPlaced event is published to EventBridge, which then routes it to multiple downstream services in real-time. For example, it triggers a Lambda function to send a confirmation email, notifies the inventory management system to update stock levels, and invokes a shipping service to generate a tracking number. This event-driven architecture ensures seamless decoupling of services, scalability, and responsiveness without direct dependencies between them.

Amazon Kinesis

Amazon Kinesis is a fully managed and scalable cloud service provided by AWS that enables real-time processing of streaming data at scale. It is designed to handle large volumes of data generated by various sources, such as websites, mobile apps, IoT devices, and more. AWS Kinesis offers a set of services that allow users to ingest, process, and analyze streaming data in real-time, making it a powerful tool for applications that require immediate insights and responsiveness. Some of the features of Amazon Kinesis family of services are listed in the following:

- **Components of AWS Kinesis**: Amazon Kinesis comprises several key components, each serving a specific purpose in the streaming data pipeline:

  o **Kinesis Data Streams**: Kinesis Data Streams is the foundational service that allows us to ingest and process real-time data. It enables us to scale the ingestion of data by adding or removing shards dynamically. Producers can publish data to a stream, and consumers can subscribe to the stream to process and analyze the data.

  o **Kinesis Data Firehose**: Kinesis Data Firehose simplifies the process of loading streaming data to AWS for storage and analytics. It automatically scales to match the volume and throughput of the data. Data Firehose can deliver data to various destinations, such as Amazon S3, Amazon Redshift, and Amazon Elasticsearch, without the need for manual intervention.

  o **Kinesis Data Analytics**: Kinesis Data Analytics enables real-time processing and analysis of streaming data using SQL queries. It allows us to derive insights, detect anomalies, and make decisions based on the continuously flowing data. This service simplifies the development of real-time analytics applications without requiring low-level programming.

- **Use cases for AWS Kinesis**: Amazon Kinesis finds applications across a wide range of industries and use cases:

  o **Real-time analytics**: Businesses can gain immediate insights from streaming data to make data-driven decisions in real-time. Analytics applications can perform aggregations, filtering, and transformations on the data as it flows through the stream.

  o **Internet of Things (IoT)**: Kinesis is well-suited for handling data from IoT devices, allowing for real-time monitoring, analysis, and response to sensor data.

  o **Log and event data processing**: Organizations can use Kinesis for processing logs and events in real-time, enabling quick identification of issues and anomalies.

  o **Clickstream analytics**: online platforms can use Kinesis to process and analyze user clickstream data, providing insights into user behavior and preferences.

- **Architecture and features of AWS Kinesis**:

  o **Kinesis data streams architecture**: Data Streams consist of shards, which are the basic building blocks of the stream. Each shard has a specified capacity for ingesting and processing data, and the total capacity of the stream scales with the number of shares.

o **Scalability and elasticity**: One of the key features of Kinesis is its ability to scale horizontally by adding or removing shards dynamically. This allows the system to handle varying workloads and adapt to changes in the data volume.

o **Durability and retention**: Data durability is ensured by replicating data across Multiple **Availability Zones (AZs)**. Kinesis allows users to define retention periods for the data, ensuring that it is available for processing during the specified time frame.

o **Kinesis Data Firehose features**: Automatic scaling of resources to match the incoming data rate. Support for various data formats, including JSON, Apache Parquet, and Apache ORC. Integration with AWS services like Amazon S3, Amazon Redshift, and Amazon Elasticsearch for seamless data delivery.

o **Kinesis data analytics capabilities**: SQL-based language for real-time analytics. Integration with Kinesis Data Streams and Kinesis Data Firehose for input and output. Automatic handling of tasks like time-based windowing and aggregation.

Best practices and considerations for AWS Kinesis implementation:

- **Data serialization and compression**:

  o Optimize data transmission by choosing efficient serialization formats.

  o Implement compression techniques to reduce the amount of data transmitted, lowering costs and improving performance.

- **Monitoring and logging**:

  o Leverage AWS CloudWatch metrics to monitor the performance and health of Kinesis streams.

  o Setup detailed logging to capture information for troubleshooting and auditing purposes.

- **Security considerations**:

  o Implement appropriate IAM roles and policies to control access to Kinesis resources.

  o Use encryption for data at rest and in transit to ensure the security of sensitive information.

- **Error handling and retry mechanisms**:

  o Implement robust error handling and retry mechanisms to handle transient failures gracefully.

  o Configure appropriate retry policies to ensure the reliability of data processing.

- **Cost optimization**:
  - o Optimize costs by carefully choosing the number of shards based on the expected data volume.
  - o Monitor and adjust the capacity dynamically to match the workload, avoiding over-provisioning.
- **Consideration for ordering**:
  - o If data order is crucial, ensure that you choose the appropriate ordering mechanism based on the requirements of your application.
  - o Consider the trade-offs between ordering and scalability when designing the streaming data pipeline.

Following is the table highlighting the differences between Amazon Kinesis Data Streams, Amazon Kinesis Data Firehose, and Amazon Kinesis Data Analytics:

Feature	Kinesis Data Streams	Kinesis Data Firehose	Kinesis Data Analytics
Purpose	Real-time data streaming and processing	Near real-time data delivery to destinations	Real-time data analysis and processing
Data retention	24 hours (default) to 7 days	No retention (immediate delivery)	N/A (processing only)
Use case	High-speed data ingestion for custom applications	Automated delivery of streaming data to AWS services	Running SQL queries and analytics on streaming data
Processing latency	Milliseconds (low latency)	Minutes (buffering before delivery)	Milliseconds to seconds
Data transformation	Requires custom consumer applications (Lambda, EC2, etc.)	Supports built-in transformations (format conversions, compression, encryption)	SQL-based transformations and aggregations
Scalability	Manual scaling via shard allocation	Fully managed, auto-scales	Scales automatically based on input
Data destinations	Custom consumers (Lambda, EC2, Kinesis Firehose, etc.)	S3, Redshift, OpenSearch, HTTP endpoints, Datadog, Splunk, etc.	Outputs to Kinesis Streams, Firehose, or AWS services
Integration	Custom applications or AWS Lambda	Direct integration with AWS services	Works with Streams or Firehose
Best For	Real-time event processing (IoT, clickstream, logs)	Simplified real-time data ingestion and delivery	Streaming analytics and real-time dashboards

Table 10.1: Comparison of Kinesis Data Services Features

AWS Kinesis provides a comprehensive solution for real-time streaming data processing, offering a range of services to meet diverse application needs. Understanding its architecture, features, and best practices is crucial for successfully implementing and optimizing streaming data solutions on the AWS Cloud platform.

AWS MQ

Amazon MQ is a fully managed messaging service offered by AWS that facilitates the decoupling of applications by enabling seamless communication between them through message queues. This service abstracts the underlying complexity of message-oriented middleware, allowing businesses to focus on building scalable, resilient, and loosely coupled applications. In this overview, we will delve into the key features, benefits, and use cases of Amazon MQ.

Amazon MQ supports industry-standard messaging protocols, such as MQTT, AMQP, and STOMP, providing flexibility for developers to choose the most suitable protocol for their applications. It is built on the Apache ActiveMQ and RabbitMQ open-source messaging engines, ensuring reliability and performance. This fully managed service automates administrative tasks such as patching, monitoring, and backups, allowing businesses to offload operational overhead and concentrate on core application development. Let us see the key features, benefits, and use cases of Amazon MQ.

Following are the key features of Amazon MQ:

- **Protocol support**: Amazon MQ supports multiple messaging protocols, making it versatile for various use cases. Whether it is lightweight and efficient MQTT for IoT applications or the widely adopted AMQP for enterprise messaging, Amazon MQ accommodates diverse communication needs.

- **Message durability and persistence**: One of the critical aspects of messaging systems is the ability to ensure message durability. Amazon MQ achieves this through message persistence, safeguarding messages against system failures. With message persistence, businesses can rely on Amazon MQ for critical and reliable message delivery.

- **Horizontal scaling and high availability**: Amazon MQ supports horizontal scaling, allowing applications to handle varying workloads by dynamically adjusting the number of message brokers. Additionally, it offers high availability by distributing broker instances across multiple AZs. This ensures that applications remain resilient and available even in the face of infrastructure failures.

- **Integration with AWS services**: Amazon MQ seamlessly integrates with other AWS services, creating a cohesive ecosystem for building scalable and robust applications. Integration with AWS IAM provides secure access control, while compatibility with AWS CloudWatch allows for comprehensive monitoring and logging.

- **Managed operations and security**: AWS takes care of the operational aspects of Amazon MQ, including software updates, patching, and routine maintenance.

The service also provides security features such as encryption in transit and at rest, ensuring the confidentiality and integrity of messages.

Following are the benefits of using Amazon MQ:

- **Simplified operations**: By opting for Amazon MQ, businesses can simplify the management of messaging infrastructure. The fully managed service handles operational tasks, freeing up valuable time and resources that can be redirected towards innovation and development.

- **Scalability and flexibility**: Amazon MQ's ability to scale horizontally enables businesses to adapt to changing workloads. The service provides the flexibility to adjust resources based on demand, ensuring optimal performance during peak times and cost-efficiency during periods of lower activity.

- **Cost-effective solution**: With a pay-as-you-go pricing model, Amazon MQ offers a cost-effective solution for messaging needs. Businesses only pay for the resources they consume, making it scalable and budget-friendly for organizations of all sizes.

Following are the use cases of AWS MQ:

- **Microservices communication**: Amazon MQ is well-suited for microservices architectures, facilitating communication between loosely coupled services. It enables the decoupling of microservices, allowing them to evolve independently without disrupting the entire system.

- **IoT applications**: For IoT applications with a massive number of connected devices, Amazon MQ's support for MQTT makes it an ideal choice. It ensures efficient and reliable communication between devices and the cloud, handling the complexities of IoT messaging.

- **Enterprise messaging**: In enterprise environments where reliable and scalable messaging is crucial, Amazon MQ provides a robust solution. The support for AMQP makes it compatible with a wide range of enterprise messaging scenarios, including financial services and healthcare.

Amazon MQ is a powerful messaging service that simplifies the complexities of building scalable and resilient applications. With support for various protocols, durability features, and seamless integration with AWS services, Amazon MQ empowers developers to focus on creating value without the burden of managing messaging infrastructure. As businesses continue to embrace cloud-native architectures, Amazon MQ stands out as a reliable and efficient solution for facilitating communication between applications in the AWS ecosystem.

AWS EventBridge

AWS EventBridge is a fully managed event bus service that makes it easy to connect different applications using events. Introduced to the AWS ecosystem in 2019, EventBridge has quickly become a crucial component for building scalable and decoupled event-driven architectures.

- **Meaning of event buses**: An event bus is a communication mechanism that enables different components or services within a software system to exchange information without having direct dependencies on each other. This decoupling is achieved through a pub/sub model, where components can publish events and subscribe to events of interest. The event bus acts as an intermediary, relaying messages between producers and consumers, allowing for asynchronous and loosely coupled communication.

  Following are the key components:

  o **Publishers**: Components or modules that generate events and send them to the event bus. These events represent occurrences or changes within the system.

  o **Subscribers**: Components or modules that express interest in specific types of events by subscribing to them. Subscribers receive and react to events that match their criteria.

  o **Event bus**: The central channel through which events flow. It manages the registration of subscribers, dispatches events to relevant subscribers, and ensures the decoupling of components.

- **Architecture of Event buses**: The architecture of an event bus can vary, but there are common patterns that provide a foundation for understanding their functioning:

  o **Pub/sub model**: Event buses are often built on the pub/sub model, where publishers and subscribers are decoupled. Publishers broadcast events to the event bus without any knowledge of who might be interested, and subscribers' express interest in specific types of events without the direct knowledge of the publishers.

  o **Event channels**: Event buses may have different channels or topics to categorize events. This allows subscribers to filter and receive only the events that are relevant to their functionality. Channels enhance the scalability and organization of the event bus.

  o **Synchronous vs. asynchronous**: Event buses can operate synchronously or asynchronously. In a synchronous model, events are immediately processed by subscribers, while in an asynchronous model, events are queued and processed at a later time. The choice between these models depends on the specific requirements of the system.

- **Applications of event buses**: The versatility of event buses makes them applicable in various scenarios across software development:

○ **Microservices architecture**: In a microservices architecture, where applications are composed of loosely coupled and independently deployable services, event buses facilitate communication between these services. Events can signify state changes, updates, or relevant information, allowing microservices to react and adapt dynamically.

○ **UI components**: Event buses are instrumental in coordinating communication between different UI components. For example, in a web application, a sidebar component may publish an event indicating a user's action, and other components, such as a data grid or a notification panel, can subscribe to and react accordingly.

○ **Decoupled systems integration**: Event buses are employed in integrating disparate systems, enabling them to communicate without direct dependencies. This is particularly beneficial when integrating third-party services or components where changes in one system should trigger actions in another.

- **Challenges and best practices**: While event buses offer numerous advantages, they also present challenges that developers need to address:

○ **Event schema evolution**: As systems evolve, the structure and content of events may change. Managing backward compatibility and evolving the event schema gracefully is a crucial consideration.

○ **Event reliability and consistency**: Ensuring the reliability and consistency of events, especially in distributed systems, requires careful consideration. Techniques such as event replay and idempotent processing are employed to handle these challenges.

○ **Debugging and monitoring**: Debugging and monitoring distributed systems with event buses can be complex. Logging, tracing, and monitoring tools become essential to gain insights into the flow of events and diagnose issues.

Event buses have emerged as a powerful and versatile tool in the arsenal of software architects and developers. By promoting loose coupling and enabling asynchronous communication, event buses enhance the scalability, flexibility, and maintainability of complex software systems. As technology continues to advance, event buses will likely play an even more integral role in shaping the landscape of modern software architecture. Understanding their principles and best practices is key for developers seeking to build resilient and responsive systems in today's dynamic software development environment.

The key features of AWS EventBridge are mentioned in the following:

- **Event bus**: EventBridge uses the concept of an event bus to connect event sources (producers) and event targets (consumers). This central hub enables the seamless flow of events across different services and applications.

- **Event patterns**: Event patterns define the structure and content of events. AWS EventBridge supports sophisticated event patterns, allowing you to filter events based on specific criteria, ensuring that only relevant events are processed.

- **Schema registry**: The schema registry feature in EventBridge allows us to define the structure of your events using JSON schema. This ensures a standardized format for events, making it easier to understand and work with data across different services.

- **Integration with AWS services**: EventBridge seamlessly integrates with a wide range of AWS services, such as AWS Lambda, Amazon SNS, Amazon SQS, AWS Step Functions, and more. This enables us to build powerful and flexible event-driven workflows.

Use cases and benefits of AWS EventBridge are mentioned in the following:

- **Microservices architecture**: AWS EventBridge is a perfect fit for microservices architectures. It enables microservices to communicate asynchronously, reducing dependencies between services. Events can be used to trigger actions or updates in response to changes in one microservice without directly calling another.

- **Serverless computing**: When combined with AWS Lambda, EventBridge becomes a powerful tool for building serverless applications. Lambda functions can be triggered by events, allowing us to respond to changes in our environment in real-time without the need to provision or manage servers.

- **Data ingestion and ETL workflows**: EventBridge simplifies the process of ingesting and processing data from various sources. By defining event schemas, we can ensure a consistent format for incoming data, making it easier to integrate with downstream data processing and analytics tools.

- **Real-time analytics**: Event-driven architectures are well-suited for real-time analytics. With EventBridge, we can capture and process events as they occur, enabling us to gain insights and take action in real-time.

- **Decoupled systems**: One of the key benefits of AWS EventBridge is the ability to build decoupled systems. Components can operate independently, reacting to events without needing direct knowledge of one another. This results in increased flexibility, scalability, and easier maintenance.

Getting started with AWS EventBridge

Getting started with AWS EventBridge involves setting up an event-driven architecture that allows you to easily connect applications using events. You begin by creating an EventBridge event bus, which acts as a central hub for receiving and managing events from various sources like AWS services, integrated applications, or custom applications. From there, you define event rules to route these events to specific targets, such as AWS Lambda,

Step Functions, or other services, enabling automation and seamless communication between your systems:

- **Setting up an event bus**: Creating an event bus is the first step in utilizing AWS EventBridge. We can use the AWS Management Console, AWS CLI, or SDKs to create an event bus within minutes.

- **Defining event patterns**: After setting up the event bus, define event patterns to filter and route events to the appropriate targets. This involves specifying conditions based on event attributes to determine which events trigger specific actions.

- **Integrating with AWS services**: AWS EventBridge integrates seamlessly with various AWS services. For example, we can configure Lambda functions as targets to process events or use SNS for event notifications. The integration possibilities are extensive, providing flexibility in building custom workflows.

- **Monitoring and debugging**: AWS provides robust monitoring and logging capabilities for EventBridge through Amazon CloudWatch. We can setup alarms, monitor event activity, and troubleshoot any issues that may arise during the event-driven process.

AWS EventBridge plays a pivotal role in modernizing application architectures by promoting flexibility, scalability, and resilience. Its ability to facilitate communication between different services and applications through events makes it a foundational element for event-driven architectures. As organizations continue to embrace cloud-native solutions, AWS EventBridge stands out as a valuable tool for building responsive and agile systems.

Conclusion

AWS offers a robust and diverse set of event and message systems that empower businesses to build scalable and resilient applications. We explored key services such as SQS and SNS, which play pivotal roles in decoupling components and facilitating asynchronous communication between microservices. SQS ensures reliable message queuing with features like message persistence and multiple message consumers, while SNS simplifies the distribution of messages to multiple subscribers, enabling real-time communication across various endpoints.

Moving beyond SQS and SNS, AWS provides advanced solutions like Amazon Kinesis and Amazon MQ to address specific use cases. Amazon Kinesis excels in handling real-time streaming data at scale, making it an ideal choice for applications requiring immediate processing of large volumes of data. Amazon MQ, on the other hand, provides managed message broker services, supporting widely used messaging protocols such as MQTT and AMQP. These services offer flexibility in designing event-driven architectures tailored to diverse business needs.

The introduction of Amazon EventBridge enhances AWS event-driven capabilities by simplifying event management and integration across services. With a central event bus, EventBridge streamlines the process of connecting various AWS services and third-party applications, fostering a more cohesive and efficient event-driven architecture. As organizations continue to leverage AWS for their event and messaging needs, the combination of these services provides a comprehensive toolkit to build scalable, decoupled, and responsive applications in the cloud.

In the next chapter, we will study AWS Logging capabilities and cloud monitoring, and we will see AWS CloudWatch and AWS CloudTrail services and how they are used to log important information about the system in your AWS account and across services.

Points to remember

- **Amazon SQS**:

  - **Messaging queue service**: SQS enables the decoupling of components in a distributed system, allowing them to communicate asynchronously.

  - **Message retention**: Messages are stored in SQS queues for a configurable retention period, ensuring reliability and Fault-tolerance.

  - **Standard and FIFO queues**: SQS provides both standard queues and FIFO queues, catering to different message processing requirements.

- **Amazon SNS**:

  - **Pub/sub model**: SNS follows a pub/sub paradigm, allowing messages to be broadcast to multiple subscribers.

  - **Topic-based communication**: SNS uses topics to organize messages, simplifying the management of communication between components.

  - **Integration with other AWS services**: Seamless integration with other AWS services for triggering events and notifications.

- **Amazon Kinesis**:

  - **Real-time data streaming**: Kinesis facilitates the ingestion and processing of real-time data streams at scale.

  - **Kinesis Data Streams**: Allows the creation of scalable and durable streams for collecting and processing large volumes of data.

  - **Kinesis Data Firehose**: Offers a simpler way to load streaming data into AWS data stores and analytics tools.

- **Amazon MQ**:

  - **Managed message broker service**: Amazon MQ provides a managed message broker service based on popular messaging protocols such as MQTT, AMQP, and more.

  - **Enterprise-grade messaging**: Designed for enterprise-level messaging with features like message persistence, encryption, and high availability.

- **Amazon EventBridge**:

  - **Event-driven architecture**: EventBridge simplifies the building of event-driven architectures by connecting different services using events.

  - **Event bus**: Allows multiple sources and targets to communicate through a central event bus, facilitating easy event routing and management.

  - **Integration with AWS services**: Seamless integration with various AWS services, enabling automation and coordination between different components.

- **AWS messaging systems**:

  - **Scalability**: All AWS messaging systems are designed to scale with the demands of applications, supporting high throughput and large workloads.

  - **Reliability and durability**: Built-in features such as message persistence and redundancy ensure reliable message delivery and durability.

  - **Security**: AWS provides security features such as encryption in transit and at rest, IAM integration, and VPC isolation to secure messages and communication.

  - **Integration with AWS ecosystem**: These services seamlessly integrate with other AWS services, providing a comprehensive ecosystem for building scalable and resilient applications.

Exercises

1. **What is Amazon SQS used for in AWS?**

    a. Managing virtual servers

    b. Storing and retrieving data

    c. Message queuing service

    d. Content delivery network

2. **What is the primary purpose of Amazon SNS?**

   a. Database management

   b. Event-driven communication

   c. Virtual private networking

   d. Load balancing

3. **Which AWS service is suitable for real-time stream processing of big data?**

   a. Amazon MQ

   b. Amazon Kinesis

   c. Amazon EventBridge

   d. Amazon SQS (SQS)

4. **What is the purpose of Amazon MQ in AWS?**

   a. Message queuing service

   b. Machine learning

   c. Managed file storage

   d. Database management

5. **Which AWS service provides a serverless event bus for connecting applications using events?**

   a. Amazon Kinesis

   b. Amazon SNS

   c. Amazon EventBridge

   d. Amazon SQS

6. **What is the primary use case for Amazon Kinesis Data Streams?**

   a. File storage

   b. Real-time stream processing of big data

   c. Virtual private networking

   d. Relational database management

7. **In AWS, what type of communication does Amazon EventBridge support for connecting different applications?**

   a. Batch processing

   b. Request-response

    c.   Event-driven

    d.   Remote procedure call

8. **What is the key feature of Amazon SQS that ensures messages are delivered exactly once and in the order, they are sent?**

    a.   Long polling

    b.   Dead-letter queues

    c.   Message deduplication

    d.   Visibility timeout

Answers

1. c

2. b

3. b

4. a

5. c

6. b

7. c

8. c

Key terms

- AWS SQS
- AWS SNS
- AWS Kinesis
- AWS MQ
- AWS EventBridge
- Event buses
- Notification services
- Queue

CHAPTER 11

AWS Cloud Monitoring

Introduction

In cloud computing, effective monitoring and alerting systems are paramount to ensuring the health, performance, and security of applications and infrastructure. **Amazon Web Services** (**AWS**) offers a comprehensive suite of tools and services tailored to meet the diverse monitoring and alerting needs of modern cloud environments. This chapter explores key AWS services, including Amazon CloudWatch, AWS CloudTrail, AWS X-Ray, Amazon CodeGuru, and AWS Health, each playing a pivotal role in providing visibility, insights, and proactive measures for managing AWS resources effectively.

Amazon CloudWatch is important in AWS monitoring, offering a centralized platform for monitoring and managing various AWS resources and applications in real time. With CloudWatch, users can collect and track metrics, set alarms to trigger notifications based on predefined thresholds, and gain deep insights into system performance and operational health. Furthermore, CloudWatch provides extensive logging capabilities, enabling the capture and analysis of log data from AWS services, custom applications, and third-party integrations, facilitating troubleshooting and optimization efforts.

AWS CloudTrail complements CloudWatch by offering detailed insights into API activity across AWS resources, delivering a comprehensive audit trail for security, compliance, and governance purposes. By capturing API calls and related metadata, CloudTrail provides visibility into user actions, resource changes, and system events, empowering organizations to monitor activity, investigate security incidents, and maintain regulatory compliance.

AWS X-Ray offers advanced tracing capabilities, allowing developers to analyze and debug distributed applications, identify performance bottlenecks, and optimize resource utilization. With CodeGuru, AWS introduces machine learning-powered code review and profiling tools, enabling developers to identify and remediate code issues, improve application performance, and enhance overall code quality. AWS Health gives personalized insights and recommendations. It helps organizations optimize their AWS infrastructure, stay informed about planned maintenance events, and mitigate potential risks to application availability and performance.

Structure

In this chapter, we will cover the following topics:

- AWS CloudWatch
- AWS CloudTrail
- AWS Trusted Advisor
- AWS X-Ray
- AWS Lambda Insight
- AWS CodeGuru
- AWS Health

Objectives

This chapter aims to provide a comprehensive understanding of key AWS monitoring and alerting services. It helps readers to effectively monitor, analyze, and optimize their AWS environments. The chapter will focus on seven core monitoring services: Amazon CloudWatch, AWS CloudTrail, AWS Trusted Advisor, AWS X-Ray, AWS Lambda Insight, Amazon CodeGuru, and AWS Health.

We will first study Amazon CloudWatch, a centralized monitoring service that offers real-time insights into AWS resources and applications. Readers will learn how to Setup custom dashboards, define alarms, and collect logs and metrics to gain actionable intelligence on system performance, resource utilization, and application health. Additionally, we will explore CloudWatch Logs Insights for advanced log analysis and CloudWatch Events for event-driven monitoring and automated responses.

Then, we will examine AWS CloudTrail, which provides a detailed record of API calls made within an AWS account. The readers will understand how CloudTrail enhances security and compliance by auditing resource changes, troubleshooting operational issues, and detecting unauthorized activity. We will study the best practices for configuring CloudTrail trails, integrating with other AWS services, and leveraging its log data for forensic analysis and compliance reporting.

We will also explore other specific tools like AWS Trusted Advisor and Lambda Insight services. AWS Trusted Advisor provides real-time guidance by analyzing your AWS environment and offering best practice recommendations across security, Fault-tolerance, performance, cost optimization, and service limits. AWS Lambda Insights enhances observability by offering detailed metrics and logs for Lambda functions, enabling developers to monitor performance, troubleshoot issues, and optimize resource utilization.

Finally, we will read about AWS X-Ray, Amazon CodeGuru, and AWS Health, three specialized services that offer advanced monitoring, performance optimization, and health insights for AWS applications and environments. The chapter will help the readers gain insights into how AWS X-Ray enables distributed tracing and performance analysis of microservices architectures, how CodeGuru provides intelligent recommendations for optimizing code quality and performance, and how AWS Health delivers personalized alerts and remediation guidance for the proactive management of AWS infrastructure and services. Through practical examples and use cases, readers will learn how to leverage these services to ensure the reliability, security, and efficiency of their AWS deployments.

AWS CloudWatch

Amazon CloudWatch is a comprehensive monitoring and observability service provided by AWS. It offers a wide range of tools and features to monitor, collect, and analyze metrics, log files, and events across your AWS resources and applications. CloudWatch enables you to gain valuable insights into the performance, health, and operational status of your AWS infrastructure, helping you optimize resource utilization, troubleshoot issues, and ensure the reliability of your applications.

Key features of AWS CloudWatch

AWS CloudWatch is a powerful monitoring and observability service that provides real-time insights into resource and application performance. It enables users to collect and track metrics, set alarms, and log data for their AWS infrastructure and applications. With CloudWatch, users can gain visibility into system health, automate responses to changes, and ensure the reliability and performance of their services. The following are the key features of AWS CloudWatch:

- **Metrics monitoring**: CloudWatch allows us to monitor various metrics related to AWS resources, such as EC2 instances, S3 buckets, RDS databases, and Lambda functions. These metrics provide valuable information about resource utilization, performance, and health, enabling us to detect anomalies and take proactive actions to optimize performance and reduce costs. For example, some metrics CloudWatch offers for EC2 instances, it tracks **CPUUtilization**, **DiskReadOps**,

NetworkIn, and **NetworkOut** to measure processing power, storage activity, and network traffic, RDS databases have metrics like DatabaseConnections and ReadLatency to assess database performance, Lambda functions are monitored using Invocations, Duration, and ErrorCount, helping developers optimize execution time and failure rates.

- **Logs monitoring**: CloudWatch Logs helps centrally collect, monitor, and analyze log files generated by applications and AWS services. We can Setup log streams to capture log events in real time, search and filter log data using CloudWatch Logs Insights, and create custom metrics based on log data to gain deeper insights into application behavior and troubleshoot issues more effectively.

- **Events monitoring**: CloudWatch Events enables us to respond to changes in the AWS environment and trigger automated actions based on predefined rules. We can create event rules to monitor changes in resource state, schedule automated tasks at specified intervals, and integrate with other AWS services, such as Lambda functions and SNS topics, to automate workflows and streamline operations.

- **Dashboards**: CloudWatch dashboards provide customizable, real-time visualizations of AWS metrics and logs, allowing us to create personalized dashboards to monitor the performance and health of applications and infrastructure. We can add widgets to display metrics, logs, and alarms and arrange them to suit our monitoring needs, providing a centralized view of the AWS environment.

AWS CloudWatch Logs

Amazon CloudWatch Logs is a monitoring and logging service provided by AWS that allows us to monitor, store, and access log files from various AWS resources and applications in real time. It enables us to centralize log data, gain insights into system and application behavior, troubleshoot issues, and maintain compliance with regulatory requirements. This section will explore the key features, benefits, and use cases of AWS CloudWatch Logs:

- **Key features of AWS CloudWatch Logs**:

  o **Log streams and log groups**: CloudWatch Logs organizes log data into log streams, representing sequences of log events from a single source, such as an Amazon EC2 instance or an AWS Lambda function. Log streams are further grouped into log groups, providing a hierarchical structure for managing and organizing logs.

  o **Real-time log monitoring**: CloudWatch Logs helps monitor log data in real time, allowing us to react quickly to events and troubleshoot issues as they occur. We can setup real-time log monitoring to trigger alarms or notifications based on predefined metrics or custom filters.

o **Storage and retention**: CloudWatch Logs provides durable storage for log data, allowing us to retain logs for as long as needed. We can specify retention policies at the log group level to automatically expire log data based on storage requirements and compliance policies.

o **Integration with AWS services**: CloudWatch Logs seamlessly integrates with various AWS services, including Amazon EC2, AWS Lambda, Amazon RDS, and Amazon API Gateway, allowing you to capture and analyze logs from different sources within the AWS environment.

o **Search and query capabilities**: CloudWatch Logs offers powerful search and query capabilities, enabling us to filter and search through large volumes of log data efficiently. We can use simple text searches or advanced queries using filter patterns and regular expressions to extract relevant information from logs.

o **Visualization and analysis**: CloudWatch Logs Insights enables us to visualize and analyze log data using interactive queries and built-in functions. It provides a user-friendly interface for exploring log data, identifying trends, and diagnosing issues across distributed systems and applications.

- **Benefits of using AWS CloudWatch Logs**:

  o **Centralized logging**: CloudWatch Logs centralizes log data from various AWS resources and applications, providing a single source of truth for monitoring and troubleshooting purposes. It eliminates managing multiple logging solutions and facilitates easier access to log data across the AWS environment.

  o **Scalability and reliability**: AWS CloudWatch Logs is a fully managed service that scales automatically to handle large volumes of log data. It offers high availability and durability, ensuring that the log data is always accessible and protected against data loss.

  o **Cost-effective logging solution**: CloudWatch Logs offers a pay-as-you-go pricing model, where we only pay for the log data ingested and stored. It eliminates the upfront costs and overhead associated with maintaining on-premises logging infrastructure, making it a cost-effective solution for organizations of all sizes.

  o **Operational insights**: Analyzing log data with CloudWatch Logs helps gain valuable insights into system performance, resource utilization, and application behavior. It helps identify operational issues, optimize resource usage, and improve the overall reliability and performance of the AWS environment.

  o **Compliance and security**: CloudWatch Logs provides features such as encryption, access control, and audit logging to help us meet compliance requirements and enhance the security of our log data. It enables us to securely store and access log data while maintaining data integrity and confidentiality.

- **Use cases of AWS CloudWatch Logs**:
  - **Application monitoring and troubleshooting**: CloudWatch Logs is commonly used for monitoring application logs to track application performance, detect errors, and troubleshoot issues in real time. By analyzing log data, we can identify bottlenecks, diagnose failures, and optimize application behavior for a better user experience.

  - **Infrastructure monitoring and management**: CloudWatch Logs enables us to monitor system logs from Amazon EC2 instances, AWS Lambda functions, and other AWS resources to gain insights into system health, resource utilization, and operational issues. We can Setup alarms and notifications to alert us of abnormal behavior or performance degradation.

  - **Security and compliance monitoring**: CloudWatch Logs plays a crucial role in security and compliance monitoring by capturing and analyzing security-related logs, such as AWS CloudTrail logs, VPC Flow Logs, and application access logs. It helps detect security incidents, investigate unauthorized access, and maintain audit trails for compliance purposes.

  - **DevOps and continuous delivery**: CloudWatch Logs integrates seamlessly with DevOps tools and workflows, allowing us to monitor application logs, infrastructure changes, and deployment activities in real time. It enables us to track deployment success, monitor application health, and automate remediation actions to ensure the smooth and reliable delivery of software updates.

AWS CloudWatch Logs is a powerful logging and monitoring solution that provides centralized log management, real-time monitoring, and actionable insights for the AWS environment. Leveraging CloudWatch Logs, we can improve operational visibility, enhance system reliability, and streamline troubleshooting processes, ultimately enabling us to deliver a better experience for our customers and stakeholders. Whether running a small-scale application or a large enterprise workload, CloudWatch Logs offers the scalability, flexibility, and reliability to effectively monitor and manage the AWS infrastructure.

AWS CloudWatch metrics

CloudWatch metrics form the backbone of this service, providing valuable insights into the performance, health, and behavior of AWS resources and applications. In this chapter, we will explore the fundamentals of CloudWatch metrics, including how they work, how to use them effectively, and their importance in maintaining the reliability and efficiency of AWS environments. Following are some CloudWatch metrics' key aspects to better understand this service:

- **Understanding CloudWatch metrics**: CloudWatch metrics are numerical data points representing the behavior of AWS resources and applications over a specific period. Depending on the type of resource being monitored, these metrics can include CPU utilization, disk usage, network traffic, and many other parameters. Metrics are collected at regular intervals and stored in the CloudWatch repository, where they can be analyzed, graphed, and used to set alarms for automated actions.

- **Types of CloudWatch metrics**: CloudWatch metrics can be categorized into two main types: Basic and detailed metrics. Basic metrics are automatically collected at 5 minutes intervals by default and are available at no additional cost. These metrics provide essential insights into the overall health and performance of AWS resources. On the other hand, detailed metrics offer more granular data with one-minute intervals, providing a more comprehensive view of resource behavior. However, detailed metrics incur additional charges, so users must carefully consider their monitoring requirements before opting for detailed monitoring.

- **Working with CloudWatch metrics**: To start monitoring AWS resources using CloudWatch metrics, users need to enable monitoring for the desired resources through the AWS Management Console, CLI, or SDKs. Once enabled, CloudWatch metrics will start collecting data points for the specified resources automatically. Users can then view these metrics through the CloudWatch console, where they can create custom dashboards, Setup alarms, and perform advanced analytics to gain insights into resource performance and behavior.

- **Importance of CloudWatch metrics**: CloudWatch metrics plays a crucial role in AWS environments by providing visibility into resource utilization, identifying performance bottlenecks, and detecting anomalies or potential issues before they impact operations. By continuously monitoring metrics such as CPU usage, memory utilization, and network traffic, users can optimize resource allocation, troubleshoot problems, and ensure the scalability and reliability of their applications and infrastructure on AWS.

To make the most of CloudWatch metrics, it is essential to follow best practices for monitoring and managing AWS resources effectively:

- **Define clear monitoring objectives**: Before configuring CloudWatch metrics, clearly define the metrics and thresholds that are most relevant to our monitoring goals and objectives.

- **Use custom metrics**: In addition to AWS-provided metrics, consider creating custom metrics to monitor specific aspects of applications and workloads that are not covered by default metrics.

- **Setup alarms**: Configure CloudWatch alarms to notify when metric values exceed predefined thresholds, allowing us to take proactive measures to address issues before they escalate.

- **Monitor trends over time**: Regularly analyze metric data over time to identify patterns, trends, and anomalies that may require further investigation or optimization.

- **Optimize costs**: Choose the appropriate level of monitoring (basic vs. detailed) based on requirements to optimize costs while ensuring sufficient visibility into resource behavior.

CloudWatch metrics are a fundamental component of AWS monitoring and observability, providing valuable insights into the performance, health, and behavior of AWS resources and applications. By effectively leveraging CloudWatch metrics and following best practices for monitoring and managing AWS environments, users can ensure the reliability, scalability, and efficiency of their applications and infrastructure on AWS.

AWS CloudWatch alarms

AWS CloudWatch is a monitoring and observability service provided by AWS that enables users to collect and track metrics, log files, and events from various AWS resources and applications. Among its suite of features, CloudWatch alarms stand out as a critical component for proactive monitoring and alerting within AWS environments. Some of the key points for CloudWatch alarms are as follows:

- **Understanding CloudWatch alarms**: CloudWatch alarms allow users to set thresholds on CloudWatch metrics and receive notifications when those thresholds are breached. These alarms can be configured to monitor various metrics, such as CPU utilization, network traffic, and application performance, across different AWS services like EC2 instances, RDS databases, and Lambda functions.

- **Creating CloudWatch alarms**: Creating a CloudWatch alarm involves several steps:

  o **Selecting metrics**: Users begin by selecting the CloudWatch metrics they want to monitor. These metrics can be either AWS-provided metrics or custom metrics generated by users.

  o **Setting thresholds**: Once the metrics are selected, users define thresholds for the alarm. Thresholds can be set for specific values or based on statistical functions like average, maximum, or minimum over a specified period.

  o **Configuring actions**: Users then configure actions to be triggered when the alarm state changes. Actions can include sending notifications via Amazon SNS, triggering auto scaling policies, or executing AWS Lambda functions.

  o **Defining alarm states**: CloudWatch alarms have three states: **OK**, **ALARM**, and **INSUFFICIENT_DATA**. Users can define what actions should be taken when the alarm transitions between these states.

To effectively utilize CloudWatch alarms, it is essential to follow the best practices, some of which are mentioned in the following:

- **Set meaningful thresholds**: Define thresholds that reflect the normal behavior of the system and trigger alarms only when necessary to avoid unnecessary alerts.

- **Use composite alarms**: Combine multiple metrics into a single composite alarm to reduce alarm noise and improve visibility into complex system behaviors.

- **Implement hysteresis**: To prevent rapid state changes and alert flapping, incorporate hysteresis by setting different thresholds for alarm activation and deactivation.

- **Regularly review and adjust alarms**: As the application evolves, regularly review and adjust the CloudWatch alarms to ensure they remain relevant and effective in detecting performance anomalies.

- **Utilize metric math**: Leverage CloudWatch metric math to create custom metrics and perform calculations on existing metrics, enabling more advanced monitoring and alerting capabilities.

AWS CloudWatch alarms provide a powerful mechanism for monitoring the health and performance of AWS resources and applications. By configuring alarms with meaningful thresholds and appropriate actions, users can proactively detect and respond to potential issues, ensuring the reliability and availability of their AWS environments. Embracing best practices for CloudWatch alarms enables organizations to maintain operational excellence and deliver exceptional user experiences in the cloud.

AWS CloudWatch custom dashboards

One of the key features of CloudWatch is the ability to create custom dashboards, which enable users to visualize their AWS resources' performance and health in a single, centralized location. In this section, we will explore CloudWatch custom dashboards, including their features, benefits, and how to create and customize them to suit specific monitoring needs.

CloudWatch custom dashboards offer several features and benefits that make them indispensable for monitoring and managing AWS resources effectively:

- **Centralized monitoring**: Custom dashboards provide a centralized location to monitor the performance and health of various AWS resources, including EC2 instances, RDS databases, Lambda functions, and more. Users can create multiple dashboards to organize and visualize different sets of metrics based on their specific monitoring requirements.

- **Customization**: CloudWatch custom dashboards give users full control over the layout, design, and content of their dashboards. They can customize the widgets, arrange them in different configurations, and choose from a variety of visualization options, such as line charts, stacked area graphs, and numerical values to represent their metrics data effectively.

- **Real-time metrics**: Custom dashboards provide real-time updates for metrics data, allowing users to monitor their AWS resources performance and health in near real-time. Users can set custom refresh intervals to ensure they have the latest information available for making informed decisions and taking timely actions.

- **Integration with CloudWatch alarms**: Custom dashboards seamlessly integrate with CloudWatch alarms, enabling users to create alarms based on metric thresholds and visualize them directly on the dashboard. This integration allows users to quickly identify and respond to any anomalies or issues detected in their AWS environment.

- **Shareability**: Users can share their custom dashboards with team members or stakeholders, facilitating collaboration and enabling everyone to stay informed about the status of AWS resources. Shared dashboards can be accessed via a unique URL or embedded into other applications or websites for wider visibility.

Creating a custom dashboard in CloudWatch involves the following steps:

- **Accessing the CloudWatch console**: Log in to the AWS Management Console and navigate to the CloudWatch service.

- **Navigating to dashboards**: In the CloudWatch console, select **Dashboards** from the navigation pane to access the list of existing dashboards or create a new one.

- **Creating a new dashboard**: Click on the **Create dashboard** button to create a new custom dashboard. Provide a name for the dashboard and optionally specify a description to help identify its purpose.

- **Adding widgets**: Once the dashboard is created, users can add widgets to visualize metrics data from various AWS resources. They can choose from a wide range of available metrics, including CPU utilization, memory usage, network traffic, and more.

- **Customizing widgets**: Users can customize each widget by selecting the desired metric, adjusting the time range, choosing the visualization type, and configuring additional settings such as alarms and annotations.

- **Arranging widgets**: Arrange the widgets on the dashboard layout according to preference, resizing them as needed to optimize the dashboard's visual representation.

- **Saving and viewing the dashboard**: After customizing the dashboard to their satisfaction, users can save their changes and view the completed dashboard, which provides a comprehensive overview of their AWS resources performance and health.

AWS CloudWatch custom dashboard example

Let us see a practical example on how to create a custom dashboard for an EC2 instance running on our AWS account.

If you do not have one EC2 running, launch a new instance following the EC2 wizard under the EC2 section in your AWS Console. You can find from the main search bar on the top or clicking the **Services** menu on the top then clicking **EC2** in the compute section.

Open a new tab and open another AWS Console. First navigate to CloudWatch service in your AWS Console then click on **Dashboards** link in the left panel. Click on **Create dashboard** and give it a name:

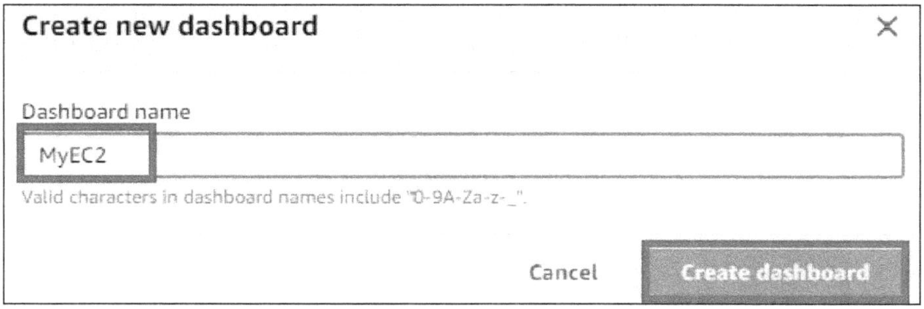

Figure 11.1: Create a new CloudWatch dashboard

We have to select a widget type to configure and add to this dashboard. Select **Line**:

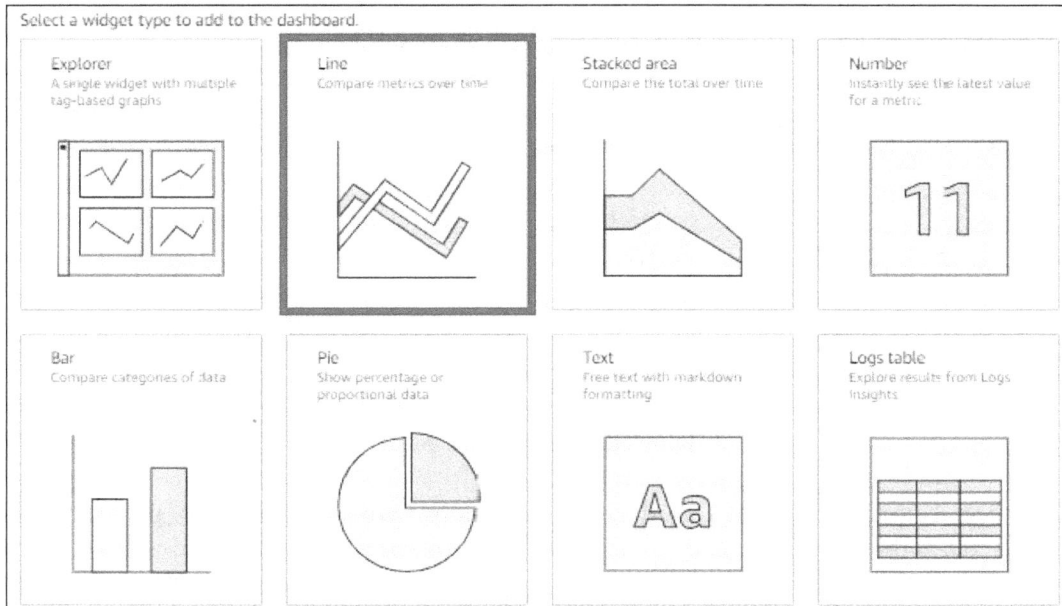

Figure 11.2: Select widget type

Select **Metrics** as data source:

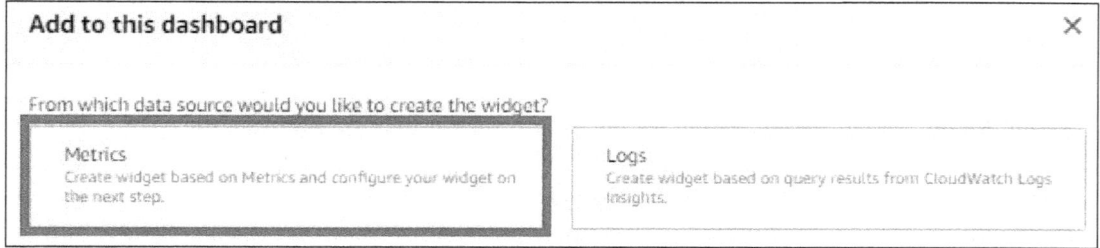

Figure 11.3: Select metrics

You will see a metric graph. Under **All** metrics, search and choose **EC2** (since we are going to watch the metrics of EC2 which we created earlier) then under **EC2** select **Per-Instance Metrics**.

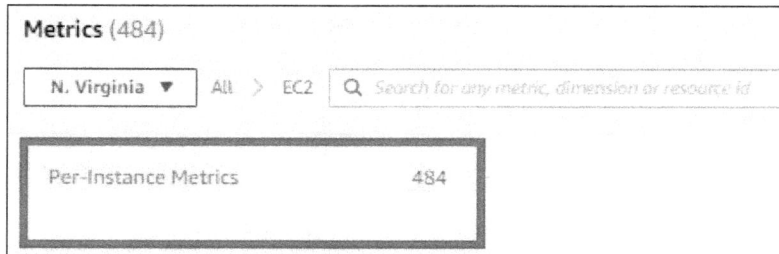

Figure 11.4: Per-Instance Metrics for EC2

In the first tab find your running EC2, copy the **Instance ID**:

Figure 11.5: Find EC2 Instance ID

In the previous tab with the CloudWatch new metric we were creating, paste the EC2 instance ID in the search bar and select the **CPUUtilization** from the metrics and click on **Create widget** button. *Figure 11.6* refers to the association of the EC2 instance ID to the new metric.

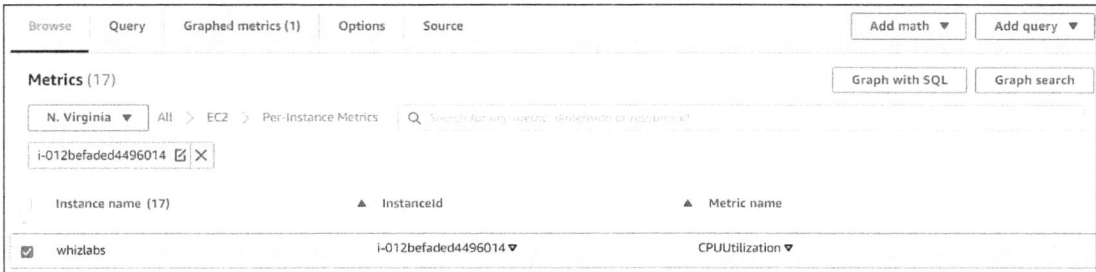

Figure 11.6: *Association of the EC2 instance ID to the new metric*

We have successfully created a **Line** widget for **CPUUtilization** If you do not see any data, wait five minutes to see some updated results. *Figure 11.7* shows the final widget:

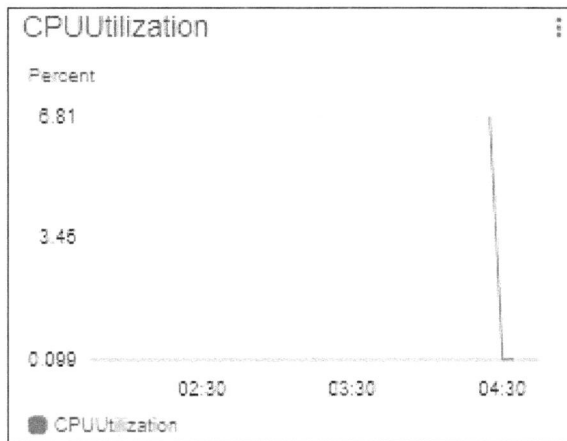

Figure 11.7: *Final widget*

AWS CloudWatch custom dashboard best practices

To make the most out of CloudWatch custom dashboards, consider the following best practices:

- **Keep it relevant**: Include only the most relevant metrics and widgets on the dashboard to avoid clutter and focus on **key performance indicators** (**KPIs**) that matter most to monitoring objectives.

- **Use annotations**: Utilize annotations to add context to the metrics data, such as deployment events, maintenance windows, or other relevant events that may impact resource performance.

- **Regular review and optimization**: Regularly review and optimize custom dashboards to ensure they remain aligned with monitoring requirements and provide actionable insights into the AWS environment.

- **Share with stakeholders**: Share the custom dashboards with relevant stakeholders, such as team members, managers, or clients, to foster collaboration and transparency in monitoring AWS resources.

- **Monitor alarms**: Carefully monitor CloudWatch alarms integrated into custom dashboards and take proactive measures to address any alerts triggered based on predefined thresholds.

AWS CloudWatch custom dashboards offer a powerful solution for monitoring and visualizing the performance and health of AWS resources in real-time. Leveraging the customization capabilities of CloudWatch dashboards, users can create tailored monitoring solutions that meet their specific requirements and enable informed decision-making. Following best practices and regularly optimizing their custom dashboards, users can ensure they have the necessary visibility and insights to effectively manage their AWS environment and maintain operational excellence.

AWS CloudTrail

AWS CloudTrail is a service provided by AWS that enables governance, compliance, operational auditing, and risk auditing of an AWS account. It provides a detailed history of AWS API calls made on an AWS account, including the identity of the entity that made the call, the time of the call, the source IP address of the caller, the request parameters, and the response elements returned by the AWS service.

Features of AWS CloudTrail

AWS CloudTrail is a service that enables the tracking and monitoring of API activity within an AWS account. It automatically records actions taken by users, roles, or AWS services, providing visibility into resource usage and helping to ensure compliance, security, and governance. CloudTrail captures detailed logs, which can be analyzed for auditing, troubleshooting, and maintaining operational integrity across AWS environments. The following are the distinguishing features of AWS CloudTrail:

- **Comprehensive logging**: CloudTrail captures API activity across various AWS services, including AWS Management Console, AWS SDKs, command-line tools, and other AWS services.

- **Detailed event history**: It provides a chronological record of every API call, including the identity of the caller, timestamp, requested action, and the response from AWS.

- **Log file integrity**: CloudTrail ensures the integrity of log files by digitally signing each log entry and storing them in a secure, immutable format.

- **Integration with AWS services**: It seamlessly integrates with other AWS services, such as Amazon S3, Amazon CloudWatch, and AWS Lambda, allowing for custom log processing, monitoring, and alerting.

- **Centralized management**: CloudTrail offers centralized management and configuration through the AWS Management Console, AWS CLI, or AWS CloudFormation templates.

Benefits of AWS CloudTrail

AWS CloudTrail provides several benefits to organizations operating in AWS environments, enhancing security, compliance, and operational visibility. Some of the key benefits include:

- **Security monitoring and auditing**: Capturing every API call made within an AWS account, CloudTrail enables organizations to monitor and audit user activity, identify unauthorized access attempts, and investigate security incidents effectively.

- **Compliance and governance**: CloudTrail assists organizations in meeting regulatory compliance requirements by providing a detailed audit trail of actions performed on AWS resources. It aids in compliance audits, incident response, and demonstrating adherence to industry standards.

- **Operational insights**: With CloudTrail, organizations gain valuable operational insights into their AWS environments, including resource utilization, changes to infrastructure configurations, and troubleshooting of operational issues.

- **Risk management**: Maintaining a comprehensive history of API activity, CloudTrail helps organizations mitigate risks associated with unauthorized access, data breaches, and configuration errors, thereby strengthening their overall security posture.

- **Forensic analysis**: In the event of a security incident or operational outage, CloudTrail facilitates forensic analysis by providing a detailed timeline of events, enabling organizations to identify the root cause and take appropriate remedial actions.

Auditing and compliance

In cloud computing, ensuring security, transparency, and adherence to regulatory standards are paramount. Auditing and compliance are two crucial concepts that play a pivotal role in achieving these objectives.

- Auditing is the systematic examination and evaluation of an organization's processes, operations, and controls to ensure they align with predefined standards, policies, and objectives. It involves tracking and analyzing various activities, events, and transactions to detect anomalies, identify potential risks, and ensure accountability. Auditing provides insights into the effectiveness of security measures, helps in identifying security gaps, and enables organizations to take proactive steps to mitigate risks.

- Compliance, refers to the adherence to specific regulations, laws, standards, or internal policies relevant to an organization's operations. Compliance ensures that organizations conduct their business ethically, protect sensitive data, and meet the requirements set forth by regulatory bodies or industry standards. Non-compliance can result in severe consequences, including legal penalties, loss of reputation, and financial repercussions.

AWS CloudTrail is a service provided by AWS that enables governance, compliance, operational auditing, and risk auditing of AWS accounts. It records and stores AWS API calls made by users, services, or AWS Management Console actions, providing a comprehensive trail of activities within an AWS environment.

Let us see how AWS CloudTrail is used in auditing:

- **Visibility into AWS API activity**: CloudTrail captures detailed information about API calls made to AWS services, including the identity of the entity making the call, the time of the call, the source IP address, and the actions performed. This visibility allows organizations to track and monitor user activity, identify unauthorized access attempts, and detect potential security breaches.

- **Security analysis and monitoring**: Analyzing CloudTrail logs, organizations can gain insights into their AWS infrastructure's security posture. They can identify patterns of suspicious behavior, monitor changes to resource configurations, and detect unauthorized modifications, helping them proactively respond to security incidents and mitigate risks.

- **Investigation and forensics**: CloudTrail logs serve as a valuable source of information for conducting investigations and forensic analysis in the event of security incidents or compliance violations. Organizations can trace the sequence of events leading to an incident, identify the root cause, and take appropriate remedial actions to prevent recurrence.

- **Compliance reporting**: CloudTrail facilitates compliance with regulatory requirements and industry standards by providing auditors with detailed logs of AWS API activity. Organizations can generate reports, analyze trends, and demonstrate adherence to compliance frameworks such as GDPR, HIPAA, PCI DSS, SOC 2, and more.

- **Policy enforcement**: CloudTrail logs can be used to enforce security policies, access controls, and governance frameworks within an AWS environment. Organizations can configure alerts and triggers based on specific API activities, enforce least privilege access principles, and ensure that only authorized actions are performed.

To maximize the benefits of AWS CloudTrail and ensure effective monitoring and auditing of AWS environments, organizations should follow best practices for its implementation and configuration. The best practices are mentioned in the following:

- **Enable CloudTrail in all AWS Regions**: Ensure that CloudTrail is enabled in all AWS Regions where resources are deployed to capture activity across the entire infrastructure.

- **Use CloudTrail with AWS Organizations**: Leverage AWS Organizations to centrally manage CloudTrail configurations across multiple AWS accounts, facilitating consistent logging and auditing practices.

- **Enable multi-region logging**: Enable multi-region logging to aggregate log data from multiple regions into a centralized Amazon S3 bucket, providing a unified view of API activity across the organization's AWS footprint.

- **Regularly monitor CloudTrail logs**: Establish processes for regularly monitoring CloudTrail logs for suspicious activity, unauthorized access attempts, or deviations from established security policies.

- **Integrate with SIEM and security tools**: Integrate CloudTrail with **security information and event management (SIEM)** systems and other security tools to correlate log data, detect anomalies, and automate incident response workflows.

Adhering to these best practices, organizations can harness the full capabilities of AWS CloudTrail to strengthen security, ensure compliance, and gain valuable insights into their AWS environments.

AWS Trusted Advisor

AWS Trusted Advisor is a valuable tool provided by AWS to help customers optimize their AWS environments, improve performance, increase security, and reduce costs. It offers proactive guidance based on AWS best practices, identifying potential issues and making recommendations to address them. In this chapter, we will explore the features, benefits, and use cases of AWS Trusted Advisor.

Features of AWS Trusted Advisor

AWS Trusted Advisor is an online resource to help users optimize their AWS environment by providing real-time guidance on best practices. It evaluates your AWS infrastructure across categories like cost optimization, performance, security, Fault-tolerance, and service limits, offering actionable recommendations to improve efficiency and reduce risks. Trusted Advisor helps users maintain a secure, high-performing, and cost-effective cloud setup. The following are the features of AWS Trusted Advisor:

- **Cost optimization**: One of the primary features of AWS Trusted Advisor is its ability to analyze your AWS infrastructure and identify opportunities to optimize costs. It provides recommendations for rightsizing instances, terminating idle resources, and utilizing Reserved Instances effectively to save money.

- **Performance improvement**: Trusted Advisor examines your AWS environment for performance inefficiencies and offers suggestions to enhance performance. It may recommend optimizing load balancers, reviewing security group rules, or optimizing database configurations to improve overall performance.

- **Security enhancement**: Security is paramount in any cloud environment. Trusted Advisor evaluates your AWS environment against security best practices and provides recommendations to enhance security posture. It may suggest enabling **multi-factor authentication (MFA)**, closing unnecessary ports, or encrypting data at rest for improved security.

- **Fault-tolerance**: Ensuring high availability and Fault-tolerance is crucial for critical applications. Trusted Advisor assesses your AWS architecture for Fault-tolerance and resilience, making recommendations to enhance reliability. It may advise implementing auto scaling, distributing resources across multiple **Availability Zones (AZs)**, or configuring health checks for improved Fault-tolerance.

- **Service limits**: AWS imposes certain limits on resources to prevent abuse and ensure fair usage. Trusted Advisor monitors your resource usage against these limits and alerts you when you are approaching or exceeding them. It helps prevent unexpected service disruptions due to reaching service limits.

Benefits of AWS Trusted Advisor

AWS Trusted Advisor offers actionable recommendations to ensure that AWS resources are being used efficiently and securely, helping organizations maintain best practices and reduce potential risks. AWS Trusted Advisor is known for the following benefits:

- **Cost savings**: Implementing the recommendations provided by Trusted Advisor, organizations can achieve some cost savings by optimizing resource usage and leveraging cost-effective options like Reserved Instances.

- **Improved performance**: Trusted Advisor helps identify performance bottlenecks and inefficiencies, leading to improved application performance and user experience.

- **Enhanced security**: Following the security recommendations of Trusted Advisor, organizations can strengthen their security posture and mitigate potential security risks and vulnerabilities.

- **Increased reliability**: Implementing Fault-tolerance and resilience recommendations from Trusted Advisor improves the reliability and availability of applications, reducing the risk of downtime and service disruptions.

- **Streamlined operations**: Trusted Advisor automates the process of analyzing AWS environments and providing actionable recommendations, allowing organizations to streamline operations and focus on strategic initiatives.

AWS Trusted Advisor is a powerful tool that empowers organizations to optimize their AWS environments for cost, performance, security, and reliability. By leveraging its proactive guidance and actionable recommendations, businesses can achieve significant benefits in terms of cost savings, performance improvement, enhanced security, and streamlined operations. Incorporating Trusted Advisor into your AWS Management strategy can help you maximize the value of your cloud investments and achieve greater success in the cloud.

AWS X-Ray

AWS X-Ray is a powerful diagnostic tool provided by AWS for analyzing and debugging distributed applications and microservices. It helps developers understand the performance and behavior of their applications by providing insights into how components interact and identifying issues in real-time. In this chapter, we will explore the features, benefits, and use cases of AWS X-Ray.

Amazon CloudWatch and AWS X-Ray serve different but complementary roles in monitoring AWS applications. CloudWatch focuses on infrastructure and application-level monitoring by collecting and analyzing metrics, logs, and events from AWS resources. It provides alarms, dashboards, and automated actions to help detect anomalies, optimize performance, and troubleshoot issues. CloudWatch is ideal for tracking resource utilization, application health, and system-wide trends across EC2, Lambda, RDS, and other AWS services.

On the other hand, AWS X-Ray is designed for distributed tracing, offering deeper visibility into application requests as they travel through microservices. It helps developers analyze latency, pinpoint bottlenecks, and debug performance issues in complex architectures like serverless applications and containerized environments. While CloudWatch provides high level operational insights, AWS X-Ray enables a detailed request flow analysis, showing how different services interact and where failures or delays occur within an application.

Understanding AWS X-Ray concepts

Before studying the details of AWS X-Ray, it is essential to understand some key concepts:

- **Traces**: A trace represents the path of a request as it travels through various components of an application. It includes information about the request's journey, such as the services it interacts with and the time taken at each step.

- **Segments**: Segments are individual units of work within a trace. They represent specific operations performed by components of an application, such as API calls, database queries, or function executions.

- **Sampling**: AWS X-Ray uses sampling to collect data efficiently. It captures traces and segments from a subset of requests based on configurable sampling rules, allowing developers to balance between performance overhead and data accuracy.

Features of AWS X-Ray

AWS X-Ray offers several features to help developers diagnose and optimize their applications:

- **Service map**: The service map provides a visual representation of the components and their interactions within an application. It helps developers understand the architecture and dependencies of their systems at a glance.

- **Trace analysis**: Developers can analyze individual traces to identify performance bottlenecks, errors, and latency issues. AWS X-Ray provides detailed information about each segment, including response times and error rates.

- **Performance insights**: With AWS X-Ray, developers gain insights into the performance of their applications over time. They can identify trends, anomalies, and areas for optimization by analyzing aggregated data and metrics.

- **Integration with AWS services**: AWS X-Ray seamlessly integrates with other AWS services, such as AWS Lambda, Amazon EC2, and Amazon ECS. Developers can instrument their applications to capture traces and segments automatically without modifying code.

- **Custom annotations and metadata**: Developers can add custom annotations and metadata to traces and segments to provide additional context for analysis. This feature is valuable for tracking user IDs, session information, or any other relevant data.

Benefits of Using AWS X-Ray

The use of AWS X-Ray offers several benefits for developers and organizations:

- **Improved application performance**: By identifying and addressing performance issues proactively, developers can improve the overall performance and responsiveness of their applications, leading to a better user experience.

- **Faster troubleshooting**: AWS X-Ray helps streamline the troubleshooting process by providing actionable insights into the root causes of issues. Developers can quickly identify problematic components and take corrective actions to resolve issues promptly.

- **Optimized resource utilization**: With insights from AWS X-Ray, developers can optimize resource utilization by identifying inefficient or underutilized components. This leads to cost savings and better resource allocation across the application stack.

- **Enhanced scalability**: By understanding the behavior of distributed systems, developers can design and implement scalable architectures more effectively. AWS X-Ray enables proactive scaling based on real-time insights, ensuring optimal performance under varying workloads.

AWS X-Ray is a valuable tool for developers building distributed applications on AWS. By providing detailed insights into application behavior, performance, and dependencies, it empowers developers to optimize their applications for better performance, scalability, and reliability. As organizations continue to embrace cloud-native architectures, AWS X-Ray will play a crucial role in ensuring the success of modern applications in the cloud.

AWS Lambda Insight

AWS Lambda Insight is a monitoring and troubleshooting solution provided by AWS to help developers gain deep insights into the performance and behavior of their AWS Lambda functions. As serverless computing continues to gain popularity, understanding and optimizing the performance of serverless functions become paramount for ensuring efficient and reliable application execution. AWS Lambda Insight offers developers a comprehensive set of tools and capabilities to monitor, analyze, and optimize the performance of their Lambda functions, thereby enabling them to deliver better user experiences and optimize resource utilization. While Amazon CloudWatch provides a broad range of monitoring capabilities for AWS resources, AWS Lambda Insights is specifically designed to enhance observability for Lambda functions. Unlike general CloudWatch metrics, Lambda Insights offers automated in-depth performance monitoring, including CPU time, memory usage, and invocation cold starts. This makes it particularly useful for troubleshooting performance bottlenecks, optimizing execution time, and reducing costs. Additionally, Lambda Insights provides enhanced logs and visualizations, giving developers a more detailed view of function behavior without requiring extensive custom metric configurations.

Prioritizing Lambda Insights over CloudWatch is beneficial when dealing with high-frequency Lambda executions or complex, event-driven architectures where function efficiency is critical. While CloudWatch provides basic invocation metrics, Lambda Insights offers detailed profiling, anomaly detection, and performance breakdowns. This level of granularity helps developers quickly identify inefficiencies, such as memory over-provisioning or excessive cold starts, leading to better cost and resource optimization. If deep-dive performance analysis for Lambda functions is the main focus, Lambda Insights is the preferred choice over standard CloudWatch metrics.

Understanding AWS Lambda Insight

AWS Lambda Insight provides developers with visibility into the behavior of their Lambda functions, helping them understand various aspects such as performance metrics, execution traces, and resource utilization. Leveraging AWS Lambda Insight, developers can gain insights into the following key areas:

- **Performance metrics**: Lambda Insight collects and presents performance metrics such as duration, invocation count, and error rates, allowing developers to monitor the overall health and efficiency of their Lambda functions.

- **Execution traces**: Developers can trace the execution path of their Lambda functions, identifying bottlenecks, latency issues, and inefficiencies in the function's code or dependencies.

- **Resource utilization**: Lambda Insight provides insights into resource utilization, including memory usage, CPU utilization, and network activity, helping developers optimize the allocation of resources for their functions.

Benefits of Using AWS Lambda Insight

The utilization of AWS Lambda Insight offers several benefits to developers and organizations looking to optimize their serverless applications, some are mentioned in the following:

- **Improved performance**: Gaining visibility into performance metrics and execution traces, developers can identify and address performance bottlenecks, leading to improved response times and better user experiences.

- **Cost optimization**: Understanding resource utilization helps developers optimize the allocation of resources for their Lambda functions, thereby reducing unnecessary costs associated with over-provisioning resources.

- **Troubleshooting and debugging**: Lambda Insight simplifies troubleshooting and debugging by providing detailed insights into the behavior of Lambda functions, enabling developers to quickly identify and resolve issues.

- **Operational efficiency**: With comprehensive monitoring and insights, developers can proactively manage and optimize their serverless applications, improving operational efficiency and reducing downtime.

Key features of AWS Lambda Insight

AWS Lambda Insight offers several key features that empower developers to monitor and optimize the performance of their Lambda functions effectively:

- **Integrated monitoring**: Lambda Insight seamlessly integrates with AWS CloudWatch, providing developers with a unified platform to monitor Lambda function metrics, logs, and traces.

- **Customizable dashboards**: Developers can create custom dashboards to visualize performance metrics and execution traces, tailoring the monitoring experience to their specific requirements.

- **Alerting and notifications**: Lambda Insight supports alerting and notifications, allowing developers to setup alarms based on predefined thresholds for performance metrics, ensuring proactive detection and response to issues.

- **Integration with AWS X-Ray**: Lambda Insight integrates with AWS X-Ray, enabling developers to trace requests across distributed architectures and gain end-to-end visibility into the performance of serverless applications.

AWS Lambda Insight plays a crucial role in enabling developers to monitor, analyze, and optimize the performance of their serverless applications built on AWS Lambda. By providing deep insights into performance metrics, execution traces, and resource utilization, Lambda Insight empowers developers to deliver high-performing, efficient, and reliable serverless applications. By leveraging Lambda Insight's capabilities, developers can proactively manage and optimize their serverless applications, ensuring optimal performance, cost efficiency, and operational excellence.

AWS CodeGuru

AWS CodeGuru is a developer tool powered by machine learning that assists developers in improving code quality and optimizing performance. It provides automated code reviews and identifies critical issues, enabling developers to deliver higher-quality software faster. This chapter explores the features, benefits, and implementation of AWS CodeGuru.

Features of AWS CodeGuru

The following are the best-known features of AWS CodeGuru:

- **Automated code reviews**: CodeGuru analyzes code repositories and automatically detects issues like code defects, security vulnerabilities, and performance bottlenecks. It provides actionable recommendations to address these issues, helping developers write cleaner and more efficient code.

- **Code profiling**: With CodeGuru Profiler, developers can identify the most expensive lines of code and performance bottlenecks in their applications. By analyzing runtime data, CodeGuru Profiler offers insights into CPU utilization, memory usage, and other performance metrics, enabling developers to optimize their applications for better efficiency and cost-effectiveness.

- **Continuous improvement**: CodeGuru continuously learns from code reviews and profiling data to improve its recommendations over time. Developers can integrate CodeGuru into their CI/CD pipelines to ensure that every code change is thoroughly analyzed for quality and performance before deployment.

Benefits of AWS CodeGuru

AWS CodeGuru is a machine learning-powered service that helps developers improve code quality and security. By providing automated code reviews and recommendations, CodeGuru enhances development efficiency, identifies potential bugs, and ensures best practices are followed. It helps teams reduce technical debt, improve maintainability, and streamline the software development process.

AWS CodeGuru ensures the following benefits:

- **Improved code quality**: Automatically identifying code defects and security vulnerabilities, CodeGuru helps developers maintain high code quality standards. Fixing issues early in the development process reduces the risk of bugs slipping into production, resulting in more reliable software.

- **Optimized performance**: CodeGuru Profiler enables developers to pinpoint performance bottlenecks and optimize resource usage in their applications. By addressing inefficiencies, developers can improve application performance, reduce latency, and lower operational costs.

- **Accelerated development**: With automated code reviews and actionable recommendations, CodeGuru accelerates the development cycle by reducing the time spent on manual code reviews and troubleshooting. Developers can focus on writing code rather than debugging, leading to faster time-to-market for new features and updates.

Implementing AWS CodeGuru

Implementing AWS CodeGuru involves integrating the service into your development workflow to analyze and improve code quality. The process typically includes setting up AWS CodeGuru Reviewer for automated code reviews, connecting it to your code repositories (for example, GitHub, Bitbucket, or AWS CodeCommit), and using CodeGuru Profiler to identify performance issues in running applications. Once configured, CodeGuru provides recommendations for improving security, efficiency, and maintainability, helping teams deliver high-quality software more efficiently. The following are the steps to implementing AWS CodeGuru in your AWS environment:

1. **Setup AWS CodeGuru**:

    a. Sign in to the AWS Management Console.

    b. Navigate to AWS CodeGuru Reviewer or AWS CodeGuru Profiler, depending on your use case.

    c. Ensure you have the necessary IAM permissions to use CodeGuru services.

2. **Enable CodeGuru Reviewer for code analysis**:

    a. Link your GitHub, Bitbucket, or AWS CodeCommit repository to CodeGuru Reviewer.

    b. Select the repository and configure CodeGuru Reviewer for automatic code reviews on pull requests.

    c. Run a manual or scheduled review to detect security vulnerabilities and performance issues.

3. **Setup CodeGuru Profiler for application monitoring**:

   a. Integrate CodeGuru Profiler SDK into your application (for Java or Python).

   b. Modify your application code to enable profiling (for example, add profiling agents in Java).

   c. Deploy the application on Amazon EC2, AWS Lambda, or containerized services.

4. **Analyze CodeGuru insights and recommendations**:

   a. Review CodeGuru Reviewer's security and performance recommendations in the AWS Management Console.

   b. Monitor CodeGuru Profiler's visualization of CPU usage, memory leaks, and latency bottlenecks.

   c. Implement suggested code improvements to optimize application performance.

5. **Automate and optimize code reviews**:

   a. Enable **continuous integration/continuous deployment (CI/CD)** pipelines with AWS CodePipeline for automated reviews.

   b. Regularly monitor CodeGuru Profiler dashboards to track application performance trends.

   c. Iterate based on feedback, fixing identified inefficiencies and security issues.

AWS CodeGuru is a valuable tool for developers seeking to enhance code quality and optimize performance in their applications. By leveraging machine learning capabilities, CodeGuru provides actionable insights and recommendations to help developers deliver high-quality software efficiently. With its automated code reviews and profiling capabilities, CodeGuru empowers developers to build better applications faster, ultimately improving the customer experience and driving business success.

AWS Health

AWS Health is a service provided by AWS that offers personalized insights and guidance to help users optimize their AWS environment for performance, security, and reliability. It provides real-time information about the health of AWS services, resources, and infrastructure, empowering users to take proactive measures to maintain the availability and performance of their applications and workloads. In this chapter, we will delve into the various aspects of AWS Health, including its features, benefits, and best practices for leveraging this service effectively. While Amazon CloudWatch provides in-depth monitoring and observability through metrics, logs, and alarms, AWS Health takes a more proactive approach by offering personalized alerts and insights about AWS resource performance and availability. AWS Health delivers real-time notifications on service disruptions, scheduled maintenance, and security advisories that could impact your environment. This makes it crucial for organizations that require proactive awareness of AWS infrastructure health beyond just resource-level monitoring.

Prioritizing AWS Health over CloudWatch is particularly beneficial in scenarios where businesses need immediate awareness of AWS service issues rather than granular operational metrics. For example, if an AWS Region experiences an outage, AWS Health provides timely notifications, allowing teams to prepare and mitigate impact. In contrast, CloudWatch might only indicate symptoms like increased latency or failed requests without pinpointing the root cause. Organizations relying on high availability and disaster recovery should leverage AWS Health to stay ahead of infrastructure-wide issues, while CloudWatch remains essential for detailed performance monitoring and automation within their AWS environment.

Features of AWS Health

AWS Health offers several features that enable users to monitor, analyze, and respond to the status of their AWS environment. Some key features include:

- **Personalized dashboards**: AWS Health provides personalized dashboards that display the current status of the user's AWS environment, including any ongoing incidents, scheduled maintenance events, and relevant notifications.

- **Insightful notifications**: Users receive timely notifications about events that may impact their AWS resources, such as service disruptions, infrastructure changes, or security vulnerabilities. These notifications can be customized based on the user's preferences and subscribed channels.

- **Integrated visibility**: AWS Health integrates with other AWS services, such as Amazon CloudWatch and AWS Trusted Advisor, to provide comprehensive visibility into the health and performance of AWS resources. This integrated approach allows users to gain actionable insights and recommendations for optimizing their AWS environment.

- **API access**: AWS Health offers programmatic access through APIs, enabling users to automate the monitoring and response to health events within their AWS environment. This API access allows for seamless integration with existing workflows and toolsets.

Benefits of AWS Health

The adoption of AWS Health offers several benefits to users across different roles and responsibilities within an organization:

- **Improved operational efficiency**: Providing real-time insights into the health of AWS resources, AWS Health helps organizations identify and resolve issues more quickly, reducing downtime and improving operational efficiency.

- **Enhanced security and compliance**: AWS Health notifies users about security vulnerabilities and compliance issues within their AWS environment, enabling them to take proactive measures to mitigate risks and maintain regulatory compliance.

- **Optimized resource utilization**: Analyzing performance metrics and utilization patterns, AWS Health helps users optimize their AWS resources for cost-effectiveness and performance, ensuring that resources are utilized efficiently.

- **Increased reliability and resilience**: With proactive monitoring and notifications, AWS Health helps organizations build more resilient and reliable applications by identifying and addressing potential issues before they impact users or business operations.

Best practices for leveraging AWS Health

To maximize the benefits of AWS Health, organizations should follow best practices for leveraging this service effectively:

- **Enable notifications**: Ensure that relevant stakeholders receive notifications from AWS Health about events and incidents that may impact their AWS environment. Customize notification settings based on the severity and urgency of the event.

- **Integrate with monitoring tools**: Integrate AWS Health with existing monitoring tools, such as Amazon CloudWatch, to gain comprehensive visibility into the health and performance of AWS resources. Leverage automation to streamline response workflows and mitigate issues more efficiently.

- **Regularly review dashboards**: Monitor the AWS Health Dashboard regularly to stay informed about the current status of AWS services, resources, and infrastructure. Take proactive measures to address any issues or recommendations highlighted in the dashboard.

- **Implement remediation actions**: Develop and implement remediation actions for common health events and incidents identified by AWS Health. Establish clear escalation paths and response procedures to ensure timely resolution of issues.

AWS Health plays a crucial role in helping organizations maintain the health, performance, and reliability of their AWS environment. By providing personalized insights, timely notifications, and integrated visibility, AWS Health empowers users to optimize their AWS resources and build resilient, secure, and cost-effective applications. By following best practices for leveraging AWS Health effectively, organizations can enhance operational efficiency, improve security and compliance, and maximize the value of their AWS investment.

Conclusion

AWS offers a comprehensive suite of monitoring and metrics tools that empower users to gain deep insights into the performance and health of their cloud infrastructure and applications. Services like Amazon CloudWatch provide real-time monitoring and actionable insights through customizable dashboards and alarms, allowing users to manage resources ensuring optimal performance.

AWS X-Ray facilitates the debugging and optimization of distributed applications by providing end-to-end visibility into requests and responses, helping developers identify bottlenecks and improve efficiency.

AWS CodeGuru leverages machine learning algorithms to analyze code quality and provide intelligent recommendations for optimization, enhancing the overall reliability and performance of applications. Automating the identification of code issues and inefficiencies, CodeGuru enables developers to streamline development workflows and deliver higher-quality software with greater speed and confidence.

AWS Health delivers personalized alerts and remediation guidance, keeping users informed about potential security vulnerabilities, service disruptions, and operational issues, thereby enabling proactive risk mitigation and ensuring continuous availability and reliability of AWS resources.

In essence, AWS monitoring and metrics tools play a central role in enabling organizations to monitor, optimize, and maintain their cloud environments with ease and efficiency. By harnessing the power of these tools, users can drive innovation, improve performance, and deliver exceptional user experiences in the ever-evolving landscape of cloud computing.

In the next chapter, we will study deployment and **infrastructure as code** (**IaC**) and we will see AWS CloudFormation and AWS CDK as the main resources to create IaC, and other services to create automatic deployments like AWS CodeBuild, AWS CodePipeline, etc.

Points to remember

- **Monitoring and metrics**:
    - AWS provides a comprehensive suite of monitoring tools to track the performance, availability, and health of your resources.
    - Amazon CloudWatch is the primary service for monitoring AWS resources, offering metrics, logs, and alarms for real-time insights.
    - CloudWatch metrics allow you to collect and track data points related to your AWS resources and applications.
    - Alarms in CloudWatch can be set to trigger notifications or automated actions based on predefined thresholds.

- CloudWatch Logs enable centralized log management and analysis for applications running on AWS.

- **Amazon CloudTrail**:
  - CloudTrail is a service that provides governance, compliance, and operational and risk auditing of your AWS account.
  - It logs all API calls made on your account, including actions taken through the AWS Management Console, SDKs, and command-line tools.
  - CloudTrail logs provide detailed information such as caller identity, the time of the API call, the request parameters, and the response elements returned by the AWS service.
  - These logs can be used for security analysis, resource change tracking, and troubleshooting operational issues.

- **AWS X-Ray**:
  - X-Ray is a distributed tracing service that helps developers analyze and debug applications by providing end-to-end visibility into requests.
  - With X-Ray, you can identify performance bottlenecks, troubleshoot errors, and optimize application performance.
  - X-Ray traces requests as they travel through your application and provides detailed insights into service dependencies and latency.
  - Integration with AWS services and third-party applications allows for comprehensive tracing across distributed architectures.

- **AWS CodeGuru**:
  - AWS CodeGuru is a machine learning-powered service for automated code reviews and performance optimization.
  - CodeGuru Reviewer analyzes code during development to identify potential defects, security vulnerabilities, and best practices violations.
  - CodeGuru Profiler continuously monitors application performance in production, identifying CPU, memory, and resource usage inefficiencies.
  - Recommendations provided by CodeGuru help improve code quality, reduce technical debt, and optimize application performance.

- **AWS Health**:
  - AWS Health provides personalized alerts and insights to help you manage the health and performance of your AWS infrastructure.
  - Health alerts notify you of events that may impact your resources, such as planned maintenance, service disruptions, or security vulnerabilities.

- o The AWS Personal Health Dashboard offers a centralized view of your AWS resource health and provides guidance on remediation steps.
- o Integrated with AWS Organizations, AWS Health enables enterprise-wide visibility and management of resource health across multiple accounts and regions.

Exercises

1. **What is the primary purpose of Amazon CloudWatch in AWS?**

   a. Database management

   b. Monitoring and observability

   c. Content delivery network

   d. Virtual private networking

2. **Which AWS service provides centralized logging and monitoring capabilities for AWS resources?**

   a. Amazon CloudFront

   b. Amazon CloudTrail

   c. Amazon X-Ray

   d. AWS CodeGuru

3. **What is the primary purpose of AWS X-Ray?**

   a. Database management

   b. Distributed tracing and analysis

   c. Load balancing

   d. Machine learning

4. **Which AWS service provides automated code reviews and recommendations for improving code quality?**

   a. Amazon CloudWatch

   b. AWS X-Ray

   c. AWS CodeGuru

   d. Amazon Inspector

5. **What is the primary use case for AWS Health?**

   a. Virtual private networking

   b. Monitoring AWS service health and incidents

    c.   File storage

    d.   Machine learning

6. **Which AWS service provides real-time monitoring and visualization of application and infrastructure metrics?**

    a.   Amazon CloudFront

    b.   Amazon CloudWatch

    c.   Amazon X-Ray

    d.   AWS CodeGuru

7. **What type of data does Amazon CloudWatch Logs primarily collect and monitor?**

    a.   Network traffic

    b.   Application logs

    c.   User activity

    d.   File storage

8. **Which AWS service provides continuous security and compliance monitoring of your AWS environment?**

    a.   AWS Trusted Advisor

    b.   AWS X-Ray

    c.   Amazon CloudWatch

    d.   AWS CodeGuru

9. **What is the primary function of AWS CloudTrail?**

    a.   Real-time monitoring

    b.   Application tracing

    c.   User activity and API tracking

    d.   Automated code reviews

10. **Which AWS service provides performance and security insights for your AWS Lambda functions?**

    a.   AWS CodeGuru

    b.   Amazon CloudWatch

    c.   Amazon X-Ray

    d.   AWS Lambda Insights

Answers

1. b
2. b
3. b
4. c
5. b
6. b
7. b
8. a
9. c
10. d

Key terms

- AWS CloudWatch
- AWS CloudWatch Logs
- AWS CloudWatch metrics
- AWS CloudWatch custom dashboards
- AWS CloudTrail
- Auditing
- Compliance
- AWS X-Ray
- AWS CodeGuru
- AWS Health
- AWS Trusted Advisor
- AWS Lambda Insight

CHAPTER 12
AWS Cloud Deployment and IaC

Introduction

In today's fast-evolving technological world, agility and efficiency are key for staying competitive. **Infrastructure as code (IaC)** and **continuous integration/continuous deployment (CI/CD)** have emerged as crucial practices for automating and streamlining software development and deployment. **Amazon Web Services (AWS)** offers tools to support both approaches. IaC enables developers to define infrastructure resources in machine-readable files, replacing manual configurations with automated and repeatable processes. This ensures consistency, scalability, and version control, reducing errors and improving infrastructure reliability. CI/CD focuses on automating the build, testing, and deployment of code, allowing developers to detect and fix issues early and deploy updates quickly. AWS services like CodePipeline, CodeBuild, and CodeDeploy support the creation of tailored CI/CD pipelines. By combining IaC with CI/CD, organizations can increase agility, scalability, and efficiency, improving their software delivery speed and security. AWS's comprehensive tools enable teams to automate infrastructure provisioning and accelerate time-to-market, making it essential for organizations aiming to innovate and succeed in the cloud.

Structure

In this chapter, we will cover the following topics:

- IaC introduction
- AWS CloudFormation
- AWS CDK
- CI/CD introduction
- AWS CodeCommit
- AWS CodeBuild
- AWS CodePipeline
- AWS CodeArtifact

Objectives

In the field of AWS IaC, the primary objective is to establish a consistent and reproducible method for provisioning and managing infrastructure resources. Utilizing tools like AWS CloudFormation or Terraform, teams can define infrastructure configurations in code, allowing for version control, automated testing, and easy replication across environments. This approach minimizes manual errors, accelerates deployment times, and fosters scalability and agility in infrastructure management.

With CI/CD, the focus shifts towards automating the software delivery pipeline from code changes to production deployment. The objective here is to achieve a continuous flow of code changes through automated testing, integration, and deployment stages. Leveraging AWS services like AWS CodePipeline, CodeBuild, and CodeDeploy, teams can implement a robust CI/CD pipeline that ensures rapid feedback, early bug detection, and reliable releases. This results in shorter release cycles, improved software quality, and greater responsiveness to customer needs.

Furthermore, the integration of AWS IaC and CI/CD brings additional objectives aimed at optimizing the overall development and deployment process. One such objective is to promote collaboration and visibility across development, operations, and other stakeholders by establishing shared practices, tools, and metrics. This fosters a culture of continuous improvement and enables teams to iterate quickly, adapt to changing requirements, and deliver value more effectively.

A key objective is to enhance security and compliance in the AWS environment through automation and policy enforcement. By incorporating security best practices and compliance checks into the IaC templates and CI/CD pipelines, teams can ensure that infrastructure and applications are deployed in a secure and compliant manner. This minimizes the risk of security breaches, reduces compliance overhead, and enables faster audits and remediation. Overall, the convergence of AWS IaC and CI/CD serves as a catalyst for innovation, efficiency, and reliability in modern cloud-based development and operations.

IaC introduction

Efficient management and provisioning of IT infrastructure have become essential for organizations to stay competitive. IaC has emerged as a powerful solution to address the challenges associated with traditional infrastructure management. By treating infrastructure configurations as code, IaC enables organizations to automate the provisioning, configuration, and management of their IT resources. In this section, we will explore IaC as a generic IT feature, discussing its benefits, implementation strategies, and potential challenges.

Understanding infrastructure as code

At its core, IaC involves managing and provisioning computing infrastructure through machine-readable definition files rather than through manual processes or interactive configuration tools. These definition files, typically written in a **domain-specific language** (**DSL**) or a configuration management tool, describe the desired state of the infrastructure components, including servers, networks, storage, and other resources. Defining IaC, organizations can leverage **version control systems** (**VCS**), automated testing, and deployment pipelines to streamline the management and deployment of their IT infrastructure.

Exploring different infrastructure as code languages

IaC is a crucial concept in modern software development and system administration. It refers to the practice of managing and provisioning computing infrastructure through machine-readable definition files rather than physical hardware configuration or interactive configuration tools. IaC allows developers and system administrators to automate the process of managing infrastructure, making it easier to scale, replicate, and maintain systems.

There are several different formats and usage patterns for IaC, each with its own advantages and disadvantages. Two popular IaC tools that illustrate these differences are Terraform and Ansible.

Terraform is a widely used IaC tool developed by *HashiCorp*. It uses a declarative language called **HashiCorp Configuration Language** (**HCL**) to define infrastructure resources and their dependencies. Terraform allows users to describe the desired state of their infrastructure in configuration files and then automatically creates, updates, and deletes resources to match that state. Terraform supports a wide range of cloud providers and other infrastructure platforms, making it a flexible choice for managing diverse environments.

A key difference in format between Terraform and other IaC tools is its use of a DSL-like HCL. While some users may find HCL more intuitive and expressive than other formats like **YAML Ain't Markup Language (YAML)** or **JavaScript Object Notation (JSON)**, others may prefer the familiarity and flexibility of more general-purpose formats. Additionally, Terraform's use of a DSL allows it to provide features like interpolation and conditionals, which can make configuration files more dynamic and reusable.

In terms of usage, Terraform typically follows a workflow of defining infrastructure in configuration files, running the Terraform plan command to preview changes, and then applying those changes with Terraform apply. This workflow aligns well with the principles of IaC, allowing users to track changes to their infrastructure over time, collaborate on configurations using VCSs like Git, and apply changes consistently across different environments.

Ansible is a different approach to IaC developed by *Red Hat*. Rather than using a DSL like Terraform, Ansible uses YAML to define infrastructure configurations in a more human-readable and easily-editable format. Ansible also takes a more imperative approach to configuration management, allowing users to define tasks and actions that should be performed on target systems rather than declaring the desired state of those systems directly.

One advantage of Ansible's YAML-based format is its simplicity and readability, which can make it easier for new users to get started with IaC. YAML's hierarchical structure also allows for more complex configurations and data structures, which can be useful for managing larger and more diverse environments.

In terms of usage, Ansible follows a workflow of defining infrastructure configurations in YAML playbooks, and then running those playbooks with the `ansible-playbook` command to apply changes to target systems. Ansible's agentless architecture also makes it easy to deploy and manage infrastructure across different environments, without requiring any additional software to be installed on target systems.

While both Terraform and Ansible are powerful tools for managing IaC, they differ in their choice of format and usage patterns. Ansible is a great tool for the management and automation of infrastructure; Terraform is best for infrastructure provisioning and managing complex environments, even in cross-cloud setups.

Terraform's use of a DSL like HCL allows for more dynamic and expressive configuration files, while Ansible's YAML-based format prioritizes simplicity and readability. The choice between these tools will depend on factors like the specific requirements of the environment, the team's familiarity with different formats, and preferences for workflow and tooling.

Example of IaC using YAML or JSON formats

IaC is an approach to managing and provisioning infrastructure resources using machine-readable definition files rather than manual processes. Two popular formats for writing IaC scripts are YAML and JSON While both formats serve the same purpose, they have distinct differences in syntax, readability, and flexibility. The following are the differences between YAML and JSON as IaC with examples in AWS.

- **Syntax**:

  o **YAML**: It uses indentation and whitespace to denote structure and hierarchy. It is known for its human-readable and concise syntax, making it easy to write and understand. Following is an example of YAML used for AWS IaC:

  ```
  Resources:
   MyEC2Instance:
   Type: AWS::EC2::Instance
   Properties:
   ImageId: ami-12345678
   InstanceType: t2.micro
  ```

  o **JSON**: It uses curly braces **{}** and square brackets **[]** to denote objects and arrays, respectively. It is more verbose than YAML but offers strict syntax rules. Here is an example of JSON used for AWS IaC:

  ```
  {
   "Resources": {
   "MyEC2Instance": {
   "Type": "AWS::EC2::Instance",
   "Properties": {
   "ImageId": "ami-12345678",
   "InstanceType": "t2.micro"
   }
   }
   }
  }
  ```

- **Readability**:

  o **YAML**: It is often considered more readable than JSON due to its minimalist syntax and lack of punctuation. It uses indentation to represent nesting, making it easier for humans to parse and understand.

  o **JSON**: It can be less readable than YAML due to its heavier use of punctuation and explicit syntax. While it is still human-readable, the syntax can become cumbersome, especially for complex structures.

- **Flexibility**:

  o **YAML**: It provides more flexibility in terms of structure and formatting. It allows for multiline strings, comments, and shorthand notation, making it suitable for expressing complex configurations concisely.

  o **JSON**: It has a stricter syntax with fewer options for formatting. While this can make JSON files more consistent and predictable, it may also limit flexibility, especially when dealing with multiline strings or comments.

- **Performance**:

  o **YAML**: Slow parsing speed due to his flexibility and complexity.

  o **JSON**: Faster parsing speed making it more efficient.

Usage in AWS

YAML and JSON are widely-used in AWS to define infrastructure resources using services like AWS CloudFormation or AWS **Cloud Development Kit (CDK)**. AWS CloudFormation templates can be written in YAML or JSON format, allowing developers to choose the best format that suits their preferences and requirements. Example of an AWS CloudFormation template in YAML is mentioned in the following:

```
Resources:
 MyS3Bucket:
 Type: AWS::S3::Bucket
 Properties:
 BucketName: my-bucket
```

Example of an AWS CloudFormation template in JSON is mentioned in the following:

```
{
 "Resources": {
 "MyS3Bucket": {
 "Type": "AWS::S3::Bucket",
 "Properties": {
 "BucketName": "my-bucket"
 }
 }
 }
}
```

While both YAML and JSON are suitable for writing IaC scripts in AWS, they have differences in syntax, readability, and flexibility. Developers can choose the format that best fits their preferences and project requirements.

Benefits of IaC

IaC in AWS allows developers to automate and manage infrastructure deployment using code, making it faster, more reliable, and scalable. By defining infrastructure in configuration files, it reduces manual errors, increases consistency across environments, and facilitates version control. IaC enables rapid provisioning of resources, simplifies infrastructure updates, and supports easier replication across different environments, empowering teams to focus more on application development and less on infrastructure management. Implementing IaC offers numerous benefits for organizations seeking to improve their IT operations:

- **Automation**: IaC enables organizations to automate the provisioning and configuration of infrastructure resources, reducing manual errors and increasing operational efficiency.

- **Consistency**: By defining infrastructure configurations as code, organizations can ensure consistency across environments, leading to more predictable and reliable deployments.

- **Scalability**: IaC allows organizations to scale their infrastructure resources rapidly and consistently, in response to changing business needs or fluctuations in demand.

- **Reusability**: IaC can be modularized and reused across projects and teams, promoting code sharing and collaboration within the organization.

- **Version control**: Infrastructure code can be stored in VCSs, enabling organizations to track changes, roll back to previous versions, and collaborate more effectively.

- **Documentation**: Infrastructure code serves as documentation for the configuration of the infrastructure, making it easier for teams to understand and maintain the system over time.

- **Speed and agility**: With IaC, organizations can deploy infrastructure changes quickly and easily, enabling them to respond rapidly to market opportunities and customer demands.

Implementation strategies

AWS provides a range of tools and services to implement IaC, enabling the automation and management of cloud resources through code. Key services like AWS CloudFormation and AWS CDK allow developers to define infrastructure in a declarative or programmatic manner, promoting consistency and scalability. These tools facilitate version control, reduce manual intervention, and improve infrastructure reliability by allowing infrastructure to be treated like software code, which can be tested, deployed, and updated in a repeatable and automated way. Also, implementing IaC for a project requires careful planning and consideration of various other factors. Here are some key strategies for successfully adopting IaC:

- **Choose the right tools**: Selecting the appropriate tools and technologies for implementing IaC is crucial. Popular choices include configuration management tools like Ansible, Puppet, or Chef, as well as cloud-native solutions like AWS CloudFormation, Azure Resource Manager, or Google Cloud Deployment Manager.

- **Define IaC**: Develop reusable templates or scripts that describe the desired state of the infrastructure. Depending on the chosen tool or framework, these templates should be written in a declarative or imperative language.

- **Use version control**: Store infrastructure code in a VCS (for example, Git), and establish best practices for branching, merging, and code review. This enables teams to collaborate effectively and track changes to the infrastructure over time.

- **Automate testing**: Implement automated testing processes to validate infrastructure code before deployment. This helps identify and mitigate errors or misconfigurations early in the development cycle.

- **Implement CI/CD**: Integrate infrastructure code into CI/CD pipelines to automate the deployment process and ensure consistency across environments. This allows for rapid and reliable delivery of infrastructure changes to production.

- **Monitor and maintain**: Monitor the deployed infrastructure continuously and establish processes for maintaining and updating infrastructure code as needed. Regularly review and optimize infrastructure configurations to ensure efficiency and security.

Challenges and considerations

IaC in AWS offers significant benefits like automation, consistency, and scalability, but it also presents challenges. These include managing complex configurations, ensuring version control, dealing with state management, and addressing security concerns. Additionally, proper testing, monitoring, and error handling are essential to avoid unintended consequences and to maintain the integrity of infrastructure during updates or changes. While IaC offers significant benefits, its adoption can also present challenges for organizations:

- **Learning curve**: Adopting IaC requires teams to learn new tools, languages, and best practices, which can initially slow down development velocity.

- **Complexity**: Managing infrastructure code and dealing with dependencies, resource relationships, and orchestration can introduce complexity into the development and deployment process.

- **Security risks**: Misconfigurations or vulnerabilities in infrastructure code can pose security risks, leading to data breaches or system downtime.

- **Legacy systems**: Integrating IaC with existing legacy systems or applications may require additional effort and coordination.

- **Cultural shift**: Adopting a DevOps culture and mindset is often necessary to fully realize the benefits of IaC, which may require organizational buy-in and cultural change.

- **Cost management**: Automated provisioning of infrastructure resources can lead to increased costs if not carefully monitored and managed.

IaC represents a paradigm shift in how organizations manage and provision IT infrastructure. By treating infrastructure configurations as code, organizations can automate and streamline the deployment process, leading to greater efficiency, scalability, and agility. However, successful adoption of IaC requires careful planning, implementation, and ongoing maintenance. By addressing the challenges and considerations associated with IaC adoption, organizations can unlock the full potential of this powerful approach to infrastructure management.

AWS CloudFormation

AWS CloudFormation is a powerful service from AWS that enables users to define and provision infrastructure resources in a predictable and repeatable manner. By using templates written in JSON or YAML, CloudFormation automates the setup of AWS resources such as EC2 instances, S3 buckets, and VPCs. This IaC approach ensures consistency, reduces the potential for human error, and simplifies the process of managing complex cloud environments. With CloudFormation, users can create, update, and manage a collection of related AWS resources as a single unit, known as a **stack**, making it an essential tool for efficient cloud operations. In this section, we will explore the features, benefits, and best practices of using AWS CloudFormation for managing IaC.

Overview of AWS CloudFormation

AWS CloudFormation is a service provided by AWS that enables users to create and manage a collection of related AWS resources, provisioning and updating them in an orderly and predictable fashion.

At its core, CloudFormation uses templates written in either JSON or YAML format to define the desired state of the infrastructure. These templates specify the AWS resources and their configurations, as well as any dependencies or relationships between them.

CloudFormation then automatically provisions and configures the resources according to the template, ensuring consistency and repeatability.

Key features of AWS CloudFormation

The following are the key features of AWS CloudFormation:

- **Declarative templates**: CloudFormation templates allow users to define the desired state of their infrastructure in a declarative manner, specifying the resources and their configurations without needing to specify the exact sequence of steps required to provision them.

- **Automation**: CloudFormation automates the provisioning and management of infrastructure resources, reducing the need for manual intervention and enabling rapid deployment and scaling.

- **Dependency management**: CloudFormation handles dependencies between resources, ensuring that resources are provisioned in the correct order and that any dependencies are satisfied before proceeding with the provisioning process.

- **Rollback protection**: CloudFormation provides built-in rollback protection, allowing users to easily revert to a previous stable state in case of errors or failures during the provisioning process.

- **Integration with AWS services**: CloudFormation integrates seamlessly with other AWS services, allowing users to define and provision a wide range of AWS resources, including EC2 instances, S3 buckets, RDS databases, and more, using a single template.

Benefits of using AWS CloudFormation

Using AWS CloudFormation has the following benefits:

- **Consistency**: By defining infrastructure resources in code, CloudFormation ensures consistency across environments, reducing the risk of configuration drift and making it easier to maintain and manage infrastructure at scale.

- **Repeatability**: CloudFormation templates can be easily reused and modified to provision identical or similar infrastructure resources in multiple environments, streamlining the deployment process and reducing the time and effort required for provisioning.

- **Scalability**: CloudFormation enables users to easily scale infrastructure resources up or down in response to changing demand, allowing for greater flexibility and efficiency in resource utilization.

- **Cost savings**: By automating the provisioning and management of infrastructure resources, CloudFormation helps to reduce operational costs and eliminate the need for manual intervention, freeing up resources for other tasks.

Best practices for using AWS CloudFormation

The following ensures maximum results from using AWS CloudFormation:

- **Use version control**: Store CloudFormation templates in version control repositories such as Git, allowing for easy tracking of changes and collaboration among team members.

- **Modularize templates**: Break down CloudFormation templates into smaller, reusable components or modules, making it easier to manage and maintain complex infrastructure configurations.

- **Parameterize templates**: Use parameters in CloudFormation templates to make them more flexible and customizable, allowing users to easily customize resource configurations for different environments or use cases.

- **Test templates**: Validate CloudFormation templates using the AWS CloudFormation Linter or other validation tools to ensure that they are syntactically correct and comply with AWS best practices before deploying them.

- **Monitor stack changes**: Monitor changes to CloudFormation stacks using AWS CloudFormation stack drift detection, CloudTrail logs, or other monitoring tools to detect and prevent unauthorized changes to infrastructure resources.

AWS CloudFormation is a powerful IaC tool that simplifies the provisioning and management of AWS infrastructure resources, enabling users to define and deploy IaC in a consistent, repeatable, and automated manner. By following best practices and leveraging the features and benefits of CloudFormation, organizations can achieve greater efficiency, scalability, and cost savings in their cloud environments.

AWS CDK

In recent years, IaC has become a crucial aspect of modern software development and deployment. With IaC, developers can manage and provision infrastructure resources in a programmatic and automated way, greatly reducing the time and effort required to setup and maintain infrastructure. AWS offers a variety of tools and services to support IaC, one of which is the AWS CDK.

Introduction to AWS CDK

AWS CDK is an open-source software development framework for defining cloud infrastructure in code and provisioning it through AWS CloudFormation. It allows developers to define infrastructure resources using familiar programming languages such as TypeScript, Python, Java, and C#. This enables them to leverage the power of modern software development practices, such as object-oriented programming, abstraction, and code reuse, to define and manage their cloud infrastructure.

Getting started with AWS CDK

To get started with AWS CDK, developers first need to install the CDK **command line interface** (**CLI**) and initialize a new CDK project. They can do this by running a few simple commands, as mentioned in the following:

```
npm install -g aws-cdk
cdk init app --language=typescript
```

This will create a new CDK project with a basic TypeScript template that developers can customize to define their infrastructure.

Defining infrastructure with AWS CDK

Once the project is setup, developers can start defining their infrastructure using the constructs provided by AWS CDK. These constructs represent AWS resources such as EC2 instances, S3 buckets, Lambda functions, and more. Developers can use these constructs to define the desired state of their infrastructure and specify any dependencies or relationships between resources.

For example, here is how we can define an S3 bucket with AWS CDK in TypeScript:

```typescript
import { Bucket } from '@aws-cdk/aws-s3';
import { Stack, App } from '@aws-cdk/core';

const app = new App();
const stack = new Stack(app, 'MyStack');

new Bucket(stack, 'MyBucket', {
 versioned: true,
 removalPolicy: RemovalPolicy.DESTROY,
});
```

This code creates a new S3 bucket with versioning enabled and sets the removal policy to **DESTROY**, which means the bucket will be deleted when the stack is deleted.

Deploying infrastructure with AWS CDK

Once the infrastructure is defined, developers can deploy it to AWS using the CDK CLI. This will automatically generate a CloudFormation template based on the CDK code and deploy it to the specified AWS account and region.

Issue this command in your terminal to deploy your infrastructure code on your AWS account:

cdk deploy

This command will deploy the stack to AWS, creating or updating the specified resources as necessary. Developers can then monitor the progress of the deployment and view the status of their resources using the AWS Management Console or the CDK CLI.

AWS CDK provides a powerful and flexible way to define and manage cloud infrastructure using familiar programming languages. Leveraging the power of IaC and modern software development practices, developers can automate the provisioning and management of their AWS resources, making it easier to build and deploy scalable and reliable applications in the cloud. With its rich ecosystem of constructs and extensive documentation, AWS CDK is a valuable tool for any developer working with AWS.

AWS CDK and CloudFormation

Both AWS CloudFormation and AWS CDK offer powerful tools for managing IaC on AWS. CloudFormation provides a simple and declarative approach to defining infrastructure using JSON or YAML templates, while CDK offers a more expressive and flexible approach using programming languages.

The choice between CloudFormation and CDK ultimately depends on the team's preferences, skills, and requirements. If a simple and straightforward way to define infrastructure is preferred, CloudFormation may be the better option. If one is comfortable with programming and wants more control and flexibility over infrastructure definitions, CDK may be the way to go.

In practice, many teams use a combination of both CloudFormation and CDK, leveraging the strengths of each tool where appropriate. For example, one may use CloudFormation for defining simple resources or managing legacy infrastructure, while using CDK for more complex or dynamic deployments.

Overall, AWS provides a robust ecosystem of tools and services for managing IaC, and both CloudFormation and CDK play important roles in that ecosystem. By understanding the strengths and weaknesses of each tool, we can make informed decisions about how best to manage AWS infrastructure in a scalable and efficient manner.

AWS CodeCommit

AWS CodeCommit is a fully managed source control service provided by AWS. It enables teams to securely store and manage their source code in the cloud, making it easy to collaborate and track changes. In this section, we will take a closer look at AWS CodeCommit, its features, and how to get started with using it effectively.

Please be aware that on July 25, 2024, AWS announced that their source code management product CodeCommit, is no longer available to new customers.

Introduction to AWS CodeCommit

AWS CodeCommit provides a secure and scalable solution for hosting private Git repositories. It integrates seamlessly with other AWS services like AWS CodeBuild, AWS CodeDeploy, and AWS CodePipeline, enabling a complete DevOps workflow. With CodeCommit, teams can collaborate on code, track changes, and manage branches effectively.

The key features of AWS CodeCommit are mentioned in the following:

- **Fully managed service**: AWS CodeCommit is a fully managed service, which means AWS handles all the infrastructure management, including server maintenance, scaling, and backups. This allows teams to focus on their code without worrying about infrastructure management.

- **Security and compliance**: CodeCommit provides built-in encryption for data in transit and at rest, ensuring that your code is always secure. It also integrates with AWS **Identity and Access Management (IAM)** for fine-grained access control, allowing controlling access repositories and what actions they can perform.

- **Scalability**: CodeCommit is designed to scale with one's needs, whether working on small projects with a few collaborators or large enterprise projects with hundreds of developers. It can handle repositories of any size and supports Git's distributed version control model.

- **Integration with AWS services**: CodeCommit integrates seamlessly with other AWS services like AWS CodeBuild, AWS CodeDeploy, and AWS CodePipeline, enabling a complete DevOps workflow. This allows to automate code builds, testing, and deployments, improving productivity and reducing manual effort.

- **Code reviews**: CodeCommit provides built-in support for code reviews, allowing team members to collaborate on code changes before they are merged into the main branch. This helps ensure code quality and consistency across projects.

- **Branching and merging**: CodeCommit supports branching and merging workflows, allowing teams to work on multiple features or bug fixes simultaneously without affecting each other's work. It provides tools for resolving merge conflicts and keeping branches in sync with the mainline.

- **Git compatibility**: CodeCommit is fully git compatible solution hosted on AWS.

Getting started with AWS CodeCommit

To get started with AWS CodeCommit, we need an AWS account. Once we have an account, we can create a CodeCommit repository using the AWS Management Console, AWS CLI, or AWS SDKs. The following is a step-by-step guide to creating a repository using the AWS Management Console:

1. **Sign in to the AWS Management Console**: Go to the AWS Management Console and sign in with AWS account credentials.

2. **Navigate to CodeCommit**: In the AWS Management Console, navigate to the CodeCommit service by typing CodeCommit in the search bar or selecting it from the list of services.

3. **Create a repository**: Click on the **Create repository** button to create a new repository. Enter a name for the repository, choose the repository description, and configure any additional settings such as repository permissions and encryption.

4. **Clone the repository**: Once the repository is created, we can clone it to the local machine using the Git CLI. This will create a local copy of the repository on our machine that we can work with.

5. **Add and commit files**: Add the project files to the local repository and commit them using the Git CLI. This will create a new commit with the changes that we can push to the CodeCommit repository.

6. **Push changes to CodeCommit**: Push the changes to the CodeCommit repository using the Git CLI. This will upload the changes to the remote repository hosted on AWS CodeCommit.

7. **Collaborate with team members**: Share the repository URL with team members so they can clone the repository and start collaborating on the project. We can use IAM to control access to the repository and manage permissions for team members.

AWS CodeCommit is a powerful source control service that provides a secure and scalable solution for hosting private Git repositories in the cloud. With features like built-in security, seamless integration with other AWS services, and support for branching and merging workflows, CodeCommit enables teams to collaborate effectively and streamline their DevOps workflow. Whether working on small projects or large enterprise projects, CodeCommit can help manage the code more efficiently and improve productivity.

CI/CD introduction

In today's fast-paced software development environment, the need for efficient and reliable processes to build, test, and deploy code has become increasingly critical CI/CD are methodologies that address this need by automating and streamlining the software delivery pipeline. In this chapter, we will explore what CI/CD is, its key concepts, and how it benefits modern software development practices.

Definition of CI/CD

CI/CD is a set of practices and principles aimed at automating the process of integrating code changes into a shared repository CI and delivering those changes to production environments in a rapid and reliable manner. CI/CD encompasses a series of steps, from code changes to production deployment, that are automated to minimize manual intervention and reduce the time it takes to deliver new features or fixes to end-users.

Key concepts of CI/CD

In AWS, CI/CD pipelines streamline code integration, automated testing, and fast, reliable deployment across environments. AWS provides various services like AWS CodeCommit, AWS CodeBuild, AWS CodeDeploy, and AWS CodePipeline, which help manage these workflows, allowing teams to deliver high-quality software quickly and consistently while minimizing manual intervention. These practices enhance collaboration, reduce errors, and speed up delivery cycles. Several key concepts underpin the CI/CD methodology, including:

- **CI**: CI involves automating the process of integrating code changes into a shared repository frequently, typically multiple times a day. With CI, developers commit their code changes to the repository, triggering automated build and test processes that validate the changes and identify any integration issues early in the development lifecycle.

- **Continuous delivery**: Continuous delivery extends the principles of CI by automating the process of deploying code changes to production-like environments for testing and validation. With CD, every code change that passes the automated tests is considered deployable and can be released to production at any time, reducing the time it takes to deliver new features or fixes to end-users.

- **CD**: CD takes automation a step further by automatically deploying every code change that passes the automated tests to production environments without manual intervention. While CD offers the potential for faster release cycles, organizations must have robust testing and monitoring in place to ensure the stability and reliability of their production environments.

- **Automated testing**: Automated testing is a crucial component of CI/CD pipelines, enabling developers to validate code changes quickly and reliably. Automated tests include unit tests, integration tests, and end-to-end tests that verify the functionality, performance, and security of the application throughout the development lifecycle.

- **IaC**: It is a practice that involves managing and provisioning infrastructure resources programmatically using code. Treating IaC, organizations can automate the deployment and configuration of infrastructure components, ensuring consistency and repeatability across environments.

Benefits of CI/CD

CI/CD offers several benefits to organizations and development teams, including:

- **Faster time-to-market**: Automating the software delivery pipeline, CI/CD enables organizations to release new features and updates to end-users more quickly, reducing time-to-market and gaining a competitive edge.

- **Improved quality**: Automated testing and validation processes in CI/CD pipelines help identify and address issues early in the development lifecycle, resulting in higher-quality software with fewer defects.

- **Increased collaboration**: CI/CD encourages collaboration among developers, testers, and operations teams by providing a shared, automated workflow for building, testing, and deploying code changes. This fosters a culture of collaboration and continuous improvement within the organization.

- **Enhanced reliability**: Automating deployment processes and implementing IaC, CI/CD helps ensure the consistency and reliability of production environments, reducing the risk of configuration drift and downtime.

AWS CodeBuild

AWS CodeBuild is a fully managed continuous integration service that compiles source code, runs tests, and produces ready-to-deploy software packages. It eliminates the need to setup, patch, update, and manage our own build servers. With AWS CodeBuild, we can quickly build, test, and deploy code to the production environment or other environments in a reliable and efficient manner.

Key features of AWS CodeBuild

The following are the key features of AWS CodeBuild:

- **Fully managed service**: AWS CodeBuild is a fully managed service, meaning AWS takes care of infrastructure provisioning, scaling, and maintenance. This allows developers to focus on writing code rather than managing build servers.

- **Customizable build environments**: CodeBuild provides preconfigured build environments for popular programming languages and frameworks such as Java, Python, Node.js, Ruby, and Docker. Additionally, we can create custom build environments tailored to our specific requirements.

- **Pay-As-You-Go pricing**: AWS CodeBuild follows a pay-as-you-go pricing model, which means we only pay for the compute resources you use during the build process. There are no upfront fees or long-term commitments, making it cost-effective for projects of any size.

- **Integration with AWS services**: CodeBuild seamlessly integrates with other AWS services such as CodePipeline, CodeCommit, and S3, allowing us to automate the entire software release process from code commit to deployment.

- **Security and compliance**: AWS CodeBuild provides a secure environment for building and testing code. It supports AWS IAM for fine-grained access control and integrates with AWS KMS for encrypting sensitive data.

Getting started with AWS CodeBuild

The following is a step-by-step guide to creating a build:

- **Setting up a build project**: To get started with AWS CodeBuild, we first need to create a build project. This involves specifying the source code repository, build environment, and build commands. We can configure build projects using the AWS Management Console, AWS CLI, or AWS SDKs.

- **Defining build specifications**: Build specifications are YAML files that define the build commands, environment variables, and other settings for our build project. These specifications are stored in the root directory of the source code repository and are used by AWS CodeBuild to execute the build process.

- **Triggering builds**: Builds can be triggered manually from the AWS Management Console or automatically in response to events such as code commits, pull requests, or changes to the build project configuration. AWS CodeBuild integrates with AWS CodePipeline to automate the entire CI/CD process.

Best practices for AWS CodeBuild

The following ensures maximum results from using AWS CodeBuild:

- **Optimize build environments**: Take advantage of preconfigured build environments provided by AWS CodeBuild whenever possible. These environments are optimized for performance and come pre-installed with common build tools and dependencies.

- **Use build caching**: Enable build caching to speed up subsequent builds by storing intermediate build artifacts and dependencies. This can significantly reduce build times, especially for large projects with complex dependencies.

- **Monitor build performance**: Monitor build performance and resource utilization using Amazon CloudWatch metrics and logs. This allows you to identify bottlenecks, optimize build configurations, and ensure reliable and efficient build execution.

- **Implement build notifications**: Setup build notifications to receive alerts when builds fail or encounter errors. This ensures timely notification of build issues and allows you to take corrective actions as soon as possible.

AWS CodeBuild is a powerful and versatile CI service that simplifies the process of building, testing, and deploying code. With its fully managed infrastructure, customizable build environments, pay-as-you-go pricing, and seamless integration with other AWS services, CodeBuild enables developers to accelerate software delivery and improve overall development productivity. By following best practices and leveraging its key features, you can streamline your build process and deliver high-quality software with confidence.

AWS CodePipeline

AWS CodePipeline is a fully managed CI/CD service provided by AWS. It allows developers to automate their software release process, from building and testing code to deploying applications. In this section we study the functionalities and features of AWS CodePipeline.

Introduction to AWS CodePipeline

AWS CodePipeline provides a streamlined way to automate the software release process. It allows developers to define a series of stages, each containing actions that perform specific tasks such as building code, running tests, and deploying applications. These stages and actions are defined in a pipeline, which serves as a visual representation of the workflow.

Key concepts

The following are the key concepts related to this section:

- **Pipelines**: Pipelines in AWS CodePipeline represent the workflow that orchestrates the steps required to release software. Each pipeline consists of stages, and each stage contains one or more actions. Pipelines can be created, edited, and managed through the AWS Management Console, AWS CLI, or AWS SDKs.

- **Stages**: Stages are the individual steps in a pipeline. They represent a logical grouping of actions that need to be executed sequentially. For example, a typical pipeline might have stages for source code retrieval, building, testing, and deployment.

- **Actions**: Actions are the tasks performed within each stage. They can be AWS-provided actions, such as deploying code to AWS Elastic Beanstalk or AWS Lambda, or custom actions defined by the user. Each action has a configuration that specifies how it should be executed, including input and output artifacts, settings, and credentials.

- **Artifacts**: Artifacts are the files generated as a result of each action. They are passed between stages in a pipeline, allowing subsequent actions to access and use the output of previous actions. Artifacts can include source code, compiled binaries, configuration files, and any other files required for the software release process.

Working with AWS CodePipeline

AWS CodePipeline enables developers to create, configure, and manage continuous integration and delivery workflows, automating the process from code commit to deployment:

- **Creating a pipeline**: To create a pipeline in AWS CodePipeline, developers need to define the stages and actions that make up the workflow. This can be done through the AWS Management Console by providing details such as the source repository, build provider, and deployment target. Alternatively, pipelines can be defined using AWS CloudFormation templates for IaC.

- **Configuring actions**: Each action in a pipeline needs to be configured with the necessary settings and parameters. This includes specifying the input and output artifacts, configuring any required permissions or credentials, and defining the action type and provider. AWS CodePipeline supports a wide range of action types, including source control, build, test, and deployment actions.

- **Managing pipelines**: Once a pipeline is created, developers can manage it through the AWS Management Console or programmatically using the AWS CLI or SDKs. This includes starting and stopping pipeline executions, viewing execution history and logs, and editing pipeline configurations. Pipelines can also be cloned or deleted as needed.

Integrations and extensibility

AWS CodePipeline integrates seamlessly with other AWS services, allowing developers to build end-to-end CI/CD workflows. For example, pipelines can trigger AWS CodeBuild for building and testing code, AWS CodeDeploy for deploying applications to EC2 instances or Lambda functions, and AWS Elastic Beanstalk for deploying and managing containerized applications.

Additionally, AWS CodePipeline supports custom integrations through the use of AWS Lambda functions and third-party tools. This allows developers to extend the functionality of pipelines by adding custom actions or integrating with external systems and services.

AWS CodePipeline provides a powerful platform for automating the software release process and streamlining CI/CD workflows. By defining pipelines with stages and actions, developers can automate tasks such as building, testing, and deploying code, enabling faster and more reliable software releases. With its integration with other AWS services and support for custom actions, AWS CodePipeline offers flexibility and extensibility for a wide range of use cases.

AWS CodeArtifact

In the rapidly evolving world of software development, managing dependencies and artifacts is a critical aspect of ensuring smooth and efficient development workflows. AWS CodeArtifact is a fully managed artifact repository service provided by AWS that simplifies the management and distribution of software packages.

Definition of AWS CodeArtifact

AWS CodeArtifact serves as a centralized repository for storing, sharing, and managing software packages and dependencies. It supports popular package formats such as npm (for JavaScript), PyPI (for Python), and Maven (for Java), making it versatile and compatible with a wide range of programming languages and ecosystems.

With AWS CodeArtifact, developers can store both public and private artifacts securely, ensuring that their dependencies are readily available and easily accessible to development teams. Additionally, CodeArtifact integrates seamlessly with existing AWS services, enabling developers to incorporate artifact management into their existing workflows.

Meaning of code repositories

Code repositories, also known as **version control repositories** or source code repositories, are essential tools in software development for managing and tracking changes to codebases. They serve as centralized storage for source code files, allowing developers to collaborate, track changes, and maintain a history of revisions. Code repositories provide a structured framework for organizing code, enabling teams to work efficiently and collaboratively on software projects. In this section, we will explore the key concepts and functionalities of code repositories:

- **Version control**: At the core of a code repository is version control, which enables developers to track changes to their codebase over time. VCS keep a record of every modification made to files within the repository, allowing developers to view previous versions, revert to earlier states, and compare changes between versions. This ensures that developers can work confidently, knowing that they can easily recover from mistakes or unexpected issues.

- **Collaboration**: Code repositories facilitate collaboration among team members by providing a centralized location for sharing code and coordinating efforts. Developers can work on different parts of the codebase simultaneously, with the ability to merge changes seamlessly and resolve conflicts when necessary. Collaboration features such as pull requests enable developers to review and discuss code changes before, they are incorporated into the main codebase, ensuring code quality and consistency.

- **Branching and merging**: Code repositories support branching, allowing developers to create separate lines of development for new features, bug fixes, or experiments. Branches provide isolation for changes, enabling developers to work on new features without affecting the main codebase. Once changes are complete, developers can merge their branches back into the main codebase, incorporating their modifications while preserving the integrity of the code.

- **History and auditing**: Code repositories maintain a comprehensive history of changes made to the codebase, including information such as who made the change, when it was made, and why it was made. This audit trail is invaluable for tracking the evolution of the codebase over time, diagnosing issues, and understanding the rationale behind specific changes. By preserving a complete history of revisions, code repositories provide transparency and accountability for the development process.

- **Backup and recovery**: Code repositories serve as a reliable backup mechanism for source code files, ensuring that code is protected against data loss or corruption. By storing code in a centralized repository, developers can easily recover from disasters such as hardware failures or accidental deletions. Additionally, many code repository platforms offer features such as data replication and backups to further enhance resilience and data protection.

- **Integration with development tools**: Code repositories integrate seamlessly with a wide range of development tools and services, including **integrated development environments (IDEs)**, CI/CD pipelines, and issue tracking systems. This integration enables developers to automate workflows, track the progress of development tasks, and streamline the software development lifecycle.

Code repositories play a crucial role in modern software development by providing a centralized and structured environment for managing source code files. By supporting version control, collaboration, branching, auditing, backup, and integration with development tools, code repositories empower developers to work efficiently, collaborate effectively, and deliver high-quality software products.

Key features of AWS CodeArtifact

AWS CodeArtifact offers a variety of features designed to streamline the management of software artifacts and dependencies:

- **Centralized artifact management**: CodeArtifact provides a single, centralized repository for storing and managing artifacts, eliminating the need for developers to maintain multiple repositories or manage dependencies manually.

- **Secure artifact storage**: CodeArtifact ensures the security of artifacts by providing granular access controls and encryption at rest. Developers can control access to repositories and artifacts using AWS IAM policies, ensuring that sensitive code and dependencies are protected from unauthorized access.

- **Support for multiple package formats**: CodeArtifact supports popular package formats such as npm, PyPI, and Maven, allowing developers to manage dependencies for a wide range of programming languages and frameworks.

- **Dependency resolution**: CodeArtifact automatically resolves dependencies and ensures that the correct versions of packages are used in development and deployment workflows. This helps prevent compatibility issues and ensures consistent builds across different environments.

- **Integration with CI/CD pipelines**: CodeArtifact integrates seamlessly with popular CI/CD tools such as AWS CodePipeline and AWS CodeBuild, allowing developers to incorporate artifact management into their automated build and deployment processes.

- **Immutable repositories**: CodeArtifact repositories are immutable, meaning that once an artifact is published, it cannot be modified or deleted. This ensures the integrity and reliability of artifacts, preventing accidental changes or tampering.

Benefits of using CodeArtifact

AWS CodeArtifact offers a flexible pricing model based on usage, with no upfront fees or long-term commitments. Developers pay only for the storage and data transfer associated with their repositories, making it cost-effective for projects of all sizes.

We will explore how to setup and configure AWS CodeArtifact, integrate it with CI/CD pipelines, and leverage its features to streamline software development workflows.

AWS CodeArtifact offers numerous benefits to developers and organizations looking to streamline their software development workflows and improve the management of dependencies and artifacts. The following are some of the key advantages of using AWS CodeArtifact:

- **Simplified dependency management**: One of the primary benefits of using AWS CodeArtifact is its ability to simplify dependency management. By providing a centralized repository for storing and managing artifacts, CodeArtifact eliminates the need for developers to maintain multiple repositories or manage dependencies manually. Instead, developers can publish and consume artifacts from a single, unified location, making it easier to track dependencies and ensure consistency across projects.

- **Enhanced security**: AWS CodeArtifact offers robust security features to help protect sensitive code and artifacts. With granular access controls and encryption at rest, developers can control access to repositories and artifacts using AWS IAM policies. This ensures that only authorized users have access to sensitive code and dependencies, helping to prevent unauthorized access and data breaches.

- **Support for multiple package formats**: Another key benefit of AWS CodeArtifact is its support for multiple package formats, including npm, PyPI, and Maven. This versatility allows developers to manage dependencies for a wide range of programming languages and frameworks within a single repository. Whether building a web application in JavaScript, a data science project in Python, or a backend service in Java, developers can rely on CodeArtifact to manage their dependencies efficiently.

- **Automated dependency resolution**: AWS CodeArtifact automates the resolution of dependencies, ensuring that the correct versions of packages are used in development and deployment workflows. This helps prevent compatibility issues and ensures consistent builds across different environments. By automatically resolving dependencies, CodeArtifact saves developers time and effort, allowing them to focus on writing code rather than managing dependencies.

- **Seamless integration with CI/CD pipelines**: CodeArtifact integrates seamlessly with popular CI/CD tools such as AWS CodePipeline and AWS CodeBuild, allowing developers to incorporate artifact management into their automated build and deployment processes. This integration enables developers to publish and consume artifacts as part of their CI/CD pipelines, ensuring that artifacts are automatically updated and distributed to downstream environments.

- **Immutable repositories**: CodeArtifact repositories are immutable, meaning that once an artifact is published, it cannot be modified or deleted. This ensures the integrity and reliability of artifacts, preventing accidental changes or tampering. Immutable repositories provide an additional layer of security and reliability, ensuring that artifacts remain unchanged throughout their lifecycle.

AWS CodeArtifact offers a wide range of benefits, including simplified dependency management, enhanced security, support for multiple package formats, automated dependency resolution, seamless integration with CI/CD pipelines, and immutable repositories. By leveraging these benefits, developers and organizations can streamline their software development workflows, improve collaboration, and deliver high-quality software more efficiently.

Conclusion

In this chapter, we have explored the powerful capabilities of AWS infrastructure as IaC and CI/CD in modern software development practices. AWS offers a comprehensive suite of services and tools that enable developers to automate the provisioning, deployment, and management of infrastructure and applications, thereby accelerating the development lifecycle and improving the reliability and scalability of software systems.

With AWS CloudFormation, developers can define infrastructure resources as code, allowing them to provision and manage AWS resources in a consistent and repeatable manner. By using declarative templates, developers can define the desired state of their infrastructure and easily manage changes over time, reducing the risk of configuration drift and ensuring the reliability and consistency of deployments.

Furthermore, AWS CodePipeline and AWS CodeDeploy provide robust CI/CD capabilities, allowing developers to automate the build, test, and deployment of code changes with ease. By defining pipelines that orchestrate the different stages of the software delivery process, developers can streamline their workflows, improve collaboration across teams, and deliver high-quality software faster and more efficiently.

AWS IaC and CI/CD are essential components of modern software development practices, enabling developers to automate and streamline the entire software delivery lifecycle. By leveraging AWS services and tools, developers can achieve greater agility, scalability, and reliability in their development processes, ultimately leading to improved software quality and faster time-to-market. As organizations continue to embrace cloud-native development methodologies, AWS IaC and CI/CD will play an increasingly important role in driving innovation and success in the digital era.

The next chapter will study identity services, and we will see AWS Cognito and **Single Sign-On (SSO)** as the main resources to create a secure identity platform, plus other services to authenticate and authorize a user.

Points to remember

- **IaC:**
    - AWS CloudFormation is a service that allows us to define and provision AWS IaC.
    - Templates are written in JSON or YAML and describe the resources and their configurations.

- o Provides a declarative way to manage AWS resources and enables automated provisioning and updates.

- **AWS CDK:**
  - o CDK is a software development framework for defining AWS infrastructure using familiar programming languages such as TypeScript, Python, and Java.
  - o Allows developers to define infrastructure using object-oriented programming constructs, making it easier to manage and reuse code.
  - o Generates CloudFormation templates under the hood, providing the flexibility of CDK with the power of CloudFormation.

- **CI/CD (CodeCommit):**
  - o AWS CodeCommit is a fully managed source control service that hosts Git repositories.
  - o Provides secure, scalable, and highly available repositories for storing source code.
  - o Integrates seamlessly with other AWS services and third-party CI/CD tools.

- **CodeBuild:**
  - o AWS CodeBuild is a fully managed build service that compiles source code, runs tests, and produces deployable artifacts.
  - o Supports various programming languages and build tools, making it versatile and adaptable to different project requirements.
  - o Enables CI by automating the build process and providing reliable and scalable build environments.

- **CodePipeline:**
  - o AWS CodePipeline is a CI/CD service that orchestrates the build, test, and deployment workflows.
  - o Allows developers to define custom pipelines that automate the release process and enforce best practices.
  - o Integrates seamlessly with other AWS services and third-party tools, enabling end-to-end automation of the software delivery lifecycle.

- **CodeArtifact:**
  - o AWS CodeArtifact is a fully managed artifact repository service that simplifies the management and distribution of software packages and dependencies.
  - o Provides a centralized repository for storing, sharing, and managing artifacts, supporting popular package formats such as npm, PyPI, and Maven.
  - o Integrates seamlessly with CI/CD pipelines, enabling developers to incorporate artifact management into their automated workflows.

- **Best practices and considerations**:
  - o Use IaC to manage AWS resources consistently and reliably.
  - o Implement CI/CD pipelines to automate the build, test, and deployment processes, improving efficiency and reducing errors.
  - o Leverage VCSs like Git and services like CodeCommit to collaborate on code changes and track revisions.
  - o Securely manage and store artifacts using services like CodeArtifact, enforcing access controls and encryption to protect sensitive data.
  - o Monitor and optimize your CI/CD pipelines for performance, scalability, and cost-effectiveness, adjusting configurations as needed to meet evolving requirements.

Exercises

1. **What is AWS CloudFormation used for?**
   a. Managing infrastructure using YAML or JSON templates
   b. Building and deploying serverless applications
   c. Managing containerized applications
   d. Analyzing logs and monitoring system performance

2. **Which AWS service allows you to define IaC using programming languages like TypeScript or Python?**
   a. AWS CloudFormation
   b. AWS CodeCommit
   c. AWS CodeBuild
   d. AWS CodePipeline

3. **What are AWS CodeCommit?**
   a. A service for building and testing code
   b. A repository service for hosting Git repositories
   c. An artifact repository for storing software packages
   d. An orchestration service for deploying applications

4. **Which AWS service is used for automating the build process and creating build artifacts?**
   a. AWS CodeCommit
   b. AWS CodeBuild

    c.   AWS CodeDeploy

    d.   AWS CodePipeline

5. **What is the purpose of AWS CodePipeline?**

    a.   To host Git repositories

    b.   To automate the build, test, and deployment process

    c.   To store and manage software packages and dependencies

    d.   To monitor and analyze application logs

6. **Which AWS service is used for storing and managing software packages and dependencies?**

    a.   AWS CodeCommit

    b.   AWS CodeBuild

    c.   AWS CodeArtifact

    d.   AWS CodeDeploy

7. **What is the benefit of using IaC tools like AWS CloudFormation or AWS CDK?**

    a.   Increased manual intervention in the deployment process

    b.   Reduced risk of errors and inconsistencies in infrastructure provisioning

    c.   Higher infrastructure costs

    d.   Longer deployment times

8. **Which AWS service allows you to define and provision AWS resources using declarative YAML or JSON templates?**

    a.   AWS CloudFormation

    b.   AWS CodeDeploy

    c.   AWS CodePipeline

    d.   AWS CodeBuild

9. **What is the primary goal of CI/CD?**

    a.   To manually deploy code changes to production environments

    b.   To automate the process of building, testing, and deploying code changes

    c.   To increase infrastructure costs

    d.   To introduce more errors into the deployment process

10. **Which AWS service is commonly used for orchestrating the CI/CD pipeline and coordinating the different stages of the deployment process?**

    a. AWS CodeCommit

    b. AWS CodeBuild

    c. AWS CodePipeline

    d. AWS CodeDeploy

Answers

1. a

2. d

3. b

4. b

5. b

6. c

7. b

8. a

9. b

10. c

Key terms

- AWS CloudFormation
- AWS CDK
- AWS CodeCommit
- AWS CodeBuild
- AWS CodePipeline
- AWS Code Artifact
- Continuous integration/continuous deployment
- Infrastructure as code
- Source repository

CHAPTER 13
AWS Billing and Organizations

Introduction

Managing costs and maintaining financial control are integral aspects of utilizing **Amazon Web Services** (**AWS**) effectively. In this chapter, we will explore the intricate field of AWS Billing and Organizations, the tools and strategies essential for optimizing expenditure and streamlining financial governance within the AWS ecosystem. As organizations increasingly adopt cloud computing, understanding billing structures and leveraging **organizational units** (**OUs**) becomes paramount for achieving cost-efficiency and operational agility.

The chapter commences by elucidating the fundamental concepts of AWS Billing and the diverse pricing models, such as pay-as-you-go, **Reserved Instances** (**RIs**), and Savings Plans. Through detailed explanations and practical examples, readers gain insights into cost allocation, budgeting, and cost optimization techniques to ensure prudent resource utilization and cost-effectiveness. Additionally, we explore the intricacies of AWS Cost Explorer, enabling users to visualize, analyze, and forecast expenditure patterns, thereby empowering informed decision-making and proactive cost management.

Furthermore, the chapter discusses the organizational constructs of AWS Organizations, elucidating how hierarchical structures, consolidated billing, and cross-account access facilitate centralized management and governance of multiple AWS accounts. By delineating best practices for organizing accounts and implementing policies, readers gain proficiency in optimizing security, compliance, and cost management across diverse OUs.

Harnessing the capabilities of AWS Billing and organizations empowers enterprises to mitigate financial risks, drive operational efficiency, and scale their cloud infrastructure in alignment with business objectives.

Structure

In this chapter, we will cover the following topics:

- AWS Billing introduction
- AWS Billing pricing models
- AWS Cost Explorer
- AWS Billing dashboard
- AWS Budgets
- Cost and usage reports for billing
- AWS Billing alarms
- AWS Organizations
- AWS Organizations service control policies
- AWS consolidated billing for AWS Organizations

Objectives

The chapter on AWS Billing and Organizations aims to provide a comprehensive understanding of managing finances and organizational structures within the AWS ecosystem. Firstly, it seeks to elucidate the intricacies of AWS Billing mechanisms, including cost management tools, billing alerts, and budgeting strategies. Readers will gain insights into optimizing cost-efficiency, understanding billing reports, and leveraging cost allocation tags to track and allocate expenses effectively. Moreover, the chapter will delve into advanced billing concepts such as AWS Cost Explorer, RIs, and Savings Plans, empowering users to make informed decisions to optimize their AWS spending.

Secondly, the chapter will explore AWS Organizations, offering guidance on setting up and managing multi-account environments. It will cover best practices for organizing accounts hierarchically, implementing governance policies, and streamlining resource provisioning across multiple AWS accounts. Furthermore, readers will learn about consolidated billing, enabling centralized management of billing and payments across multiple accounts. By the end of this chapter, users will be equipped with the knowledge and tools necessary to navigate AWS Billing complexities with confidence and efficiently manage organizational structures within the AWS Cloud platform.

AWS Billing introduction

In the vast ecosystem of AWS, effective management of billing and cost is essential for businesses seeking to optimize their cloud resources. Understanding AWS Billing components and tools is fundamental for ensuring cost-efficiency and maintaining budgetary control.

In this chapter, we will delve into the intricacies of AWS Billing, exploring its tools and components that empower users to monitor, analyze, and manage their cloud expenses effectively.

AWS Billing components

At the core of AWS Billing lies a set of components designed to provide users with insights into their cloud spending.

These components form the foundation for billing management and enable users to track, analyze, and optimize costs. Let us examine these components in detail:

- **AWS Cost Explorer**: AWS Cost Explorer is a powerful tool that provides comprehensive visibility into AWS usage and spending. It offers graphical representations, customizable reports, and forecasting capabilities, allowing users to analyze historical data, identify trends, and forecast future spending. With Cost Explorer, users can drill down into their costs by services, regions, accounts, and more, facilitating informed decision-making and cost optimization strategies.

- **Billing dashboard**: The Billing dashboard serves as a centralized hub for monitoring and managing AWS Billing and usage. It offers an overview of current spending, cost trends, and budget status, empowering users to track expenses in real-time and stay within budgetary constraints. Additionally, the dashboard provides access to cost allocation tags, which enable users to categorize resources and allocate costs accurately across departments or projects.

- **AWS Budgets**: It is a feature that allows users to set custom budgets and receive alerts when spending exceeds predefined thresholds. By defining budgets based on cost, usage, or custom metrics, users can proactively monitor their spending and take corrective actions to avoid unexpected charges. AWS Budgets help organizations maintain cost control and align cloud spending with business objectives.

- **Cost and usage reports**: Cost and usage reports (CURs) provide detailed insights into AWS usage and spending, enabling users to analyze resource utilization and identify cost drivers. These reports offer granular data on hourly usage, pricing, and metadata, facilitating deep analysis and optimization of cloud costs. Moreover, CURs can be integrated with third-party tools or billing systems for further analysis and automation.

- **Consolidated billing**: Consolidated billing is a feature designed for organizations with multiple AWS accounts, allowing them to centralize billing and receive a single invoice for all accounts. This simplifies cost management, streamlines accounting processes, and provides a holistic view of cloud spending across the organization. With consolidated billing, businesses can leverage volume discounts and optimize costs more effectively.

In conclusion, AWS Billing encompasses a range of tools and components that enable users to monitor, analyze, and manage their cloud expenses efficiently. From cost explorer and the Billing dashboard to AWS Budgets and CURs, these components offer valuable insights and capabilities for controlling costs, optimizing resource utilization, and aligning cloud spending with business objectives. By leveraging these tools effectively, organizations can navigate the complexities of AWS Billing, maximize cost-efficiency, and drive business success in the cloud.

AWS Billing pricing models

AWS Billing encompasses a complex interplay of usage-based pricing, resource provisioning, and service-specific charges.

At its core, AWS operates on a pay-as-you-go model, where customers are billed based on their actual resource consumption. This model offers unparalleled flexibility, allowing businesses to scale resources up or down in line with fluctuating demands without being tied down by fixed costs.

The overview of pricing models is mentioned in the following:

- **On-demand pricing**: The on-demand instances provide instant access to computing resources with no long-term commitments. Customers pay for what they use on an hourly or per-second basis, making it ideal for workloads with unpredictable traffic patterns or short-term projects. While on-demand pricing offers maximum flexibility, it tends to be more expensive compared to other models for sustained workloads.

- **RIs**: They offer significant cost-savings for stable workloads with predictable usage patterns. Customers commit to a specific instance type, region, and term length (one or three-years) in exchange for a discounted hourly rate. RIs provide cost predictability and can result in substantial savings, especially for steady-state applications.

- **Spot Instances**: They allow customers to bid on unused EC2 capacity, enabling access to compute resources at deeply discounted rates. While Spot Instances offer substantial cost-savings, they come with the risk of interruption if the spot price exceeds the bid price. Spot Instances are well-suited for fault tolerant and flexible workloads that can withstand potential interruptions.

- **Savings Plans**: Savings Plans offer flexible pricing options for EC2 instances and AWS Fargate usage. Customers commit to a consistent amount of usage (measured in dollars per hour) over a one or three-year term, in exchange for discounted rates compared to on-demand pricing. Savings Plans provide significant cost-savings with the added benefit of flexibility, allowing customers to allocate their usage across any instance family, region, or operating system.

- **Pay-as-you-go**: This pricing encompasses a wide range of AWS services, including storage, databases, networking, and more. Customers are billed based on their actual usage, with pricing varying across different services and resource types. Pay-as-you-go pricing offers maximum flexibility, making it suitable for businesses with dynamic or evolving needs.

Optimizing AWS costs

Effective cost optimization on AWS requires a combination of proactive planning, continuous monitoring, and leveraging cost management tools and best practices. Some key strategies include:

- **AWS Well-Architected Framework**: The cost optimization pillar of the AWS Well-Architected Framework provides strategies for managing and reducing expenses. It emphasizes rightsizing resources, such as using appropriate instance types and sizes, and identifying underutilized resources. Utilizing Savings Plans or RIs for predictable workloads can significantly lower costs. Monitoring usage with tools like AWS Cost Explorer and Trusted Advisor helps uncover inefficiencies, ensuring you only pay for what you need.

- **Leveraging automation to reduce costs**: Automating resource management with services like AWS Lambda, auto scaling, and Instance Scheduler helps ensure you are only running resources when required. For instance, scheduling non-production EC2 instances to shut down during off-hours or using auto scaling to match resource capacity with demand can reduce waste. Additionally, automation in storage management, such as transitioning data to lower cost tiers with S3 Lifecycle policies, minimizes ongoing storage costs effectively.

- **Rightsizing**: Analyzing resource utilization to match instance types and sizes with actual workload requirements.

- **Instance lifecycle management**: Leveraging RIs, Savings Plans, or Spot Instances to optimize costs based on workload characteristics and usage patterns.

- **Usage monitoring and alerts**: Setting up billing alarms and utilizing AWS Cost Explorer to monitor usage trends and identify opportunities for optimization.

- **Tagging and cost allocation**: Implementing resource tagging and cost allocation strategies to track and allocate costs accurately across departments, projects, or teams.

- **Reserved capacity planning**: Strategically planning and purchasing RIs or Savings Plans based on long-term workload projections to maximize cost-savings.

Navigating AWS Billing and pricing models can be a daunting task, given the multitude of options and variables involved. However, with a solid understanding of the different pricing models, coupled with effective cost optimization strategies, businesses can harness the power of AWS while keeping costs under control. By adopting a proactive approach to cost management and leveraging the right pricing models for their specific use cases, organizations can unlock the full potential of cloud computing without breaking the bank.

AWS Cost Explorer

AWS Cost Explorer is a comprehensive cost management tool that enables users to visualize, understand, and manage their AWS spending.

It provides a detailed breakdown of costs across various AWS services, allowing users to identify cost drivers, track spending trends, and forecast future expenses. With its intuitive interface and robust analytics capabilities, AWS Cost Explorer empowers businesses to make informed decisions to optimize their AWS infrastructure costs.

The key features are mentioned in the following:

- **Cost visualization**: AWS Cost Explorer offers interactive visualizations, such as line graphs, pie charts, and bar graphs to represent cost data dynamically. Users can easily navigate through different dimensions such as services, accounts, regions, and tags to gain insights into cost allocation and utilization patterns.

- **Cost analysis**: Users can perform ad-hoc analyses using filters and custom queries to drill down into specific cost metrics. Whether it is analyzing costs by resource type, usage type, or billing period, AWS Cost Explorer provides granular visibility into cost breakdowns, enabling users to identify areas for optimization.

- **Cost forecasting**: One of the standouts feature of AWS Cost Explorer is its ability to forecast future costs based on historical usage data. By leveraging machine learning algorithms, it generates predictive cost estimates, helping businesses anticipate budgetary requirements and plan resource allocation effectively.

- **Budgeting and alerts**: AWS Cost Explorer allows users to set custom budgets and receive alerts when actual spending exceeds predefined thresholds. This proactive approach to cost management empowers businesses to mitigate cost overruns and maintain budgetary discipline.

- **Resource optimization recommendations**: In addition to cost tracking and analysis, AWS Billing Cost Explorer offers recommendations for optimizing resource utilization. These recommendations may include rightsizing instances, leveraging RIs, or adopting cost-effective pricing models, thereby helping businesses maximize **return on investment (ROI)** on their AWS allocations.

The benefits are mentioned in the following:

- **Cost transparency**: AWS Billing Cost Explorer provides transparent insights into AWS spending, enabling stakeholders to understand cost implications associated with different services, projects, or departments.

- **Cost control**: By monitoring costs in real-time and setting budgetary controls, businesses can proactively manage their AWS spending and prevent unexpected expenses.

- **Operational efficiency**: The ability to visualize and analyze cost data allows businesses to identify inefficiencies and optimize resource allocation, leading to improved operational efficiency.

- **Forecast accuracy**: With accurate cost forecasting capabilities, businesses can make informed decisions about resource provisioning and budget planning, minimizing financial risks.

- **Continuous optimization**: AWS Billing Cost Explorer facilitates continuous optimization of AWS infrastructure costs by providing actionable insights and recommendations for cost-saving opportunities.

AWS Cost Explorer is a vital tool for businesses operating in the AWS Cloud environment, offering a comprehensive suite of features for cost management and optimization. By leveraging its capabilities to track, analyze, and forecast AWS spending, businesses can achieve greater cost transparency, control, and efficiency, ultimately maximizing the value derived from their AWS investments.

AWS Billing dashboard

The AWS Billing dashboard serves as a central hub for managing all aspects of Billing and Cost Management within the AWS ecosystem.

Upon accessing the dashboard, users are greeted with an intuitive interface that provides a snapshot of their current billing status, including total costs, usage trends, and cost breakdowns by service.

The key features of the AWS Billing dashboard are mentioned in the following:

- **Cost visualization and analysis**: One of the key features of the AWS Billing dashboard is its robust cost visualization and analysis tools. Users can easily drill down into their spending patterns, identify cost drivers, and track usage across various AWS services. Graphical representations such as charts and graphs offer insights into cost trends over time, enabling users to forecast future expenses and allocate resources more effectively.

- **Cost allocation tags**: AWS Billing dashboard allows users to assign custom cost allocation tags to their resources, providing granular insights into spending across different projects, departments, or teams. By tagging resources appropriately, organizations can accurately track and allocate costs, facilitating better cost accountability and budget management.

- **Budgeting and alerts**: Effective budgeting is essential for controlling costs and preventing unexpected expenses. The AWS Billing dashboard enables users to setup budgets based on their projected spending and receive alerts when actual costs approach or exceed predefined thresholds. These alerts serve as early warnings, allowing users to take corrective actions promptly and avoid cost overruns.

- **Cost optimization recommendations**: In addition to monitoring spending, the AWS Billing dashboard offers cost optimization recommendations to help users maximize their ROI. These recommendations leverage AWS extensive knowledge of cloud best practices and cost-saving opportunities, ranging from rightsizing instances to leveraging reserved capacity.

- **Integration with AWS Cost Explorer and Trusted Advisor**: The AWS Billing dashboard seamlessly integrates with other AWS Cost Management tools, such as Cost Explorer and Trusted Advisor. Cost Explorer provides advanced analytics capabilities, allowing users to analyze historical spending, forecast future costs, and identify areas for optimization. Trusted Advisor, on the other hand, offers personalized recommendations for improving performance, security, and cost-efficiency.

In conclusion, the AWS Billing dashboard is a powerful tool for managing and optimizing cloud costs within the AWS ecosystem. Its intuitive interface, robust visualization tools, and integration with other AWS services make it indispensable for businesses looking to control expenses and maximize the value of their cloud investments.

AWS Billing dashboard versus Cost Explorer

The AWS Billing Dashboard and AWS Cost Explorer are both tools within AWS for managing and understanding your costs, but they serve different purposes and provide distinct functionalities.

The AWS Billing dashboard offers a high level overview of your account's billing and payment information. It provides a snapshot of your current and past usage costs, payment history, and any outstanding invoices. This dashboard is ideal for administrative tasks such as viewing your payment methods, managing budgets, and ensuring invoices are paid on time. Its focus is more on financial management rather than deep analytical insights.

On the other hand, AWS Cost Explorer is a robust tool designed for analyzing and visualizing your AWS cost and usage data in greater detail. It enables users to generate reports, track spending trends, and understand how costs are distributed across services, accounts, or regions. Cost Explorer is ideal for identifying cost-saving opportunities, understanding usage patterns, and forecasting future expenses. While the Billing dashboard gives you a summary, Cost Explorer empowers you with granular data and filtering options for detailed cost management.

In essence, the Billing dashboard is your starting point for financial transactions and summaries, whereas Cost Explorer is your analytical toolkit for diving deep into your AWS expenditure. Both tools are complementary and essential for effective AWS cost management.

AWS Budgets

AWS Budgets provides organizations with the ability to set custom cost and usage budgets that align with their financial goals and objectives. By leveraging AWS Budgets, businesses can gain greater visibility into their AWS spending, identify cost trends, and take proactive measures to optimize resource allocation and control expenses.

Setting budgets

The first step in effective cost management with AWS Budgets is setting appropriate budgets tailored to the specific needs and priorities of the organization. AWS Budgets allows users to define budgets based on various parameters, including overall cost, usage, and specific services or resources. Organizations can setup multiple budgets to track spending across different departments, projects, or environments, providing granular insights into cost allocation and consumption patterns.

Monitoring and tracking spending

Once budgets are set, AWS Budgets provides real-time monitoring and tracking of spending against predefined thresholds. Users can easily view their current spending status, projected costs, and budget utilization through intuitive dashboards and reports. This visibility enables businesses to identify potential cost overruns or unexpected spikes in spending early on, allowing for timely intervention and corrective actions.

Custom notifications and alerts

AWS Budgets offers customizable notifications and alerts to keep stakeholders informed about budget status and spending trends. Users can configure notifications based on predefined triggers, such as reaching a specified percentage of the budget or exceeding a certain spending threshold. These proactive alerts empower organizations to stay on top of their AWS spending and take preemptive measures to mitigate risks and optimize resource utilization.

Cost optimization strategies

In addition to monitoring spending, AWS Budgets facilitates the implementation of cost optimization strategies to maximize ROI and minimize wastage. By analyzing spending patterns and identifying areas of inefficiency, businesses can fine-tune their resource allocation, leverage cost-effective pricing models, and explore opportunities for rightsizing or downsizing infrastructure. AWS Budgets catalyze continuous improvement, driving ongoing optimization efforts to align AWS usage with business objectives and financial constraints.

Best practices and recommendations

In order to leverage AWS Budgets effectively, organizations should adhere to best practices and recommendations outlined by AWS. This includes regularly reviewing and adjusting budgets based on changing business requirements, conducting a thorough analysis of cost and usage data to identify optimization opportunities, and fostering collaboration between finance, IT, and operations teams to align spending with organizational goals. By embracing a proactive and holistic approach to cost management, businesses can unlock the full potential of AWS while ensuring financial sustainability and accountability.

In conclusion, AWS Budgets play a pivotal role in enabling organizations to manage their AWS spending effectively and efficiently. By providing granular visibility, proactive alerts, and actionable insights, AWS Budgets empowers businesses to take control of their cloud costs, optimize resource utilization, and drive continuous improvement.

Cost and usage reports for billing

AWS CURs provide comprehensive insights into the usage and costs incurred by various AWS resources within an account. These reports are generated in a customizable format, allowing users to tailor them according to their specific needs and preferences. By leveraging CURs, businesses can gain granular visibility into their AWS spending, enabling them to make informed decisions regarding resource optimization, budgeting, and cost allocation.

The key features and benefits are mentioned in the following:

- **Granular data**: CURs offer detailed information on usage metrics, including resource utilization, data transfer, and service-specific charges. This granularity enables users to identify cost drivers and pinpoint areas for optimization.

- **Customization options**: Users can configure CURs to suit their requirements, selecting specific data fields, time intervals, and billing dimensions. This flexibility empowers organizations to tailor reports according to their unique operational and financial needs.

- **Cost allocation tags**: AWS CURs support cost allocation tags, allowing users to categorize expenses based on custom-defined tags. This feature facilitates accurate cost attribution across departments, projects, or business units, enhancing accountability and financial transparency.

- **Historical analysis**: CURs retain historical data, enabling users to analyze spending trends over time. This historical perspective is invaluable for forecasting future expenses, identifying cost-saving opportunities, and optimizing resource utilization. You can review up to 13 months of historical billing data, which enables you to identify spending trends over time, analyze cost patterns, and create forecasts for future expenses. Additionally, you can access detailed usage data through AWS CUR, which provides granular insights into service usage and associated costs. These reports can be retained in Amazon S3 for as long as needed, allowing you to maintain historical records beyond the 13 month limit of Cost Explorer. After 2023 AWS announced that you can now access up to 38 months of historical data at monthly granularity, allowing for more comprehensive long-term trend analysis. For more details see: **https://aws.amazon.com/blogs/aws-cloud-financial-management/extended-history-and-more-granular-data-available-within-aws-cost-explorer/**.

Best practices for cost management are mentioned in the following:

- **Regular review and analysis**: Establish a cadence for reviewing CURs to monitor spending patterns, identify anomalies, and track cost-saving initiatives. Regular analysis ensures proactive cost management and helps mitigate overspending risks.

- **Utilize cost allocation tags effectively**: Leverage cost allocation tags to categorize resources and expenses accurately. Implement consistent tagging strategies across your organization to facilitate seamless cost attribution and reporting.

- **Set budgets and alerts**: Define budgets and configure budget alerts within AWS to receive notifications when spending exceeds predefined thresholds. Proactive budget management enables timely interventions and prevents unexpected cost overruns.

- **Optimize resource utilization**: Continuously assess resource utilization and identify opportunities for optimization. Implement cost-saving measures such as rightsizing instances, leveraging reserved capacity, and adopting serverless architectures to maximize efficiency and minimize waste. Serverless architectures can lead to significant cost-savings by eliminating the need for organizations to provision and manage servers. Instead of paying for idle computing resources, users only pay for the actual computing time their applications consume. This is particularly useful for applications with variable or unpredictable traffic, as it ensures that resources scale automatically with demand. Serverless is also beneficial when developers want to focus solely on writing code without managing infrastructure, making it ideal for rapid development cycles, microservices, and event-driven architectures. However, it might not be the most cost-effective for consistently high workloads.

AWS CURs are indispensable tools for effective cost management in the AWS Cloud environment. By leveraging the granular insights provided by these reports, organizations can gain a deeper understanding of their AWS spending, optimize resource utilization, and align their cloud strategy with business objectives. Through careful analysis, proactive budgeting, and strategic optimization efforts, businesses can harness the full potential of AWS while maintaining cost-efficiency and financial accountability.

AWS Billing alarms

AWS Billing alarms are pivotal components of the AWS Billing and Cost Management suite, designed to empower users with real-time visibility into their expenditure. These alarms serve as proactive mechanisms, alerting users when their AWS costs exceed predefined thresholds.

By setting up billing alarms, organizations can establish proactive cost controls, ensuring that budgetary constraints are respected and unexpected expenses are promptly identified and addressed.

Configuring AWS Billing alarms

Configuring AWS Billing alarms involves a straightforward process within the AWS Management Console. Users can define billing thresholds based on various metrics such as total costs, usage volume, or specific service expenses. Once these thresholds are set, users can specify the actions to be taken when these thresholds are breached, such as sending notifications via email or triggering automated responses.

Best practices for utilizing AWS Billing alarms

In order to derive maximum benefit from AWS Billing alarms, it is essential to adhere to the best practices mentioned in the following:

- **Granular threshold setting**: Define precise thresholds tailored to your organization's budgetary constraints and usage patterns. Granular thresholds allow for more nuanced cost monitoring and better responsiveness to changes in expenditure.

- **Regular review and adjustment**: Regularly review and adjust billing alarms as your usage patterns evolve. This ensures that your cost monitoring remains aligned with your organization's current needs and objectives.

- **Integration with cost allocation tags**: Leverage AWS cost allocation tags to allocate costs to specific departments, projects, or teams. Integrating billing alarms with cost allocation tags enables more targeted cost monitoring and allocation, facilitating better cost accountability and optimization efforts.

- **Automated remediation**: Implement automated remediation actions in response to billing alarms to mitigate potential cost overruns promptly. This could include scaling down resources, modifying usage patterns, or implementing budget constraints to align with organizational priorities. Automating remediation of modifying usage patterns to save costs on AWS can be achieved by using AWS services like AWS Cost Explorer, AWS Lambda, and AWS Auto Scaling. For instance, you can setup AWS Lambda functions triggered by AWS CloudWatch alarms to automatically adjust EC2 instance types or scale down unused resources during off-peak hours. AWS Cost Explorer can analyze usage patterns and identify cost optimization opportunities, while Lambda can implement changes such as resizing instances, stopping idle resources, or switching to more cost-effective RIs, all based on predefined criteria, helping to automatically adjust usage patterns and reduce costs.

- **Collaborative monitoring**: Foster a culture of collaborative cost monitoring within your organization by involving relevant stakeholders in the monitoring process. Encourage cross-functional collaboration between finance, operations, and IT teams to ensure a holistic approach to cost management.

AWS Billing alarms play a pivotal role in enabling organizations to proactively monitor and manage their AWS expenditure effectively. By leveraging AWS Billing alarms in conjunction with best practices, organizations can establish robust cost control mechanisms, mitigate financial risks, and optimize resource utilization within the AWS ecosystem. As cloud computing continues to proliferate, mastering the art of cost management through tools like AWS Billing alarms becomes increasingly essential for maintaining competitiveness and sustainability in the digital age.

AWS Organizations

AWS Organizations emerges as a powerful solution, offering a comprehensive suite of tools and features to streamline management and governance across AWS accounts. This section explores the intricate details of AWS Organizations, exploring its functionalities, benefits, and best practices for implementation.

Understanding AWS Organizations

At its core, AWS Organizations serves as a central hub for managing multiple AWS accounts within an organization. Whether dealing with a handful of accounts or a sprawling network of resources, AWS Organizations simplifies the process of orchestrating and governing these environments. Through a hierarchical structure, organizations can establish policies, permissions, and budgetary controls across their entire AWS infrastructure.

Key features and functionality

AWS Organizations provides a plethora of features designed to enhance operational efficiency and enforce governance standards. One of its standout features is the ability to create and manage OUs, allowing for the categorization and grouping of accounts based on specific criteria, such as departments, teams, or projects. This hierarchical arrangement facilitates targeted management and policy enforcement tailored to the needs of each unit.

Moreover, AWS Organizations empowers organizations with fine-grained control over permissions and access through the use of **service control policies** (**SCPs**). By defining SCPs at the organizational level, administrators can restrict access to certain AWS services or resources, ensuring compliance with security protocols and regulatory requirements. This granular control mechanism minimizes the risk of unauthorized actions and data breaches, bolstering the overall security posture of the organization.

Additionally, AWS Organizations offers consolidated Billing and Cost Management features, enabling organizations to track expenditures and allocate costs across multiple accounts. With the ability to set budgets, monitor spending patterns, and visualize cost allocation, administrators can optimize resource utilization and mitigate financial risks effectively.

Benefits of AWS Organizations

The adoption of AWS Organizations yields a multitude of benefits for organizations seeking to streamline their cloud operations, as mentioned in the following:

- **Centralized management**: By centralizing account management and governance functions, AWS Organizations simplifies administrative tasks and fosters consistency across the organization's AWS environment.

- **Enhanced security**: Through the enforcement of SCPs and centralized policy management, AWS Organizations strengthen security controls, mitigating risks associated with unauthorized access and data breaches.

- **Cost optimization**: With consolidated Billing and Cost Management features, organizations gain greater visibility into their AWS spending, enabling them to optimize resource usage and adhere to budgetary constraints effectively.

- **Scalability and flexibility**: As organizations scale their operations, AWS Organizations accommodates growth seamlessly, providing the scalability and flexibility needed to adapt to evolving business requirements.

- **Compliance and governance**: By implementing standardized policies and controls, AWS Organizations aid organizations in achieving compliance with industry regulations and internal governance standards.

Best practices for implementation

In order to maximize the benefits of AWS Organizations, organizations should adhere to best practices for its implementation, as mentioned in the following:

- **Establish a clear organizational structure**: Define a logical hierarchy of OUs that aligns with the organization's structure and objectives, facilitating efficient management and governance.

- **Define comprehensive policies**: Craft SCPs that encompass the organization's security, compliance, and operational requirements, ensuring consistent enforcement of policies across all accounts.

- **Implement tagging strategies**: Leverage tagging strategies to categorize resources and track spending effectively, enabling granular cost allocation and optimization.

- **Regular monitoring and review**: Continuously monitor the effectiveness of SCPs and organizational policies, conducting regular reviews to identify areas for improvement and optimization.

- **Employee training and awareness**: Provide comprehensive training and awareness programs to educate employees on AWS Organizations capabilities and best practices, fostering a culture of compliance and accountability.

In conclusion, AWS Organizations serves as a cornerstone for efficient management and governance in the AWS Cloud, offering a robust set of tools and features to streamline operations and enhance security. By embracing AWS Organizations and adhering to best practices, organizations can unlock the full potential of their AWS infrastructure while maintaining control, compliance, and cost-effectiveness.

AWS Organizations service control policies

AWS Organizations emerges as a powerful tool for managing multiple AWS accounts within an organization. Central to its functionality are SCPs, which allow administrators to exert granular control over the actions and resources available to different accounts.

This section explores the nuances of AWS Organizations SCPs, exploring their significance, implementation, and implications for organizational governance.

AWS Organizations and service control policies

AWS Organizations simplifies the management of multiple AWS accounts by enabling administrators to govern policies, compliance, and security centrally. At its core, AWS Organizations establishes a hierarchy of accounts, with a master account at the apex, overseeing subordinate member accounts. This hierarchical structure facilitates the implementation of SCPs, which serve as guardrails governing the actions and resources permissible within each account.

SCPs act as guardrails by defining the permissions available to member accounts within an organization. Unlike **Identity and Access Management (IAM)** policies, which operate at the individual account level, SCPs operate at the organizational level, exerting control across all member accounts. Administrators can use SCPs to allow or deny access to AWS services and resources, effectively shaping the operational boundaries of the organization's cloud environment.

Implementation and configuration of SCPs

The implementation of SCPs within AWS Organizations involves a systematic approach to defining and enforcing governance policies across the organizational hierarchy. Administrators access the AWS Management Console or leverage AWS **Command Line Interface (CLI)** and **software development kits (SDKs)** to create and manage SCPs.

Creating an SCP involves specifying the desired permissions by allowing or denying access to specific AWS services or actions. Administrators can craft SCPs tailored to the organization's requirements, considering factors such as compliance standards, security protocols, and operational best practices. Once created, SCPs are applied to OUs or individual member accounts, cascading down the hierarchy to enforce consistent policy enforcement.

Implications for organizational governance

AWS Organizations SCPs play a pivotal role in strengthening organizational governance by enforcing compliance, enhancing security, and optimizing resource utilization. By delineating the boundaries of permissible actions and resources, SCPs mitigate the risk of unauthorized access and prevent inadvertent breaches of security protocols. Furthermore, SCPs facilitate regulatory compliance by aligning cloud operations with industry standards and internal policies.

Effective governance through SCPs fosters operational efficiency by streamlining resource allocation and optimizing cost management. By restricting access to unnecessary services and resources, SCPs prevent resource sprawl and mitigate the risk of overspending. Additionally, SCPs enable organizations to uphold data privacy and confidentiality by controlling access to sensitive information and ensuring compliance with data protection regulations.

In conclusion, AWS Organizations SCPs emerge as a cornerstone of effective governance in the cloud computing landscape. By centralizing policy management and enforcement, SCPs empower organizations to maintain compliance, enhance security, and optimize resource utilization. As organizations navigate the complexities of cloud adoption, leveraging AWS Organizations SCPs proves instrumental in achieving operational excellence and safeguarding against potential risks. Embracing SCPs within AWS Organizations heralds a new era of governance, where organizations can confidently harness the full potential of cloud computing while safeguarding their assets and upholding regulatory compliance.

AWS consolidated billing for AWS Organizations

Consolidated billing allows AWS Organizations service to consolidate payment for multiple AWS accounts under a single paying account. This means that instead of receiving separate bills for each AWS account, all charges are aggregated into one comprehensive bill.

This simplifies the billing process and provides a centralized view of spending across various AWS resources and accounts. To use consolidated billing, you will need to Setup and link all your AWS accounts under an AWS Organizations service if, for example, you have one master AWS account only or if you have different AWS accounts not already linked together under an AWS Organizations service.

The benefits of consolidated billing are mentioned in the following:

- **One bill**: You will get a single bill for multiple AWS accounts.

- **Cost-efficiency**: By consolidating billing, organizations can take advantage of volume discounts and reserved instance pricing, leading to cost savings.

- **Centralized management**: With consolidated billing, administrators can manage all AWS accounts and resources from a single dashboard, making it easier to track usage, set budgets, and allocate costs.

- **Enhanced reporting**: Consolidated billing provides detailed reports on usage and spending, enabling better decision-making and resource optimization.

- **Simplified accounting**: Instead of dealing with multiple invoices and payment processes, finance teams can streamline accounting tasks with a single, consolidated bill.

Implementation of consolidated billing

Setting up consolidated billing involves linking existing AWS accounts to a single paying account, known as the **master account**. Here is a step-by-step guide to implementing consolidated billing:

1. **Identify the master account**: Choose an existing AWS account to serve as the master account for consolidated billing.

2. **Invite member accounts**: Invite other AWS accounts to become member accounts under the master account.

3. **Accept invitations**: Once invited, member accounts need to accept the invitation to join the consolidated billing family.

4. **Link accounts**: Link member accounts to the master account using AWS Organizations or the AWS Billing Console.

5. **Configure billing preferences**: Setup billing preferences, such as payment methods and billing addresses, for the master account.

Best practices for consolidated billing are mentioned in the following:

- **Establish a tagging strategy**: Use tags to categorize resources and allocate costs accurately across departments or projects. This is important because with tags, you will be able to easily check how your cloud spending is going and follow the spending of a single project precisely.

- **Implement budgeting and alerts**: Setup budgets and billing alerts to monitor spending and prevent unexpected charges.

- **Regularly review and optimize**: Analyze billing reports regularly to identify cost optimization opportunities, such as unused resources or inefficient configurations.

- **Leverage AWS Cost Explorer**: Use AWS Cost Explorer to gain insights into spending patterns and forecast future costs.

Consolidated billing is a valuable feature offered by AWS for organizations with multiple accounts and complex cloud infrastructure. By centralizing billing management, organizations can achieve cost efficiency, streamline operations, and gain better visibility into their AWS spending.

Conclusion

This chapter has highlighted the intricate details of AWS Billing, emphasizing the importance of monitoring usage, leveraging cost management tools, and implementing budget controls to optimize expenditure. With AWS Billing, Organizations can gain insights into their usage patterns, identify cost-saving opportunities, and allocate resources efficiently.

Moreover, by utilizing AWS Organizations, businesses can centralize and streamline the management of multiple AWS accounts, enabling better governance, security, and compliance across their infrastructure.

Furthermore, AWS Organizations provide a robust framework for organizing and managing AWS accounts within an organizational hierarchy. This facilitates the implementation of consistent policies, access controls, and resource-sharing strategies across various departments or teams. By utilizing features such as consolidated billing and SCPs, organizations can achieve greater visibility and control over their AWS infrastructure, leading to improved cost management and operational efficiency. Additionally, AWS Organizations support the implementation of best practices for security and compliance, helping businesses mitigate risks and adhere to regulatory requirements.

In summary, mastering AWS Billing and AWS Organizations is essential for organizations seeking to optimize their cloud operations and maximize the value of their AWS investments. By adopting proactive cost management strategies, leveraging the capabilities of AWS Billing tools, and implementing effective governance structures through AWS Organizations, businesses can achieve greater agility, scalability, and cost-effectiveness in their cloud journey. Embracing these concepts empowers organizations to harness the full potential of AWS while maintaining control, security, and compliance across their cloud environment.

In the next chapter, we will discuss AWS advanced identity services and explore AWS Cognito, used to authorize and customize access to your users, we will see how it can be integrated using social media logins and **single sign-on** (**SSO**) for enterprise authentication, and then we will check out other identity services like STS and directory services.

Points to remember

- **AWS Billing basics**:
  - Understand the different components of AWS Billing, including usage charges, AWS support plans, and data transfer fees.
  - Familiarize yourself with the AWS Free Tier and its limitations to avoid unexpected charges.

- **Cost optimization strategies**:
  - Implement cost optimization strategies such as rightsizing instances, leveraging RIs, and utilizing Spot Instances for non-critical workloads.
  - Monitor and analyze your usage patterns using AWS Cost Explorer and Trusted Advisor to identify cost-saving opportunities.

- **Budgeting and cost allocation**:
  - Setup budgets and alerts to track your AWS spending and prevent cost overruns.
  - Allocate costs accurately to different departments or projects using tags and cost allocation reports.

- **AWS Organizations overview**:
  - Learn about AWS Organizations, a service that enables centralized management of multiple AWS accounts.
  - Understand the benefits of using AWS Organizations, including consolidated billing, centralized security controls, and simplified resource sharing.

- **OUs and accounts**:
  - Structure your AWS accounts using OUs to reflect your organizational hierarchy and manage permissions more effectively.

- o Use SCPs to enforce security and compliance policies across all accounts and OUs.

- **Consolidated billing**:

  - o Take advantage of consolidated billing to aggregate the charges of multiple AWS accounts onto a single bill.

  - o Streamline cost management and invoicing for organizations with multiple accounts and teams.

- **Cross-account access and resource sharing**:

  - o Enable cross-account access to securely share resources such as Amazon S3 buckets or Amazon RDS instances across multiple AWS accounts.

  - o Use AWS **Resource Access Manager (RAM)** to share AWS resources across-accounts within an organization or with other AWS accounts.

- **Governance and compliance**:

  - o Implement governance and compliance policies using AWS Organizations to ensure consistency and security across your organization's AWS environment.

  - o Utilize AWS Config and AWS CloudTrail to monitor and audit changes to your AWS resources and account activities.

- **Integration with Other AWS services**:

  - o Integrate AWS Organizations with other AWS services such as AWS SSO and AWS Control Tower to further streamline account management and security.

  - o Leverage AWS Organizations APIs and SDKs for programmatic management of accounts, OUs, and SCPs.

- **Best practices and recommendations**:

  - o Regularly review and optimize your AWS Billing and Organizational structure to align with changing business requirements and usage patterns.

  - o Stay informed about new AWS features and updates related to billing and AWS Organizations to continuously improve efficiency and cost-effectiveness.

Exercises

1. **What is the primary purpose of AWS Organizations?**

   a. To manage multiple AWS accounts under one umbrella

   b. To provide a Billing dashboard for AWS services

   c. To offer technical support for AWS infrastructure

   d. To automate deployment processes on AWS

2. **How can AWS Organizations help in controlling costs across multiple AWS accounts?**

   a. By providing consolidated Billing and Cost Management tools

   b. By offering discounts on AWS services

   c. By automatically optimizing resource usage

   d. By restricting access to AWS services

3. **What is the benefit of using AWS Organizations for billing purposes?**

   a. It reduces the overall cost of AWS services

   b. It simplifies the process of managing billing across multiple accounts

   c. It provides free credits for new AWS users

   d. It offers unlimited usage of AWS services

4. **Which AWS service allows you to visualize and analyze your AWS Billing and usage data?**

   a. AWS Organizations

   b. AWS Cost Explorer

   c. AWS Budgets

   d. AWS Billing dashboard

5. **How does AWS Organizations help in enforcing policies and security across multiple AWS accounts?**

   a. By providing built-in security features for each account

   b. By automatically applying AWS best practices to all accounts

   c. By allowing the creation of OUs with custom policies

   d. By restricting access to the AWS Management Console

6. **What is the purpose of AWS Budgets?**

   a. To allocate funds for AWS services

   b. To forecast future AWS spending

   c. To track expenses in non-AWS Cloud platforms

   d. To automate resource provisioning on AWS

7. **How can AWS Organizations help in managing compliance requirements across multiple AWS accounts?**

   a. By providing built-in compliance tools

   b. By automatically ensuring compliance with industry standards

   c. By enabling centralized policy enforcement and monitoring

   d. By restricting access to AWS services based on compliance status

8. **Which AWS service can help you Setup budgets and alerts for your AWS spending?**

   a. AWS Cost Explorer

   b. AWS Budgets

   c. AWS Organizations

   d. AWS Billing dashboard

9. **What is the main benefit of using AWS Organizations for large enterprises?**

   a. Reduced operational complexity

   b. Higher performance of AWS services

   c. Lower overall cost of AWS usage

   d. Unlimited scalability of AWS resources

10. **How does AWS Organizations simplify the process of creating and managing AWS accounts?**

    a. By providing a graphical user interface for account management

    b. By automating the account creation process

    c. By offering pre-configured AWS account templates

    d. By providing free AWS credits for new accounts

Answers

1. a
2. a
3. b
4. b
5. c
6. b
7. c
8. b
9. a
10. b

Key terms

- AWS Billing
- AWS Cost Explorer
- AWS Budgets
- AWS Billing alarms
- Billing: Cost and usage reports
- AWS Organizations
- Organizational units
- Service control policies
- Consolidated billing for AWS Organizations

Join our book's Discord space

Join the book's Discord Workspace for Latest updates, Offers, Tech happenings around the world, New Release and Sessions with the Authors:

https://discord.bpbonline.com

CHAPTER 14

AWS Advanced Identity Services

Introduction

In this chapter, we will explore the advanced identity services offered by **Amazon Web Services** (**AWS**), which play a pivotal role in securing and managing access to resources within cloud environments. As we saw in the previous chapters, AWS provides a comprehensive suite of **Identity and Access Management** (IAM) tools that cater to a wide range of authentication and authorization needs. Among these services, we found more advanced identity services.

For example, Amazon Cognito is a powerful solution for managing user identities and authentication in web and mobile applications. Cognito's flexible and scalable architecture enables developers to integrate user sign-up, sign-in, and access control functionalities seamlessly into their applications, thus enhancing user experience while ensuring robust security practices.

Additionally, we explore AWS **Single Sign-On** (**SSO**), **Security Token Service** (**STS**), and directory services, which complement Cognito in managing access across AWS services and resources.

AWS SSO simplifies user access management by providing centralized account access to multiple AWS accounts and business applications using a single set of credentials. STS, on the other hand, offers temporary security credentials that can be used to grant fine-grained access permissions for users and applications. Finally, AWS Directory Service facilitates seamless integration with existing on-premises directories or enables the creation of new directories in the cloud, ensuring a smooth transition and unified identity management experience for organizations leveraging AWS's advanced identity services.

Structure

In this chapter, we will cover the following topics:

- AWS Cognito introduction
- Identity federation for access
- Identity federation in IAM
- AWS Security Token Service
- AWS Directory Service

Objectives

The objective of this chapter is to provide a comprehensive understanding of the services and advanced capabilities of identity services in AWS, focusing on Cognito, SSO, STS, and directory services.

The chapter aims to discuss Amazon Cognito, an AWS fully managed identity service, to explore its advanced features, such as user authentication, authorization, and user management for web and mobile applications. This includes understanding how to integrate Cognito with other AWS services and third-party **identity providers** (**IdPs**) for seamless and secure user authentication workflows. Additionally, the chapter will cover best practices for managing user identities, implementing **multi-factor authentication** (**MFA**), and leveraging Cognito identity pools for fine-grained access control to AWS resources.

Secondly, the chapter will focus on advanced identity services: AWS SSO, STS, and AWS Directory Services. This includes exploring how SSO simplifies user access to multiple AWS accounts and third-party applications through a single set of credentials, and how STS enables temporary, limited-privilege credentials for applications and users. Furthermore, the chapter will discuss AWS Directory Services, including Managed Microsoft **Active Directory** (**AD**) and Simple AD, to highlight their role in managing user directories and enabling seamless integration with AWS resources for hybrid cloud environments.

Overall, the chapter aims to equip readers with the knowledge and skills to design, implement, and manage advanced identity solutions using these AWS services effectively.

AWS Cognito introduction

Amazon Cognito is a robust identity and user management service provided by AWS that enables developers to easily add authentication, authorization, and user management to their applications. It is a comprehensive solution that helps developers focus on building great user experiences while offloading the complexities of user identity management to AWS.

Purpose of AWS Cognito

AWS Cognito is designed to simplify the implementation of secure authentication and authorization workflows in applications. Whether you are developing a web application, mobile application, or any other type of application, Cognito provides the necessary tools and services to handle user authentication, manage user profiles, and secure access to resources.

Key features of AWS Cognito

AWS Cognito offers a wide range of features that make it a powerful identity and user management solution. Some key features are mentioned in the following:

- **User authentication**: Cognito supports multiple authentication methods, including username/password, social IdPs, such as *Google, Facebook,* and *Amazon,* and federated identities via **Security Assertion Markup Language (SAML)** or **OpenID Connect (OIDC)**.

- **User pools**: User pools are a core component of Cognito and allow you to create and manage a repository of user identities. You can define custom attributes, configure password policies, and enable MFA for added security.

- **Identity federation**: Cognito supports identity federation, allowing your users to sign-in using their existing identities from third-party IdPs such as Google, Facebook, or corporate IdPs.

- **User profiles**: With Cognito, you can manage user profiles and store user-specific data such as preferences, settings, and custom attributes. This data can be securely accessed and updated by both the user and your application.

- **Authorization**: Cognito provides fine-grained access control through user roles and groups. You can define permissions based on these roles and groups to control access to different resources within your application.

- **Security**: Cognito implements industry-standard security practices, such as encryption, secure token-based authentication, and secure password storage. It also supports adaptive authentication and risk-based policies to detect and respond to suspicious activities.

- **Scalability**: As an AWS service, Cognito is designed for scalability and can handle millions of users and authentication requests. It integrates seamlessly with other AWS services for enhanced functionality and scalability.

Features of AWS Cognito

Let us look into some of the key features of AWS Cognito that make it an advanced identity service:

- **User pools**: User pools are a fundamental feature of AWS Cognito that allows you to manage user identities within your applications. Here are some key capabilities of user pools:

- **Sign-up and sign-in**: User pools provide APIs and UI components to enable user registration, email or phone verification, and user sign-in using various authentication methods.

- **User attributes**: You can define custom attributes for user profiles, such as name, email, address, and custom data relevant to your application. These attributes can be used for personalization and segmentation.

- **Authentication options**: User pools support a variety of authentication options, including username/password, social IdPs like Google and Facebook, and federated identities using SAML or OIDC.

- **MFA**: Enhance security by enabling MFA for user logins. Cognito supports SMS-based, email-based, and application-based **Time-based One-time Password (TOTP)**, MFA methods to add an extra layer of protection.

- **Identity federation**: AWS Cognito allows you to integrate with external **providers** IdPs for identity federation. This feature offers several benefits, some are mentioned in the following:

  - **SSO**: Users can sign-in once with their existing credentials from IdPs, such as Google, Facebook, or corporate IdPs, and gain access to multiple applications and services without re-entering their credentials.

  - **Secure token exchange**: Cognito handles the exchange of tokens between different IdPs securely, ensuring that the user's identity is trusted across the federation.

  - **Custom IdPs**: You can configure custom IdPs using SAML or OIDC, allowing you to integrate with enterprise identity systems or third-party providers.

- **User management and profiles**: Cognito provides comprehensive user management capabilities to manage user accounts and profiles efficiently, some factors are mentioned in the following:

  - **User lifecycle management**: You can manage user lifecycle events such as account creation, verification, password resets, and account deletion using Cognito's APIs and triggers.

o **User attributes and customization**: Store and retrieve user attributes and custom data in user profiles. This data can be used for personalized user experiences and targeted communication.

o **User groups and roles**: Organize users into groups and assign roles and permissions based on group membership. This allows for fine-grained access control within your application.

User management with AWS Cognito

Effective user management is crucial for maintaining the security and usability of your applications. AWS Cognito offers robust tools and features for managing users efficiently.

Here are some examples of Cognito user flow authentication in some diagrams:

- **API-based authentication flow**:

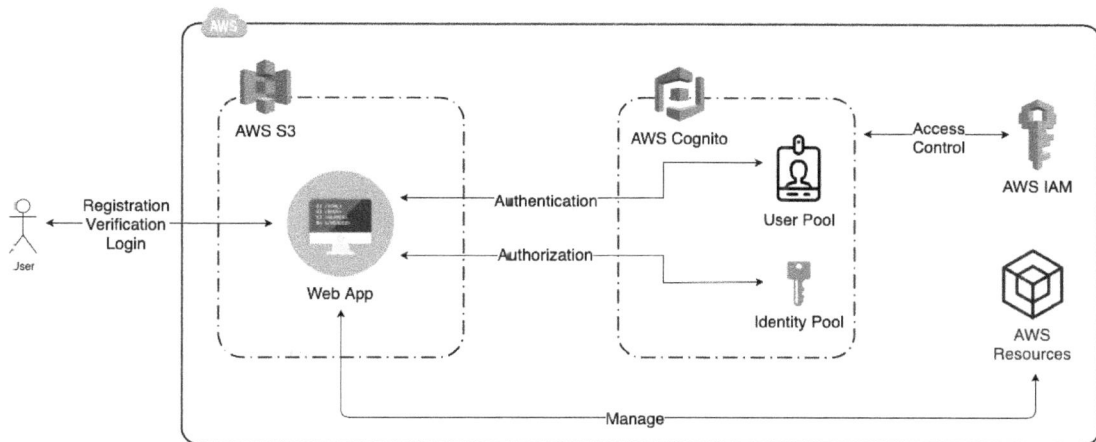

Figure 14.1: API-based user authentication in Cognito

- **Social sign-in authentication flow**:

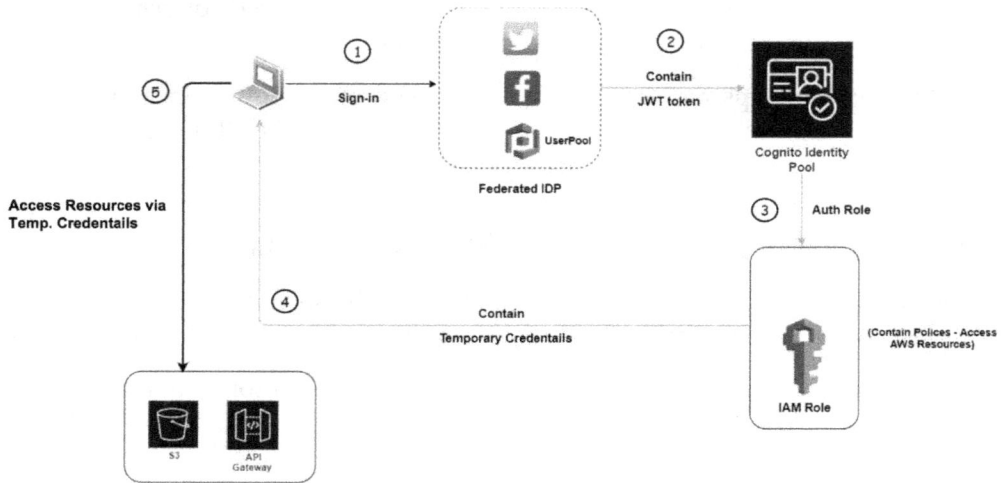

Figure 14.2: *Social sign-in based user authentication in Cognito*

User authentication flows

Cognito supports various authentication flows to suit different application requirements, such as:

- **User pool hosted UI**: Use Cognito's pre-built, customizable UI for user sign-up and sign-in experiences.

- **API-based authentication**: Integrate authentication directly into your application using Cognito's API endpoints for user authentication and token management.

- **Social sign-in**: Enable users to sign-in using their social media accounts (for example, Google, and Facebook) with minimal friction.

User management APIs

Cognito provides APIs for programmatically managing users and user data. Refer to the following points for clarity:

- **User CRUD operations**: **Create, read, update, and delete** (**CRUD**) user accounts using Cognito's APIs. This includes managing user attributes, passwords, and user statuses.

- **User group management**: Create and manage user groups to organize users and assign roles and permissions based on group membership.

- **Custom authentication challenges**: AWS Cognito enables custom authentication challenges for advanced authentication workflows. These are implemented using Cognito triggers (events) and AWS Lambda functions.

Security and compliance

AWS Cognito prioritizes security and compliance to protect user data and ensure regulatory adherence. Refer to the following points for a better understanding:

- **Data encryption**: User data, credentials, and tokens are encrypted both in transit and at rest using industry-standard encryption protocols.

- **Compliance controls**: Cognito offers features and configurations to help you comply with regulations, such as *General Data Protection Regulation (GDPR)*, *Health Insurance Portability and Accountability Act (HIPAA)*, and *Payment Card Industry Data Security Standard (PCI DSS)*, including data retention policies and user consent management.

- **Monitoring and auditing**: Use AWS CloudTrail and Amazon CloudWatch to monitor and audit user authentication and access patterns for security analysis and compliance reporting.

AWS Cognito is a powerful and versatile identity and user management service that empowers developers to build secure and scalable applications with advanced authentication and authorization capabilities. By leveraging Cognito's features, such as user pools, identity federation, and comprehensive user management APIs, developers can streamline the implementation of identity workflows and focus on delivering exceptional user experiences. With its emphasis on security, scalability, and compliance, AWS Cognito is an asset for modern application development on the AWS Cloud platform.

Identity federation for access

Identity federation plays a pivotal role in managing access and authentication across distributed systems. Amazon Cognito provides robust capabilities for managing user identities. This section will discuss the concept of identity federation within Amazon Cognito, exploring its significance, implementation strategies, and benefits.

Understanding identity federation

Identity federation is a mechanism that allows users to access multiple systems or services using a single set of credentials. It facilitates seamless authentication and authorization across disparate platforms without the need for separate user accounts.

This approach enhances user experience, simplifies identity management, and promotes security best practices.

Amazon Cognito leverages identity federation to integrate with external IdPs, such as social IdPs (for example, Google, and Facebook) SAML-based IdPs, and custom IdPs. This integration enables applications to authenticate users against these external sources while leveraging AWS services securely.

Implementing identity federation in Amazon Cognito

In order to implement identity federation in Amazon Cognito, follow these key configuration steps:

- **Create an Amazon Cognito user pool**: Start by creating a user pool in Amazon Cognito, which serves as the user directory for your application.

- **Setup IdPs**: Configure the desired IdPs within the Amazon Cognito user pool settings. This includes specifying details such as client IDs, client secrets, and scopes required for authentication.

- **Enable federation**: Enable federation for your user pool and select the IdPs you want to federate with.

- **Define federation rules**: Define federation rules to map attributes from the external IdP to attributes in the Amazon Cognito user pool.

Here is an example of a Cognito federation rule that uses AWS Cognito with SAML-based IdP federation. In this example, you are federating users from a corporate IdP using SAML into your Cognito user pool. You want to map the SAML attribute email to the Cognito attribute email and the SAML attribute role to a custom attribute **custom:role**.

```
{
  "RulesConfiguration": {
    "Rules": [
      {
        "Claim": "email",
        "MatchType": "Equals",
        "Value": "*",
        "RoleARN": "arn:aws:iam::123456789012:role/CognitoUser",
        "RoleSessionName": "CognitoSession"
      },
      {
        "Claim": "role",
        "MatchType": "Contains",
        "Value": "Admin",
        "RoleARN": "arn:aws:iam::123456789012:role/CognitoAdmin",
        "RoleSessionName": "CognitoAdminSession"
      }
    ]
  },
  "AttributeMapping": {
```

```
    "email": "email",
    "custom:role": "role"
  }
}
```

Here is the explanation for this code example:

1. **RulesConfiguration**:
   a. Defines how incoming claims from the SAML assertion are evaluated.
   b. Maps specific claims (email and role) to IAM roles for user permissions.

2. **AttributeMapping**:
   a. Maps SAML attributes to Cognito user pool attributes.
   b. The email SAML attribute is mapped to the Cognito standard email attribute.
   c. The role SAML attribute is mapped to a custom attribute called **custom:role**.

3. **IAM Role ARN**:
   a. Specifies the IAM roles users will assume based on the evaluated claims.

4. **RoleSessionName**:
   a. Defines the name for the session, which can help identify the user in AWS CloudTrail logs.

Supported identity providers

Amazon Cognito supports a wide range of IdPs, including:

- **Social IdPs**: This includes Google, Facebook, Amazon, etc.
- **SAML-based IdPs**: This includes Microsoft Azure AD, Okta, Ping Identity, etc.
- **Custom IdPs**: Implement custom federation using AWS Lambda functions or third-party solutions.

Authentication flows

Amazon Cognito supports various authentication flows, such as:

- **User pool authentication**: Users authenticate directly with Amazon Cognito user pools.
- **Identity federation**: Users authenticate with external IdPs and federate tokens with Amazon Cognito.
- **Hybrid flows**: Combining user pools and identity federation for enhanced flexibility and functionality.

The benefits of identity federation with Amazon Cognito are mentioned in the following:

- **SSO experience**: Users can access multiple applications seamlessly using a single set of credentials, enhancing convenience and productivity.

- **Centralized identity management**: Manage user identities centrally across different platforms, reducing administrative overhead and ensuring consistency.

- **Enhanced security**: Leverage the security mechanisms of external IdPs and AWS services to enforce strong authentication and access controls.

- **Scalability and flexibility**: Scale your applications and accommodate diverse authentication requirements by integrating with various IdPs and authentication flows.

The best practices and considerations are mentioned in the following:

- **Security policies**: Define granular security policies to control access based on user roles and attributes.

- **Token management**: Implement token expiration and renewal strategies to maintain security and session integrity.

- **Monitoring and logging**: Monitor authentication events and logs to detect anomalies and ensure compliance with security policies.

Identity federation in Amazon Cognito empowers developers and organizations to build secure, scalable, and user-friendly applications. By leveraging external IdPs and authentication standards, Amazon Cognito simplifies identity management and enhances the overall user experience. Embracing identity federation best practices ensures robust security and seamless integration across cloud-based systems.

Identity federation in IAM

AWS IAM is a powerful service that enables users to control access to AWS resources. Within IAM, the identity federation plays a crucial role by allowing organizations to integrate their existing identity systems with AWS, providing a seamless and secure authentication and authorization mechanism.

This section will discuss the concept of identity federation in IAM, its benefits, implementation best practices, and real-world use cases.

Understanding identity federation in AWS IAM

Identity federation is the process of linking an external identity system with AWS IAM to grant users from that system access to AWS resources. This external system could be an enterprise directory service like AD, **Lightweight Directory Access Protocol** (**LDAP**), or an IdP that supports standards, such as SAML or OIDC. By leveraging identity federation, organizations can centralize identity management and enforce consistent access policies across both on-premises and cloud environments.

The benefits of the identity federation are mentioned in the following:

- **SSO**: Identity federation enables SSO, allowing users to log in once to access multiple applications and services, including AWS resources, without the need to re-enter credentials.

- **Centralized access control**: Organizations can enforce access policies centrally through their existing IdP, ensuring consistent security across different systems and platforms.

- **Simplified user management**: User provisioning and de-provisioning can be streamlined by integrating with the enterprise's identity system, reducing administrative overhead.

- **Enhanced security**: Federation reduces the reliance on long-term AWS credentials, minimizing the risk of credential compromise and improving overall security posture.

- **Compliance and auditing**: Identity federation facilitates compliance with regulatory requirements by providing detailed logs and audit trails of user access and activities.

Implementing Identity Federation in AWS IAM

Let us see step by step how to implement Identity Federation in AWS IAM:

- **Configure IdP**:
  - Setup your preferred IdP (for example, Azure AD, Okta, and ADFS) and configure trust relationships with AWS IAM.
  - Generate or obtain necessary metadata, such as SAML metadata for SAML-based IdPs.

- **Create IAM roles**:
  - Define IAM roles in AWS IAM that specify the permissions users or groups from the federated IdP should have.
  - Establish trust relationships between IAM roles and the IdP using the IdP's metadata or manually configuring trust policies.

- **Configure federation settings**:
  - In the AWS Management Console, navigate to IAM and access the IdPs section.
  - Add your IdP and configure relevant settings, such as SAML assertions, attribute mappings, and session duration policies.

- **Test federation**:
  - o Conduct thorough testing to ensure that users from the federated identity system can successfully authenticate and assume IAM roles within AWS.
  - o Verify that permissions are correctly applied based on the IAM roles and policies defined.

Here is an example of a SAML assertion for AWS Cognito, with attributes for roles and groups. This example assumes a scenario where the user is part of specific roles and groups and is using Cognito for federated authentication:

```xml
<saml:Assertion xmlns:saml="urn:oasis:names:tc:SAML:2.0:assertion"
    xmlns:xsi="http://www.w3.org/2001/XMLSchema-instance"
    ID="_abc12345" IssueInstant="2024-12-24T12:00:00Z" Version="2.0">
    <saml:Issuer>https://idp.example.com/</saml:Issuer>
    <saml:Subject>
        <saml:NameID Format="urn:oasis:names:tc:SAML:1.1:nameid-
format:emailAddress">
            user@example.com
        </saml:NameID>
        <saml:SubjectConfirmation
Method="urn:oasis:names:tc:SAML:2.0:cm:bearer"/>
    </saml:Subject>
    <saml:Conditions NotBefore="2024-12-24T11:59:00Z" NotOnOrAfter="2024-
12-24T13:00:00Z">
        <saml:AudienceRestriction>
            <saml:Audience>urn:amazon:cognito:sp</saml:Audience>
        </saml:AudienceRestriction>
    </saml:Conditions>
    <saml:AttributeStatement>
        <!-- Role Attribute -->
        <saml:Attribute Name="https://aws.amazon.com/SAML/Attributes/Role">
            <saml:AttributeValue>arn:aws:iam::123456789012:role/CognitoRole
,arn:aws:iam::123456789012:saml-provider/ExampleIdP</saml:AttributeValue>
        </saml:Attribute>

        <!-- Group Attribute -->
        <saml:Attribute Name="https://aws.amazon.com/SAML/Attributes/
RoleSessionName">
            <saml:AttributeValue>user@example.com</saml:AttributeValue>
        </saml:Attribute>

        <!-- Groups Attribute -->
        <saml:Attribute Name="http://schemas.xmlsoap.org/claims/Group">
```

```
            <saml:AttributeValue>AdminGroup</saml:AttributeValue>
            <saml:AttributeValue>DeveloperGroup</saml:AttributeValue>
        </saml:Attribute>
    </saml:AttributeStatement>
    <saml:AuthnStatement AuthnInstant="2024-12-24T12:00:00Z"
SessionIndex="_session123">
        <saml:AuthnContext>
            <saml:AuthnContextClassRef>
          urn:oasis:names:tc:SAML:2.0:ac:classes:PasswordProtectedTransport
            </saml:AuthnContextClassRef>
        </saml:AuthnContext>
    </saml:AuthnStatement>
</saml:Assertion>
```

Example key elements explanation:

1. **Roles**: The **https://aws.amazon.com/SAML/Attributes/Role** attribute specifies the AWS IAM roles that the user is allowed to assume. The format is **role_arn, provider_arn**.

2. **Groups**: The **http://schemas.xmlsoap.org/claims/Group** attribute lists the groups the user belongs to.

3. **RoleSessionName**: Provides a unique identifier for the user session, often their email or username.

You would replace the placeholders (for example, role ARNs, group names, and user information) with your actual data.

The best practices for the identity federation are mentioned in the following:

- **Use role-based access control (RBAC)**: Implement fine-grained access controls by assigning IAM roles based on users roles and responsibilities within the organization.

- **Enable MFA**: Enhance security by requiring users to authenticate using MFA in addition to their primary credentials.

- **Regularly review and rotate credentials**: Periodically, review and rotate credentials associated with IAM roles and IdPs to mitigate security risks.

- **Monitor and audit federation activity**: Utilize AWS CloudTrail and logging mechanisms to monitor federation activity, detect anomalies, and generate audit reports for compliance purposes.

- **Implement least privilege principle**: Grant users the minimum privileges necessary to perform their tasks, reducing the potential impact of compromised credentials.

Some real-world use cases are mentioned in the following:

- **Enterprise integration**: Large enterprises with existing identity systems, such as AD or LDAP can federate these systems with AWS IAM for seamless access management across cloud and on-premises environments.

- **Cross-account access**: Organizations with multiple AWS accounts can use identity federation to enable users to assume roles in different accounts based on their permissions requirements.

- **Partner and customer access**: Extend federated access to external partners, vendors, or customers, allowing controlled access to specific resources or applications hosted on AWS.

- **Compliance and governance**: Implement federated access controls to meet compliance requirements, such as PCI DSS, HIPAA, or GDPR, while maintaining a centralized identity management approach.

Identity federation in AWS IAM offers a robust solution for organizations seeking to integrate their identity systems with AWS Cloud services. By leveraging identity federation, businesses can enhance security, streamline access management, and maintain compliance while providing a seamless user experience across diverse IT environments. Understanding the principles, best practices and real-world applications of identity federation is crucial for designing and implementing secure and scalable identity solutions in AWS.

AWS Security Token Service

The AWS STS is a powerful and versatile service that allows you to grant temporary, limited-privilege credentials for accessing AWS resources.

It plays a crucial role in enhancing security and managing access control within AWS environments.

In this section, we will discuss the advanced capabilities of STS, its key features, and how it can be leveraged to implement robust security measures.

Understanding temporary security credentials

One of the core concepts of STS is the issuance of temporary security credentials. These credentials are short-lived, typically valid for a few hours, and are used to authenticate and authorize requests to AWS services. By using temporary credentials, you can reduce the risk of long-term credential exposure and enhance your overall security posture.

STS provides three main following types of temporary security credentials:

- **Access key ID and secret access key**: These are similar to the long-term credentials associated with an IAM user but are only valid for a limited time. They can be used to make programmatic calls to AWS services.

- **Session tokens**: Along with access key ID and secret access key, STS issues a session token that provides temporary security credentials. These session tokens are used for API calls and command line tool requests.

- **Federated user tokens**: STS supports federated authentication, allowing you to grant temporary security credentials to users authenticated by external IdPs, such as **AD Federation Services** (**AD FS**), Okta, or PingFederate. This enables seamless integration with existing identity systems and facilitates SSO experiences.

Role of STS in cross-account access

STS plays a pivotal role in enabling cross-account access within AWS environments. Through IAM roles and role assumption mechanisms, STS allows users and applications in one AWS account to securely access resources in another AWS account without the need for long-term credentials or sharing sensitive information.

By defining trust relationships between accounts and configuring IAM roles with appropriate permissions, you can establish a granular and controlled access model across multiple AWS accounts. STS facilitates this process by issuing temporary credentials when a user or application assumes a role, enforcing least privilege principles, and ensuring security boundaries are maintained.

Advanced features and use cases

The AssumeRole API operation provided by STS is instrumental in programmatically assuming IAM roles. This API call enables applications and services to obtain temporary credentials for a specified role, subject to IAM policies and trust relationships. It is widely used in automated workflows, where applications need temporary access to resources with elevated privileges.

Cross-account role access

STS supports cross-account role access, allowing organizations to implement centralized security policies and governance models. By defining roles with specific permissions and establishing trust between AWS accounts, you can facilitate seamless resource sharing while maintaining a strong security posture. This feature is particularly beneficial in multi-tenant environments and scenarios involving collaboration between different teams or business units, for example if you need to use an external database provider in your AWS account, to communicate between services you will need to create a cross-account role to enable access to some specific AWS services for an external entity from your organization but granting some limited-privileges and improve security. Another example could be enabling different AWS accounts to handle different environments to develop one application, it could be common for example to have one account for code repositories and development pipelines, then another one for staging/development and another one for production. To limit the possible security breaches and errors during the development it is common to create a cross-account role between the code and pipeline account and the production and development account, to enable only some AWS services used to trigger cloud infrastructure changes and code deploy updates in the specific environment selected.

Some of the use cases for STS for cross-account roles access:

- **RBAC for applications**: STS enables RBAC for applications running on AWS infrastructure. By assigning IAM roles to EC2 instances, Lambda functions, or other compute resources, you can ensure that applications operate with the principle of least privilege. STS dynamically provides temporary credentials based on the assigned roles, reducing exposure and enhancing security for application workloads.

- **Temporary security credentials for third-party applications**: In addition to IAM users and roles, STS supports temporary security credentials for federated users and third-party applications. This capability is crucial for integrating external systems and services with AWS, enabling secure and controlled access without sharing long-term credentials. By leveraging identity federation and SAML integration, organizations can extend their identity boundaries and enforce consistent access policies across diverse environments.

Best practices for using STS effectively

In order to maximize the benefits of AWS STS and ensure a secure identity management strategy, consider the following best practices:

- **Implement RBAC**: Define granular IAM roles with minimal permissions required for specific tasks or resources. Avoid overly permissive policies to adhere to the principle of least privilege.

- **Use IAM conditions**: Leverage IAM conditions to further restrict access based on time, IP address, or other contextual factors. This adds an extra layer of security and control over temporary credentials.

- **Define IAM permission boundaries**: Set permission boundaries for roles and users to enforce maximum allowable permissions.

- **Monitor and audit role assumptions**: Enable AWS CloudTrail logging to track role assumption events and monitor for unauthorized or anomalous access attempts. Regularly review access logs and conduct security audits to ensure compliance and detect potential security incidents.

- **Grant least privilege**: Assign only the permissions users need to perform specific tasks via IAM roles or policies.

- **Use session policies**: Restrict STS session permissions using inline session policies for fine-grained control.

- **Use short session durations**: Reduce the risk of credential misuse by minimizing session token validity.

- **Leverage MFA**: Require MFA for users and applications accessing roles via STS. MFA adds an additional layer of security by verifying identity through multiple factors, such as passwords and **one-time passwords (OTP)**.

AWS STS is a fundamental component of AWS IAM, providing flexible and secure mechanisms for managing temporary credentials and role-based access control. By understanding its advanced features, integrating best practices, and leveraging STS in your AWS environment, you can strengthen security, enhance governance, and enable seamless collaboration across diverse organizational boundaries.

AWS Directory Service

In today's cloud computing landscape, managing identities and access control is a critical aspect of ensuring security and compliance within organizations. AWS offers a suite of advanced identity services that empower businesses to efficiently manage user identities, enable secure access to resources, and streamline authentication processes. Among these services, AWS Directory Service plays a pivotal role in providing scalable and reliable directory solutions for modern cloud environments.

Overview of AWS Directory Service

AWS Directory Service is a managed service that simplifies the deployment and management of directories in the AWS Cloud. It offers different directory types to meet various use cases, including AWS Managed Microsoft AD, AD Connector, Simple AD, and Amazon Cloud Directory. Let us explore each of these offerings to understand their features, benefits, and best use cases.

AWS Managed Microsoft AD

AWS Managed Microsoft AD is a fully managed AD service built on *Microsoft's Windows Server* architecture. It provides compatibility with Microsoft AD features and APIs, making it seamless for organizations to extend their on-premises AD infrastructure to the AWS Cloud. The key features of AWS Managed Microsoft AD include:

- **Integration with AWS services**: It enables seamless integration with AWS services, such as Amazon EC2, Amazon RDS, and AWS SSO, simplifying authentication and authorization processes.

- **High availability**: It offers Multi-AZ deployment options for high availability and Fault-tolerance, ensuring reliable directory services.

- **Security and compliance**: It supports features like Group Policy, **LDAP over SSL (LDAPS)**, and fine-grained password policies, enhancing security and compliance capabilities.

AWS Managed Microsoft AD is ideal for enterprises that require native AD compatibility in the cloud, centralized user management, and seamless access to AWS resources using familiar AD tools and workflows.

AD Connector

AD Connector is a lightweight directory proxy service that enables AWS workloads to authenticate and authorize against on-premises AD without requiring directory synchronization. It acts as a bridge between AWS services and on-premises AD infrastructure, allowing users to leverage their existing identities for accessing AWS resources. The key features of AD Connector include:

- **Secure authentication**: It facilitates secure authentication using existing AD credentials without storing passwords in the cloud.

- **Low latency**: It minimizes latency by directly proxying authentication requests to on-premises AD infrastructure.

- **No directory synchronization**: It eliminates the need for directory synchronization, reducing management overhead and ensuring real-time access control.

AD Connector is well-suited for organizations that want to maintain a centralized identity source in their on-premises AD environment while securely extending access to AWS services.

Simple AD

Simple AD is a cost-effective directory service that is powered by Samba 4, an open-source implementation of the **Server Message Block (SMB)** or **Common Internet File System (CIFS)** networking protocol. It provides basic AD-compatible features and is suitable for lightweight directory needs within AWS environments. The key features of Simple AD include:

- **User management**: It supports user and group management functionalities similar to traditional AD environments.

- **Authentication**: It enables authentication using standard AD protocols such as Kerberos and Windows **New Technology Lan Manager (NTLM)**.

- **Basic features**: It provides basic AD features without the complexity and cost associated with full-fledged AD deployments.

Simple AD is a good fit for small to medium-sized businesses or departments within larger enterprises that require basic directory services without the overhead of managing a full AD infrastructure.

Amazon Cloud Directory

Amazon Cloud Directory is a flexible, scalable directory service designed for hierarchically organized data storage. Unlike traditional directory services focused on user and group management, Cloud Directory is schemaless and allows organizations to create custom directory hierarchies for a wide range of use cases, such as organizational charts, device registries, and more. The key features of Amazon Cloud Directory include:

- **Custom schema**: This enables organizations to define custom schemas and hierarchies based on their specific data models.

- **Scalability**: This provides scalability to handle large datasets and complex data relationships.

- **Integration**: This integrates with other AWS services for data storage, access control, and analytics.

Amazon Cloud Directory is suitable for applications and systems that require highly customizable directory structures and support for complex data relationships beyond user management.

AWS Directory Service offers a comprehensive suite of directory solutions tailored to diverse organizational needs. Whether it is leveraging managed Microsoft AD for seamless AD integration, utilizing AD Connector for hybrid cloud scenarios, deploying Simple AD for basic directory requirements, or harnessing Amazon Cloud Directory for custom data hierarchies, AWS provides the flexibility and scalability to support modern IAM strategies in the cloud. By leveraging these advanced identity services, businesses can enhance security, streamline operations, and enable seamless access to AWS resources for their users and applications.

Conclusion

This chapter has highlighted the details of the most sophisticated identity services in AWS, emphasizing the importance of security and custom configurations.

The advanced identity services offered by AWS, including Amazon Cognito, AWS SSO, AWS STS, and AWS Directory Service, form a robust framework for managing user identities, federated access, and access control in cloud environments.

Amazon Cognito stands out as a versatile solution for user authentication and authorization, providing features, such as user pools, identity pools, and social IdPs. Its integration with other AWS services and ability to scale seamlessly make it a top choice for developers building secure and scalable applications.

Furthermore, the use of federated identity allows organizations to extend their existing identity systems to AWS, enabling users to access resources using their existing credentials. SSO simplifies access management by allowing users to sign-in once and access multiple applications and services without the need to re-enter credentials. AWS STS plays a crucial role in providing temporary credentials. Then using IAM role policies allow for fine-grained access control, enhancing security posture, and minimizing the risk of unauthorized access. Lastly, AWS Directory Service offers managed directories, such as Microsoft AD, making it easier for enterprises to manage user identities and integrate with on-premises resources.

Together, these advanced identity services empower organizations to maintain a strong security posture while enabling seamless and efficient access to AWS resources.

In the next chapter, we will learn about other important AWS services, explore AWS solutions for machine learning like Polly, and show a panoramic view of other specific AWS services useful for specific needs like Amplify, IoT Core, etc.

Points to remember

- Cognito is a managed identity service that provides user authentication, authorization, and user management for web and mobile applications. It supports multiple authentication methods, including username/password; social IdPs, such as Google, Facebook, and Amazon; and federated IdPs, like SAML-based IdPs.

- Cognito user pools manage user identities and provide features like sign-up, sign-in, and user profile management.

- Cognito identity pools (federated identities) enable users to obtain temporary AWS credentials to access AWS services securely.

- Federated identity allows users to access multiple systems or applications using a single set of credentials across different IdPs.

- AWS supports federated identity through services, like Cognito identity pools, which allow users to authenticate via external IdPs, such as Google, Facebook, or enterprise SAML providers, and obtain temporary AWS credentials.

- SSO is a mechanism that allows users to authenticate once and gain access to multiple applications or services without needing to re-authenticate for each one.

- AWS SSO is a service that simplifies SSO management for AWS accounts and business applications by centrally managing user access.

- STS is a web service that enables you to request temporary, limited-privilege credentials for AWS IAM users or federated users.

- STS supports various use cases, such as providing temporary credentials to applications running on EC2 instances or allowing federated users to access AWS resources securely.

- AWS Directory Service provides managed directories that you can use with AWS services and resources. It supports multiple directory types, including AWS Directory Service for Microsoft AD (Enterprise Edition), AWS Directory Service for Microsoft AD (Standard Edition), and Simple AD (a Microsoft AD-compatible service). These directories enable integration with on-premises AD environments, user authentication for AWS resources, and centralized user management.

- Understanding how these identity services integrate with each other and with other AWS services is crucial for designing secure and scalable applications.

- Consider use cases such as mobile and web application authentication with Cognito, federated access to AWS resources using identity pools and STS, centralizing user access with AWS SSO, and integrating with on-premises directories using AWS Directory Service.

- Implement least privilege access by granting users only the permissions they need to perform their tasks.

- Use MFA to add an extra layer of security to user authentication.

- Regularly review and audit permissions and access patterns to ensure compliance and security.

- Follow AWS security best practices and stay updated with the latest security features and enhancements.

Exercises

1. **What is the primary purpose of Amazon Cognito?**

   a. To manage AWS IAM users and groups

   b. To authenticate and authorize users for web and mobile applications

   c. To provision virtual servers in AWS

   d. To manage AWS Lambda functions

2. **Which AWS service allows users to federate existing identities with AWS resources?**

   a. AWS IAM

   b. Amazon Cognito

   c. AWS SSO

   d. AWS STS

3. **What is the benefit of using SSO in AWS?**

   a. Reducing the number of passwords users need to remember

   b. Increasing the cost of managing user identities

   c. Limiting access to AWS resources

   d. Making authentication more complex

4. **What does AWS STS provide?**

   a. Long-term user credentials

   b. Temporary, limited-privilege credentials

    c. Virtual private network access

    d. Secure email communication

5. **Which AWS service can be used to integrate AWS resources with an on-premises Microsoft AD?**

    a. Amazon Cognito

    b. AWS SSO

    c. AWS STS

    d. AWS Directory Service

6. **What is the primary purpose of AWS IAM?**

    a. Managing AWS resources such as EC2 instances and S3 buckets

    b. Providing authentication and authorization for AWS services

    c. Integrating on-premises directories with AWS resources

    d. Creating virtual private networks within AWS

Answers

    1. b

    2. b

    3. a

    4. b

    5. d

    6. b

Key terms

- AWS IAM
- AWS Cognito
- Identity Federation
- Single Sign-on (SSO)
- AWS Security Token Service (STS)
- AWS Directory Service

CHAPTER 15

Machine Learning and Other AWS Services

Introduction

In the evolving field of technology, the fusion of cloud computing and **artificial intelligence** (**AI**) has revolutionized the way businesses operate and innovate. At the forefront of this transformation stands **Amazon Web Services** (**AWS**), a juggernaut in providing scalable, reliable, and secure cloud solutions. Within the expansive arsenal of AWS services lies a treasure trove specifically tailored for machine learning applications, empowering developers and organizations to harness the full potential of their data.

However, AWS is not solely focused on machine learning. Beyond the field of predictive analytics and neural networks, AWS offers a diverse array of services designed to amplify development, streamline operations, and connect the physical and digital worlds seamlessly.

From Amplify's swift application development to AppSync's real-time data synchronization, from **Internet of Things** (**IoT**) Core's management of connected devices to Ground Station's satellite data processing, AWS provides a comprehensive suite of tools to address a multitude of challenges across industries.

This chapter will explore other important AWS services used for machine learning and computation, focusing on the pivotal role they play in enabling innovation, enhancing efficiency, and driving progress.

Structure

In this chapter, we will cover the following topics:

- AWS machine learning services
- Other useful AWS services

Objectives

In this chapter, our primary objective is to elucidate the multifaceted field of AWS offerings specifically tailored for machine learning applications and other compute services used in particular scenarios. We aim to provide a comprehensive overview of AWS services integral to machine learning workflows, elucidating their functionalities, advantages, and best practices for implementation. By exploring AWS services such as SageMaker, Comprehend, and DeepLens, among others, we endeavor to equip readers with the requisite knowledge to leverage AWS robust infrastructure for developing, deploying, and scaling machine learning models effectively.

Furthermore, we extend our scope beyond traditional machine learning services to encompass complementary offerings like Amplify, AppSync, IoT Core, and Ground Station, elucidating their roles in enhancing applications functionality, scalability, and real-world integration. Through a structured exploration of these services, we aspire to empower readers with a holistic understanding of AWS's ecosystem, enabling them to harness its full potential in their machine learning endeavors.

AWS machine learning services

In today's digital age, data is more than just a collection of numbers and figures, it is the cornerstone of innovation, driving businesses to unprecedented heights of success. With the explosive growth of data, harnessing its potential has become important. machine learning is the transformative technology that enables computers to learn from data and make predictions or decisions. However, leveraging machine learning effectively requires sophisticated algorithms and scalable infrastructure capable of handling vast amounts of data.

This is where AWS emerges as a game-changer. AWS, the cloud computing arm of *Amazon.com Inc.*, offers a comprehensive suite of services tailored to meet the diverse needs of machine learning practitioners. From data pre-processing and model training to deployment and monitoring, AWS provides a rich ecosystem of tools and resources to streamline the machine learning lifecycle.

Navigating the field of AI AWS can be overwhelming, especially for those new to the platform. With a plethora of services spanning compute, storage, networking, and more, understanding which ones are relevant for machine learning can be a daunting task. In this chapter, we will explore the AWS ecosystem, focusing on the services that support and enhance machine learning workflows.

AWS offers a diverse array of services for machine learning, each serving a unique purpose within the broader context of AI and data science. From foundational services like Amazon S3 for data storage to cutting-edge tools like Amazon SageMaker for building, training, and deploying machine learning models at scale, AWS caters to the needs of both beginners and seasoned practitioners alike.

As we explore the world of AWS for machine learning, we will explore the capabilities of key services, such as Amazon SageMaker, Amazon Comprehend, Amazon Rekognition, and more. We will uncover how these services empower organizations to extract valuable insights from their data, automate decision-making processes, and drive innovation across industries.

Furthermore, we will examine real-world use cases and success stories, showcasing how leading companies leverage AWS to solve complex challenges and stay ahead of the curve in today's competitive landscape. Whether you are a data scientist looking to experiment with new algorithms or a business leader seeking to unlock the full potential of your data assets, AWS offers the tools and resources you need to succeed in the era of machine learning.

Join us on this exploration of AWS services for machine learning, where we will demystify the technology, uncover best practices, and inspire you to harness the power of the cloud to revolutionize your approach to data-driven decision-making.

AWS Polly

In the continuously evolving field of digital communication, the ability to effectively convey information is mandatory. While text has long been the primary medium for information exchange, the rise of voice technology has opened up new avenues for communication. However, generating high-quality, natural-sounding speech traditionally required complex infrastructure and expertise. Enter AWS Polly, AWS's revolutionary **text-to-speech (TTS)** service. In this chapter, we explored the world of AWS Polly, its features, applications, and the transformative impact it has on various industries.

Understanding AWS Polly

At its core, AWS Polly is a cloud-based service that converts text into lifelike speech using advanced deep learning technologies. With Polly, developers can effortlessly integrate speech synthesis capabilities into their applications, enabling them to deliver dynamic, engaging content in multiple languages and voices. Polly supports a wide range of use cases, from enhancing accessibility for individuals with disabilities to creating immersive user experiences in gaming and entertainment.

The key features of AWS Polly are mentioned in the following:

- **Natural-sounding voices**: AWS Polly offers a diverse selection of lifelike voices, including male and female options in various accents and languages. These voices are meticulously crafted to mimic human speech patterns, ensuring an authentic listening experience.

- **Customization options**: Developers can fine-tune the speech output by adjusting parameters such as pitch, speed, and volume. This level of customization allows for the creation of tailored voice experiences that align with specific branding or user preferences.

- **Speech Synthesis Markup Language (SSML) support**: Polly supports SSML, a markup language that provides granular control over speech synthesis. SSML enables developers to add pauses, emphasis, and other expressive elements to the generated speech, further enhancing its naturalness and clarity.

- **Real-time synthesis**: With Polly, text can be converted into speech in real-time, making it ideal for applications that require dynamic content generation or live interaction. Whether it is generating voice prompts for virtual assistants or streaming audio for live broadcasts, Polly delivers high-quality speech synthesis with minimal latency.

- **Scalability and reliability**: As part of the AWS ecosystem, Polly benefits from the scalability and reliability of Amazon's infrastructure. Whether serving a handful of users or millions of requests, Polly can seamlessly scale to meet demand while maintaining a high level of performance and uptime.

Applications of AWS Polly

The versatility of AWS Polly makes it suitable for a wide range of applications across various industries. Here are just a few examples:

- **Accessibility**: For individuals with visual impairments or reading difficulties, Polly provides a lifeline by converting written text into spoken words. Websites, e-books, and educational materials can be made accessible to a broader audience through integrated speech synthesis.

- **E-learning and training**: In e-learning platforms and training applications, Polly can enhance the learning experience by narrating course content, quizzes, and instructions. By offering audio alternatives to text-based materials, Polly accommodates different learning styles and preferences.

- **Customer engagement**: Businesses can leverage Polly to enhance customer engagement through **interactive voice response** (**IVR**) systems, virtual assistants, and voice-enabled applications. By providing natural-sounding voice interactions, companies can deliver personalized and immersive experiences that drive customer satisfaction and loyalty.

- **Media and entertainment**: In the field of media and entertainment, Polly opens up new possibilities for creating compelling audio content. From podcast narration to character dialogue in video games, Polly's lifelike voices breathe life into storytelling and entertainment experiences.

- **IoT and smart devices**: With the proliferation of IoT devices and smart speakers, voice has become a primary interface for interacting with technology. Polly enables developers to integrate speech synthesis capabilities into IoT devices, enabling seamless communication and interaction with users.

AWS Polly represents a paradigm shift in the field of TTS synthesis, democratizing access to high-quality speech technology and empowering developers to create immersive voice experiences. With its natural-sounding voices, robust customization options, and seamless integration capabilities, Polly is poised to revolutionize communication across industries. Whether it is improving accessibility, enhancing customer engagement, or unlocking new possibilities in media and entertainment, AWS Polly is transforming the way we interact with information in the digital age.

AWS Rekognition

In a world inundated with digital imagery, the ability to extract meaningful information from visual data has become important. From surveillance and security to retail analytics and content moderation, businesses across various sectors are increasingly turning to computer vision technology to gain insights and streamline operations. AWS Rekognition stands at the forefront of this revolution, offering a comprehensive suite of tools and services for image and video analysis.

Understanding AWS Rekognition

AWS Rekognition is a cloud-based service that harnesses the power of deep learning to analyze images and videos at scale. With a wide array of capabilities, Rekognition empowers developers to integrate advanced computer vision functionalities into their applications with ease. Its key features include:

- **Object and scene detection**: Rekognition can identify thousands of objects and scenes within images and videos, enabling applications to automatically tag and categorize visual content.

- **Facial analysis**: Leveraging facial recognition technology, Rekognition can detect faces, analyze facial attributes, such as age, gender, emotions, and facial expressions, and even recognize individuals across different images and videos.

- **Text detection**: Rekognition can extract text from images, making it invaluable for tasks such as document analysis, **Optical Character Recognition** (OCR), and content moderation.

- **Content moderation**: By analyzing visual content for inappropriate or unsafe material, Rekognition helps businesses maintain brand integrity and ensure a safe user experience.

Use cases and applications

AWS Rekognition is a powerful image and video analysis service that uses machine learning to identify objects, scenes, and activities, as well as detect inappropriate content. It offers a range of use cases, including facial recognition for identity verification, object and scene detection for security and surveillance, and text extraction from images for document processing. With its scalable and cost-effective features, Rekognition is ideal for businesses looking to incorporate advanced visual recognition into their applications for automation, insights, and improved user experiences. The versatility of AWS Rekognition lends itself to a myriad of use cases across diverse industries:

- **Security and surveillance**: Rekognition's facial recognition capabilities are instrumental in enhancing security systems, enabling real-time identification of individuals in crowded spaces, monitoring access control, and identifying suspicious activities.

- **Retail analytics**: Retailers can utilize Rekognition to analyze customer demographics, track foot traffic within stores, optimize product placement, and personalized shopping experiences based on customer preferences.

- **Media and entertainment**: Content creators leverage Rekognition for automatic tagging of images and videos, content moderation to ensure compliance with regulations and community guidelines, and enhancing search capabilities within media libraries.

- **Healthcare**: In healthcare, Rekognition facilitates medical image analysis, assisting in tasks, such as diagnosing diseases from medical images, tracking patient outcomes, and enhancing medical imaging workflows.

Implementation and integration

Integrating AWS Rekognition into existing applications is straightforward, thanks to its robust API and comprehensive documentation. Developers can access Rekognition through **software development kits** (**SDKs**) for popular programming languages such as Python, Java, and JavaScript, allowing for seamless integration into web and mobile applications.

Furthermore, AWS provides pre-built solutions and frameworks that leverage Rekognition for specific use cases, such as the AWS DeepLens for deep learning-enabled video analytics and the AWS Panorama for edge computer vision applications.

Challenges and considerations

While AWS Rekognition offers a powerful set of tools for computer vision applications, there are several challenges and considerations to keep in mind, as mentioned in the following:

- **Data privacy and ethics**: The use of facial recognition technology raises concerns about privacy, surveillance, and potential biases. Developers must adhere to ethical guidelines and regulatory frameworks to ensure responsible use of Rekognition.

- **Accuracy and performance**: While Rekognition boasts high accuracy in many scenarios, its performance may vary depending on factors such as image quality, lighting conditions, and the diversity of the dataset. Continuous evaluation and fine-tuning are necessary to maintain optimal performance.

- **Cost management**: As with any cloud service, the cost of using AWS Rekognition can accumulate, particularly for applications with high volumes of image and video processing. Developers should carefully monitor usage and implement cost optimization strategies to avoid unexpected expenses.

AWS Rekognition empowers developers to unlock the full potential of computer vision, revolutionizing industries and transforming the way we interact with visual data. By leveraging its advanced capabilities, businesses can gain valuable insights, enhance security, improve customer experiences, and drive innovation.

AWS Comprehend

In the era of big data, understanding and making sense of vast amounts of unstructured text data is a formidable challenge. Traditional methods of analyzing text data often fall short due to their limited scalability and effectiveness. However, with the advent of AWS Comprehend, AWS has revolutionized the landscape of **natural language processing (NLP)**.

AWS Comprehend is a fully managed NLP service that enables developers to extract insights and meaning from text data effortlessly. Leveraging cutting-edge machine learning techniques, AWS Comprehend empowers businesses to unlock the value hidden within their textual data, thereby driving innovation and informed decision-making.

Key features and capabilities

Here, we will explore the core features and capabilities of AWS Comprehend that make it a powerful tool for NLP tasks:

- **Text extraction**: AWS Comprehend excels at extracting valuable information from a variety of text sources, including documents, social media posts, emails, and web pages. Through its advanced text extraction capabilities, developers can effortlessly identify key entities, phrases, and sentiments within the text data.

- **Entity recognition**: One of the standouts feature of AWS Comprehend is its ability to recognize and classify entities mentioned in the text, such as people, organizations, locations, dates, and more. This functionality enables businesses to gain valuable insights into the entities mentioned in their text data, facilitating tasks such as customer relationship management, content categorization, and trend analysis.

- **Sentiment analysis**: Understanding the sentiment expressed in text data is crucial for gauging customer satisfaction, brand perception, and market trends. AWS Comprehend offers state-of-the-art sentiment analysis capabilities, allowing developers to accurately classify text as positive, negative, neutral, or mixed sentiment. This functionality enables businesses to gauge the overall sentiment of their customers, identify emerging trends, and make data-driven decisions.

- **Language detection**: With the proliferation of multilingual content on the internet, the ability to detect the language of text data is essential for effective analysis. AWS Comprehend provides robust language detection capabilities, enabling developers to automatically identify the language of text documents and analyze them accordingly. This functionality is particularly valuable for businesses operating in global markets, allowing them to process multilingual text data with ease.

Real-world applications and use cases

Here, we explore real-world applications and use cases of AWS Comprehend across various industries:

- **Customer feedback analysis**: By leveraging AWS Comprehend's sentiment analysis capabilities, businesses can analyze customer feedback from sources such as social media, surveys, and reviews to gain insights into customer satisfaction levels, identify areas for improvement, and tailor their products and services to meet customer needs.

- **Content categorization**: AWS Comprehend's entity recognition capabilities enable businesses to automatically categorize and tag large volumes of textual content, such as news articles, blog posts, and product descriptions. By organizing content into relevant categories, businesses can enhance content discoverability, improve **search engine optimization** (**SEO**), and deliver personalized experiences to their audience.

- **Brand monitoring and reputation management**: In today's digital age, maintaining a positive brand image is important for businesses. AWS Comprehend enables organizations to monitor mentions of their brand across various online channels and analyze sentiment to gauge brand perception. By promptly identifying and addressing negative sentiment, businesses can mitigate reputational risks and preserve brand equity.

- **Market intelligence**: AWS Comprehend empowers businesses to extract valuable insights from unstructured text data, such as market reports, news articles, and social media discussions. By analyzing market trends, competitor activities, and customer sentiments, businesses can make informed decisions, identify emerging opportunities, and stay ahead of the competition.

As businesses continue to grapple with the challenges of analyzing vast amounts of text data, AWS Comprehend emerges as a valuable ally, enabling them to extract actionable insights and unlock the full potential of their textual data assets.

Amazon Lex

Amazon Lex is a cloud-based service by AWS that enables developers to build conversational interfaces using voice and text. Leveraging the same deep learning technologies that power Amazon Alexa, Lex provides **automatic speech recognition** (**ASR**) and **natural language understanding** (**NLU**) to create intelligent chatbots and virtual assistants. With its easy integration into AWS services, businesses can use Lex for customer support, automation, and interactive applications without requiring extensive AI expertise.

Designed for scalability and flexibility, Amazon Lex supports multi-turn conversations, context management, and fulfillment of user intents. It allows developers to deploy chatbots across multiple platforms, including web, mobile, and messaging applications like *Slack* and *Facebook Messenger*. By integrating with AWS Lambda, Lex can trigger custom business logic, making it a powerful tool for enhancing user experiences and streamlining workflows.

Key features and capabilities

Here, we will explore the core features and capabilities of Amazon Lex:

- **Customizable chatbots**: Allows developers to define intents, slots (parameters), and responses to tailor chatbot behavior to business needs.

- **Conversational AI**: Uses NLP and ASR to understand and respond to text and voice inputs.

- **Multi-turn Conversations**: Supports multi-step interactions, enabling context-aware conversations.

- **Built-in support for speech and text**: Handles both voice and text-based interactions seamlessly.

- **Multi-language support**: Supports multi-languages to cater to global audiences.

- **Pre-built integrations**: Includes built-in connectors for enterprise applications like Salesforce and Zendesk.

Real-world applications and use cases

Here are some real-world use cases of Amazon Lex across various industries:

- **Customer support chatbots**: Many businesses deploy Amazon Lex-powered chatbots to automate customer service inquiries, providing 24/7 assistance for order tracking, FAQs, refunds, and troubleshooting without needing human agents.

- **Virtual assistants for banking**: Financial institutions use Amazon Lex to enable users to check account balances, make transactions, and get financial advice through conversational AI in banking apps and websites.

- **HR and employee self-service portals**: Companies integrate Lex chatbots into **human resource (HR)** systems to help employees with leave requests, payroll inquiries, IT support, and benefits enrollment without needing HR personnel intervention.

- **Healthcare and telemedicine assistants**: Hospitals and telemedicine providers use Amazon Lex to create virtual health assistants that help patients schedule appointments, check symptoms, refill prescriptions, and get health tips.

- **E-commerce shopping assistants**: Online retailers use Amazon Lex chatbots to assist customers in finding products, comparing prices, getting personalized recommendations, and managing orders through natural conversations.

- **Automated travel and hospitality booking**: Airlines, hotels, and travel agencies use Amazon Lex to provide chatbot-based booking assistants that help customers reserve flights, hotels, and rental cars while answering common travel-related queries.

- **IVR systems**: Businesses integrate Amazon Lex into call centers to automate phone interactions, directing calls based on intent, handling common queries, and reducing wait times for human agents.

- **Smart home voice control**: Lex-powered voice assistants enable users to control smart home devices, such as adjusting thermostat settings, turning lights on/off, and checking security cameras through natural speech.

- **Workplace productivity bots**: Organizations use Amazon Lex for AI-powered assistants that help schedule meetings, send reminders, automate workflows, and provide quick access to enterprise data via chat or voice.

- **Survey and feedback collection**: Businesses deploy Lex chatbots to conduct interactive surveys, collect customer feedback, and analyze responses using NLP to gain insights.

Amazon Lex with his seamless integration into AWS services, scalability, and multi-platform deployment capabilities, simplifies the development of intelligent, responsive, and automated customer interactions. Its cost-effectiveness, pre-built templates, and robust security features make it an excellent choice for businesses looking to enhance user engagement and streamline operations through conversational AI.

AWS Transcribe

We know that in the digital era, data is king, but it often exists in forms that are not readily accessible or actionable. The ability to extract insights from various forms of media, such as audio and video, can unlock a treasure trove of information. This is where AWS Transcribe, a cutting-edge service offered by AWS, emerges as a game-changer. In this chapter, we will continue exploring the world of AWS Transcribe, exploring its capabilities, applications, and the benefits it brings to businesses and individuals alike.

Understanding AWS Transcribe

At its core, AWS Transcribe is a fully managed ASR service that makes it easy to convert speech to text. Leveraging advanced machine learning algorithms, AWS Transcribe can accurately transcribe audio files into written text in multiple languages. Whether it is capturing customer interactions, converting recorded meetings into searchable archives, or generating subtitles for videos, AWS Transcribe streamlines the process with remarkable precision and efficiency.

How AWS Transcribe works

The underlying technology powering AWS Transcribe is a sophisticated blend of deep learning algorithms, neural networks, and NLP models. When an audio file is submitted to AWS Transcribe, it undergoes a series of steps to extract meaningful text.

The audio is segmented into smaller chunks, which are then analyzed using acoustic models to identify phonemes and words. Then, language models contextualize the recognized words to improve accuracy and coherence. Finally, the transcribed text is output, along with confidence scores for each word, providing insights into the reliability of the transcription.

Applications of AWS Transcribe

The versatility of AWS Transcribe opens up a myriad of applications across various industries. In healthcare, for instance, medical professionals can use it to transcribe patient-doctor interactions, facilitating accurate documentation and analysis. In the legal sector, transcription of court proceedings and depositions becomes seamless, enabling lawyers to focus on core aspects of their cases.

Moreover, AWS Transcribe revolutionizes the accessibility of audiovisual content by generating captions and subtitles for videos. This not only enhances the viewing experience for individuals with hearing impairments but also improves SEO by making video content more discoverable and indexable.

Benefits of AWS Transcribe

The adoption of AWS Transcribe offers a plethora of benefits to businesses and organizations, as mentioned in the following:

- **Increased efficiency**: By automating the transcription process, AWS Transcribe reduces the time and effort required to convert audio to text, allowing employees to focus on higher-value tasks.

- **Enhanced accuracy**: With state-of-the-art machine learning algorithms, AWS Transcribe delivers highly accurate transcriptions, minimizing errors and ensuring reliability.

- **Scalability**: As a fully managed service on AWS Transcribe scales seamlessly to handle transcription tasks of any scale, from small audio clips to extensive archives.

- **Cost-effectiveness**: The pay-as-you-go pricing model of AWS Transcribe means users only pay for what they use, eliminating the need for upfront investment in infrastructure or software.

- **Accessibility**: By providing transcriptions and captions, AWS Transcribe promotes inclusivity, making content accessible to a wider audience, including those with disabilities.

AWS Transcribe represents a significant leap forward in the field of ASR and transcription. Its advanced capabilities, coupled with the reliability and scalability of AWS, empower businesses to unlock the full potential of their audio and video content. AWS Transcribe stands as a testament to the transformative power of machine learning and cloud computing in shaping the future of communication and information accessibility.

AWS SageMaker

Machine learning has emerged as a transformative force, empowering businesses to uncover patterns, make predictions, and automate processes. However, the journey from raw data to actionable insights is often fraught with challenges, from data preprocessing to model deployment. Enter AWS SageMaker, a comprehensive platform designed to streamline the entire machine learning workflow. In this chapter, we will explore the intricacies of AWS SageMaker, discussing its features, benefits, and real-world applications.

Understanding AWS SageMaker

AWS SageMaker epitomizes AWS commitment to democratizing machine learning. At its core, SageMaker is an end-to-end machine learning platform that facilitates every step of the machine learning lifecycle. Whether you are a seasoned data scientist or a novice enthusiast, SageMaker provides the tools and infrastructure necessary to build, train, and deploy machine learning models at scale.

The components of SageMaker are mentioned in the following:

- **Notebook instances**: SageMaker offers managed Jupyter Notebook instances, enabling data scientists to explore, visualize, and preprocess data seamlessly. These instances come pre-configured with popular libraries and frameworks, empowering users to kickstart their machine learning experiments with minimal setup overhead.

- **Built-in algorithms**: SageMaker boasts a rich repository of pre-built algorithms spanning various domains, from computer vision to NLP. By leveraging these algorithms, users can expedite model development without sacrificing performance or scalability.

- **Custom models with SageMaker SDK**: For more advanced use cases, SageMaker provides a Python SDK that facilitates the development and training of custom machine learning models. With the SDK's intuitive APIs, developers can harness the full power of AWS infrastructure while retaining the flexibility to implement bespoke solutions tailored to their specific requirements.

- **Automated model tuning**: Hyperparameter optimization is a critical aspect of machine learning model development. SageMaker simplifies this process through automated model tuning, which systematically explores the hyperparameter space to identify the optimal configuration for a given dataset and objective.

- **Model deployment**: Once a model is trained, deploying it into production is seamless with SageMaker's built-in deployment capabilities. Whether you prefer real-time inference or batch processing, SageMaker offers scalable and cost-effective deployment options to suit your needs.

Real-world applications

The versatility of AWS SageMaker transcends industry boundaries, empowering organizations across sectors to harness the power of machine learning for innovation and growth.

Here are some examples of usage of SageMaker in the industry:

- **Healthcare**: In the healthcare sector, SageMaker is revolutionizing patient care through predictive analytics and personalized medicine. By analyzing **electronic health records (EHRs)** and medical imaging data, healthcare providers can identify at-risk patients, optimize treatment plans, and improve clinical outcomes.

- **Retail**: Retailers leverage SageMaker to enhance customer experience and drive revenue through targeted marketing and demand forecasting. By analyzing historical sales data and customer demographics, retailers can optimize pricing strategies, recommend personalized product offerings, and anticipate market trends with unparalleled accuracy.

- **Finance**: In the finance industry, SageMaker is instrumental in fraud detection, risk management, and algorithmic trading. By analyzing transactional data and market signals in real-time, financial institutions can detect fraudulent activities, mitigate risks, and capitalize on lucrative investment opportunities with confidence.

AWS SageMaker epitomizes the democratization of ML, empowering organizations of all sizes to harness the transformative power of AI. From streamlined model development to scalable deployment, SageMaker accelerates innovation and drives tangible business value across industries. As the machine learning landscape continues to evolve, SageMaker remains at the forefront, enabling enterprises to unlock new possibilities and chart a course towards a data-driven future.

AWS Kendra

In today's fast-paced world, businesses are inundated with vast amounts of data, making it increasingly challenging to access relevant information quickly and efficiently. Traditional search engines often fall short when it comes to retrieving precise answers from complex data sources such as documents, databases, and even unstructured text. However, with the advent of AI and machine learning, there emerges a solution: AWS Kendra.

Understanding AWS Kendra

AWS Kendra is a powerful enterprise search service designed to address the limitations of traditional search engines. Leveraging advanced machine learning algorithms, NLP techniques, and sophisticated search capabilities, Kendra enables organizations to unlock the full potential of their data repositories. Whether it is finding critical information buried within documents, extracting insights from large datasets, or retrieving answers from FAQs, Kendra empowers users to access the right information at the right time with unprecedented accuracy and speed.

At the core of Kendra lies its ability to understand natural language queries, allowing users to pose questions in everyday language without the need for complex search syntax. This feature, powered by cutting-edge NLP models, enables Kendra to grasp the intent behind queries and deliver highly relevant results, even from unstructured data sources. Moreover, Kendra continuously learns from user interactions and feedback, improving its search accuracy and relevance over time, a hallmark of AI-driven systems.

Key features and benefits

AWS Kendra offers a plethora of features and benefits that distinguish it from traditional search solutions, some are mentioned:

- **NLU**: Kendra's advanced NLP capabilities enable it to comprehend complex queries, including synonyms, acronyms, and colloquial language, ensuring accurate results regardless of how users phrase their questions.

- **Enterprise-grade search**: Kendra supports a wide range of data sources, including documents, websites, databases, and file systems, making it a versatile solution for diverse enterprise environments.

- **Rich document understanding**: Unlike conventional search engines, Kendra goes beyond keyword matching by understanding the context and semantics of documents, thereby delivering precise answers and insights from even the most complex content.

- **FAQ integration**: Kendra excels at answering FAQs by extracting relevant information from structured sources and providing concise responses, thereby enhancing customer support and self-service experiences.

- **Continuous improvement**: Through machine learning, Kendra continuously learns from user interactions, feedback, and content updates, ensuring that its search results remain relevant and up-to-date over time.

Real-world applications and use cases

AWS Kendra is a highly intelligent enterprise search service powered by machine learning. It helps organizations quickly find relevant information across vast amounts of unstructured data, such as documents, emails, websites, and knowledge bases. By understanding natural language queries, Kendra delivers precise and contextual search results, making it an ideal solution for enhancing productivity in industries like healthcare, legal, retail, and customer support. The versatility and intelligence of AWS Kendra make it suitable for a wide range of applications across various industries:

- **Customer support and self-service**: Organizations can deploy Kendra to enhance customer support by providing instant access to relevant information and troubleshooting guides, reducing the need for human intervention and improving customer satisfaction.

- **Knowledge management**: Kendra serves as a powerful knowledge management tool, enabling employees to quickly find relevant documents, policies, and best practices, thereby fostering collaboration and accelerating decision-making processes.

- **Compliance and regulatory compliance**: In industries such as finance, healthcare, and legal, where compliance is paramount, Kendra can help organizations navigate complex regulatory requirements by providing accurate and up-to-date information from diverse sources.

- **E-commerce and product discovery**: By integrating Kendra into e-commerce platforms, retailers can enhance product discovery and recommendation systems, helping customers find the products that best match their needs and preferences.

- **Research and data analysis**: Researchers and data scientists can leverage Kendra to sift through vast amounts of scientific literature, patents, and research papers, accelerating the discovery of insights and driving innovation in various fields.

In conclusion, AWS Kendra represents a paradigm shift in enterprise search, offering unprecedented accuracy, relevance, and scalability. By harnessing the power of AI and machine learning, Kendra empowers organizations to unlock the full potential of their data assets, driving innovation, efficiency, and competitive advantage.

Other useful AWS services

Let us dive in exploring other interesting AWS services not covered in previous chapters. We will find some extra services used in specific industries and that can be really useful to know to better prepare you for your exam and your future professional career using AWS.

AWS Amplify

AWS Amplify, a comprehensive platform provided by AWS, offers developers a robust set of tools and services to build and deploy full-stack applications quickly and efficiently. In this chapter, we will discover the capabilities of AWS Amplify and explore how it empowers developers to accelerate their development processes and deliver exceptional user experiences.

Introduction to AWS Amplify

AWS Amplify simplifies the development process by providing a unified framework for building scalable and secure applications. At its core, Amplify offers a wide range of features, including authentication, data storage, analytics, and more. Whether you are developing a web application, mobile application, or even a backend service, Amplify streamlines the development workflow and enables developers to focus on building great features rather than managing infrastructure.

Key features of AWS Amplify

One of the standouts feature of AWS Amplify is its seamless integration with other AWS services. Developers can leverage the power of services like Amazon DynamoDB for database management, Amazon Cognito for user authentication, and AWS Lambda for serverless computing. This tight integration simplifies the development process and allows developers to build highly scalable and resilient applications without worrying about the underlying infrastructure.

Another key feature of AWS Amplify is its support for multiple programming languages and frameworks. Whether you prefer to use JavaScript with React, Angular, or Vue.js for web development, or Swift or Kotlin for mobile app development, Amplify has you covered. This flexibility enables developers to choose the tools and technologies that best fit their needs while still taking advantage of the powerful capabilities of AWS.

Accelerating development with AWS Amplify CLI

The AWS Amplify **Command Line Interface** (**CLI**) is a powerful tool that further simplifies the development process. With the CLI, developers can easily create and configure Amplify projects, add authentication and authorization to their applications, and deploy their code to the cloud with just a few simple commands. The CLI also provides features for managing backend resources, automating common tasks, and integrating with popular development tools like Git and CI/CD pipelines.

Building scalable and resilient applications

Scalability and reliability are critical factors in modern application development. especially as user demand grows and evolves over time. AWS Amplify provides developers with the tools they need to build applications that can scale effortlessly to accommodate millions of users while maintaining high performance and availability.

One of the ways Amplify achieves this is through its support for serverless computing with AWS Lambda. By leveraging Lambda functions, developers can build highly responsive and scalable backend services without provisioning or managing servers. This serverless architecture allows applications to scale automatically in response to changes in demand, ensuring a smooth and seamless user experience.

AWS Amplify is a game-changer for developers looking to build modern, scalable, and reliable applications. With its comprehensive set of features, seamless integration with other AWS services, and powerful CLI, Amplify empowers developers to accelerate their development processes and deliver exceptional user experiences. Whether you are building a web application, mobile application, or backend service, AWS Amplify provides the tools and services you need to succeed in today's competitive marketplace.

AWS AppSync

In the world of modern application development, creating robust and responsive APIs is fundamental. AWS AppSync, a fully managed service provided by AWS, empowers developers to build scalable GraphQL APIs (**https://graphql.org/**) effortlessly. This chapter delves into the intricacies of AWS AppSync, exploring its features, benefits, and practical applications.

Introduction to AWS AppSync

AWS AppSync simplifies the process of building real-time and offline-enabled applications by allowing developers to define flexible APIs with GraphQL. GraphQL, a query language for APIs, enables clients to request only the data they need, resulting in more efficient and performant applications.

AWS AppSync offers a range of features that streamline the development process, as mentioned in the following:

- **Real-time data synchronization**: With built-in support for real-time data synchronization, AWS AppSync enables developers to create applications that instantly reflect changes made to the underlying data sources. This feature is crucial for applications requiring live updates, such as collaborative tools and messaging platforms.

- **Offline data access**: By leveraging AWS AppSync's offline data access capabilities, developers can build applications that remain functional even when users are offline. Data changes made by users while offline are automatically synchronized with the backend once connectivity is restored, ensuring a seamless user experience.

- **Built-in authorization and authentication**: AWS AppSync integrates seamlessly with AWS IAM and Amazon Cognito to provide robust authentication and authorization mechanisms. Developers can define fine-grained access controls to ensure that only authorized users can access specific resources within the API.

- **Integration with data sources**: AWS AppSync supports integration with various data sources, including Amazon DynamoDB, AWS Lambda, Amazon Aurora, and more. This flexibility allows developers to leverage existing data sources and services, reducing development time and effort.

Practical applications

AWS AppSync finds applications in various domains, including but not limited to the following:

- **Real-time collaboration tools**: Developers can use AWS AppSync to build collaborative applications such as collaborative document editors, project management tools, and whiteboard applications. Real-time data synchronization ensures that all users see the latest changes made by their collaborators in real-time.

- **E-commerce platforms**: They can benefit from AWS AppSync's real-time capabilities to provide a dynamic shopping experience to customers. For example, inventory updates, price changes, and product availability can be instantly reflected in the user interface, enhancing the overall shopping experience.

- **Offline-first applications**: The applications that need to remain functional even when users are offline, such as field service management apps or data collection tools, can leverage AWS AppSync's offline data access feature. Users can continue to interact with the application and make updates, which are then synchronized with the backend once connectivity is restored.

Getting Started with AWS AppSync

In order to get started with AWS AppSync, developers can follow these steps:

- **Create an AppSync API**: Using the AWS Management Console or the AWS CLI, developers can create a new AWS AppSync API and define its schema.

- **Define data sources and resolvers**: Next, developers can define data sources such as DynamoDB tables or AWS Lambda functions and create resolvers to map GraphQL operations to these data sources.

- **Implement authorization and authentication**: Developers can configure authentication and authorization settings using Amazon Cognito or IAM to secure access to the API.

- **Test and deploy**: Developers can test their API using the AppSync console or GraphQL IDEs such as Apollo Studio and deploy it to production once satisfied with its functionality.

AWS AppSync revolutionizes the way developers build APIs by providing a fully managed service for creating scalable and responsive GraphQL APIs. With its real-time data synchronization, offline capabilities, and seamless integration with AWS services, AWS AppSync empowers developers to build modern applications that deliver exceptional user experiences. As organizations increasingly embrace GraphQL for their API needs, AWS AppSync emerges as a valuable tool for accelerating the development of innovative and dynamic applications.

AWS IoT Core

The IoT has emerged as a transformative force, connecting smart devices and systems to enable seamless communication and automation. At the heart of many IoT solutions lies AWS IoT Core, a robust platform offered by AWS. In this chapter, we will explore the intricacies of AWS IoT Core, exploring its features, capabilities, and the myriads of possibilities it offers for building scalable and secure IoT applications.

Understanding AWS IoT Core

AWS IoT Core serves as the backbone for IoT deployments, facilitating the effortless integration of devices and applications with the cloud. At its core, AWS IoT provides a set of services that enable secure and bi-directional communication between IoT devices and the cloud. Whether it is collecting data from sensors, controlling actuators, or orchestrating complex workflows, AWS IoT Core simplifies the development and management of IoT solutions.

The key features and capabilities are mentioned in the following:

- **Device management**: AWS IoT Core offers comprehensive device management capabilities, allowing users to securely onboard, organize, and monitor IoT devices at scale. With features like device registry and device shadows, developers can seamlessly manage device connectivity and state, ensuring reliable communication between devices and the cloud.

- **Message broker**: Central to AWS IoT Core is its highly scalable message broker, which facilitates efficient communication between devices and cloud applications. Using protocols like MQTT and HTTP, devices can publish data to topics, which are then routed to subscribed clients or backend systems in real-time. This pub/sub architecture forms the backbone of many IoT solutions, enabling seamless data exchange and event-driven processing.

- **Security and identity**: Security is important in IoT deployments, and AWS IoT Core provides a robust set of tools for ensuring end-to-end security and privacy. Through features, like device authentication, fine-grained access control, and encryption, AWS IoT Core helps mitigate security risks and safeguard sensitive data from unauthorized access or tampering.

- **Scalability and flexibility**: As IoT deployments continue to grow in scale and complexity, AWS IoT Core offers unparalleled scalability and flexibility to meet evolving demands. Whether you are connecting thousands or millions of devices, AWS IoT Core can seamlessly scale to accommodate varying workloads, ensuring high availability and low latency for mission-critical applications.

Use cases and applications

The versatility of AWS IoT Core opens up a plethora of use cases across diverse industries, as mentioned in the following:

- **Smart manufacturing**: In manufacturing environments, AWS IoT Core enables real-time monitoring of equipment health, predictive maintenance, and process optimization. By connecting sensors and machinery to the cloud, manufacturers can streamline operations, reduce downtime, and improve overall efficiency.

- **Connected healthcare**: In healthcare, AWS IoT Core powers innovative solutions, such as remote patient monitoring, asset tracking, and medication adherence. By securely transmitting vital data from medical devices to healthcare providers, AWS IoT Core empowers personalized patient care and improves health outcomes.

- **Smart cities**: In urban settings, AWS IoT Core facilitates the creation of smart infrastructure for managing traffic, monitoring environmental conditions, and enhancing public safety. By deploying IoT sensors and actuators across cities, municipalities can optimize resource utilization, reduce congestion, and create more sustainable communities.

AWS IoT Core serves as a foundational building block for realizing the full potential of the IoT. With its robust features, scalable infrastructure, and comprehensive security model, AWS IoT Core empowers developers to build innovative IoT solutions across a wide range of industries and use cases. As IoT continues to proliferate and reshape our world, AWS IoT Core remains at the forefront, driving innovation and enabling transformative experiences for businesses and consumers alike.

AWS Ground Station

In the vast expanse of space, satellites orbit, capturing invaluable data and imagery that shape our understanding of the world. However, the process of acquiring and managing this data has traditionally been complex, expensive, and often inaccessible to many organizations. Enter AWS Ground Station, a groundbreaking service by AWS that is revolutionizing satellite data acquisition, making it more accessible, affordable, and scalable than ever before.

Introduction to AWS Ground Station

AWS Ground Station is a fully managed service that enables customers to control satellite communications, process data, and scale their operations without having to invest in ground station infrastructure. Launched in 2018, it marked a significant shift in the satellite industry, democratizing access to space-derived data and empowering a wide range of users, from startups to large enterprises, to leverage satellite data for various applications.

Key features and capabilities

At its core, AWS Ground Station offers a comprehensive suite of features and capabilities designed to streamline the entire satellite data acquisition process, these include:

- **Global ground station network**: AWS has strategically positioned ground stations around the world, allowing customers to access satellite data from anywhere on the planet with low latency and high reliability.

- **On-demand scheduling**: With AWS Ground Station, users can schedule satellite contacts on-demand, eliminating the need to pre-allocate resources and providing flexibility to adapt to changing requirements and priorities.

- **Fully managed service**: From antenna maintenance to data processing, AWS handles all aspects of ground station operations, freeing users from the burden of managing infrastructure and allowing them to focus on extracting insights from satellite data.

- **Integration with AWS services**: AWS Ground Station seamlessly integrates with other AWS services, such as Amazon S3, AWS Lambda, and Amazon EC2, enabling customers to store, process, and analyze satellite data using familiar tools and workflows.

Use cases and applications

AWS Ground Station is a fully managed service that enables users to control satellite communications and process data from space. It simplifies the integration of satellite data into cloud-based applications, enabling real-time data processing for industries such as agriculture, defense, and environmental monitoring. By providing direct satellite connectivity, AWS Ground Station supports applications like remote sensing, weather forecasting, and disaster response, helping organizations leverage space-derived data for decision-making and analysis. The versatility of AWS Ground Station opens up a myriad of use cases and applications across various industries:

- **Earth observation**: Environmental monitoring, agriculture, urban planning, and disaster response are just a few examples of how satellite imagery acquired through AWS Ground Station can be used to gain insights into Earth's dynamic systems and phenomena.

- **Communications and connectivity**: Satellites play a crucial role in global communications networks, and AWS Ground Station enables organizations to establish and maintain reliable satellite communications for telecommunication, IoT connectivity, and remote operations.

- **Science and research**: They can leverage satellite data for a wide range of studies, including climate research, atmospheric science, oceanography, and biodiversity conservation, benefiting from the rich and continuous stream of data facilitated by AWS Ground Station.

Future outlook and impact

As the demand for satellite data continues to grow across industries, the impact of AWS Ground Station is poised to expand exponentially. With ongoing advancements in satellite technology, including the proliferation of small satellites and constellations, AWS Ground Station is well-positioned to play a pivotal role in shaping the future of space-based data acquisition and analytics.

AWS Ground Station represents a paradigm shift in satellite data acquisition, democratizing access to space and empowering organizations of all sizes to leverage satellite data for a wide range of applications. By eliminating barriers to entry and providing a scalable, cost-effective solution, AWS Ground Station is catalyzing innovation and driving positive change across industries, ultimately unlocking new insights into our planet and beyond.

Conclusion

In conclusion, the advent of cloud computing has ushered in a new era of possibilities for machine learning and other innovative technologies. AWS stands at the forefront of this revolution, offering a comprehensive suite of services tailored to the diverse needs of developers, data scientists, and businesses alike. Throughout this chapter, we have explored a range of AWS services specifically designed to support machine learning initiatives, as well as other services such as Amplify, IoT Core, and Ground Station, which augment and complement these capabilities.

AWS machine learning services, including Amazon SageMaker, Amazon Comprehend, Amazon Rekognition, and Amazon Polly, provide robust tools for training, deploying, and managing machine learning models at scale. With SageMaker, developers can streamline the entire machine learning workflow, from data preprocessing to model deployment, all within a single, integrated platform. Comprehend and Rekognition offer powerful NLP and computer vision capabilities, enabling applications to extract insights from unstructured text and images. Polly extends this functionality further by enabling the generation of lifelike speech from text, opening up new possibilities for voice-enabled applications.

Furthermore, AWS Amplify empowers developers to build full-stack web and mobile applications quickly and efficiently, with built-in support for authentication, data storage, and real-time updates. By abstracting away much of the underlying infrastructure complexity, Amplify accelerates the development process and enables teams to focus on delivering value to their users. Similarly, AWS IoT Core simplifies the development and management of IoT applications, providing scalable infrastructure for securely connecting devices and ingesting telemetry data. With features such as device shadowing and a rules engine, IoT Core facilitates the implementation of sophisticated IoT solutions across various industries.

In addition to these services, AWS Ground Station offers a novel solution for satellite data processing and analysis. By leveraging AWS Global Infrastructure, Ground Station enables customers to downlink satellite data directly to the cloud, where it can be processed, stored, and analyzed using familiar AWS tools and services. This eliminates the need for costly ground infrastructure and reduces the time and effort required to access and utilize satellite data for various applications, including environmental monitoring, disaster response, and precision agriculture.

Collectively, these AWS services represent a powerful toolkit for building and deploying cutting-edge applications that leverage ML, IoT, and satellite technologies. Whether it is predicting customer behavior, analyzing sensor data from connected devices, or monitoring environmental changes from space, AWS provides the scalable infrastructure and advanced tools needed to turn ideas into reality. As organizations continue to embrace digital transformation and seek innovative solutions to complex challenges, AWS remains a trusted partner in their journey toward success.

In the next and final chapter of this book, we will show some tips and resources for preparing for your AWS exam for the Cloud Practitioner exam and certification.

Points to remember

- **Amazon SageMaker:**
    - A fully managed service for building, training, and deploying machine learning models at scale.
    - Provides a wide range of algorithms and frameworks, along with built-in Jupyter Notebooks for data exploration and model development.

- Offers features like automatic model tuning, hosting, and monitoring to streamline the entire machine learning workflow.

- **Amazon Rekognition**:
  - A deep learning-based image and video analysis service.
  - Allows for object and scene detection, facial analysis, and text recognition in images and videos.
  - Useful for tasks like content moderation, sentiment analysis, and facial recognition in various applications.

- **Amazon Comprehend**:
  - A NLP service that uses machine learning to extract insights and relationships from text.
  - Capable of detecting entities, key phrases, language, sentiment, and more from unstructured text data.
  - Enables sentiment analysis, trend analysis, and content categorization in applications dealing with large volumes of textual data.

- **Amazon Polly**:
  - A TTS service that uses advanced deep learning technologies to synthesize human-like speech from text.
  - Supports multiple languages and voices, with customizable pronunciation and speech styles.
  - Useful for creating audio content for applications like IVR systems, e-learning platforms, and accessibility features.

- **AWS Transcribe**:
  - An ASR service that converts speech to text.
  - Supports real-time and batch transcription of audio files in various formats, including streaming audio.
  - Empowers applications with features like voice-enabled search, closed captioning, and transcription of customer support calls.

- **AWS Kendra**:
  - An intelligent search service powered by machine learning.
  - Enables organizations to build powerful search capabilities for their content repositories, databases, and applications.

o Utilizes NLU to provide accurate and contextual search results, improving productivity and decision-making.

- **AWS Amplify**:

  o A set of tools and services for building full-stack applications quickly and efficiently.

  o Supports frontend web and mobile development, providing features like authentication, analytics, and offline data synchronization.

  o Integrates seamlessly with other AWS services like Amazon S3, Amazon DynamoDB, and AWS AppSync to simplify application development and deployment.

- **AWS AppSync**:

  o A fully managed GraphQL service for building real-time and offline-enabled applications.

  o Simplifies data fetching and synchronization between clients and backend data sources, such as databases, APIs, and AWS services.

  o Supports automatic conflict resolution, offline data caching, and subscription-based real-time updates for enhanced user experiences.

- **AWS IoT Core**:

  o A managed cloud service for securely connecting IoT devices to the cloud and other devices.

  o Provides device management, secure communication, and data processing capabilities for IoT applications.

  o Enables features like device provisioning, message routing, and integration with other AWS services for IoT data analytics and automation.

- **AWS Ground Station**:

  o A fully managed service for satellite communications, allowing customers to control and downlink data from satellites.

  o Provides access to a global network of ground stations, eliminating the need for building and maintaining custom ground infrastructure.

  o Enables real-time data processing and analysis of satellite data for applications like weather monitoring, disaster response, and agricultural monitoring.

Exercises

1. **What AWS service is primarily used for natural language search and discovery within large volumes of unstructured data?**

   a. Kendra

   b. SageMaker

   c. Polly

   d. Rekognition

2. **Which AWS service facilitates the training, building, and deployment of machine learning models at scale, with minimal effort and cost?**

   a. Kendra

   b. SageMaker

   c. Polly

   d. Rekognition

3. **Which AWS service converts text into lifelike speech, enabling developers to create applications that talk with human-like voices?**

   a. Kendra

   b. SageMaker

   c. Polly

   d. Rekognition

4. **Which AWS service provides deep learning-based image and video analysis for object and scene detection, facial recognition, and text extraction?**

   a. Kendra

   b. SageMaker

   c. Polly

   d. Rekognition

5. **Amplify is an AWS service primarily used for what purpose?**

   a. Natural language search and discovery

   b. machine learning model training and deployment

   c. Text-to-speech conversion

   d. Building scalable mobile and web applications

6. **What AWS service provides GraphQL APIs for building scalable, secure, and real-time data-driven applications?**

    a. Amplify

    b. AppSync

    c. IoT Core

    d. Ground Station

7. **IoT Core is an AWS service designed for what purpose?**

    a. Building scalable mobile and web applications

    b. Providing GraphQL APIs

    c. Managing IoT devices securely

    d. Real-time data-driven applications

8. **Ground Station is an AWS service used for what specific function?**

    a. Natural language search and discovery

    b. machine learning model training and deployment

    c. IoT device management

    d. Satellite data processing and analysis

Answers

1. a

2. b

3. c

4. d

5. d

6. b

7. c

8. d

Key terms

- Machine learning
- Natural language processing
- Text-to-speech
- Automatic speech recognition
- AWS Polly
- AWS Rekognition
- AWS SageMaker
- AWS Comprehend
- Amazon Lex
- AWS Transcribe
- AWS Kendra
- AWS Amplify
- AWS AppSync
- AWS IoT Core
- AWS Ground Station

Join our book's Discord space

Join the book's Discord Workspace for Latest updates, Offers, Tech happenings around the world, New Release and Sessions with the Authors:

https://discord.bpbonline.com

CHAPTER 16
Preparing for the Exam

Introduction

In this last chapter, we discussed the essential resources provided by **Amazon Web Services (AWS)** to equip aspiring Cloud Practitioner with the knowledge necessary to ace the certification exam. AWS offers a plethora of study materials, ranging from comprehensive documentation and whitepapers to interactive online courses and practice exams. We will navigate through these resources, highlighting their significance in understanding AWS Cloud services, architectures, and best practices. Whether you are a seasoned IT professional or a newcomer to the cloud landscape, AWS educational offerings cater to diverse learning styles, ensuring a solid foundation for exam preparation.

As the exam day approaches, meticulous preparation becomes paramount. Whether opting for an in-person examination or a proctored online session, candidates must familiarize themselves with the exam format, rules, and logistics. We will guide you through the exam day preparations, covering everything from technical requirements for online proctoring to tips for managing time effectively during the exam. With these tips and tricks, you will be well-equipped to navigate the AWS Certified Cloud Practitioner exam with confidence and finesse.

Structure

In this chapter, we will cover the following topics:

- AWS resources for exam preparation
- Other resources from third-parties
- Mock exam
- Exam day preparation
- Tips and exam discounts

Objectives

In this chapter, we aim to equip aspiring AWS Certified Cloud Practitioner with the resources available to effectively prepare for the examination. We will explore the plethora of study materials and resources provided by AWS, offering a comprehensive overview of the core concepts and services crucial for success in the exam. By understanding the breadth of AWS offerings and honing in on key areas of study, candidates will be better prepared to navigate the exam content and demonstrate their proficiency in cloud computing fundamentals.

Furthermore, we will provide detailed guidance on exam day preparations, whether opting for an in-person testing center or a proctored online environment. From understanding the logistics of the exam process to familiarizing oneself with the exam interface and timing constraints, we will ensure candidates are well-equipped to approach the examination with confidence and composure. Additionally, we will address strategies for managing exam anxiety and optimizing performance under pressure, empowering candidates to showcase their knowledge and skills effectively on exam day.

Finally, this chapter will offer a host of additional tips and tricks designed to augment exam preparation and maximize success. From leveraging practice exams and simulation tools to refining time management and test-taking strategies, we will provide actionable insights to enhance the efficiency and effectiveness of study efforts. Moreover, we will highlight common pitfalls to avoid and best practices to adopt throughout the exam preparation journey, empowering candidates to navigate the certification process with clarity and proficiency. By synthesizing key resources, exam day preparations, and expert tips, this chapter aims to serve as an invaluable roadmap for aspiring AWS Certified Cloud Practitioner seeking to excel in their certification journey.

AWS resources for exam preparation

Congratulations on taking the first step towards becoming an AWS Certified Cloud Practitioner. This certification is an excellent foundation for anyone looking to start a career in cloud computing or enhance their existing skills in AWS. In this chapter, we will explore the main resources offered by AWS to help you prepare for the exam.

Understanding AWS Certified Cloud Practitioner exam

Before exploring the preparation resources, it is essential to understand the structure and objectives of the AWS Certified Cloud Practitioner exam (**https://aws.amazon.com/ certification/certified-cloud-practitioner/**). The exam validates your overall understanding of the AWS Cloud, including its basic architectural principles, key services, security, compliance, and the AWS shared responsibility model. It is designed for individuals who have the knowledge and skills necessary to effectively demonstrate an overall understanding of the AWS Cloud.

The exam format typically consists of multiple-choice questions, and candidates are required to demonstrate their knowledge across various domains. These domains include:

- Cloud concepts
- Security
- Technology
- Billing and pricing

Each domain contributes to a percentage of the overall exam content, and it is crucial to have a solid grasp of all these areas before attempting the exam.

The exam structure and domains asked during the exam are listed in the official exam guide here: **https://d1.awsstatic.com/training-and-certification/docs-cloud-practitioner/ AWS-Certified-Cloud-Practitioner_Exam-Guide.pdf**

AWS Training and Certification

AWS offers a variety of training and certification resources to help you prepare for the Cloud Practitioner exam. These resources cater to individuals with different learning preferences and levels of expertise. Here are some of the main resources offered by AWS:

- **AWS training courses**: AWS provides both digital and classroom-based training courses tailored to different certification levels under their main courses website: **https://explore.skillbuilder.aws/learn**. For the Cloud Practitioner exam, you can enroll in courses such as AWS Cloud Practitioner Essentials (**https:// explore.skillbuilder.aws/learn/course/external/view/elearning/134/aws-cloud- practitioner-essentials**) to build a foundational understanding of AWS services and concepts.

- **AWS Documentation**: The AWS Documentation (**https://docs.aws.amazon. com/**) serves as a comprehensive source of information on all AWS services and features. It is an invaluable resource for understanding service-specific details, best practices, and architectural patterns. Make sure to familiarize yourself with the AWS Documentation, especially the services covered in the exam blueprint.

- **AWS whitepapers and FAQs**: AWS publishes whitepapers and FAQs documents that delve deeper into specific topics such as security, compliance, and cost optimization. These resources provide valuable insights and can help clarify complex concepts covered in the exam.

- **Practice exams**: Practice exams are an excellent way to assess your readiness for the Cloud Practitioner exam. AWS offers official practice exams that mimic the format and difficulty level of the actual exam questions. Taking practice exams allows you to identify areas of weakness and focus your study efforts accordingly, for example this one: **https://explore.skillbuilder.aws/learn/course/external/view/ elearning/14050/aws-certified-cloud-practitioner-official-practice-question-set- clf-c02-english**.

- **AWS Certified Cloud Practitioner exam guide**: The AWS Certified Cloud Practitioner exam guide (**https://d1.awsstatic.com/training-and-certification/ docs-cloud-practitioner/AWS-Certified-Cloud-Practitioner_Exam-Guide.pdf**) is a comprehensive resource that covers all the exam objectives in detail. It provides sample questions, practice exercises, and tips for exam preparation. Utilize this guide as a roadmap for your study plan.

- **AWS training partners**: If you prefer instructor-led training, consider enrolling in courses offered by AWS Training Partners. These partners deliver instructor-led training in various formats, including virtual classrooms and on-site sessions, to accommodate different learning preferences.

AWS Educate

AWS Educate is a global initiative to provide students and educators with the resources needed to accelerate cloud-related learning. Whether you are new to the cloud or looking to enhance your AWS skills, AWS Educate offers a variety of resources to support your journey.

One of the key benefits of AWS Educate is its focus on providing hands-on experience through labs, tutorials, and real-world scenarios. By leveraging these resources, you can gain practical experience working with AWS services, which is essential for success in the AWS Certified Cloud Practitioner exam.

AWS Educate also offers access to AWS Cloud services at no cost, allowing you to experiment and build projects in a risk-free environment. This hands-on experience not only helps solidify your understanding of AWS concepts but also provides valuable practical skills that can be applied in real-world scenarios. Additionally, AWS Educate provides access to training modules, learning pathways, and certification exam preparation resources tailored to the AWS Certified Cloud Practitioner exam objectives. These resources include study guides, practice exams, and interactive quizzes to help you assess your knowledge and identify areas for improvement.

You can find more information about AWS Educate here: **https://aws.amazon.com/education/awseducate/**.

AWS Cloud Quest for Cloud Practitioner

As the journey towards becoming an AWS Cloud Practitioner progresses, it becomes imperative to engage in targeted practice sessions that simulate real-world scenarios. AWS understands the significance of hands-on experience in mastering their services. Hence, they have devised a unique offering called the Cloud Quest (**https://aws.amazon.com/training/digital/aws-cloud-quest/**) an immersive game experience designed to hone the skills necessary for success in the Cloud Practitioner exam.

Understanding the game

The Cloud Quest for Cloud Practitioner certification is a free 3D interactive learning experience tailored to mimic the challenges one might encounter in the AWS Cloud Practitioner exam. This role-playing game is structured to reinforce key concepts, test decision-making abilities, and instill confidence in navigating AWS services.

Gameplay mechanics

The game operates on a scenario-based approach, where players are presented with simulated scenarios resembling real-world AWS implementations. These scenarios cover a wide array of topics, including cloud concepts, security, billing, and pricing, among others. Players must leverage their knowledge of AWS services and best practices to solve these challenges effectively.

Here there are some features and benefits of the Cloud Quest game:

- **Scenario repository**: The game offers a diverse repository of scenarios, each focusing on different aspects of AWS. This ensures comprehensive coverage of exam topics and prepares players for any challenge they might face.

- **Realistic simulations**: The scenarios are meticulously crafted to mirror real-world situations, providing players with a practical understanding of how AWS services are utilized in various scenarios.

- **Feedback and guidance**: After completing each scenario, players receive detailed feedback and guidance on their performance. This feedback helps identify areas of improvement and reinforces learning objectives.

- **Scalable difficulty levels**: The game adapts to the player's skill level, gradually increasing the difficulty as they progress. This ensures a challenging, yet manageable learning curve tailored to individual learning pace.

The benefits of the game are mentioned in the following:

- **Skill enhancement**: By engaging in hands-on scenarios, players develop practical skills essential for success in the AWS Cloud Practitioner exam and real-world AWS implementations.

- **Confidence building**: The immersive nature of the game instills confidence in players, equipping them with the kno wledge and skills needed to tackle any challenge thrown their way.

- **Time efficiency**: The game optimizes learning time by focusing on targeted practice sessions, allowing players to maximize their preparation efficiency.

- **Cost-effective**: Compared to traditional training methods, the Cloud Quest: Cloud Practitioner offers a free solution for exam preparation, eliminating the need for expensive training programs.

In the road to becoming an AWS Cloud Practitioner, mastery of AWS services and concepts is paramount. The Cloud Quest: Cloud Practitioner game provides a dynamic platform for honing skills, refining decision-making abilities, and ultimately achieving success in the AWS Cloud Practitioner exam. Embrace the challenge, immerse yourself in the scenarios, and embark on your journey towards AWS expertise.

AWS Workshops

An AWS Workshops **https://workshops.aws/** is a hands-on learning experience designed to immerse participants in the world of AWS Cloud computing. These workshops are typically conducted by AWS Certified trainers or authorized training partners, who guide participants through a series of interactive sessions, practical exercises, and real-world scenarios. The workshops cover various AWS services, concepts, best practices, and use cases, catering to individuals with diverse backgrounds, from beginners to experienced professionals.

There are more than 100 free workshops created by AWS experts that are comprehensive of each AWS key service.

The key components of an AWS workshop are mentioned in the following:

- **Introduction to AWS**: The workshop begins with an overview of AWS, including its history, Global Infrastructure, and core services. Participants gain insights into the benefits of cloud computing, such as scalability, flexibility, and cost-efficiency, as well as the AWS shared responsibility model.

- **Core services**: Participants delve into key AWS services, such as Amazon EC2, Amazon S3, Amazon RDS, and Amazon VPC, among others. Through hands-on exercises and demonstrations, they learn how to provision resources, configure settings, and deploy applications on the AWS platform.

- **Security and compliance**: Security is important in cloud computing, and workshops emphasize best practices for securing AWS resources, implementing **Identity and Access Management (IAM)**, encrypting data, and adhering to compliance standards such as GDPR and HIPAA.

- **Scalability and high availability**: Participants explore strategies for designing scalable and highly available architectures on AWS, leveraging services like auto scaling, Elastic Load Balancing, and Amazon Route 53. They learn how to optimize performance, minimize downtime, and ensure resilience in their applications.

- **Cost management**: Efficient cost management is essential for maximizing the value of AWS services. Workshops cover strategies for optimizing costs, monitoring usage, and leveraging pricing models such as On-Demand, Reserved Instances, and Savings Plans.

- **Real-world use cases**: Throughout the workshop, participants are presented with real-world use cases and scenarios drawn from various industries, such as e-commerce, healthcare, finance, and media. They apply their knowledge to solve practical challenges and design solutions using AWS services.

The benefits of participating in an AWS Workshop are mentioned in the following:

- **Hands-on learning**: Workshops provide a hands-on learning experience, allowing participants to gain practical skills by working directly with AWS services in a guided environment.

- **Expert guidance**: Certified trainers offer expert guidance and support, clarifying concepts, answering questions, and providing valuable insights based on their real-world experience.

- **Networking opportunities**: Participants have the opportunity to network with peers, exchange ideas, and collaborate on group activities, fostering a sense of community and shared learning.

- **Preparation for certification**: AWS Workshops serve as excellent preparation for AWS Certification exams, equipping participants with the knowledge and skills needed to succeed in their certification journey.

- **Career advancement**: By acquiring proficiency in AWS Cloud computing, participants enhance their career prospects and open doors to new opportunities in the rapidly growing field of cloud technology.

In conclusion, AWS workshops play an interesting and fun hands-on experience in equipping individuals and organizations with the knowledge, skills, and confidence to thrive in the cloud computing landscape. Through interactive sessions, practical exercises, and expert guidance, participants gain a deep understanding of AWS services, best practices, and real-world applications.

Other resources from third-parties

We can start studying for the exam using AWS official documentation and workshops offered by AWS for free, but on the internet, there are many other tutorials, blog posts and paid courses to improve your AWS skills and have more confidence during the exam.

Here we will try to list some ideas of where to find other external resources to study and we will see some nice paid courses that can make you ace your certification exam.

There are plenty of resources available online to prepare for the AWS Certified Cloud Practitioner exam apart from the official AWS resources, like official documentation or AWS Educate. Here are some suggestions:

- **Online courses**: Platforms like Coursera, Udemy, Pluralsight, and LinkedIn Learning offer courses specifically tailored for AWS Certifications. Look for courses with high ratings and good reviews.

- **Books**: There are many books available that cover AWS Certified Cloud Practitioner exam topics in detail. Some popular ones include *AWS Certified Cloud Practitioner Study Guide* by *Ben Piper* and *AWS Certified Cloud Practitioner Complete Study Guide* by *Scott Patterson* or for example this book you are reading right now.

- **Practice exams**: Taking practice exams can help you familiarize yourself with the format of the real exam and identify areas where you need to focus your studies. Websites like TutorialDojo, Whizlabs, Udemy, and Linux Academy offer practice exams for AWS Certifications.

- **Online communities**: Joining online communities like the AWS subreddit or the AWS Certification forums can provide you with valuable insights and tips from people who have already taken the exam.

- **YouTube tutorials**: There are many YouTube channels dedicated to AWS tutorials and exam preparation. Watching video tutorials can be a helpful supplement to your study materials.

- **Study groups**: Joining or forming a study group with other individuals preparing for the same exam can provide support and accountability. You can discuss difficult topics, quiz each other, and share resources.

- **Blogs and articles**: Many AWS experts and professionals share their insights and experiences through blogs and articles. Reading these can give you different perspectives and deepen your understanding of AWS concepts.

Remember to create a study plan and schedule dedicated study time regularly. Consistent practice and review are key to success in passing the AWS Certified Cloud Practitioner exam.

Mock exam

Let us dig more into an example of what kind of questions you will encounter in your AWS exam using a mock exam.

This is a sample mock exam with some questions that could possibly be shown in the real exam.

Real exam details

In the real certification exam, you could find multiple-choice questions with a single correct answer, or sometimes also multiple-choice questions with two or more correct answers. In this specific case, every question will instruct you to choose, for example, Choose three possible answers. But usually, most of the questions will be with a single correct answer to choose.

Also, check out the official AWS sample questions for Cloud Practitioner certification here: **https://d1.awsstatic.com/training-and-certification/docs-cloud-practitioner/AWS-Certified-Cloud-Practitioner_Sample-Questions.pdf**, so you can make a feeling for the kind of topics you could find in the real thing.

The real exam will be more or less 90 minutes long as maximum time, you will be asked 65 questions, and the score is calculated from 0 to 1000 points. To pass this exam, you need to score at least 750 points (so 75% of 1000 points in total).

We suggest you to try to practice some mock exams like this one, and when you do this take note of the time you spend on each question, if for some reason you see you are taking too much time for a single question, it is better to pass to the next one, and complete the old one only after you have finished all the other questions you are more comfortable with.

Instructions to mock exam

So, here we go. This is a mock exam to see what kind of topics AWS could ask you during the exam day.

The instructions are mentioned in the following:

- This mock exam consists of multiple-choice questions designed to test your knowledge and understanding of key concepts covered in the AWS Certified Cloud Practitioner exam.

- Read each question carefully and select the best answer from the options provided.

- There is only one correct answer for each question.

- The list of all correct answers is at the end of this mock exam. Check them only after you have completed all the questions by yourself. This will help you to train in a similar real-world scenario where the answer will not be seen near each question.

- If you do not know the answer, no need to worry. But it is important to have good time management skills, so please always be considerate about how much time passes between each question.

- Do not limit yourself only to this mock exam. Check out on the internet for more, so you can be more and more at ease when the real exam day will take off.

- Take note also when you miss a question, and try to re-read this book and other materials about the specific topic you have missed.

Questions

1. **Which of the following is a fundamental characteristic of cloud computing?**

    a. High cost of ownership

    b. Limited scalability

    c. On-premises infrastructure

    d. On-demand self-service

2. **What is the primary benefit of using Amazon Simple Storage Service (S3)?**

    a. Low latency

    b. Unlimited storage capacity

    c. High durability

    d. Real-time analytics

3. **Which AWS service provides a scalable and fully managed database?**

    a. Amazon S3

    b. Amazon Relational Database Service (RDS)

    c. Amazon Elastic Compute Cloud (EC2)

    d. Amazon Glacier

4. **Which AWS service is used to route traffic to different AWS resources based on DNS requests?**

    a. Amazon Route 53

    b. Amazon CloudFront

    c. Amazon API Gateway

    d. AWS Lambda

5. **What is the purpose of AWS IAM?**

   a. Monitoring AWS resource usage

   b. Managing user permissions and access control

   c. Scaling applications automatically

   d. Optimizing costs

6. **Which AWS pricing model allows users to pay only for the compute capacity they use?**

   a. Reserved Instances

   b. On-Demand Instances

   c. Spot Instances

   d. Dedicated Hosts

7. **Which AWS service enables users to create, publish, maintain, monitor, and secure APIs at any scale?**

   a. Amazon EC2

   b. Amazon API Gateway

   c. Amazon RDS

   d. AWS Lambda

8. **Which AWS storage service is designed for long-term archival and backup of data?**

   a. Amazon S3

   b. Amazon Elastic Block Store (EBS)

   c. Amazon Glacier

   d. Amazon Elastic File System (EFS)

9. **What is the primary benefit of using AWS CloudWatch?**

   a. Real-time monitoring of AWS resources

   b. Data encryption

   c. Application load balancing

   d. Content delivery network (CDN)

10. **Which AWS service provides a fully managed Kubernetes service?**

    a. Amazon Elastic Container Service (ECS)

    b. Amazon Elastic Kubernetes Service (EKS)

    c.   AWS Lambda

    d.   Amazon RDS

11. **Which AWS service allows users to automate the deployment, scaling, and management of containerized applications?**

    a.   Amazon S3

    b.   Amazon EC2

    c.   AWS Lambda

    d.   Amazon ECS

12. **What is the primary function of AWS CloudFormation?**

    a.   Real-time monitoring

    b.   Infrastructure as code (IaC)

    c.   Content delivery

    d.   Container orchestration

13. **Which AWS service is used to deliver content to end-users with low latency and high transfer speeds?**

    a.   Amazon Route 53

    b.   Amazon CloudFront

    c.   Amazon RDS

    d.   AWS Lambda

14. **What is the primary benefit of using Amazon VPC?**

    a.   High durability

    b.   Low latency

    c.   Enhanced security

    d.   Real-time analytics

15. **Which AWS service enables users to run code without provisioning or managing servers?**

    a.   Amazon EC2

    b.   AWS Lambda

    c.   Amazon RDS

    d.   Amazon S3

You can find all the correct answers in the following.

Try to answer all questions autonomously and without any external help to try to simulate the real exam experience.

Answers

1. d
2. c
3. b
4. a
5. b
6. b
7. b
8. c
9. a
10. b
11. d
12. b
13. b
14. c
15. b

Exam day preparation

When gearing up for the AWS Cloud Practitioner exam, one of the first decisions you will encounter is choosing between an in-person or proctored online exam. Each option has its own set of advantages and considerations to keep in mind, as mentioned in the following:

- **In-person exam**: They are conducted at designated testing centers. They offer a controlled environment where you can focus solely on the exam without any distractions. You will be provided with a quiet space equipped with all the necessary resources, including a computer and internet access. Additionally, trained proctors are present to monitor the exam and ensure fairness.

- **Proctored online exam**: They provide the convenience of taking the test from the comfort of your own space. With a stable internet connection and a suitable environment, you can complete the exam without the need to travel to a testing center. However, it is essential to note that stricter security measures are in place to maintain exam integrity. This may include webcam monitoring, screen sharing, and verifying your identity through government-issued identification.

Each option offers its own set of benefits, so it is crucial to choose the one that aligns with your preferences and circumstances.

Basic installation setup for proctored online exam

If you opt for the proctored online exam, ensuring your setup meets the necessary requirements is paramount for a smooth testing experience. Here is a basic installation setup guide to help you prepare:

- **Technical requirements**: Before scheduling your exam, review the technical requirements outlined by AWS. Ensure your computer meets the specified criteria for the operating system, browser compatibility, and internet speed.

- **Secure environment**: Find a quiet and well-lit space where you will not be disturbed during the exam. Clear your workspace of any unauthorized materials or devices. It is essential to maintain exam integrity and avoid any potential accusations of cheating.

- **Webcam and microphone**: Verify that your computer's webcam and microphone are functional. These will be used to monitor you throughout the exam. Adjust their settings and positioning to ensure clear visibility and audio.

- **System check**: Perform a system check using the provided exam preparation software. This tool will assess your system's readiness for the exam, flagging any potential issues that need to be addressed beforehand.

- **Practice session**: Take advantage of any practice sessions offered by AWS or the exam proctoring service. This will familiarize you with the exam interface and the proctoring process, reducing anxiety on exam day.

By following these steps, you will be well-prepared to tackle the AWS Cloud Practitioner exam in a proctored online setting.

Basic prerequisites for taking the exam

Before diving into your exam preparation, it is essential to ensure you meet the basic prerequisites set by AWS. Here is what you need to know:

- **Familiarity with AWS services**: While the Cloud Practitioner exam is designed for individuals with little to no AWS experience, having a basic understanding of cloud computing concepts and AWS services will undoubtedly benefit you. Familiarize yourself with core services, such as Amazon EC2, S3, and IAM, as well as fundamental concepts like elasticity, scalability, and security.

- **Study resources**: Gather study materials tailored to the Cloud Practitioner exam, such as official AWS Documentation, whitepapers, and practice exams. Online courses and tutorials can also provide valuable insights and structured learning paths.

- **Exam registration**: Once you feel adequately prepared, register for the exam through the AWS Training and Certification portal. Select your preferred exam type (in-person or proctored online) and schedule a convenient date and time.

- **Payment**: Pay the exam fee online to secure your spot. Keep in mind that exam fees are non-refundable, so ensure you are fully prepared before scheduling your exam.

- **Identification**: On the day of the exam, ensure you have valid government-issued identification with a clear photo and signature. This will be used to verify your identity before starting the exam.

By meeting these prerequisites and following a structured study plan, you will be well-equipped to excel in the AWS Cloud Practitioner exam and kickstart your journey into the world of cloud computing.

Tips and exam discounts

Here we will explore various strategies and tips to help you succeed in your exam preparation and to get some discounts or vouchers to reduce the cost of the exam.

Leveraging AWS meetups

One of the fantastic opportunities AWS provides is access to meetups. These gatherings are not only great for networking and learning from industry experts but can also be valuable for exam preparation. Many meetups offer sessions specifically tailored to AWS Certifications, including Cloud Practitioner. These sessions often cover key concepts, exam tips, and even hands-on labs to reinforce your learning.

Attending these meetups can provide you with insights into real-world scenarios and best practices, enhancing your understanding of AWS services. Additionally, engaging with the AWS community can help clarify any doubts or questions about exam topics. Take advantage of these meetups to supplement your study materials and interact with like-minded individuals on their certification journey.

Discounts for exams

AWS frequently offers discounts and promotions for certification exams, including the Cloud Practitioner. Keep an eye out for these opportunities, as they can significantly reduce the cost of taking the exam. AWS often announces these discounts through its official channels, such as the AWS Training and Certification website or their social media platforms.

Moreover, AWS occasionally runs special promotions in collaboration with training partners or during events like *AWS re:Invent*. By taking advantage of these discounts, you can save money while pursuing your certification goals. Be proactive in seeking out these opportunities and plan your exam schedule accordingly to maximize savings.

Tips for the exam

Preparing for any certification exam requires a strategic approach. Here are some tips to help you effectively study for the AWS Cloud Practitioner exam:

- **Understand the exam guide**: Familiarize yourself with the AWS Certified Cloud Practitioner exam guide provided by AWS. It outlines the topics covered in the exam and the level of knowledge required for each domain.

- **Use multiple resources**: Do not rely solely on one study material. Utilize a combination of official AWS Documentation, online courses, practice tests, and hands-on labs to reinforce your understanding of AWS services and concepts.

- **Hands-on practice**: AWS offers a Free Tier that allows you to experiment with various services at no cost. Take advantage of this to gain practical experience and deepen your understanding of how AWS works in real-world scenarios.

- **Time management**: Practice answering exam questions within the allocated time limit. Time management is crucial during the exam, so simulate exam conditions during your practice sessions to improve your speed and accuracy.

- **Review and reinforce**: Periodically review the topics you have covered and revisit areas where you feel less confident. Repetition is key to retention, so reinforce your learning through regular review sessions.

- **Join study groups**: Consider joining study groups or forums where you can discuss exam topics with peers, ask questions, and share insights. Collaborating with others can provide valuable perspectives and support throughout your preparation journey.

By following these tips and dedicating sufficient time and effort to your exam preparation, you will be well-equipped to tackle the AWS Cloud Practitioner exam with confidence.

Preparing for the AWS Cloud Practitioner exam requires dedication, persistence, and a strategic approach. By leveraging resources such as AWS meetups, taking advantage of exam discounts, and following effective study strategies, you can enhance your chances of success. Remember to stay focused, manage your time effectively, and continuously review and reinforce your understanding of AWS services and concepts. Good luck on your certification journey.

Conclusion

In conclusion, the journey to become an AWS Certified Cloud Practitioner is not merely about obtaining a certification, it is about acquiring a foundational understanding of cloud concepts and AWS services that can fundamentally reshape one's career trajectory. Through this last chapter, we have discussed the vital strategies and resources necessary for effective exam preparation. From grasping core AWS services to mastering exam-taking techniques, every aspect contributes to building a solid foundation in cloud computing.

As AWS continues to dominate the cloud market, possessing a Cloud Practitioner certification becomes increasingly invaluable for professionals aiming to establish themselves in the field. This certification signifies not only a deep understanding of AWS services but also an ability to navigate the complexities of cloud computing effectively. Moreover, the journey of preparing for this exam fosters a mindset of continuous learning and adaptation, crucial traits in an evolving technological field.

Ultimately, achieving AWS Cloud Practitioner Certification is a significant milestone, marking the beginning of a journey filled with opportunities for growth and advancement. By embracing the knowledge gained through preparation and leveraging it in real-world scenarios, individuals can carve out successful careers in cloud computing, contributing meaningfully to the innovation and transformation of businesses worldwide.

Congratulations on the hard work and dedication you have put into mastering the foundational concepts of cloud computing on AWS. Throughout this book, you have explored the core principles, services, and best practices of AWS, equipping yourself with the knowledge and skills needed to excel in the world of cloud technology.

As you continue on the final leg of your exam preparation, remember to trust in your abilities and approach the test with confidence. You have covered a wealth of material, from understanding the essential AWS services to navigating the intricacies of cloud security and pricing models. Now, it is time to showcase your expertise and demonstrate your proficiency in AWS Cloud Practitioner concepts.

Join our book's Discord space

Join the book's Discord Workspace for Latest updates, Offers, Tech happenings around the world, New Release and Sessions with the Authors:

https://discord.bpbonline.com

Index

B